Contemporary Government and Business Relations

Contemporary Government and Business Relations

Third Edition

Martin C. Schnitzer

Virginia Polytechnic Institute

69257

HOUGHTON MIFFLIN COMPANY   **BOSTON**

Dallas   Geneva, Illinois   Lawrenceville, New Jersey   Palo Alto

Library of Congress Catalog Card Number: 86-81981

ISBN: 0-395-35715-2

ABCDEFGHIJ-BP-89876

Contents

List of Cases

List of Tables

List of Diagrams

Preface

The purpose of this book is to fill a void in government and business courses: the lack of coverage of all areas of government regulation that directly affect business operations. Some books on government fail to show or do not sufficiently emphasize the fact that government influence has expanded into a number of areas totally unrelated to antitrust policies and public utility regulation. In fact, most business firms are far more likely to be affected by the federal government's environmental and affirmative action policies than by its antitrust policies. The federal government has expanded so greatly that today it has become the largest purchaser of business products. Moreover, government economic policies exercise a powerful influence over business. Two examples, the deficit in the federal budget and the tax reform legislation of 1986, have or will have a direct impact on business operations.

The composition of this book reflects the many and diverse areas in which government and business interact. Chapter 1 is about how government affects business — in public finance, regulation and control, as an employer, and as an owner of industry. Chapters 2 and 3 present the background of the development of government and business relations in the United States. Chapters 4, 5, 6, 7, 8, and 9 cover market models, industrial concentration, and antitrust laws. Chapters 10, 11, 12, and 13 deal with the subject of social regulation of business and include such areas as affirmative action and comparable worth, consumer protection, and environmental policy. Chapters 14 and 15 cover government regulation of so-called natural monopolies and deregulation of air transportation, banking, natural gas and other industries. Chapters 16 and 17 outline various ways in which government provides support to business, with emphasis placed on foreign trade and protectionism. Chapters 18 and 19 discuss government economic policies including "Reaganomics," and the declining competitive position of the United States in a global economy.

Operating within the constraints of time, I have tried to update this book to include as many changes as possible in a subject area that is prone to rapid change. Included in the book are the 1986 Supreme Court decisions on affirmative action. I have also utilized the most current data available and have relied where possible on firsthand sources. I am indebted to William Young of the law firm of Hunton and Williams who provided me the material for most of the antitrust cases used in the book and to Judith Johnson, Director of Equal Employment/Affirmative Action Programs at Virginia Tech. I also wish to thank the Attorney General's Office of Virginia, the Antitrust Division of the Justice Department, and the Federal Trade Commission for providing me with firsthand sources of information on antitrust; and the Interstate Commerce Commission for sending me data on railroad and trucking deregulation.

M. S.

Contemporary Government and Business Relations

PART I
INTRODUCTION TO
GOVERNMENT AND
BUSINESS RELATIONS

In many ways it is correct to say that the future of the steel industry is made right here in Washington. We must regard the federal establishment as having a preeminent influence on capital investment decisions — preeminent and, unfortunately, unconstructive on many occasions. This is so because of a combination of two different aspects of Federal power: in the first place, it is broad and pervasive, affecting virtually every aspect of our business, and second, in many instances, the power is being exercised to meet special and often political objectives and not to achieve goals which will bring the greatest benefit to the nation in the long run.*

This statement by the president of Republic Steel defines quite well the significance of the relationship between government and business. Today no business firm is free from some form of government control. For example, a little more than a decade ago, most business firms were mainly unregulated private enterprises. They were free to design the kinds of products they pleased, subject to product acceptance. Marketing practices were also free from control, and pricing policies, depending on the size of the company, were geared to provide a high return on capital, based on a standard volume concept. But now, business firms are subject to detailed government regulations in which almost all phases of design, marketing, management, and at times even pricing policies are responses to specifications laid down in Washington. Therefore, the subject of business-government relations is even more important to students because there is an enormous interaction between these two major institutions in American society, and it is necessary to establish a framework within which a discussion of this interaction can take place.

---

*William DeLancey, president, Republic Steel Corporation, "The Federal Presence in Steel," speech delivered at Cold Finished Bar Institute Annual Meeting, Washington, D.C., December 4, 1975, pp. 2-3.

Chapter 1
The Influence of Government on Business

To use a botanical analogy, government and business are two genera of the social and economic system of the United States. Each of these genera contains species, such as federal, state, and local political bodies in the case of government, and corporations, partnerships, and proprietorships in the case of business. Sometimes there are even hybrid species, joint government/business or public/private enterprises such as the Communications Satellite Corporation (COMSAT). There is an interrelationship between these two genera because government provides the institutional foundation on which business rests, the legal framework within which it functions, and many of the instruments through which its activities are carried out. The economic system within which business functions is also shaped by government, and its performance depends on decisions made by government. The system's expectations of profit or loss depend to some extent on the policies adopted by central banking authorities to control the volume of credit and on the policies pursued by the federal government to balance its budget, to accumulate a surplus, or to run a deficit.

To be more specific, government relates to business in at least the following ways: it regulates the particular functions of all businesses, such as competition, foreign trade, product safety, the issuance and sale of securities, labor relations, and the impact of a business on the environment. Government participates in the management of the so-called public utilities by regulating entry, service, output, investment, prices, and other variables of the utilities' operation. Government also sells or regulates a wide variety of goods and services, including postal services, nuclear fuel, electricity, and police and fire protection. It taxes business, and it makes business a collector of taxes such as those levied on alcohol, gasoline, and tobacco. In addition, it purchases many kinds of equipment, supplies, goods and services from business. Government also subsidizes some business enterprises, particularly those connected with farming and shipbuilding; it finances other enterprises through direct loans, loan guarantees, and insurance. Finally, and perhaps most important, government attempts to stabilize the economic environment within which business must operate through its use of fiscal and monetary policies.

The government's participation in America's business life has grown enormously. From the beginning of the republic in 1787, the federal government has been interested in promoting manufacturing, and it soon passed tariff laws to protect American business interests. Subsidies were used to develop canals, roads, and various forms of transportation, from which business benefited directly. As industrialization and business concentration increased, the government passed laws to regulate specific segments of business — for example, railroads — or to control business practices. This trend began in the latter part of the last century and continued, with some interruptions, until 1940. After World War II, government participation in business took the form of increasing consumption of a wide variety of goods and services, the bulk of which have been items considered essential for the national defense. One result of this process is that many industries and enterprises have become dependent on government spending.

In recent years in American society there has been a shift in emphasis from market to political decisions, largely in response to the increase in societal problems. Not much more than a decade ago, most business firms were largely unregulated, free to produce whatever kinds of products they pleased, as long as consumers would accept them. Today, these firms are subject to detailed government regulations in almost all phases of their operations. One example of this is the controversial affirmative action programs set in motion by the federal government, which apply to business firms and unions alike. Protection of the environment is another area in which the government has encroached on the activities of most business firms. The prime example of this is the automobile industry, which must now comply with emission control standards that require a radical reduction in the amount of hydrocarbons and carbon monoxide emitted by motor vehicles. Safety standards require automobile designers to accommodate various restraints, including seat belts and buzzer systems, specifications for brakes, safety glass, and the padding of bumpers. Government constraints on business can be expected to increase in the future in accordance with new social and ideological demands.

For the purpose of organization, government intervention and participation in the American economy can be divided into four areas, which provide the subject matter of the remainder of this chapter. First, there is public finance, in which government is a purchaser of goods and services as well as a tax collector. Government economic stabilization policies may also be considered a part of this area. Second, government regulation and control prescribe specific conditions under which private business activity can or cannot take place. Government may interpose itself as a part of management in certain industries, such as public utilities, and regulate rates and the provision of services. It may also influence private business operations both directly and indirectly through antitrust and other laws. Third, government is the single largest employer in the American economy and, as such, competes directly with private industry for labor. The government also affects the level of wages and salaries. Fourth, government owns and operates business enterprises and is a major provider of credit. In fact, few, if any, changes in the market structure of the American economy have as much social and political significance as does this movement of government into areas previously reserved for private enterprise.

THE ROLE OF PUBLIC FINANCE

Public finance is the clearest and probably the most important example of the extent of government participation in the "mixed" economy of the United States. Taxes give the government control over the nation's resources and also affect the distribution of income. Government expenditures for goods and services divert resources from the private to the public sector of the economy. Through its own expenditures, the government has literally created business firms and whole industries, has conducted much of the basic research in certain industries, and has given impetus and direction to technological change. Indeed, the direct subsidies and indirect benefits offered business by government are too numerous to mention. In addition, preferential tax treatment is accorded to some firms and industries. So great is the impact of taxes and so great are the benefits of favorable tax treatment that businesses take immense interest in, and attempt to influence the writing of, tax legislation. Examples of special tax treatment include the investment credit, depletion allowances, and accelerated depreciation.

The importance of the public sector to business can be explained in three ways. First, there is the general level of government expenditures and taxation in relation to the gross national product (GNP). Economists prefer, however, to use changes in the share of the GNP taken off the market rather than total government expenditures as a guide to the public sector's economic influence. Second, there is the actual composition of expenditures and taxes. For example, direct government expenditures for goods and services would have an impact on business different from that exerted by transfer payments, which return no equivalent value in either products or services. The composition of taxes is also important, and in recent years more attention has been paid to the role of tax policies in promoting economic growth. Third, there has been a general acceptance of public policy measures designed to maintain a high level of employment, economic growth, stable prices, and other economic and social goals. Both fiscal and monetary policies have thereby come to be important to the management of the American economy.

The Level of Expenditures and Taxation

The importance of the federal government's budget to the business community cannot be overemphasized. The budget exerts an influence on the national economy and also on business regarding the level of expenditures and taxes, whether or not it is balanced, and the specific expenditures and taxes it authorizes. The federal budget tends to be the focal point of the presentation and implementation of the government's economic policy, and it is often used as a means of publicizing the government's policies toward particular sectors, groups of people, or industries, either in an attempt to improve the chances of success of the proposed measures or, at times, as a substitute for any specific measures. Moreover, the budget can be used to alter the level of economic activity. Taxes represent a withdrawal of income from the income stream, whereas government expenditures represent an injection of income into it.

The significance of the federal budget can be measured by its size in relation to GNP. Budgetary receipts for 1986 are estimated at $771.1 billion, and expenditures are estimated at $979.9 billion.[1] When these tax revenues are compared to the estimated GNP for 1986 of approximately $4 trillion, it is apparent that the federal budget diverts approximately 21 percent of GNP from the private to the public sector. The budgetary outlays of around $980 billion take the form of direct expenditures for goods and services, most of which are provided by business firms, and of transfer payments and subsidies of various types, many of which also benefit business firms. Government purchases of goods and services also directly increase the total demand for output in the economy; government transfer payments and taxes exert a more indirect influence on total demand.

State and local government taxes and expenditures also have to be considered. In 1985, for example, total receipts, including taxes, for all levels of government amounted to $1.3 trillion and total expenditures amounted to $1.4 trillion.[2] However, some of the state and local receipts are federal grants-in-aid. In the same year, total government purchases of goods and services amounted to $814.6 billion, in comparison with a GNP of $4.0 trillion.[3] Of the total $814.6 billion, federal government expenditures on goods and services accounted for $353.9 billion and state and local government expenditures accounted for $460.7 billion. It can be said that in regard to the actual purchases

1. *Budget of the U.S. Government, Fiscal Year 1987* (Washington, D.C.: U.S. Government Printing Office, 1986), p. M-4.
2. *Economic Report of the President 1986* (Washington, D.C.: U.S. Government Printing Office, 1986), table B-77, p. 344.
3. Ibid., table B-1, p. 253.

of goods and services, state and local governments have more of an impact on business than the federal government does.

The economic influence of the public sector has intensified steadily throughout this century and has become particularly pervasive during the last thirty years. To some extent, this increase in influence can be attributed to a growing acceptance of the government's taking charge of public welfare. But in fact, government expenditures for the national defense have been the most important single factor in the growth of public expenditures during the last three decades. Indeed, in 1980 this type of expenditure accounted for about 25 percent of the total purchases of goods and services by all government units. Economic growth has also spurred a trend toward urban living. As a larger proportion of the nation's population has concentrated in urban areas, the inevitable result has been a greater demand for services that must be provided through the public sector. Increased industrialization has changed the size and complexity of business enterprises, and the government's regulatory operations have had to be expanded. But regardless of the causes, the growth of both the absolute and the relative importance of the public sector is clear, as Table 1-1 indicates. (The table excludes government transfer payments to individuals and business firms.)

Table 1-1 Government Expenditures on Goods and Services Compared to Gross National Product for Selected Years

Year	Gross National Product (billions of $)	Government Expenditures on Goods and Services (billions of $)
1929	103.4	8.8
1933	55.6	8.0
1939	90.8	13.5
1945	213.4	83.0
1950	288.3	38.8
1960	515.3	100.6
1970	1,015.5	218.9
1980	2,732.0	530.3
1981	3,025.6	588.1
1982	3,166.0	641.7
1983	3,401.6	675.7
1984	3,774.7	736.8
1985	3,992.5	814.6

Source: *Economic Report of the President 1986* (Washington, D.C.: U.S. Government Printing Office, 1986), table B-1, p. 253.

The Composition of Taxes and Expenditures

The pie charts in Figure 1-1 present a breakdown of government taxes and expenditures by categories. To business firms the actual composition of taxes and expenditures is more important than the level of taxes and expenditures. Taxes represent an outflow of revenue from business firms and individuals to the government, and expenditures represent an outflow from the government to individuals and business firms. As the chart indicates, the three major sources of government revenues are individual income taxes, social insurance receipts, and borrowing. Government expenditures include direct payments to individuals and business firms, which includes subsidies and transfer payments, national defense expenditures, and interest payments on the national debt. Interest payments, when expressed as a percentage of total government expenditures, have more than doubled since 1975.

The Composition of Taxes

The composition of taxes is important to business firms. Government expenditures are normally covered by taxes, including taxes on business; thus, where taxes are levied ultimately determines who will pay for government expenditures. Many of those who make public policy believe that variations in the rate of economic growth can be attributed to tax policies. A hallmark of the Reagan administration was a shift in tax policy to stimulate economic growth. The Economic Recovery Tax Act of 1982 was designed to stimulate the rate of savings and capital formation by cutting both individual and corporate income taxes. Various tax breaks can be used to encourage specific types of economic activity. An example is the investment credit, which has been used both in this country and abroad to stimulate investment in the capital goods industries.

Taxes can be used manipulatively by granting exemptions and special tax rates to certain types of persons, corporations, and activities. An example is the corporate income tax, which is used by the federal government. The maximum tax rate on all corporate income is 46 percent,[4] though favorable treatment of particular types of income has been used to influence shifts in corporate behavior by reducing the income on which the tax has to be paid. One such example is the provision in the corporate income tax law that allows firms in certain extractive industries to deduct an allowance for depletion before computing taxable income.[5] This allowance reduces the amount of

4. The rate will change to 34% as a result of the new tax law.
5. The provision is supposed to be deleted as a part of the reforms.

Diagram 1-1 The Budget Dollar (Fiscal Year 1987 Estimate)

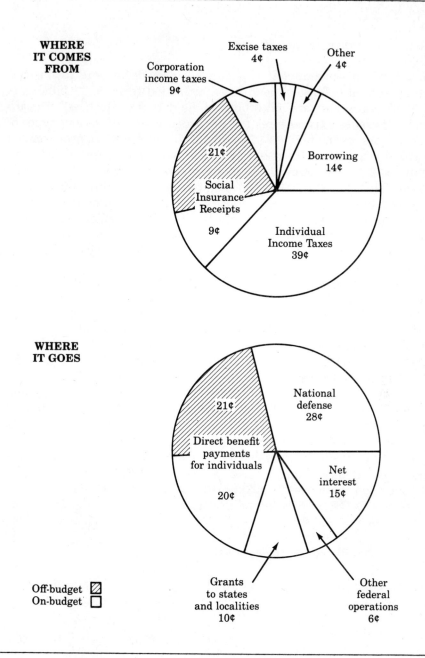

Source: *Budget of the U.S. Goverment, Fiscal Year 1987* (Washington, D.C.: U.S. Government Printing Office, 1986), p. M-2.

taxes that these industries have to pay, which often results in additional investment in this area.

The Composition of Expenditures

Many types of government expenditures provide income to business firms. National defense expenditures, estimated to be $282 billion for the 1987 fiscal year, are important to the defense industries.[6] Department of Defense expenditures for the procurement of various types of weapons are estimated at $77 billion. In addition to procurement expenditures, outlays for research and development are projected to be around $32 billion. Almost all these expenditures help the high-technology industries. Operation and maintenance expenditures, estimated to be $81 billion, include expenditures for ship and aircraft fuel, overhaul of ships, aircraft, other weapons, and medical supplies and services, thus providing income for still other industries. Expenditures on the construction of military bases and family houses, projected at $7.1 billion, benefit the construction industry. Atomic energy defense activities, conducted by the Department of Energy, also provide revenue to business firms.

Business firms are also the beneficiaries of other types of government expenditures — shipbuilding, for example. The cost of building a ship in the United States is about twice what it would be elsewhere, and if it were not for the subsidies and the various laws confining U.S. commercial shipping to American built and operated ships, there would be better shipbuilding in this country. In 1987, expenditures for ship construction and operating differential subsidies are estimated at around $300 million.[7] Then there are the business development loans made by federal agencies at interest rates lower than those prevailing at the usual lending sources. The federal government sponsors and encourages the development of small businesses through loans financed out of budget revenues. The Export-Import Bank (Eximbank) makes direct loans to U.S. exporters and importers.[8]

Economic Stabilization Policies

It is the consensus that the economic objectives of American society are a high level of employment, price stability, economic growth, and

---

6. *Budget of the U.S. Government, Fiscal Year 1987* (Washington, D.C.: U.S. Government Printing Office, 1986), p. 5-5.
7. Ibid., p. 6-142.
8. Total guaranteed loans of Eximbank are estimated at $12 billion for 1986.

a balance-of-payments equilibrium. Each goal does not lend itself to precise definition, and the attainment of one may not help achieve the others. Considerable government intervention is necessary. This intervention takes the form of macroeconomic stabilization of fiscal and monetary policies that are implemented by the government's use of taxation, transfer payments, and purchases, and by the Federal Reserve's control over the money supply and interest rates.

Fiscal Policy

Fiscal policy refers to the tax and expenditure policies of the federal government. Its objective is to increase or decrease the level of aggregate demand through changes in the level of government expenditures and taxation. An expansionary fiscal policy would stimulate economic growth and employment through an increase in government spending, decreases in taxes, or both. Conversely, fiscal policy can be used to contract the level of aggregate demand. Taxes can be raised, expenditures can be reduced, or a combination can be used. The federal budget is the fulcrum of fiscal policy. It provides a system of planning and control over government activities by the executive and legislative branches of government. The budget, because of its sheer dollar size, exercises a potent influence on the economy.

Monetary Policy

Monetary policy is used by the Federal Reserve to control the level of national output and the price level through variations in the money supply.[9] An increase in the money supply will lower interest rates and stimulate private and public spending; a decrease in the money supply will raise interest rates and reduce private and public spending. The Federal Reserve cannot fix the amount of credit and its cost independently. If it wants to restrain the rate of growth in the money supply, it must allow interest rates to rise as high as possible. If it wants to keep interest rates low, it has to accept the consequences of an increase in the money supply. It differs from fiscal policy in that control over it is not in the hands of the federal government.

9. The money supply is the total quantity of money existing in an economy at a particular time. It consists of coins and currency, demand deposits, and other checkable account balances. It includes M1, which represents the more liquid types of money, and M2, which represents less liquid assets such as savings and certificates of deposits. M1 + M2 equals the total money supply.

Impact on Business

Government economic policies provide parameters within which both American domestic and multinational business firms have to operate. Monetary policy affects the cost of credit available to domestic and multinational corporations. Changes in interest rates can affect currency exchange rates between countries. Exports or imports can be stimulated, which will either positively or negatively affect the U.S. balance of payments. Fiscal policy also has an impact on both domestic and multinational corporations. On the tax side of the government budget, changes in tax rates can affect earnings; on the expenditure side, changes in expenditure can affect earnings. Whether or not the budget is balanced can also affect business. The deficit in the budget, which is around $220 billion as of early 1986, has kept interest rates high and has contributed to a negative balance in the U.S. merchandise trade accounts with other countries, particularly Japan.

GOVERNMENT REGULATION AND CONTROL OF BUSINESS

The regulation and control of business is a second area in which government has become firmly entrenched. This sphere of public sector activity has developed sporadically. The demand for some form of government regulation or control arose as various crises or problems occurred. In the 1880s the trust movement threatened to envelop much of American industry, which brought about a demand for some sort of government control over the trusts, with the result that the Sherman Antitrust Act was passed in 1890. The Depression, which began with the stock market crash of 1929 and continued until the wartime mobilization of the early 1940s, was a crisis. In response, many new government agencies were created, most of which encroached in some way on the activities of business firms. By the end of the Depression, the federal government extensively regulated and controlled business. But after that time there was little increase in government intervention until the late 1960s and early 1970s when environmental protection, employment of minorities, and consumer protection became dominant issues.

Government regulation and control of business became necessary for several reasons, all of which are associated with certain failures of the market system. Over time, many industries came to be dominated by a relatively few large firms, instead of the many small firms that create the strict competitive conditions required for a pure market economy. In some cases, a single large firm or trust achieved control of a large part of an industry's productive capacity, or a few large firms were able to act together to achieve monopolistic control of output. Thus it follows that the results of operating under the conditions of monopoly or oligopoly can be quite different from those anticipated under the conditions that would prevail in a true market system. One reason is that firms operating under the conditions of monopoly or oligopoly have some control over output and are able, within limits, to ask a price that is not reflective of market forces.

The distribution of income and wealth can be considered a second flaw in the market system. In a purely competitive market economy, market forces are supposed to enable people to be compensated on the basis of their contributions to total output. In regard to reward for labor, those persons, whose skills are scarce in relation to demand would enjoy a high level of income, whereas those persons whose skills are not scarce would not. But this concept of reward had to be modified when it became apparent that large incomes accrued to some persons not on the basis of their contributions to national output but through inherited wealth and other accidents of birth or through the exercise of special privileges. Moreover, capricious economic and social factors often impeded the most productive of individuals. The Social Darwinist concept of "survival of the fittest" made little sense when a depression caused millions of efficient and productive people to be out of work.

Finally, the market system, with its price mechanism, failed to furnish individuals or society with a satisfactory means for achieving certain wants, for example, the desire for a clean environment. Although great importance is attached to this want, it is difficult to achieve on the basis of price-cost relationships in the market. Initiative for the provision of a clean environment therefore falls to public agencies, which use controls that inevitably have a major impact on the operations of business firms. There are also certain services, such as education, that are not suitable for production and sale on a private basis and are provided by the public sector.

Antitrust Laws

In a market economy, competition is necessary to provide the discipline needed for the efficient allocation of resources. Any departure from competition can work against the public welfare. A prime example was the development of trusts and other forms of business combinations in the United States in the latter part of the last century. The trusts were aimed at eliminating competitors and many industries fell under the control of a single trust. Discriminatory pricing and other anticompetitive business practices were numerous, and companies colluded to restrain competition. For these reasons, antitrust laws were passed to protect the public. These laws are designed to maintain competition by limiting monopoly power, whether achieved by internal growth or by mergers. They are also directed at specific business practices: anticompetitive price fixing, price discrimination against buyers or sellers, tying agreements, interlocking directorates, and other coercive practices. Each device can be used to restrain competition. For example, the aim of a price-fixing agreement, if successful, is the elimination of price competition. The power to fix prices, whether exercised reasonably or not, involves power to control the market.

Public Utility Regulation

Public utilities are those enterprises that are in some degree characterized by monopoly. In these enterprises, government accepts monopoly as being natural or desirable and establishes maximum rates to protect the public against unreasonable charges. In some instances, the government may also set minimum rates to ensure that a given utility will not arbitrarily reduce rates to injure other enterprises. Public utilities are recognized by the courts as being affected with a public interest, and as such, their property is subject to regulation. If they do business intrastate, they are subject to control by the public service or public utility commission in the particular state. Utility companies engaged in interstate commerce are subject to regulation by the federal government.

Social Regulation

There is also government social regulation of business — hiring of the handicapped, occupational safety, consumer protection, environmental protection, affirmative action, and so forth. The rationale for social regulation is that the market system does not work to solve such problems as sex and race discrimination, negative wants, and externalities created by rising living standards. Pollution is an example of externalities. There was no price imposed upon business for using the air or water to store or discharge its waste, and so the cost to society of polluting the air or water was not taken into consideration by market forces. Thus the federal government stepped in to improve regulation and to create the Environmental Protection Agency. It and other social regulatory agencies have come to have a great influence on business for the simple reason that few business firms can avoid dealing with them.

GOVERNMENT AS AN EMPLOYER

One measure of the public sector's size and its impact on business is the number of persons employed by governmental units. When the armed forces are included, some 16 percent of the total labor force is employed by the public sector, and since the demand for social services is likely to increase, so is this percentage likely to, particularly at the state and local levels of government.[10] In addition, numerous other jobs are related indirectly to government employment. An army base, defense plant, or state university often supports the economy of a whole town or area.[11] In many areas, the public sector sets the wage standards and competes against the private sector for labor and other resources. There can be an adverse effect on productivity. Although comparisons with the private sector are difficult to make, the available evidence suggests that productivity in the federal government sector has risen less rapidly than that in the private sector.[12]

Two sets of administrative hierarchies, one public and the other private, have grown at different times for different reasons to carry out different functions. The public hierarchy developed much later than the private hierarchy. In 1929, the federal government's working force in Washington was a great deal smaller than that at U.S. Steel or General Motors; today it is much larger than both companies combined. Numerous federal agencies have been created, and a new administrative culture has developed. The work, attitudes, and perspective of the business administrator and the government administrator have become and will remain almost as distinct and separate as those of the scientist and humanist. The attitudes of these two hierarchies define business and government relations. This relationship over time has been anything but amicable. One reason is cultural: business leaders are usually older and have different educational and career backgrounds than the public officials with whom they must deal.

10. A major objective of the Reagan administration is to reduce the role of the federal government in the American economy. If he is successful over the long run, the role of state and local governments in the American economy will increase. The likelihood, at least for the immediate future, is for a more rapid increase in state and local government employment than in federal government employment.
11. An example is Blacksburg, Virginia, where Virginia Tech is by far the largest employer in the area.
12. U.S. Congress, Joint Economic Committee, *Productivity in the Federal Government* (Washington, D.C.: U.S. Government Printing Office, May 1979).

GOVERNMENT OWNERSHIP OF BUSINESS

In the United States, all levels of government own and operate productive facilities of many kinds. Airports, but not railway terminals, are usually government owned. Governmental units own and operate the plants that provide water, gas, and electricity to thousands of cities and towns, as well as owning local transportation systems, heating plants, warehouses, printing companies, and many other facilities. The government also produces, either directly or indirectly, all of our artificial rubber, atomic power, and many other goods, and it runs projects connected with reforestation, soil erosion, slum clearance, rural electrification, and housing. All of this does not mean that government ownership and operation is necessarily preferred to private ownership and operation. In many cases, the resources required were too large, the risks too great, or the likelihood of profit too small to attract private enterprise, and so the government was compelled to perform the tasks.

One example of this is the Tennessee Valley Authority (TVA), a major public enterprise for the production and distribution of electrical power in the southeastern United States. At one time, the area adjacent to the Tennessee River was among the most impoverished in the United States. Flooding and soil erosion were common, and almost all homes in the area were without electricity. The area was also generally unattractive to industry, and so TVA was created to erect dams and hydroelectric plants to provide electric power, to improve navigation on the Tennessee River, to promote flood control, to prevent soil erosion, to reforest the land, and to contribute to the nation's defense through the manufacture of artificial nitrates. It was opposed by private companies, in particular the utility companies, because it was empowered to sell electricity in direct competition with them, even though the utility companies in the Tennessee Valley area had never considered it profitable to provide any but the most minimal amount of service. TVA was also supposed to serve as a yardstick of efficiency, though government ownership and operation of power facilities do not always mean lower rates or greater efficiency. Opinion on TVA's efficiency is mixed: TVA is efficient compared with other government agencies, but not so compared with private business.

Government credit programs are a gray area in that they do not involve outright state ownership of industry. Federal credit programs, however, do have an impact on private industry that should be mentioned. Direct, insured, and federally sponsored agency loans passed the $500 billion mark in 1980 and have continued to increase. These programs have three main functions: the elimination of gaps in the credit market, the provision of subsidies to encourage socially desirable activity, and the stimulation of the economy. The first two of these functions are microeconomic in that they are supposed to affect the types of activity for which credit is made available, the geographical location of that activity, and the types of borrowers who have access to credit. For example, Federal Housing Administration (FHA) and Veterans' Administration (VA) mortgage insurance programs have resulted in a greater demand for housing. The third function is macroeconomic in that federal lending affects the level of economic activity on a large scale, in particular, the gross national product and employment.

THE BUSINESS–GOVERNMENT INTERFACE

President Calvin Coolidge once said that the business of America is business. But that was long ago when business was supreme and government was small, and business firms had the power to shift business-government relations in their favor.[13] Presidents were probusiness usually, and businessmen were appointed to cabinet positions and to other key government jobs where they could gain approval of such measures as a protective tariff and could transform the Federal Trade Commission and other federal government regulatory agencies into having a more probusiness attitude. These businessmen were not necessarily the "greedy capitalists" who inspired government regulations in the first place. Often they were like evangelists who believed in the fervor of their cause.[14] Many saw success in business as a service to society, not just as the pursuit of private gain.

But times have changed. Not only does government now control a significant share of the national product, its expenditures and regulatory and redistributive activities affect virtually every kind of private activity. Even though business firms have been the beneficiaries of many government activities, many business leaders and some politicians would like to reduce the role of the federal government in the marketplace. They believe that a responsibly managed private sector can solve many social problems more efficiently than government.[15] They feel that government intrusion into private decisions, bureaucracy, and the uncertainty of political and economic policy all frustrate capital investment planning.[16] This reduces the capacity of the private sector to

13. The time was the 1920s, which has been called the golden age of American capitalism.
14. Evangelism was a powerful religious force during the 1920s. Aimee Semple MacPherson and Billy Sunday were the counterparts of Billy Graham and Oral Roberts today.
15. Private enterprise is now running prisons and hospitals.
16. They have some justification here as witnessed by the inability of President Reagan and Congress to balance the budget.

create jobs, products, and services. Moreover, many government regulatory agencies are regarded as too intrusive into business affairs.

Conversely, it can be argued that much of the government regulations and intervention that business desires was brought about by business itself. This regulation occurred because there was a failure on the part of business either to recognize or to accede to the public's stake in their activities. They would always react when compelled to do so, but they would never act to solve a problem. Despite the desire of the public for clean air and water, safer goods and working conditions, and truthful advertising, it took government legislation and regulation to make business respond. Moreover, many persons see business as being willing to use its power to frustrate the public interest and to oppose social change, so that government intervention in the process of business decision making is mandatory if the public interest is to be served.

It is necessary to go back to the last century to understand the relationship of government and business. The coming of the large railroads and then of large industrial enterprises brought about government regulation. The regulation of business became the paramount domestic issue in American politics for the period from 1880 to 1920. In the 1930s, business, in particular big business, took much of the blame for the Depression. Then in the 1960s and 1970s, business was blamed for the depletion of resources and the pollution that resulted, as well as for other social problems of the day. By then the standard response to complex economic problems was to pass laws creating regulatory commissions to monitor the activities of the businesses involved. During the 1980s, the Reagan administration has made an attempt to reduce the extent of government regulation of business and the overall role of the federal government in the American economy. Whether it will succeed in its objectives remains to be seen.

SUMMARY

Some government intervention is necessary for the establishment of even the freest type of economic system. The very atmosphere for the conduct of business is created by the ability of government to establish and maintain private property, freedom of enterprise, money and credit, and a system of civil laws for adjudicating the private disputes of individuals. Such institutions make possible an elaborate system of private planning in which individuals, rather than government, organize and direct the production of goods and services in response to the desires of consumers.

Government regulation of business has been established for a number of reasons. One reason is the failure of the market mechanism to allocate resources properly. When there is a breakdown in competitive market forces, monopoly, oligopoly, and otherwise imperfectly competitive market structures cause inefficient resource allocation and socially undesirable market performance. Antitrust policies are designed to deal with industry conduct, such as price fixing, and with industry structure that might foster monopolistic powers. There is also government regulation of the so-called natural monopolies — industries so large or so vital that competition is simply not feasible. Another area of regulation is the use of public resources such as air and water. There are two issues here: first, balancing the amount of tolerable pollution against the value of the goods or services produced and, second, choosing the appropriate instruments to minimize the cost of achieving this balance. Government regulation can also intervene between sellers and consumers to protect either or both from certain conditions that might emerge in the absence of regulation. Since research is expensive to conduct, the government itself often collects data rather than having the market participant do it. The government then uses the research data to determine whether or not a product should be available to the public. For example, it is unlawful to market certain drugs unless they have been approved by the Federal Drug Administration (FDA).

QUESTIONS FOR DISCUSSION

1. Discuss the various ways in which the activities of government have an impact on business.
2. Explain the reasons for the increase in the government's intervention in business affairs.
3. Government expenditures and taxes affect almost every business firm in the U.S. economy. Discuss this statement.
4. Explain the reasons for the increase in expenditures at all levels of government.
5. In what ways has the U.S. government provided aid to business firms?
6. Why is it important for students to learn about the relationship between business and government?
7. What is government social regulation of business?
8. Government ownership of business in the United States is limited to a few areas. Discuss.

PART II
HISTORICAL BACKGROUND OF GOVERNMENT AND BUSINESS RELATIONS

Government regulation of business can be divided into three periods. The first period, which is the subject of Chapter 2, lasted from 1870 to 1930. During this time, government intervention in business was sporadic and essentially microeconomic. This intervention was in the form of laws to regulate railroads and to curb the power of monopolies. Only when the competitive, self-adjusting market mechanism broke down did the government undertake to correct its most serious failings. The first laws to protect the interests of consumers were also passed during this period. Those laws regulating the railroads and monopolies usually were initiated by the state governments and only later by the federal government. Laws were also passed to improve the lot of laborers, particularly with respect to working conditions and tax income and wealth. But for the most part, the laws directed against industrial concentration and the accumulation of wealth did not have much effect, and by 1920 industrial concentration was more pronounced than it had been in 1880.

The second period covers the Depression of the 1930s, probably the most active period ever in business-government relations during which much legislation was passed to stimulate business recovery. Because it was believed that certain defects in the business system were at least partly responsible for causing the Depression, laws regulating business were enacted in a number of areas, and the number of regulatory agencies multiplied. It was evident, when the decade of the Depression ended, that the federal government had begun extensive regulation of most segments of business activity. The Depression marked the decline of laissez faire and the advent of the mixed economy, which was reflected in increased governmental intervention in all spheres of business activity. The federal debt, which had been reduced to less than $2 billion by 1929, had increased to $40 billion by 1939. The machinery for the government's macroeconomic intervention was started during the 1930s and was completed with the passage of the Employment Act of 1946.

The third period of increased government control of business extends from roughly 1960 to the present. Before this period, most legislation affecting business was economic in nature. The Sherman Antitrust Act, the Clayton Act, the Federal Trade Commission Act, the Robinson-Patman Act, and many other acts all dealt with specific economic issues: monopoly power, pricing, concentration of industry, and corporate economic power and its uses and abuses. The focus of more recent legislation, however, has been on the attainment of certain social goals: environmental protection, consumerism, minority employment, employment of women, job safety, and so forth. These goals are associated with a change in societal values that is characterized by the terms *rising entitlements* and *a better quality of life*. Examples of such legislation include the Clean Air Act of 1970, the Consumer Product Safety Act of 1972, and the Equal Employment Opportunity Act of 1972. This kind of legislation also has created a new type of regulatory agency that is broader based in its control over business activities and is more oriented toward accomplishing social objectives than the older regulatory agencies were. An example of this kind of agency is the Environmental Protection Agency, which can regulate any type of business that pollutes the atmosphere.

Chapter 2 provides a historical framework to explain why government intervention into business affairs became necessary. Because there was a concentration of economic power in many industries, terms like *competition* and *free enterprise* had ceased to have much meaning. In addition, there were great inequalities in the distribution of income and wealth, since there were no countervailing forces to big business. Labor unions were weak because they were denied due process under the law, and the authority of government was circumscribed by its adherence to the philosophy of laissez faire. The concentration of economic power in the hands of a few persons and corporations hindered the democratic process because it tended also to promote the concentration of political power, and many economic and political abuses ensued that worked to the detriment of the country's social welfare. These abuses angered farmers, consumers, and small business owners, who felt at a disadvantage in comparison with big business, trusts, and the eastern banks. Organized pressure from these groups was the catalyst that eventually resulted in government intervention in the form of railroad regulation and action against the industrial monopolies.

Chapter 2
The Development of Government Regulation of Business

This chapter and the one following it provide the historical background necessary to understand the reasons for government intervention into business affairs. Once this background has been presented, it will be possible to explore in more detail the role of government in today's business world. It can be said that business-government relations as they exist today have evolved from the last century as the United States began its transformation from an agrarian to an industrial society. Following the Civil War, industry became increasingly complex, and mass production techniques enabled producers to expand their output. The industrial capitalists began to rise above those who were so much a part of the American economy before the war — merchants, shippers, farmers, and artisans. The economic pendulum, which before the Civil War had favored competition among a large number of sellers, swung over to the large-scale enterprise with an ever-increasing need for capital. Various business abuses followed that contributed to a decline in competition.

Industrial and railroad monopolies were formed around 1880 and continued into this century. The primary reason for the creation of this type of combination was the manufacturer's desire to restrict or eliminate competition and thus establish monopoly prices. This was done through control of supply. A monopoly price is likely to be higher than a competitive price, for the monopolist can limit supply and in this way prevent prices from falling to the level determined by competition. A second reason for business monopolies was the development of the business cycle. As recessions became more severe, business firms merged to achieve some sort of control over the market. A third reason for monopolies was that those organizing them hoped they would achieve the economies of the trust: a trust could almost always secure raw materials more cheaply than would be possible in a state of competition.

INDUSTRIAL CONSOLIDATION AND THE
DECLINE OF COMPETITION

The period from the end of the Civil War to around 1890 can be called the golden age of laissez faire capitalism. Business had just about everything its own way. The government, in particular the federal government, did nothing to intervene until business abuses of the market system became so prevalent that some form of intervention became necessary. Business, after a period of fierce competition, was characterized not only by the rise of the corporation as the dominant business unit but also by the growth of large-scale production and the beginning of business combinations. These combinations, of which the trust was the most important, were organized to eliminate competition and to regulate output and thereby stabilize prices, control production, and acquire greater profit. They were united under one central management of a large number of production units either turning out the same product or operating different stages of the process necessary to prepare the final product for market.

The growing concentration of economic power also created another problem — extremes of poverty and wealth. The new aristocracy of the country was made up of wealthy entrepreneurs and business leaders whom some called *robber barons*. The prototypes of the industrial capitalists were John D. Rockefeller and Andrew Carnegie. They epitomized the Protestant work ethic, successful in a competitive race in which victory went to the swift and resourceful. They also were not particularly scrupulous, taking advantage of every loophole, corrupting government officials, and bribing rivals' employees in a no-holds-barred effort to ruin competitors. But they were supported by a philosophy that helped explain and justify their preeminent position — the philosophy of Social Darwinism. To put it simply, Social Darwinism was the application of Darwin's biological theory to economics.[1] It was the "survival of the fittest" principle applied to the business world. The Carnegies and the Rockefellers reached their positions through a competitive selection process, proved themselves the fittest, and were therefore entitled to the fruits of their labor. Society was the beneficiary of their efforts. Social Darwinism opposed government intervention in the operation of the economy and upheld industrial capitalism as a system in which each contributing group received a just reward.

There is some merit in Social Darwinism. Carnegie, Rockefeller and others of their type possessed certain attributes that encouraged

---

1. Social Darwinism was conceived by the English philosopher Herbert Spencer. His disciples in the United States were William Graham Sumner and John B. Clark. Sumner, a professor of moral philosophy at Yale, had a particularly strong influence on American thought.

success.[2] They were energetic, shrewd, and resourceful men who worked hard and expanded their business by plowing profits back into it. But there also were hardworking people at the opposite end of the income spectrum. In 1890, Marshall Field's income was calculated at $600 an hour; his shopgirls, earning salaries of $3 to $5 a week, had to work more than three years to earn that amount.[3] The working conditions for almost all the workers were deplorable, and working twelve hours a day, seven days a week was not uncommon. Wages were low, and there was no government intervention in the form of laws designed to provide unemployment benefits, worker's compensation, or any form of social security taken for granted in the industrial societies of today. There were no child labor laws — children of eight and even younger worked in the mills and coal mines. Social and economic inequities divided the United States, and by 1890, 1 percent of the population owned as much of the nation's wealth as the remaining 99 percent did.

The Decline of Competition

Edward Bellamy, a social critic of the time and the author of the well-known utopian novel *Looking Backward*, offers some rather incisive insights into the industrial society that existed in the United States during the latter part of the last century.[4] He feared the consequences of the ever-increasing concentration of business in the hands of fewer and fewer individuals — individuals responsible neither to society nor to government. He saw that smallness was no remedy for bigness, however, and that if the concentration of business continued, government control would be the only means of protecting the public from exploitation. The following excerpt from *Looking Backward* summarizes conditions as they existed at the time:

> The next of the great wastes was that from competition. The field of industry was a battleground as wide as the world, in which the workers wasted in assailing one another, energies which, if expended in concentrated effort would have enriched all. As for mercy or quarter in this warfare, there was absolutely none of it. To deliberately enter a field of business and destroy the enterprises of

2. Hacker, *The Triumph of American Capitalism*, p. 401.
3. Cited in Otto L. Bettman, *The Good Old Days — They Were Terrible* (New York: Random House, 1974), p. 67.
4. Edward Bellamy, *Looking Backward* (New York: NAL, 1963). The main protagonist in the story is a wealthy young Bostonian named Julian West who is transported in time from the year 1887 to the year 2000. There has been a complete transformation of society during the interval.

those who had occupied it previously, in order to plant one's own enterprise on their ruins, was an achievement which never failed to command popular admiration....[5]

This description of competition during the late nineteenth century was not far from the truth. Competition among companies took many forms, including physical violence. For example, an independently owned railroad, the Albany and Susquehanna, had been constructed between Albany and Binghamton, New York. One of its major objectives was to haul coal between the Pennsylvania coal fields near Binghamton and the New England users of coal beyond Albany. The line was adjacent to the territory served by the Erie Railroad, which saw the desirability of possessing the Albany and Susquehanna. First the Erie tried to buy a majority of the shares of stock in the line but failed. It then attempted through legal maneuvering to gain a clear majority on the line's board of directors but failed in this, too. The Erie finally tried by armed assault to gain control of the Albany terminus of the line but was repulsed, though it did succeed in taking the line's facilities at the Binghamton end. The Albany and Susquehanna planned to retaliate by sending out several hundred men from Albany to retake the terminus. The Erie Railroad sent out its own men from Binghamton. The trains carrying the two factions met head-on, and passengers in both trains were killed. A battle between the two groups of men ensued. The Erie group lost and retreated, tearing up tracks and bridges as they went. Only then did the Erie group give up trying to gain control of the Albany and Susquehanna.[6]

The market system, if working well, can produce many generally good results. It can play on self-interest to produce results in the interest of others. It can use the lures of profits, income, and material rewards to induce individuals and business enterprises to behave in ways that are supposed to benefit others. The market system does not, however, eliminate all the disadvantages of economic interdependence among persons and groups. At times it is a hard taskmaster, exacting heavy penalties on those who fail to conform to its demands. Thus there are not only winners under a market system but losers, too, and many manufacturers learned the hard way that competition can have the effect of reducing prices and profits. At least to some extent, the more some win, the more others lose. A business, for example, may lose its local market to a distant rival now able to compete because of a new mode of transportation. Therefore business firms began to seek

5. Ibid., pp. 156–157.
6. For a detailed description of this and other practices, see Matthew Josephson, *The Robber Barons* (New York: Harcourt, Brace & World, 1934). The Erie Railroad was controlled by the Erie Ring, a combination put together by Jay Gould.

ways to make sure that they, rather than someone else, were the winners. In the absence of laws and government regulation to force them to play the free enterprise game by the rules, it became easy for business firms to circumvent competition through collusive practices and various forms of combinations.

Modern technology was partly responsible for the decline of competition. As mentioned previously, there were numerous inventions after the Civil War that made possible the use of highly specialized and sometimes quite elaborate and complex machinery. Efficient ways to organize production in large units were also being discovered. One outcome of this was an increase in the average size of many businesses and a decline in the numbers of firms in many industries. Many of these larger firms had a considerable investment tied up in durable and highly specialized equipment. Interest, maintenance, and depreciation costs were incurred regularly whether or not the equipment was being used. Fixed costs were beginning to be very large and therefore very important for some firms. When the volume of output was below capacity, additional amounts of product could be produced without any increase in fixed costs and, therefore, with relatively little total additional cost. In these circumstances, the managers of these firms were eager to find ways to sell all the output that could be produced at full capacity.

A third factor leading to the decline of competition was the business cycle. As the United States became an industrial nation, there were more and more periods of boom and bust. During a business depression, competition for survival led to falling prices and output. Business firms learned that the reductions in the price of goods they offered for sale often did not encourage consumers to buy more of them, particularly when the demand for the goods was inelastic, in other words, when a change in price was accompanied by a less than proportionate change in the quantity demanded. The small increases in the volume of sales of these goods also were accompanied by declining profits. An advantage of the business combine or monopoly was that output could be controlled and prices stabilized. Business consolidation was facilitated by the depressions. In the depression of 1893, Andrew Carnegie was able to take advantage of his competitors' economic distress to acquire a wide variety of holdings. He bought iron deposits, ore ships, ports, docks, warehouses, and railroad lines to link his coal, coke, limestone, furnaces, and mills into a single chain. The end of that depression saw the Carnegie Company, later the United States Steel Corporation, in control of the heavy-steel field and the fixer of prices for the finished-steel manufacturers.

Devices for Achieving Monopoly Power

The era of industrial expansion that began after the end of the Civil War resulted in two related developments important to policy. The first was a trend toward the concentration of production in the hands of a limited number of firms. This was in part a logical concomitant of changing technology: as the technically optimum size of firms grew larger, some firms went under. The high proportion of fixed costs associated with the elaborate equipment that the new technology had made possible increased the efforts of each firm to take over the market sales of other firms. In many industrial fields competition was virtually unimpaired, but in others a few enterprises came to dominate enough of the market to allow them to control prices. The second development, which had more important implications for public policy, was a trend by business firms to limit competition through various types of combinations designed to promote monopoly power.

These combinations usually came in cycles. The first cycle, lasting roughly from 1870 to 1890, used the pool and the trust as monopoly devices.[7] The pool was devised first but was superseded by the trust, which proved to be a more effective type of combination. A wave of federal and state antimonopoly legislation, culminating with the Sherman Antitrust Act, made the trust a rather unpopular vehicle for combination. The trust began to decline in popularity, and by the end of the last century the holding company had achieved dominance. The second cycle was the period of the holding company. There was an intensive phase of consolidation facilitated by the holding company device that lasted from 1897 to 1903. A third cycle of industrial combination occurred during the 1920s, when mergers in the form of holding companies or outright mergers between companies were used to consolidate and reduce the number of firms in new industries such as radios, automobiles, and electrical appliances. The fourth cycle of the combination movement, which came after the end of World War II and continued into the 1950s, was characterized by horizontal and vertical merger arrangements.

We should emphasize that the results of various business combinations were often disappointing. There were many reasons for this. Combinations were unable to increase profits or even to perpetuate them in industries subject to stagnation; on the other hand, accelerated growth in a new industry created an industrial climate in which combinations were able to prosper. Industrial combinations were also affected by the vagaries of the business cycle and were often incapable of forestalling sharp decreases in profits in years of general business depression. When combinations acquired unmanageable financial

---

7. The terms *pool* and *trust* are discussed on p. 29.

structures that subjected them to fixed charges above their minimum earnings capacity, they were often unable to readily adapt themselves to new situations. Many of the earlier combinations were made up of equal producers who sought to curb the excesses of cutthroat competition by allocating production and fixing prices; sooner or later, however, almost all such arrangements ended in failure because one of the participants violated the agreements. The large corporation had to appear first, based on horizontal and vertical integration, before combinations could be truly effective. Finally, combinations did not automatically guarantee competent management.

Pools

The pool was used widely in the 1870s among the railroads and in some manufacturing companies. Under this arrangement, all or almost all the producers of some good or service reached an agreement, usually informally, to share customers, sales, profits, or territories in some fashion. In this way, they hoped to avoid price reductions and the more ruthless kinds of competition among themselves. Pooling arrangements took a number of forms. Two railroads could decide to divide freight revenues evenly, regardless of which one actually transported the freight. For example, in the 1870s, the five or six railroads that controlled the shipment of anthracite coal in the five counties of northeastern Pennsylvania divided the total shipment among themselves. Some pools attempted to corner the market for a given product; often though pooling agreements were violated soon after their initiation when one or more of the parties would find it irresistible to undercut the others. Other reasons for the short duration of the pools were competition from a large number of small firms operating in local markets made pooling agreements ineffective, and the pools could not adapt rapidly to changing market conditions.

Trusts

In the 1880s, trusts began to replace or exist alongside pools as the primary means for eliminating competition. Under a trust arrangement, owners of a controlling interest in all or almost all an industry's firms would agree to entrust their ownership shares to the control of one or a few people, called trustees, and to receive trust certificates in return. These certificates were issued on the basis of the amount of stock held in trust, and the board of trustees controlled the business policies of the combination. The trustees would direct all firms in the trust as though they were one large firm. With monolithic power, they confronted the competition. They maximized profits, not by being best, but by being biggest. Trusts had a highly centralized form of management in which the trustees were able to elect members of the board of directors of the operating companies whose common stock was deposited with them. Although the trust eventually gave way to other arrangements, it first gave its name to the general government campaign against monopolies.

The trust par excellence was the Standard Oil Trust formed in 1879, forever to be associated with John D. Rockefeller. By 1884, Standard Oil was selling more than 80 percent of all the oil that flowed out of domestic wells. It controlled not only the refining of petroleum but also its retail sales. The trust was organized to eliminate competition at these two levels of operation. In areas in which the competition with the products of other oil companies was keen, the trust reduced the retail prices of its products to attract customers from competing retailers. In many cases, these outlets were unable to compete and sold out to Standard Oil. In areas in which there was no competition, Standard Oil would charge artificially high prices. The trust also tried to control the transportation of petroleum. It was able to negotiate secret rebates from railroads, which were eager to carry Standard's petroleum, and it was even able to force one railroad to give it a rate of ten cents a barrel and to charge other companies thirty-five cents a barrel, of which twenty-five cents went back to Standard Oil.[8]

Holding Companies

Holding companies replaced trusts as a device to ensure the firms' survival and to prevent economic warfare among them. A holding company is a corporation that has among its assets shares of stock in other corporations. Controlled corporations are subsidiaries of the holding company, which may be a managing company or an operating company. Those who control a holding company are able through their ownership of stock in other companies to dictate business policies. Competition among companies can be controlled by the holding company. As a direct corporate entity, it can issue stock and borrow money through the issuance of corporate bonds. The proceeds from the sale of either or both of these types of securities have often been used to purchase common stock in other holding companies, thus creating a pyramid arrangement. In the 1920s, pyramiding corporate issues in public utility companies channeled power and control over vast corporate empires into the hands of a few utility magnates.

8. Ida M. Tarbell, *The History of the Standard Oil Company* (New York: McClure, Phillips, & Co., 1904).

Mergers

The merger was another device used to eliminate competition. Mergers may take several forms. One company may purchase the physical assets or the shares of stock of a previously competing company. Two companies may exchange their stock, and a new company may be formed to buy up the assets or shares of two or more older companies. The General Electric Company, the American Sugar Refining Company, and the International Harvester Company[9] all were born of mergers. The results of mergers are similar to those of holding companies. The power to make decisions about such things as production techniques and selling arrangements is transferred to a single group of persons, among whom coordination is achieved largely by central command. As a method of controlling large industries, the merger was somewhat impractical since it required the consent of each class of security holder to the merger and involved complex negotiations on the terms of exchange.

Mergers also can be classified on the basis of horizontal and vertical arrangements. A horizontal merger is one between firms engaging in the same or similar activities — a union of railroads, bakeries, or shoe manufacturers, for example. There is nothing illegal about a horizontal merger unless it is used to restrict competit·on, which all too often has been the case. A vertical merger is one between firms engaging in different parts of the producing and selling process. An example would be the union of a shoe manufacturer and a shoe retail store. A steel mill could acquire a coal mine and use its entire output in its own furnace. In a vertical merger, various phases of the production and distribution process are integrated. Again, there is nothing illegal about a vertical merger unless it can be demonstrated that competition is lessened. During the last century, both types of mergers were common, and no laws controlled their impact on competition. The merger arrangement itself did not guarantee success, for profits were often affected by other factors, including business recessions, over which a combination had no control.

Cartels

Cartels are international associations of firms in the same industry established to allocate world markets among their members, regulate the prices in those markets, eliminate competition, and restrict output. The cartel arrangement was less a product of the period that produced the trust and the holding company than of a later period when busi-

9. International Harvester is now known as Navistar.

ness firms had more global operations. Almost all cartels have been made up of companies in the production of chemicals, electrical equipment, and synthetic products like plastics. Their control is usually over the cross-licensing of patents, which has often led to worldwide control of production and trade by what almost amounts to a private government. The cartels may also control the use of trademarks, with each cartel member granted the exclusive right to use a trademark in its own territory.

Interlocking Directorates

An interlocking directorate is an arrangement in which one person sits on the board of directors of two or more companies. In a complex network of many interlocking directorates, it is possible for the interlocked firms to eliminate or reduce competition. The interlocking device has been used not only by industrial firms but also by banks. The latter would place one of their members on the board of directors of companies with which they did business, and in this way, the banks were in a position to dictate corporate policy and regulate competition. Thus, supposedly independent firms collaborated rather than competed with each other. Although it is now illegal for one person to serve on the board of directors of two companies that produce the same goods and services, interlocking directorates are still used, with interlocks between competitors and between companies and their suppliers or customers.

Anticompetitive Business Practices

A variety of anticompetitive business practices began during the last century, and many still remain in effect. As laws were passed to correct existing abuses, new abuses would arise. Some of the devices used to eliminate competition are presented below. It should be emphasized that trusts, pools, and other monopoly arrangements were originally devised to circumvent some of the more ruthless kinds of competition. But this certainly did not mean that the trust was free from anticompetitive business practices; if anything, it refined them.

Preemptive Buying

One tactic that has been used to eliminate competition is preemptive buying. Using this technique, a company would buy up all the supplies or resources needed to make its product. The company does not necessarily need all that it buys, but in this way it can deny vital supplies to its competitors. In the last century, the Southern Pacific Railroad, in an attempt to ensure for itself a monopoly on rail transport eastward out of the state of California, bought up land and constructed rail lines in the few suitable passageways through the Sierra mountains. It did this not to provide services through these places but to block the construction of competing lines. More recently (during the 1920s and 1930s), the Aluminum Company of America (Alcoa) acted similarly. According to the government charges levied against it, Alcoa acted to acquire bauxite deposits, water power sites, and plants in excess of its needs with the intent of denying their use to competitors.[10]

Exclusive Sales Arrangement

In exclusive sales arrangement, manufacturing companies agree to allow distributors and retailers to handle their products only if they agree not to handle similar products made by other manufacturers. A case in point is the American Tobacco Trust, a trust comparable in power and ruthlessness to the Standard Oil Trust. During the latter part of the nineteenth century, the trust controlled distributors at the wholesale and retail levels by offering large discounts to jobbers who agreed to handle exclusively the products of American Tobacco. A commission of 2.5 percent was paid to jobbers who agreed to sell only to the retail trade and only at prices fixed by the trust. If they agreed to handle only the products of the trust, they received an additional 7.5 percent commission. The objective of the arrangement was to leave no room for the products of other tobacco manufacturers. American Tobacco was able to do this because of its economic power: it almost completely controlled the supply of cigarettes and other tobacco products.

Tying Agreements

Tying agreements are somewhat similar to exclusive sales arrangements. In a tying agreement, a company requires a buyer to purchase one or more additional products as a condition for purchasing the desired product. For the tying agreement to be successful, the desired product must have few substitutes and also be relatively less interchangeable than the tied item. In one well-known case, the International Salt Company, which had patents on two salt dispensing machines, would

10. Robert F. Lanzilloti, *The Structure of American Industry: Some Case Studies*, ed. Walter Adams, 3rd ed. (New York: Macmillan, 1961), chap. 6.

lease the machines only if the lessee would agree to buy all salt to be used in the machine from International Salt. The United Shoe Machinery Company once compelled shoemakers to purchase other materials and intermediate products from it as a condition for purchasing shoe machinery, which limited the other sellers of the tied products from competing in the market. But the courts have generally disallowed tying agreements in which the end result is the lessening of competition, particularly when the tied product is a legal monopoly such as a patent.

Patent Control

To stimulate invention, the federal government grants patents, which give exclusive control over articles and processes for seventeen years. These legal grants sometimes have been used to establish and maintain a monopolistic position. Patent rights are property and can be rented with conditions of use specified. They thus have formed the basis of agreements to maintain prices, allocate markets, and restrict production. Patents promote invention by granting temporary monopolies to inventors, but they have often had the effect of subverting competition. An example of this was the Ethyl Gasoline Corporation, jointly owned by Standard Oil of New Jersey and General Motors, which held the patent on tetra-ethyl, "antiknock" gasoline. It licensed all refiners and eleven thousand independent retail distributors, forcing them to agree to maintain a price differential over ordinary gasoline and to follow the big oil companies' price policies before they would be allowed to make and use tetra-ethyl.

Price Discrimination

Discriminatory pricing policies are almost too numerous to describe. One example is the basing point system. To avoid giving mills located near a consuming center an advantage in obtaining business, steel corporations adopted the idea of selling all iron and steel products, except rails, at delivered prices only. The delivered prices were the sum of the base price added to the cost of transportation from Pittsburgh to the destination, regardless of the origin of the shipment or the actual freight cost. Thus the "Pittsburgh-plus" system was born. Prices were quoted on the basis of Pittsburgh, even though the product may have been made in Chicago. Buyers in the Chicago area, for example, were required to pay $7.50 a ton in phantom freight — the freight "plus" from Pittsburgh — on steel produced in Chicago by the local subsidiaries of U.S. Steel. In 1948, the Supreme Court declared that the basing point system was a monopolistic form of pricing.

In attempting to eliminate competition, business firms have also used predatory pricing practices. Firms with several products or with sales in more than one market area were able to use predatory pricing. A firm with a chain of grocery stores, for example, might lower prices at one of its outlets that was in close competition with an independent grocery store. It could sustain the resulting temporary losses at the one outlet by relying on the profits it received from other outlets. In this way, the chain could drive the independent store out of business. Then it could raise its prices in what had become its own local monopoly. Firms with many products used similar tactics to eliminate rival firms with one product. Price discrimination occurs when a seller charges different prices to the same or different buyers for the same good. This in itself is not necessarily unfair, for it may be more economical for a firm to sell in bulk, and those economies can be passed on to the consumer. But often discriminatory pricing has been used to undercut the competition of other firms.

Business firms also have resorted to price fixing. This approach has always been tempting because firms can reduce or even eliminate the risk of economic loss. The power to fix prices requires having the power to control the market. Price fixing may take two forms, either overt collusion between business firms to set prices or price leadership, in which one firm sets the price. Collusion may occur when several firms agree to fix bids on government contracts, with each firm taking its turn in submitting the lowest bid. In some industries there is a relatively small number of firms, and one dominates the market by virtue of its size and economic power. The dominant firm acts as the price leader, and the others set their prices accordingly, because of fear of the consequences if they do not or because of the benefit of the price stability that will occur if they do. Price competition disappears, and often the prices are higher than they would be in a competitive market. The potential harm to competition from adopting the same prices as those of the industry leader is as great as that stemming from an outright conspiracy to fix prices.

Reciprocal Agreements

Reciprocal agreements are arrangements in which firms agree to purchase certain products from each other. This kind of thing happens all the time, and there is nothing inherently wrong with reciprocal agreements unless the end result is the lessening of competition. This may well happen. Company A may refuse to buy products from Company B unless it in turn agrees to buy Company A's products. Company A may be able, through the volume of its purchases, to compel Company B to reciprocate by buying its products, and Company A can threaten to purchase its goods elsewhere unless such an arrangement is made. In one case, Consolidated Foods was able to use its buying power to force its suppliers to purchase products from one of its affiliates. In another case, General Motors told the railroads that unless they bought their locomotives, GM would take its shipping business to other lines. In both cases, the courts found these activities to constitute a substantial lessening of competition and ordered them stopped.

RAILROAD REGULATION

In his novel *Giants in the Earth*, O. E. Rolvaag describes the coming of the railroad to South Dakota:

> One fine day a strange monster came writhing westward over the prairie, from Worthington to Luverne; it was the greatest and most memorable event that had yet happened in these parts. The monster crawled along with a terrible speed, but when it came near, it did not crawl at all; it rushed forward in tortuous windings, with an awful roar, while black, curling smoke streaked out behind it in the air. People felt that day a joy that almost frightened them; for it seemed now that all their troubles were over, that there could be no more hardships to contend with — at least, that was what the Sognings solemnly affirmed. For now that the railway had come as far as this, it wouldn't take long before they would see it winding its way into Sioux Falls.[11]

Few inventions have had more impact on American life than the railroad. To the farmers, the railroads brought many blessings. They enabled the farmers to get their produce to market, supplied them with agricultural implements, catalogues, and other accoutrements of the outside world, and ended rural isolation as passenger trains connected the farms with the cities. The railroads contributed to the development of mass transportation and distribution and to large-scale corporations in their modern form. They also helped urbanize the American economy by carrying laborers and supplies to newly built factories in the cities. Many railroad innovations and inventions improved the economy — for example, the Pullman car and the creation of a standard gauge, which enabled the integration of the nation's rail system. Methods of financing and promoting railroad expansion also influenced the economy. Railroad securities were one of the largest outlets for the Ameri-

11. O. F. Rolvaag, *Giants in the Earth* (New York: Harper & Row, 1927), p. 327.

can peoples' savings. State and local governments also extended financial aid to the railroads in the form of loans, grants, and property tax exemption. Almost all railroads tended to rely on bonds for financial expansion; however, the heavy fixed interest charge they incurred often led to financial disaster.

The railroad industry had many of the same characteristics of industrial capitalism described in the last chapter — increasing costs leading to large-scale production, keen competition, and a resulting tendency toward monopoly. But it was in the railroads that the country first encountered the problems that arise under such conditions. There was a period of competition that eventually degenerated into a struggle for the survival of the fittest. One condition that contributed to undesirable practices by the railroads was the high ratio of fixed to operating costs. In addition, the railroads' total fixed costs bore no relation to the volume of traffic once these fixed costs had been incurred or once the railroads had been constructed. Rate wars were common, and in response, railroad operators began to expand and consolidate their holdings in order to operate more efficiently and secure greater profits. The earliest type of combination is exemplified by the railroad empire created by Cornelius Vanderbilt, who bought control of the competing lines operating from New York City to Albany and from Albany to Buffalo, and out of them formed the New York Central system.[12] A later form of railroad combination was the pool, formed to apportion business, fix rates, and thus avoid ruinous competition. For example, the five or six railroads that controlled the shipment of anthracite coal in northeastern Pennsylvania allocated to each of themselves certain percentages of the total shipment of coal. Fines were collected from those railroads that exceeded their allocations, and in turn, the money from the fines was distributed among the railroads that had carried less than their allocated portions of coal.

Reasons for Railroad Regulation

In the railroads' early days, the prevailing government policy was one of aid rather than regulation. The promise of swift transportation, industrial development, and access to market enhanced the value of the railroads, and the public interest was identified with the railroads' interests. But there were a number of abuses, resulting in part from cutthroat competitive practices in which railroads disregarded the interests of consumers and shippers. Rate discrimination was one abuse, which entailed setting different rates for different places, for different

12. Matthew Josephson, *The Robber Barons* (New York: Harcourt, Brace & World, 1934), pp. 134-138.

commodities, or for different firms. Railroads charged more for short hauls than for long hauls, and rates were higher between local, noncompetitive points. Deviations from published tariffs were a common means of rate discrimination, and rebates were given to favored shippers and localities. One of the reasons for these practices was the high ratio of fixed costs to operating costs. Traffic attracted by charging rates that brought in anything at all over operating costs was better than no traffic at all; at least it brought in something to help defray fixed costs.

Immediately after the Civil War, the farmers and small businessmen began pressing for railroad regulation. The farmers were particularly hard hit because they were absolutely dependent on the railroads, which, unregulated by any government body, practiced various forms of price discrimination, the money from which often went to pay dividends on watered stock. The prices for agricultural products fluctuated widely in domestic markets, and a high protective tariff prevented foreign manufactured goods from competing effectively with American manufactured goods, whose prices remained high. The farmers' discontent coalesced in the Grange movement, which became an important political force at the state level.[13] The Grange wanted the regulation of railroads to bring about lower freights and fares and to ban discriminatory rates for different places and persons. It also wanted cheap money, an income tax, and a reduction of the protective tariff except on agricultural products. But the Grange's main impact was on the passage of laws to regulate the railroads.

State Regulation of Railroads

The Grange, together with its allies — merchants and other small businessmen who also resented rate discrimination — gained control of a number of midwestern state governments and enacted a series of regulatory laws since known as *Granger legislation.*[14] In 1871, Illinois created a railroad and warehouse commission authorized to fix maximum rates for intrastate freight and passenger service on the railroads, as well as rates for storing grain in public warehouses and grain elevators. The commission was empowered to prosecute when a railroad charged a higher rate for a short than for a long haul over the same line in the same direction. Also in 1871, the Minnesota legislature prescribed maximum rates for passengers and freight and appointed a railroad commission to enforce the railroad laws. In 1874, a board of railway commissioners was authorized to fix maximum rates. The Iowa

13. Broadus Mitchell, *American Economic History* (Boston: Houghton Mifflin, 1947), p. 697.
14. Ibid., p. 701.

Railroad Act of 1874 followed the Minnesota model of setting maximum rates, with provisions for a railroad commission empowered to reduce rates below the maximum when that could be done without injury to the railroad. Wisconsin and other states followed the Minnesota and Iowa examples.

Federal Regulation of Railroads

The farmers' anger over railroad abuses also affected the federal government. The railroads continued to combine and strengthen, and the farmers continued to find themselves exploited, suffering from high rates and rate discrimination. Stock watering and manipulation and bribing of state legislatures injured a further section of the population. Between 1875 and 1880, pooling arrangements spread rapidly all over the United States. Whenever competition promised to regulate railroad rates through supply and demand, the pool was used to preserve dividends on watered stock and interest on fixed obligations. To a certain extent the railroads were caught up in a frenetic round of speculation and overbuilding, and they resorted to frequent issues of common stock to provide investment funds. Competition on interstate rail routes brought rate wars: in one year, the rate for fourth-class mail from New York to Chicago fell from $1.80 a pound to $.25 a pound.[15] In turn, the rate wars, particularly on trunk lines, led to the first pooling arrangement in 1874 when, at the Saratoga Conference, the owners of the Erie, Pennsylvania, and New York Central railroads met to devise a means for suppressing competition in trunk line traffic.

But the pools, far from being a remedy for the evils of excess competition, only aggravated the problem they attempted to cure. The high rates they were able to maintain often attracted the attention of speculators and led to the creation of rival roads. After prolonged railroad wars, in which competing promoters neglected the interest of the shippers and all others, E. H. Harriman achieved control of the Union Pacific and Southern Pacific, and James J. Hill, with Morgan backing, gained control of the Great Northern and the Northern Pacific. The New York Central and the Pennsylvania Railroad established a community of interest between themselves; the Pennsylvania Railroad obtained stock control of the Baltimore and Ohio and the Norfolk and Western, and the New York Central acquired the Lake Erie and Western and leased the Baltimore and Albany. These two major roads also controlled the Chesapeake and Ohio. These railroad combinations were possible because stock ownership had become so diffused that

15. Chester W. Wright, *Economic History of the United States*, 2nd ed. (New York: McGraw-Hill, 1949), p. 597.

often a comparatively small block of shares was sufficient to give one railroad decisive control over the management of another railroad.

Federal government regulation of the railroads began with the passage of the Interstate Commerce Act of 1887. It created the Interstate Commerce Commission, the first major federal regulatory agency. It outlawed certain discriminatory acts used by railroads against shippers; for example, the act made it unlawful for railroads to charge a higher rate for short hauls on shipments on the same line in the same direction. Schedules of freight rates and passenger rates alike had to be made public to prevent discrimination against shippers, and rate increases could be made only after ten days' advance public notice had been given. The Interstate Commerce Act was followed by the Hepburn Act of 1906, which broadened the jurisdiction of the Interstate Commerce Commission to cover other forms of transportation such as pipelines and express companies. The Mann-Elkins Act of 1910 extended this jurisdiction further to include telephone, telegraph, and cable and wireless companies engaged in interstate commerce.

GOVERNMENT REGULATION OF TRUSTS

As was mentioned in the last chapter, the enormous growth in the size of business units, often with consequent damage to competition, took place in the period following the end of the Civil War and continued unabated until the end of the century. To circumvent competition, various types of business combinations were formed — the pool, the trust, and the holding company. These combinations engaged in various forms of abuses that aroused the general public. Freedom of enterprise was threatened as combinations were able to restrict entry into many business fields. Consumers were at the mercy of the trusts, for through control over markets, they were able to set prices on many basic necessities. In particular, there was public resentment against the Standard Oil Trust and the Sugar Trust. The former was criticized for its goal of monopoly and for the practices it used to eliminate competition; the latter was charged with fixing prices and eliminating competition. The Standard Oil, Sugar, and other trusts were able to apply political pressure to achieve their goals; for example, the Sugar Trust engineered the passage of protective tariffs to protect itself against foreign competition, and then it was free to raise the domestic prices of sugar.

The Influence of Populism

Public indignation by itself was not enough to enact antitrust laws, but the same political force was present that had contributed to the passage of federal and state laws to regulate railroads. Even though the influence of the Grange had declined by 1880, various farm-labor parties, the most important of which was the Farmers' Alliance, were created as part of the general political movement known as populism. Populism expressed the anger of the farmer, the factory worker, and the small businessman against the trusts, railroads, and big banks. The trusts, they felt, overcharged them for the necessities of life they had to buy, the railroads overcharged them for what they had to transport, and the banks charged them usurious rates when they had to borrow. These groups felt that the politicians of both the major political parties represented vested business interests; therefore, it would be better for them to elect their own representatives. The farmers, together with the nascent labor movement, were able in the decade between 1880 and 1890 to elect many senators, congressmen, and state legislators supporting their interests. A national third party, the Populist Party, emerged in the presidential election of 1892.[16] Pragmatic Republican and Democrat politicans took notice and concluded that the best way to defeat a competing political movement was to incorporate some of its more important ideas.

State Antitrust Laws

We should emphasize that the state courts rather than the state legislatures were the first to regulate trusts under the provisions of common law, which is a system of unwritten law not necessarily expressed in written statutes. Until 1889 there were no state laws covering industrial combinations and trusts, but there was a large body of common doctrine on which courts could rely. Early in English law it was established that contracts or agreements in restraint of trade were void and, therefore, unenforceable. English common law was carried over into U.S. law and generally accommodated the rising American antitrust movement; in fact, the state courts used the common law to outlaw trusts. In what is probably the most important common law antitrust case, the Ohio Supreme Court in 1892 declared the Standard Oil Trust to be illegal.[17] The state charged that the Standard Oil Company of Ohio had violated the law by placing the control of its affairs in the hands of trustees, nearly none of whom were residents of the state. In its decision, the court ruled that the Standard Oil Trust, domiciled in New York, exerted a virtual monopoly over petroleum production, refining, and distribution all over the country and ordered the Standard Oil Company of Ohio to dissociate itself from the trust.

16. The Populist Party gained twenty-two electoral votes and more than a million popular votes in 1892.
17. *State* v. *Standard Oil Company*, 49 Ohio 137 (1892).

The first antitrust laws were enacted by the states rather than by the federal government because the impact of populism was felt first at the state level. In 1889, the state of Kansas passed a law outlawing trusts, which were defined as combinations formed to restrict trade, fix prices, or prevent competition. In the same year, similar laws were passed in Michigan, Tennessee, and Texas. By 1895, seventeen states had passed various types of antitrust laws. These laws varied considerably in content, but almost all forbade monopolies and combinations in restraint of trade and provided criminal penalties and administrative machinery for prosecution. In addition, they attacked particular forms of agreements and specific practices that were thought likely to bring about control of the market. The state antitrust laws, however, were limited, because in the American system of government the states can regulate only intrastate commerce.

Federal Antitrust Laws

The application of common law to business combinations did little to slow down their growth. Remedies were difficult to enforce and rarely succeeded in restoring competition. What is more, these applications of common law were statewide only, and a large combination could operate in other states even after being declared illegal in one. States varied in their interpretation and application of the law, and there was no all-encompassing federal law. State antitrust statutes were at best in an embryonic stage and applied only to intrastate commerce. Thus the movement toward industrial concentration was viewed with concern by many people, and this concern crystallized in the populist reform programs. In 1888, both the major political parties referred in their presidential platforms to the dangers inherent in trusts, and in 1890, during President Benjamin Harrison's administration, the Sherman Antitrust Act was passed.

The Sherman Act is the most important of all the federal antimonopoly laws, and it probably is one of the most important measures ever passed by Congress. It marked a major milestone in business-government relations, for with the passage of the act there was no turning back to complete laissez faire capitalism, and the federal government began the long task of regulating business. In 1914, the Clayton Act and the Federal Trade Commission Act were passed concurrently. Both acts increased the federal government's role in the area of antitrust policy.

The Standard Oil Trust[18]

The Standard Oil Trust, the most powerful monopoly in the history of the United States, was created as the Standard Oil Company of Ohio in 1870 by the consummate industrial capitalist of the last century, John D. Rockefeller. He was the living embodiment of the Protestant work ethic that was associated with John Calvin, the religious reformer who preached a doctrine of salvation that later proved to be consistent with the principles of a capitalist system. According to Calvin, hard work, diligence, and thrift were earthly signs that persons were fully using the talents given to them by God. Salvation was associated with achievement on this earth, and Rockefeller was an achiever. In 1856, at the age of 16, he went to work as a bookkeeper at a salary of $15 a month; by 1880, he was the richest man in the world. In three years of work as a bookkeeper, he saved $800, with which he eventually created the Standard Oil Company. Rockefeller was pious. He read the Bible every night.

When Rockefeller created Standard Oil in 1870, it was one of thirty oil companies in Cleveland alone.[19] By 1880, his was the only oil company left in Cleveland, left indeed in Ohio. Expanding into Pennsylvania, Standard Oil gained control over the oil fields in that state.[20] It became not only a refiner, but a producer of oil. Thus it could control and direct the flow of crude petroleum into its refineries. By doing this, it could drive out competitors and compel customers to buy oil at its prices. It could also compel the railroads to give it special freight rates. Before Standard Oil gained control over the Pennsylvania oil fields, cutthroat competition was the order of the day. Prices on a given day could vary from five to fifteen cents a gallon for crude oil. By gaining control of the supply of oil, Standard Oil changed that; it set prices at twenty cents a gallon.

By 1880, Standard Oil was on its way to becoming a national entity. To do this, it had to attract more capital and expand. In 1881, the Standard Oil Trust was created. All companies that were a part of Standard Oil conveyed their shares "in trust" to Standard Oil. For the shares they deposited, they received trust certificates. The trustees then

---

18. The sources used are Matthew Josephson, *The Robber Barons* (New York: Harcourt, Brace & Company, 1984); Ida M. Tarbell, *The History of the Standard Oil Trust*, vols. 1 and 2 (New York: The MacMillan Co., 1925); and *U.S. v. Standard Oil of N.J.*, 221 U.S. 106 (1911).

19. Rockefeller had a partner named Henry M. Flagler who later became a railroad tycoon and a Florida real estate developer. Standard Oil originally was a refiner of oil.

20. The U.S. Oil industry had its start in Pennsylvania when oil was discovered there after the Civil War. Pennsylvania was the major oil producing state until oil was discovered in Texas.

became the direct stockholders of all the companies in the system and were empowered to serve as directors. They could dissolve any corporation within the system and form new ones. The trust arrangement enabled Standard Oil to get its hands on large amounts of capital, which it used to expand its control over the oil industry. In 1886, net earnings amounted to $15 million on invested capital of $70 million, a return of better than 20 percent. The earnings of the Standard Oil Trust provided it with the capital to gain control of oil production in other parts of the United States.

The Standard Oil Trust was directly responsible for the passage of antitrust laws, first at the state level and then, when the Sherman Act was passed in 1890, at the federal level. Investigations took place in Ohio and New York. Standard Oil was accused of blowing up the refinery of a competitor in Buffalo. Standard Oil, though sued for damages, was acquitted. Nevertheless, hearings held by the State of New York indicated that the refinery was blown up by Standard Oil. In Ohio, Standard Oil was accused of bribing politicians and violating the state charter laws by creating a trust. When a prosecuting attorney in Cleveland began a suit to annul the charter of the Standard Oil Company, he was told by the state chairman of his political party: "You have been in politics long enough to know that no man in public office owes the public anything." Nevertheless, the charter was revoked, and the company moved to New Jersey.

The Standard Oil Company reorganized itself as a holding company after the Ohio decision of 1892. This holding company, the Standard Oil Company of New Jersey, was given voting control over the other companies of the Standard Oil group, and it exchanged its stock for the stocks of the firms that formerly had been controlled by the Standard Oil Trust. Through this process of exchange, the holding company obtained $97 million in stock, practically the same amount of trust certificates as had been issued at the time the Standard Oil Trust was dissolved in 1892. Standard Oil of New Jersey had massive economic power. In 1906, the Bureau of Corporations reported that about 91 percent of the refining industry was directly or indirectly under Standard control.[21] In 1904, the Bureau of Corporations reported that Standard Oil controlled 85 percent of domestic sales of refined oil.[22] In the same year, the total production of refined oil in the United States was 27.1 million barrels; of this total, Standard Oil and its affiliates produced 23.5 million barrels, or around 86 percent of domestic output.[23]

21. *Brief for the United States*, 1, no. 725 (1909), 8.
22. Ibid., p. 9.
23. *Brief for the United States*, vol. 2, p. 18.

Some indication of the Standard Oil Trust's economic power can be seen in Table 2-1, which presents the ratio of net earnings to the value of Standard Oil's property from 1890 to 1906. The net earnings of Standard for the ten years ending in 1906 averaged more than 25 percent of the average value of its property. During the same ten-year period, the ratio of net earnings to capital ranged from 48.8 percent to 84 percent, the average for the period being more than 61 percent. The ratio of dividends to capital ranged from 30 percent to 48 percent, with the average for the period being more than 40 percent. The ratio would have been much higher if allowance had been made for the fact that Standard was overcapitalized by $30 million.

Theodore Roosevelt distinguished between "good" trusts and "bad" trusts. A good trust was one that gained its position through economies engendered by large-scale operations short of complete monopoly and took no unfair advantage of competitors or consumers. A bad trust competed unfairly and abused its monopoly power. Standard Oil was in the latter category. It had perpetrated a number of abuses on competitors and consumers. It had secured rebates and other discriminatory

Table 2-1 Dividends and Profits of the Standard Oil Company, 1890–1906

Year	Percent Rate of Dividends	Percent of Net Earnings to Capital Stock	Percent of Net Earnings to Property
1890	12.0	19.7	17.6
1891	12.0	16.8	13.8
1892	12.2	19.7	15.4
1893	12.0	15.9	11.9
1894	12.0	16.0	11.6
1895	17.0	24.8	17.3
1896	31.0	35.0	23.5
1897	33.0	48.8	27.6
1898	30.0	48.8	27.6
1899	33.0	48.8	27.6
1900	48.0	57.0	27.6
1901	48.0	53.7	25.1
1902	45.0	66.3	29.2
1903	44.0	83.5	32.4
1904	36.0	62.6	21.7
1905	40.0	58.4	18.7
1906	40.0	84.5	24.6

Source: *Brief for the United States*, 1, no. 725 (1909), 6; 2, 8–9.

favors from the railroads, and it had bribed railway and other employees for information about competitors. Through its ownership of
almost all the oil pipelines in the United States, Standard controlled
the flow of crude oil and was able to fix prices. The independent refiners were unable to obtain crude oil except from Standard itself, and
Standard would allow them only as much crude oil as it chose and thus
was able to prevent them from expanding their business. Standard
allocated sales areas among its subsidiaries so as to eliminate competition among them. Because of the rebates and other favors it obtained
from the railroads, Standard was able to sell oil in competitive areas at
prices that were profitable to it but that left no profit for its competitors. And then when it had eliminated the competition, Standard
raised its prices.

SUMMARY

Industrial and railroad monopolies were created around 1880 and
continued into this century. The primary reason for instituting the
various types of combinations was the manufacturers' desire to restrict
or eliminate competition and thus to establish monopoly prices. This
was done by having business monopolies control supply. A monopoly
price is likely to be higher than a competitive price, for the monopolist
can limit supply and by this means prevent prices from falling to the
level they would if determined by competition. A second reason for
establishing monopolies was the hope of those organizing them that
they would thus achieve the economies of the trust. This is because a
trust can almost always secure raw materials more cheaply than would
be possible in a state of competition. A trust can often save money by
vertically integrating so that it is assured of an ample supply of raw
materials at cost. A trust is also supposed to achieve certain economies
of production through specialization of plant and machinery and also
of business talents.

QUESTIONS FOR DISCUSSION

1. The philosophy of Social Darwinism was used as a rationale to
   justify the accumulation of great wealth by Carnegie, Rockefeller,
   and other great industrial magnates of the nineteenth century.
   Define Social Darwinism, and explain how it was used as a justification by such magnates.
2. Discuss the factors that led to the decline of competition in many
   industries during the latter part of the nineteenth century.

3. Differentiate among the following types of business combinations: pools, trusts, and holding companies.
4. What is preemptive buying?
5. What prompted railroads to form combinations such as pools?
6. Discuss the methods used by the Standard Oil Company to eliminate competition.
7. What is a reciprocal agreement?
8. What was the "Pittsburgh-plus" system?

RECOMMENDED READINGS

Burns, Arthur. *The Decline of Competition.* New York: McGraw-Hill, 1936.

Chandler, Alfred D., Jr., ed. *The Railroads: The Nation's First Big Business.* New York: Harcourt, Brace & World, 1965.

Clark, John D. *The Federal Trust Policy.* Baltimore: Johns Hopkins Press, 1931.

Faulkner, Harold V. *The Decline of Laissez Faire, 1897–1917.* New York: Holt, Rinehart & Winston, 1951, chaps. 5, 8, and 15.

Hofstadter, Richard, *Social Darwinism in American Thought.* Boston: Beacon Press, 1969.

Josephson, Matthew. *The Robber Barons.* New York: Harcourt, Brace & World, 1934.

Jones, Edward. *The Trust Problem in the United States.* New York: Macmillan, 1921.

Mitchell, Broadus. *American Economic History.* Boston: Houghton Mifflin, 1947.

Chapter 3
Extension of Government Control over Business: The New Deal to the Present

During the Depression decade of the 1930s, government regulation and control of business greatly expanded. By the end of the decade, much of the legislative framework for government's current relations with business had been completed. Direct government regulation was extended over the electrical power and airline industries. Antitrust laws were strengthened by the passage of new legislation, including the Robinson-Patman Act, and consumer protection, particularly in the area of false or misleading advertising, also was improved with the passage of the Wheeler-Lea Amendment. A number of changes were made in the banking system, including the creation of the Federal Deposit Insurance Corporation to insure individual deposits against loss in the event of a bank failure. The position of the individual investor was also improved by federal legislation designed to regulate the securities market. Moreover, there was direct government intervention to support business. In 1932, the Reconstruction Finance Corporation was created and financed by the federal government to make loans to business firms in economic difficulty. The first effort at national economic planning occurred in 1933 when the National Industrial Recovery Act was passed. The federal government also entered the mortgage market through the creation of the Home Owners Loan Corporation to refinance the mortgages of financially distressed homeowners.

Other New Deal measures had a more indirect impact on business. The National Labor Relations Act, passed in 1935, greatly enhanced the bargaining power of unions and made them a countervailing force to business. New Deal efforts to regulate hours, wages, and working conditions culminated in the passage of the Walsh-Healey Act and the Fair Labor Standards Act. The Walsh-Healey Act illustrated the leverage that the federal government could use to enforce compliance with an economic or social goal. It required business firms with federal contracts for $10,000 or more to limit working hours to eight per day or forty per week and to pay wages that were no less than the industry's minimum. The Fair Labor Standards Act enacted minimum wages and maximum hours for labor engaged in interstate commerce or in the production of goods sold in interstate commerce. In the area of social welfare, the Social Security Act provided for federal pensions for persons sixty-five years and older and for survivors' benefits to widows and orphans. The cost of social security was financed in part by a payroll tax on employers.

Until the 1960s, almost all government legislation affecting business was economic. Within the past twenty years, however, the pattern of legislation has changed to reflect shifts in societal values. These shifts have occurred in several areas — ecology, consumerism, civil rights, and women's liberation. The legislative approach that has been used attempts to influence private decision makers to achieve specific social ends. New government regulatory agencies have been created in such areas as affirmative action, consumer protection, and environmental protection, and their regulatory efforts have cut across virtually every form of private industry. Changes in societal values also have caused an increase in the amount of federal funds allocated for social welfare programs. The federal government, through a variety of programs, has made a commitment to alleviate social inequalities but, in the process, has drastically altered the distribution of the federal budget. In 1950, federal budget outlays for social welfare amounted to one-fourth of the total outlays; by 1981, the outlays for social welfare had increased to one-half of what had become a much larger total of the budgetary outlays.[1]

THE GREAT DEPRESSION

The Great Depression was an economic and social catastrophe with no previous parallel in American history. Before the 1930s, there had been periods of unemployment and falling prices, but they were rarely of long duration, and they were generally followed by a reasonably prompt recovery. But all this changed with the Great Depression, which began with the collapse of the stock market in the fall of 1929 and continued until 1941, when preparation for war eventually created full employment in the American economy. Prolonged mass unemployment became the norm for the decade of the 1930s — at its worst, 25 percent of the labor force was out of work.[2] But the Depression meant more than unemployment; it also meant idle production capacity, loss of profits, business bankruptcies, a fall in the standard of living, decreases in the value of property, the closing of many banks, and considerable social unrest. It can be said that the Depression did

1. *The Budget of the United States Government, 1982* (Washington, D.C.: U.S. Government Printing Office, 1981), p. 480.
2. *Economic Report of the President, 1976* (Washington, D.C.: U.S. Government Printing Office, 1976), p. 380.

more to reshape the American economic system than any other event of the nineteenth or twentieth centuries, with the possible exception of the Civil War, for the government's efforts to alleviate it changed the market system.

The Causes of the Depression

Economists disagree on the causes of the Great Depression.[3] One theory suggests that during the 1920s many business firms enlarged their productive capacity at a rate that was too rapid to be sustained into and through the 1930s. These businesses expanded by ordering and installing new equipment, building additional floor space, and adding to their inventories of materials and products. As long as the spending continued, jobs were plentiful and times were prosperous. Indeed, the 1920s was a period of prosperity, with the mass production of the automobile stimulating the development of a number of related industries. But beginning in 1929, business firms discovered they had been creating too much productive capacity, and consequently, decreased their spending. Workers who had jobs necessitated by the previous expansion were either discharged or required to work fewer hours for lower wages. Earning less income, these workers inevitably spent less. A cumulative decline in employment, earnings, and income, in spending on the expansion of productive capacity, and in expenditures on products ensued.

Still, the Depression might have been avoided, at least in part, if the market system had functioned the way it was supposed to. In an ideal market economy, the forces of supply and demand should have caused price readjustments, and there should have been a series of reactions to price changes. Consumer and capital goods in oversupply would have declined in price, and those types of labor and other resources in oversupply would also have declined in price. The fall in the price of consumer goods would eventually have induced buyers to purchase larger quantities of them, and the fall in the price of labor would have prompted business firms to hire more labor. In other words, an ideal market system would have been self-correcting because all markets were assumed to be competitive and labor and capital able to go wherever needed. Competition among sellers or buyers would have set an equilibrium price that would have cleared the market of any surplus product or resource.

It can be argued that the pattern of response was defective. There was resistance to reducing prices because business firms held monopo-

3. John Kenneth Galbraith, *The Great Crash* (Boston: Houghton Mifflin, 1972), chap. 9.

listic power over their products and chose not to permit their prices to fall. Instead, they restricted the volume of physical output of their products to amounts that could be sold at prices higher than would prevail in a purely competitive market. Holding companies controlled large segments of the utilities and railroads and curtailed investment in operating plants to maintain dividends, the interruption of which meant default on bonds and the collapse of the holding company structure. Unionized labor, although at that time lacking the economic power of big business, did try to resist wage cuts, even though the consequence was unemployment. Income was also distributed unequally, with the top 1 percent of all income earners in 1929 receiving 14.5 percent of the total income and the top 5 percent receiving around a third of the total income.[4] This unequal income distribution meant the economy was dependent on a high level of investment or a high level of luxury consumer spending, or both.

The Depression's Effect on Public Policy

Regardless of the cause or causes of the Great Depression, however, forces were set in motion that produced an increase in federal economic and political power unequaled in scope and purpose. As the Depression grew worse, public policy was pushed far beyond the traditional regulatory techniques that had been devised for railroad regulation and antitrust. The principal concern became the stability of the nation's whole economy; the problems that called for action transcended the boundaries of any single industry. Public policy was increasingly forced to cope with the broader issues of large-scale unemployment and poverty and with ways of stimulating production and new investment. The Depression also changed the country's political and social milieu. Politically, as the prestige of corporate managers and financiers declined, the federal government became more sensitive to the claims of labor, farmers, and small business firms. President Franklin D. Roosevelt's New Deal provided a vehicle for the organization of these groups, thereby counterbalancing the power of the large business firms. In addition, the New Deal instituted new laws to regulate business.

When Franklin D. Roosevelt became president in March 1933, the nation was near economic collapse. Industry was operating at less than half its full capacity, the rate of unemployment had reached 25 percent, prices were at their lowest point during the whole Depression, the banking system was on the verge of disintegration, and the gross national product of the country had declined 50 percent from its 1929

---

4. Maurice Leven, Harold G. Moulton, and Charles Warburton, *America's Capacity to Consume* (Washington, D.C.: Brookings Institution, 1934), chap. 5.

level. A number of economic measures were enacted, some of which were temporary and cosmetic, but others of which permanently restructured the American economy. New Deal measures related directly to business can be divided into several broad categories: increased regulation and control of industry, reforms of the banking system, closer government control of the securities market, regulation of public utilities and airlines, and consumer protection.

GOVERNMENT REGULATION OF BUSINESS

It should not be assumed that increased government intervention in business began with the New Deal, for some changes were initiated by the Hoover administration. In the early stages of the Depression, President Herbert Hoover followed the traditional policy of laissez faire and waited for the self-correcting forces of the market to work. Gradually, however, he began to use governmental powers and influence to relieve economic distress.[5] The Reconstruction Finance Corporation was organized to assist banks, railroads, insurance companies, and other enterprises threatened with insolvency. The federal government contributed $500 million in capital, and the corporation was empowered to borrow an additional $1.5 billion through the sale of debenture bonds. The creation of the corporation put the federal government in the business of making loans to private firms and set a precedent for a later time when the government would decide to make loans to firms faced with bankruptcy, such as Lockheed and Penn Central. By 1933, the Reconstruction Finance Corporation had advanced more than $2 billion to business, and during the Roosevelt administration it was enlarged so that it could also make loans to newly created public financial institutions. During its twelve-year life the corporation lent $50 billion to businesses.

The National Industrial Recovery Act, 1933

The purpose of the National Industrial Recovery ACT (NIRA) was to relax antitrust policies designed to promote competition and instead to permit business firms to modify or even to eliminate competition. The devices used included restricting an industry's total production and assigning quotas to individual producers. Although deliberate attempts to reduce competition and restrict output were socially unjustifiable, it was felt that once the industrial system was stabilized, an economy

5. Herbert Stein, *The Fiscal Revolution in America* (Chicago: University of Chicago Press, 1969), pp. 6-26.

of abundance would result. But the NIRA did not work as well in practice as it did in theory. One effect it had was the creation of a price structure unfair to the interests of consumers. It was also felt that the codes of fair competition were breeding monopolies, and large firms did engage in price fixing under the codes. Moreover, the degree of government control necessary to prevent abuses of the codes was immense, beyond what business and the general public were willing to accept. In May 1935, in the Schechter Poultry case, the Supreme Court held the NIRA to be unconstitutional on the grounds that it had provided for an unconstitutional delegation of legislative power to the president in his code-making authority and that the wages and hours of employees working in local plants were not subject to regulation because the processes of production did not come under the constitutional meaning of interstate commerce.[6]

Revival of Antitrust Policies

With the end of the NIRA, there was renewed interest in enforcing measures designed to promote competition and to halt various types of price-fixing arrangements. There now was a new trend in American business, namely, the development of large-scale organizations in the area of distribution. Of particular importance was the creation of chain stores. Chain stores were organized around the turn of this century to take advantage of discounts offered to them by manufacturers in return for purchasing in volume. Chain stores also standardized the packaging and labeling of consumer goods, which tended to lower production costs. The next step was the introduction of self-service, so as to lower the cost of handling goods. Particularly during the 1920s, chain stores began to multiply, and their impact on retailing and wholesaling was significant: many types of specialty stores disappeared entirely or became much fewer in number. And as chain stores increased, the wholesale function of the marketing process was absorbed by the chain itself, and independent wholesale outlets were eliminated.

Chain stores were the focus of independent stores' resentment, which was partly caused by the various forms of price discrimination used by the chains.[7] One form of price discrimination was the manufacturers' awarding discounts for volume purchases by the chains that could not be justified on the basis of a lower cost for selling and delivering the larger quantity. A second form of discrimination took the form

6. *Schechter* v. *U.S.*, 295 U.S. 495 (1935).
7. The history of the anti-chain store movement is summarized in Frederick M. Rowe, *Price Discrimination Under the Robinson-Patman Act* (Boston: Little, Brown, 1962), pp. 8-11.

of "loss leaders." The chains would often sell nationally advertised products or unbranded staples familiar to the buying public at a price below cost. These loss leaders would entice buyers into the chain stores where they would buy other products as well. The device had a particularly deleterious effect on single-line independent stores, which might lose their entire trade to multiline chains using the same line of merchandise as a loss leader. Independent druggists and tobacco stores were particularly hurt by the loss leaders employed by drug and food chains. A third form of price discrimination was what is called whipsawing. When a chain, or any large seller, operated in several geographic markets, prices were cut in one market but maintained in others. This device was used to eliminate local sellers who, unlike the chains, could not make up a portion of their losses in other geographic areas. The chains also had a competitive advantage in that manufacturers would grant advertising and promotional allowances for large-scale purchases — allowances that were not granted equally to independent buyers.

The Depression created all sorts of demands for government assistance to small business firms. The growth of the large chain stores, like A & P and Peoples Drugs, placed great competitive pressures on individual business firms engaged in distribution, particularly the independent retail groceries and retail drug stores, and also attracted the hostility of the state legislatures, which enacted legislation to regulate the chains. To some extent, A & P became a symbol similar to what Standard Oil had been earlier.[8] The Roosevelt administration passed two laws designed to help small business firms. The first was the Robinson-Patman Act, commonly known as the "Chain Store Act." Its objective was to limit certain unfair pricing practices and to aid competition.[9] The second act, the Miller-Tydings Act, legalized resale price-maintenance agreements covering branded goods. It permitted the manufacturer or distributor of a branded product to set the minimum retail price at which the product would be sold. The purpose was to protect independent retail stores against the chains.[10]

FEDERAL REGULATION OF THE SECURITIES MARKET

The stock market crash of 1929 was a traumatic experience for many Americans. Millions of investors lost their savings, and many were

8. There was no reliable evidence of widespread monopoly abuses by the chains during the 1930s, and they were largely exonerated by the Federal Trade Commission from the charges of anticompetitive practices.
9. The Robinson-Patman Act will be discussed in detail in Chapter 6. It is regarded by some experts as protecting inefficient companies at the expense of consumers.
10. The Miller-Tydings Act was repealed by Congress in 1976.

forced into bankruptcy. After a decade of unprecedented prosperity, during which investors hoping for quick profits speculated feverishly in stocks, the economy began to sour. By autumn, the indexes of industrial and factory production had turned downward. The stock market, which is a mirror of economic conditions, began to reflect investors' deepening concern about the state of the economy. On October 24, 1929, more than 12 million shares were traded on the major exchanges. October 29 was the most devastating day in the history of the stock market; 16.4 million shares changed hands, as the average price of fifty leading stocks fell forty points.[11] This crash was followed by repeated declines in stock prices throughout the period from 1929 to 1932; the average value of fifty industrials fell from $252 to $61 per share, that of twenty railroads from $167 to $33 per share, and that of twenty public utilities from $353 to $99 per share.[12]

Business Abuses of the Securities Market

The stock market crash eventually brought to light many corporate abuses that had occurred during the 1920s.[13] Some of these abuses involved the issuance of securities to the general public. Business firms were caught up in the general optimism of the time, and, undoubtedly, American capitalism was at its productive best: automobile production alone increased from 2.3 million new cars in 1921 to 5.4 million in 1929.[14] The general public, traders on the exchanges, and investment trusts found the stock market an appropriate vehicle for investment, and the demand for securities was high. To capitalize on the demand for securities, business firms would often continue to issue stock until it was so "watered down" as to be almost worthless in book value. Another abuse was the use of various accounting methods to overstate the value of assets or to understate the extent of liabilities. Many business firms issued stock far beyond their need for financing and would use the proceeds to invest in the stock market through loans to brokers. The public also lacked adequate information to make rational buying decisions, for firms often did not reveal relevant data or when they did, often misrepresented the facts.

Other abuses were not necessarily related to business firms. Insiders on the stock exchanges who could learn about corporate earnings in advance were able to make financial gains by manipulating the market. They would run up the price of stocks to induce buying by the general

11. Galbraith, *The Great Crash*, pp. 103-110.
12. Ibid., p. 146.
13. See U.S., Congress, Senate, Committee on Banking and Currency, *Stock Exchange Practices*, 73rd Cong., 2nd sess., 1934.
14. Galbraith, *The Great Crash*, p. 7.

public and then sell out, thus causing prices to decline. They would also depress the price of stocks by selling "short," thus prompting the public to sell. Then, of course, they would repurchase the stocks at a lower price. Brokers were usually unlicensed and unregulated, and their records were not subject to inspection.

Banks, too, were guilty of unsound practices with respect to the stock market, for they often made loans to brokers and investors to buy securities. When the stock market crashed, the banks were caught short because they were unable to recoup their loans and to pay their depositors on demand.

Investment banking practices also contributed to the stock market crash. Senate hearings conducted from 1932 to 1934 revealed many instances of irresponsibility and abuse of trust by investment bankers, particularly in the flotation of foreign securities, which often turned out to be worthless. Investment banks would get large underwriting margins for handling the securities; the public enthusiastically purchased them; competition among banks to handle the securities was keen; and the bribery of foreign officials was a way of life. In one case, the son of the president of Peru was paid $450,000 for services rendered to a New York investment bank in the flotation of a $50 million loan for the Peruvian government.[15] No attention was paid to the fact that Peru had a bad debt record, with defaults on previous loans, and an unstable economic and political situation. A similar pattern held true for other Latin American countries. About one-half of all foreign securities floated by investment banks ended in default. The Depression particularly wrecked havoc on the Latin American countries, for their economies were almost wholly dependent on world prices for their exports.

The distribution of domestic securities by investment banks often did not fare much better. It is estimated that American investors lost some $25 million on worthless domestic and foreign securities acquired from 1923 to 1929.[16] One source of abuse, since terminated by legislation, was in the interrelationship of commercial and investment banking. Large commercial banks would organize affiliated investment companies and use them to speculate in stock and to manipulate the market price for securities. In numerous instances, investment bankers sponsored the flotation of issues that created unsound and unsafe corporate structures. In fact, the promoters of business mergers and consolidations during the 1920s were often investment bankers, who would profit from the result because these mergers would create new securities for flotation. Perpetual option warrants were issued, which

15. Ibid., p. 187.
16. U.S., Congress, Senate, Committee on Banking and Currency, *Regulation of Securities*, Senate Report No. 47, 73rd Cong., 1st sess., 1933, p. 2.

enabled the sponsoring banker to purchase common stock at a fixed price over an unlimited time. In 1929, for example, J. P. Morgan and Company received, for $1 apiece, 1,514,200 option warrants on United Corporation stock.[17] Within two months Morgan and Company was in a position to sell these warrants at $40 each, and it netted a profit of $60 million.

Reforms of the Securities Market

The stock market crash, and the abuses that led to it, created a need for reforms in the securities market. A series of laws were passed to achieve such reforms, beginning with the Securities Act of 1933, which prohibited the public sale of securities in interstate commerce or through the mails unless detailed information concerning the securities had been filed with the Federal Trade Commission. In 1934, the Securities and Exchange Act extended federal regulation to the securities market through the creation of the Securities and Exchange Commission (SEC), with which information about securities had to be registered. In 1935, the Public Utility Holding Company Act extended the power of the commission into the field of public utility holding companies. Subsequently, the commission was given broadened authority with respect to over-the-counter markets, was enabled to participate in corporate reorganizations, and was authorized to regulate trust indentures and investment trusts.

The Securities Act, 1933

The Securities Act, or as it is commonly known, the Truth-in-Securities Act, was passed in 1933. Its objective was to protect the unwary investor from the sale of fraudulent securities through the mail and by door-to-door salesmen who peddled "get-rich-quick" schemes in, among other things, Florida real estate ventures and Nevada silver mining stock. Various states had enacted legislation, later called blue-sky laws, to regulate the sales of securities. The laws varied widely in their scope and character, with some providing penalties for fraud and others requiring the registration of security salesmen, but not the registration of securities. State laws were limited in their effectiveness because they did not have adequate provisions for enforcement. Thus more comprehensive federal legislation became necessary to protect the public.

17. U.S., Congress, Senate, Committee on Banking and Currency, *Stock Exchange Practices*, p. 115.

The heart of the Securities Act is the requirement that new securities offered for sale in interstate commerce, unless exempted, be registered with the Securities and Exchange Commission (SEC). The registration statement must contain all the information about the issuing company and its business that the SEC considers necessary to the investors' interest. Although the requirements for different types of issuers vary, they generally include a full description of the kind of business conducted, the services or products sold, the physical assets owned, the identity of the directors and officers, detailed financial statements for the past three years, the terms of the issuer's contract with investment bankers, and many other details.

The Securities Exchange Act, 1934

As mentioned previously, widespread and flagrant abuses in the securities markets existed during the 1920s. Through such abuses, prices of securities were either pushed up or forced down for the benefit of those in control, with corresponding losses for investors. Uncontrolled margin requirements, in which a buyer puts up only a small percentage of the cost of securities and has his or her broker use the purchased securities as collateral for loans to finance the rest of the cost, caused much speculation and accentuated the instability in the stock market. When market prices declined, there was a deflationary spiral in which falling prices reduced collateral values, causing loan liquidations, which put a further downward pressure on prices.

The Securities Exchange Act created the Securities and Exchange Commission, consisting of five members appointed by the president with the consent of the Senate, and each holding office for five years. The act condemns a number of manipulative practices and gives the SEC the authority to check their use. Manipulation of stock prices in any manner is outlawed. Under the act, corporate directors, officers, and insiders are not permitted to sell their company's stock short, and they must make public any intent to exercise stock options; furthermore, willful violation of an unfair practice is punishable by a fine of not more than $10,000 or imprisonment for not more than two years, or both. The act also requires that all securities listed in national securities exchanges be registered with the SEC by the issuer, and that the financial reports contained in the registration of securities be in a form prescribed by the SEC.

The Public Utility Holding Company Act, 1935

There were several reasons for the passage of the Public Utility Holding Company Act. One was to protect investors from a recurrence of what had happened during the 1920s, namely, the loss of billions of dollars in the collapse of the public utility holding companies. Another reason was the inability of state regulatory commissions to exercise any effective control over rate making. The magnitude of the holding company systems put them beyond the reach of the state commissions. The ease with which inflated property values could be worked into the rate base and the lack of access to holding company books led state commissions to accept almost any valuation put on properties by the holding companies. Proponents of public utility holding company regulation also wanted to reduce the concentration of control of the electric and gas industries. In 1930, for example, the nineteen largest holding company groups received 77 percent of the gross revenues for electricity in the United States, and in 1932, thirteen holding companies controlled three-fourths of all privately owned public utilities.[18] This concentration, it was felt, circumvented the natural processes of a free enterprise economy.

The Public Utility Holding Company Act declared gas and electric holding companies to be responsible for the public interest because of their sale of securities in interstate commerce. The act requires public utility holding companies to register with the Securities and Exchange Commission. The registration statement must include copies of the charter of incorporation, and it must show the organization, financial status, directors and officers, balance sheets, and related information. Unless a holding company is registered, it is unlawful for it to sell, transport, or distribute gas or electricity across state lines. The act also has an antipyramiding provision, in that it requires the dissolution of holding companies above the second degree. In other words, there can be no more than two tiers of holding companies above the operating companies: the first-degree holding company, which controls the operating companies directly through stock ownership, and the second-degree holding company, which controls the first holding company.

Reforms of the Banking System

The collapse of the banking system was one of the cataclysmic results of the Depression. In 1929, the banking system was inherently weak, in part because of the large number of speculative loans made by bankers during the 1920s and in part because of the large number of independent banks free from any form of government control.[19] When the economy collapsed, these loans went into default, as the market

18. Galbraith, *The Great Crash*, p. 106.
19. Paul Studenski and Herman E. Krooss, *Financial History of the United States* (New York: McGraw-Hill, 1952), chap. 25.

value of the borrowers' goods or the value of their collateral declined. When debtors defaulted on their loans, banks were unable to satisfy the demands of depositors who came to claim their deposits. Whenever one bank failed, it would act as a warning to depositors to go to their other banks and withdraw deposits. Thus, one bank failure would lead to other bank failures, and these spread, dominolike, throughout the country. As income, employment, and property values fell as a result of the Depression, bank failures quickly became epidemic, and the eventual collapse of the entire banking system became a real possibility. In March 1933, President Roosevelt declared a moratorium on bank operations until ways could be found to resuscitate the banking system. Congress passed an Emergency Banking Act providing for the inspection of banks and the reopening of solvent banks under license.

The Glass-Steagall Act, 1933

The Glass-Steagall Act was an effort by the Roosevelt administration to place the banking system under more centralized government control. The act was designed to strengthen the commercial banks, weaken the link between speculation and banking, and give added power to the Federal Reserve system. It created the Federal Deposit Insurance Corporation to guarantee bank deposits.[20] The purpose of this guarantee was to prevent runs on banks by depositors fearful of losing their money. It required commercial banks to give up their securities affiliates and to abstain from investment banking. It also limited the investment securities that member banks in the Federal Reserve system could have in their investment portfolio. To prevent a recurrence of speculative transactions in corporate securities, real estate, and commodities financed by commercial banks, Federal Reserve banks were required to supervise the use of credit made by them. The act also created an Open Market Committee, which was given control over commercial bank policies.

The Banking Act of 1935

The Banking Act of 1935 marked a further extension of government control over banking. With the passage of this act, the banking structure became inseparably connected with federal government monetary and fiscal policy, and the Federal Reserve and the U.S. Treasury operated in tandem. The act is also important because it provided for certain

20. The original amount was up to $2,500. The amount today is $100,000.

forms of centralized credit and monetary controls. It made the president's power to appoint and remove members of the Federal Reserve Board practically unlimited. The old Federal Reserve Board was dissolved and replaced by a board of governors composed of seven members appointed by the president. The board was given broader rediscounting power and mandatory power over legal reserve requirements against customer demand and time deposits. Each reserve bank was required to restate its rediscount rate every two weeks, and approval of the rate had to be given by the board.

REGULATION OF PUBLIC UTILITIES

Public utility regulation began in the 1870s when various states passed special laws and granted charters for the railroads. The first federal law regulating the railroads was the Interstate Commerce Act of 1887, which created the Interstate Commerce Commission. Subsequent acts reinforced the powers of the commission. The regulation of transportation was expanded to include motor carriers, first at the state level. State regulation of trucks and buses, introduced in the 1920s, was at first concerned with safety, physical characteristics of vehicles, licensing of drivers, and the number of hours that a driver might work. Soon, however, the states began to regulate the rates and services of common carriers. To prevent the evasion of such regulation, these controls were extended to contract carriers. But the impossibility of the states' regulating interstate motor carriers led to the federal regulation of motor carriers through the Motor Carrier Act of 1935.

Government regulation of the electric power industry also began at the state level. As with the railroads, early public policy was largely promotional, primarily concerned with encouraging the development of the industry. Later, as abuses ensued, particularly in the form of high rates, consumer dissatisfaction laid the groundwork for state regulation. Starting in 1907, regulatory commissions were established in New York and Wisconsin and spread rapidly to other jurisdictions. With the growing importance of interstate transmission of electricity, federal intervention became inevitable. In 1920, the Federal Power Commission (FPC) was established, with the authority to issue permits or licenses for private and public power projects involved in interstate commerce. In 1935, by which time about 18 percent of all generated electric power was used in interstate commerce, the authority of the FPC was extended to cover the regulation of rates, earnings, financial transactions, and accounting practices. In 1938, control over the interstate transmission of natural gas, as well as planning control over all river basins, was also placed under the FPC.

The New Deal and Public Utility Regulation

The large-scale entry of the federal government into the field of public utility regulation began with the New Deal. This was not primarily a result of any change in the government's philosophy; it was merely a recognition of the forces of the time. The utility industries had crossed state lines and were beyond the power of the state regulatory commissions. The rapidly growing communications industry had always been national or international. At the same time, the arrival of the air age introduced a new facet to the regulation of transportation, and two important acts were passed, the Motor Carrier Act of 1935 and the Civil Aeronautics Act of 1938, which created a major regulatory commission, the Civil Aeronautics Board.

The Motor Carrier Act of 1935

The Motor Carrier Act of 1935 extended the jurisdiction of the Interstate Commerce Commission (ICC) to motor carriers engaged in interstate commerce. But the ICC cannot interfere with the exclusive rights of the states to regulate intrastate motor carriers, and permission from the ICC to engage in interstate commerce does not thereby convey any right to do intrastate business. The act established different degrees of regulation for common carriers, contract carriers, private carriers, and transportation brokers. A common carrier may operate only under a certificate from the ICC, after a finding that it is able to perform the proposed service and that the proposed service is required for public convenience and necessity. Rates and fares must be published and must not be discriminatory. The ICC is also charged with enforcing safety standards. Although general publication of rates is not required, minimum rates must be made public and filed with the ICC, which can prescribe minimum but not maximum rates. Private carriers, not available for hire and carrying their own goods, are subject only to controls over hours of service for employees, safety, and equipment. Brokers must be licensed by the commission.

The Civil Aeronautics Act, 1938

After 1918, the federal government had indirect control over air routes and types of planes allowed through its granting of conditional airmail contracts. The airmail acts of 1934 and 1935 gave the postmaster general the power to regulate schedule frequencies, departure times, stops, speed, load capacity, and so forth. Regulation of air transportation, however, culminated in the passage of the Civil Aeronautics Act, which created the Civil Aeronautics Board (CAB) and gave it regulatory authority over entry, routes, rates, airmail payments, and subsidies of common carriers. The Civil Aeronautics Board is authorized to issue a certificate of convenience and necessity, which gives an air carrier the right to serve a particular route. Rates had to be approved, published, and observed by the board. Pooling, combinations, intercorporate relations, and abandonment of services were subject to control, but the CAB had no authority over security issues. The Civil Aeronautics Act was modified by an executive order in 1940 that created within the Department of Commerce a Civil Aeronautics Authority (CAA), which maintains the national airway system, plans and administers the airport program, and enforces safety, licensing, and traffic control regulations.

Communication facilities were also made subject to federal government control. The first federal regulation of communications was authorized by the Post Roads Act of 1866, which encouraged the construction of telegraph lines. In 1888, Congress gave the Interstate Commerce Commission the power to require telegraph companies to interconnect their lines. Regulation of rates and practices of communications carriers was introduced in the Mann-Elkins Act of 1910, which also extended certain provisions of the Interstate Commerce Act to cover wireless service. When the radio became the principal form of mass communications, regulatory problems arose, for the ICC had been created to regulate railroads, not telephone and telegraph services and radio broadcasting. So in 1927, Congress created the Federal Radio Commission and in 1934, passed the Communications Act.

The Communications Act, 1934

The Communications Act of 1934 created the Federal Communications Commission (FCC) to regulate interstate and foreign commerce in wire and radio communications. The commission replaced the Federal Radio Commission and was given the jurisdiction over communications previously held by the ICC. The FCC has control over the telephone and telegraph industries as well as over radio and television broadcasting. The latter is not a utility, and its regulation is based on the principle of competition. The FCC has power over rates, services, accounts, interconnections, facilities, combinations, and finances. For example, the FCC grants licenses to radio stations, assigns them frequencies, fixes their hours of operations, and prevents interference among stations. With respect to rates, the FCC has control over interstate and foreign telephone and telegraph companies but not over broadcasting charges. Telephone and telegraph companies must file their rates with the FCC and make them available for public inspection.

Notice must be given of rate changes. If a new rate is filed, the commission may suspend it for a period not exceeding three months and hold hearings on its reasonableness. The burden of proving reasonableness is on the company.

The Federal Power Act, 1935

The Federal Power Act of 1935 gave the Federal Power Commission jurisdiction over securities, combinations, and the interstate rates and services of all interstate electric utilities. The commission was also empowered to make special studies of electric rates, the interstate transmission of electricity, national defense problems, and other matters. A corollary act, the Natural Gas Act of 1938, enlarged the commission's responsibilities by also giving it jurisdiction over the interstate transportation and wholesale of natural gas. These powers were similar to those exercised over the nation's interstate electric utilities. In subsequent acts, the commission was authorized to make water basin studies and was given control of the Tennessee Valley Authority's accounting and use of bond proceeds.

THE NEW CYCLE OF GOVERNMENT
REGULATION OF BUSINESS

A new wave of federal government regulation of business began during the 1960s and continued into the 1970s. This cycle is marked by the appearance of social goals in business legislation: eliminating discrimination in employment, ensuring better and safer products for the consumer, reducing environmental pollution, creating safer working conditions, and so forth. These goals resulted in the creation of a number of new federal agencies with regulatory functions — the Consumer Product Safety Commission, the Environmental Protection Agency, the Equal Employment Opportunity Commission, the Federal Energy Administration, the Occupational Safety and Health Administration, and a myriad of others. These new agencies follow a fundamentally different pattern from that of the older regulatory agencies such as the Interstate Commerce Commission. They are broader in scope, and they are not limited to a single industry. Their jurisdiction extends throughout most of the private sector and, at times, into the public sector. There are advantages as well as disadvantages in this type of federal regulation. An advantage is that the wide range of these agencies makes it impossible for any one industry to exercise a controlling influence on their activities. A disadvantage is that these new types of agencies are concerned only with the limited segment of operations that falls under their jurisdiction. This limitation often results in an agency's lack of concern or understanding about the effects of its actions on an entire company or industry.

More recent government legislation is the subject of Chapters 10, 11, 12, and 13. Almost all the legislation falls into three categories — consumer protection and safety, environmental protection, and equal employment opportunities. These laws have specific objectives, including reduction of product hazards, elimination of job discrimination, and environmental cleanup. Many of these laws are meritorious on the surface, but they are not without their costs. For example, the basic purpose of the Occupational Safety and Health Act of 1970 is to achieve a higher level of job safety. This act places the responsibility for safeguarding a person's well-being on the employer. In some cases, investment in employees' safety and health can add up to a considerable part of an industry's total capital spending.

Consumer Protection

Several consumer protection laws were enacted between 1962 and 1975. These laws, and a summary of what they are supposed to accomplish, are presented in Table 3-1. They were the manifestation of a consumer movement that has fluctuated in intensity from the beginning of the twentieth century but that has never coalesced into an organized pressure group. Occasional waves of popular indignation and, more frequently, identity of common interests between consumers and organized groups have produced several kinds of special government protection for the consumer — protection against adulteration or misrepresentation of foods, drugs, and cosmetics; labeling of consumer products; product safety; and so forth.

Environmental Protection

Concern about the quality of the environment, which has come from the ecology movement, is a second area currently affecting government and business relations. Although laws to protect the environment against industrial pollution have been on the books for many years, it was not until the 1970s that any major legislation was passed. Protection of the environment is partly a reflection of changing societal values, the new emphasis on the quality of life as opposed to mindless material consumption. More and more citizens have come to object to the increasing annoyances and assaults on health and aesthetic sense that result from various forms of pollution. The probability that pollution causes health hazards, some of which may endanger life itself, and the possibility that pollution may in time upset the balance of nature to such an extent that earth can no longer support human life create anxiety and have led to demands for stringent regulation of pollution. Unfortunately, the issue of environmental protection has become entangled with emotionalism, and ascertaining the true effects of pollution has become difficult.

Table 3-1 Consumer Protection Laws, 1962–1975

Year of Enactment	Law	Purpose
1962	Food and Drug Amendments	Require pretesting of drugs for safety and effectiveness.
1965	Cigarette Labeling Act	Requires labels disclosing hazards of smoking.
1966	Fair Packaging and Labeling Act	Requires producers to state what a package contains and how much it contains.
1967	Wholesome Meat Act	Offers to states federal assistance in establishing inspection standards.
1968	Consumer Credit Protection Act	Requires full disclosure of terms and conditions of finance charges in credit transactions.
1968	Wholesome Poultry Products Act	Increases protection against impure poultry.
1970	Public Health Smoking Act	Extends warnings about hazards of cigarette smoking.
1970	Poison Prevention Packing Act	Authorizes creation of standards for child-resistant packaging of hazardous substances.
1972	Consumer Product Safety Act	Establishes commission authorized to set safety standards for consumer products.
1975	Consumer Product Warranty Act	Establishes warranty standards to which business firms must adhere.

The most important pollution laws are quite new. The Air Quality Act of 1967 directed the federal government to establish atmospheric areas for the country and created the Presidential Air Quality Advisory Board. The Clean Air Act Amendments of 1970 set air quality standards and required that by 1975 new cars be virtually pollution-free.[21] The National Environmental Policy Act of 1970 created a permanent Council on Environmental Quality, consisting of three members and a professional staff, whose functions are to advise and assist the president in environmental matters. The act also requires all federal agencies to consider the effect of their actions on the environment. In 1970, the Environmental Protection Agency was established to enforce the environmental protection laws and to assume responsibility for environmental functions previously given to other federal agencies. In 1972, the Water Pollution Control Act was passed to regulate the discharge of industrial pollution into navigable waters, and in the same year the Noise Pollution and Control Act was passed to regulate the noise limits of products and vehicles. In addition to these major laws, a number of minor laws, mostly concerned with relatively limited matters such as the effluents from navigable vessels, have also been enacted.

Affirmative Action

A third new area that touches the operations of business firms is affirmative action. This also reflects a shift in societal values, which was prompted by three movements: the civil rights movement, the women's liberation movement, and an increased emphasis on egalitarianism. The civil rights movement was begun to end economic and social discrimination based on race or color. Because a large proportion of minority members have among the lowest incomes in our society, the movement also advocates the concept of entitlement, based on the idea that since society over time has deprived certain groups of their rights, the members of these groups are now entitled to compensatory incomes and education, more representation at all levels of management, and so forth. The women's liberation movement is somewhat similar to the civil rights movement. It asks for the elimination of sex discrimination, and it also advocates entitlement. Egalitarianism is somewhat more difficult to define. Essentially, it rejects merit as a desideratum for promotion and reward and instead stresses equality of result. An example is the use of mandatory quotas for minority groups, including women, in hiring and promotion policies, education, and job training.

These movements have resulted in the passage of laws that affect business. In 1963, the Equal Pay Act was passed to eliminate wage

21. These amendments have subsequently been amended several times.

differentials based on sex when the type of work performed by either sex was the same. In 1964, the Civil Rights Act was enacted to eliminate job discrimination based on such factors as sex, race, color, or religion, and it created the Equal Employment Opportunity Commission to investigate charges of job discrimination. In 1967, the Age Discrimination in Employment Act was passed to prohibit job discrimination against persons aged forty to sixty-five. In 1972, the Equal Employment Opportunity Act broadened the authority of the Equal Employment Opportunity Commission so that it could sue employers accused of job discrimination. In addition to these laws, a series of executive orders have extended the federal government's authority to cover the personnel practices of business. These executive orders are the framework for affirmative action, which seeks to redress any racial, sexual, or other imbalance that may exist in an employer's work force. Affirmative action applies to all nonconstruction contractors and subcontractors of the federal government and to all government entities.

SUMMARY

Legislation affecting government and business relations tends to come in cycles. One cycle occurred during the Depression of the 1930s, when much of the existing government regulatory framework was created. New Deal legislation, for the most part, was crisis oriented. The banking system was in a state of collapse, and so it was necessary to pass laws to preserve and support banking. Abuses in the securities market contributed to the stock market crash of 1929, and a thoroughgoing reform of the market followed. Massive unemployment and an increase in business failures stimulated a shift in emphasis in government antitrust policy and a reliance on a form of state planning under the National Industrial Recovery Act, which was to influence market conditions in ways previously prohibited by the antitrust laws. But the desire, especially of small business firms, for protection against the rigors of competition was reflected after the demise of the NIRA in their pressure for such measures as the Robinson-Patman Act. The New Deal also provided a vehicle for the organization of labor and other groups, thereby counterbalancing the power of big business. The federal government assumed greater responsibility for the functioning of the economy and for overall coordination of economic activity.

The second cycle of government-business legislation began in the 1960s but has run its course. This cycle was the result of several factors, including ecology, consumerism, and civil rights. Legislation was concentrated in three areas — consumer protection, ecology, and employment. A new set of regulatory agencies was created that has had a rather broad effect on business, in that their functions are not limited to a specific industry. With the new legislation, no business firm can operate today without contending with a multitude of government restrictions and regulations. Moreover, virtually every major department of a typical industrial corporation in the United States has one or more counterparts in a federal agency that controls or strongly influences its internal decision making. As will be pointed out, government regulation can have many adverse effects on business and consumers — a stultification of incentives and innovations by business and an increase in the costs that consumers pay for products, as government regulation increases the cost of production. Because these costs are not the result of any measurable output, they are reflected in a lower rate of productivity.

QUESTIONS FOR DISCUSSION

1. In what ways did the New Deal change business-government relations?
2. The National Industrial Recovery Act represented an attempt by the Roosevelt administration to relax the antitrust laws. Was it successful?
3. Discuss the reasons for the passage of the Robinson-Patman Act.
4. What is meant by *whipsawing* and *loss leader*?
5. Describe the activities of the Securities Exchange Commission.
6. The epidemic of bank failures between 1929 and 1932 can be attributed to basic defects in the banking system. Discuss.
7. Explain the reasons for the New Deal's regulation of air and motor carrier transportation.
8. Discuss the purposes of the Communications Act of 1934 and the Federal Power Act of 1935.

RECOMMENDED READINGS

Allen, Frederick Lewis. *The Big Change: America Transforms Itself, 1900–1959.* New York: Harper & Row, 1952, chap. 10.

Elias, Erwin A. "Robinson-Patman: Time for Rechiseling." *Mercer Law Review,* 26 (1975), 689–697.

Galbraith, John Kenneth. *The Great Crash.* Boston: Houghton Mifflin, 1972.

Mitchell, Broadus. *Depression Decade: From New Era Through New Deal.* New York: Rinehart & Co., 1941.

O'Connor, James F. *The Banking Crisis and Recovery Under the Roosevelt Administration.* Chicago: Callaghan & Co., 1938.

Posner, Richard A. *The Robinson-Patman Act.* Washington, D.C.: American Enter-
prise Institute for Public Policy Research, 1976.
Rowe, Frederick M. *Price Discrimination Under the Robinson-Patman Act.* Boston:
Little, Brown, 1962.
Studenski, Paul, and Herman E. Krooss. *Financial History of the United States.*
New York: McGraw-Hill, 1952.

PART III
INDUSTRIAL CONCENTRATION
AND ANTITRUST

The concentration of many industries in the hands of a few firms is a fact of life in the United States and other major industrial countries, although attitudes toward concentration may vary from country to country. In the United States, there is a deeply rooted tradition dating back to the last century that concentrated wealth in any form was bad, and that big business would eliminate the small firms. It is not surprising that by statute and common law our legal system has been concerned with the maintenance of a competitive market system. This concern is reflected in the existence of antitrust laws that have several major objectives — the promotion of competition by outlawing monopolies and prohibiting unfair competition, the protection of consumer welfare by prohibiting unfair business practices, and the protection of small business firms from economic pressures exerted by large firms.

Antitrust policy in the United States has had an uneven course. Historically, enforcement has had political overtones, with laws resulting from political reaction to a problem considered pressing at the time. The Sherman Act was passed in 1890 in response to public (including business) reaction to the economic power of the trusts. The Clayton Act was passed in 1914 in part as a result of public concern over the power of the investment banks. The Robinson-Patman Act was passed in 1936 in response to pressure exerted by small firms that wanted protection against the large chain stores. Since that time, antitrust policy has moved in spurts, with long interim periods in which there has been little activity. Moreover, attitudes toward antitrust regulation of business have changed. There is less worry about the size of companies and the degree of concentration in an industry and more attention to their actual impact on economic efficiency and productivity.

U.S. antitrust laws also must be considered within the framework of global market competition. Once unassailable U.S. industries are losing their edge in foreign competition. The mystique of American management superiority has been shaken by such events as the Japanese rise to prominence in the world auto industry. International considerations have come to the fore in reference to U.S. antitrust laws. There

71

has been a broadening of the focus of antitrust policy, away from a narrow legal attempt to curb anticompetitive business behavior to a broader policy of promoting the competitive position of U.S. industry at home and abroad. Put into practice by the Reagan administration, this policy involves a more relaxed approach toward corporate size, concentration, and corporate mergers.

Chapter 4
Market Structure: Competition, Monopoly, and Oligopoly

In a market economy, business firms are supposed to make most of their economic decisions on the basis of prices, price changes, and price relationships. Demand and supply forces acting in several separate market situations are supposed to determine prices. In any given market situation, some degree of competition is assumed to exist, although the degree of competition varies considerably from one situation to another. In one market situation there may be a large number of sellers and buyers of a given product; in another situation a few sellers and a number of buyers; and in a third situation one seller and a number of buyers. In price theory, pure competition and monopoly can be considered opposite points on the competitive spectrum. The essential feature of competition is that there are so many sellers and buyers of a good that no one seller or buyer is able to influence prices in the marketplace; the essential feature of monopoly is control over supply by a single seller. This control can be translated into control over the price of a good in the marketplace.

COMPETITION

Clearly, competition in the economic sense is not a natural thing but is a social pattern produced by the operation of various supporting institutions, including private property ownership and freedom of enterprise. Its justification, like that of the other capitalistic institutions, is that it contributes to the social welfare. When the industries and markets of an economy are organized competitively, certain supposedly desirable results will ensue.

First, competition should bring about efficiency in the operation of industry and business by granting economic success to those firms efficiently operated and by relentlessly eliminating those inefficiently and wastefully operated. Thus to survive, each enterprise must use the best machines and productive methods available and eliminate waste at all points in its organization. The removal of inefficient producers from the market is meant to leave the productive factors in the hands of those firms that use them most effectively.

Second, competition should lead to innovation and technological progress. Better productive methods, machines that increase efficiency or lower cost, or a product that appears to satisfy a human want more effectively than similar products from other business firms give certain firms a greatly prized advantage over the others with respect to income. But such advantages tend to be lost sooner or later in a competitive industry, and the continuing result should be the consumers' ability to obtain better and better products at lower and lower prices.

Finally, competition is said to be a regulator of economic activity, a means by which the productive efforts of numerous business firms are correlated through prices with the desires of consumers as expressed in the market. Success in competition depends on the ability to give consumers the right amount, quality, and kinds of goods, at the right price. Firms that supply goods not suited to consumers' desires or that cost more than similar products of other firms, usually fall by the wayside. If the total output of a good is small in relation to the demand for it, the possibility of making a profit will stimulate a competitive industry to expand production and, if necessary, its plant facilities. But if competitive producers turn out far more goods than are demanded, the lack of profits will force some firms from the industry and adjust output to demand.

Economic Concepts of Competition

Competition as an economic concept can mean a number of things, the most common of which is pure competition. Certain elements must be present for pure competition to exist in a market. First, there must be a large number of buyers and sellers of a standardized product. Second, there must be complete freedom of entry and exit into and out of the market. Third, no one buyer or no one seller can influence the price of the product sold. Fourth, there must be no collusion of any form between the buyers and the sellers. Finally, there can be no interference in the market from outside forces — government, labor unions, and so forth.

Pure competition is a theoretical concept. It can be used to define a desirable market situation, which, if it existed, would redound to the advantage of the consumer for the simple reason that supply and demand forces acting in a given market would determine the price and output of a product. No single seller or buyer could affect the market in any way. The hallmark of competition is the existence of many producers, each of which contributes only a small part of the output traded in the market. A competitive market price is decided by an equilibrium of supply and demand, which is determined independently of the actions of any single seller or buyer. Sellers may sell all they please, and buyers may buy all they please, but only at the price set in the market by supply and demand.

Diagram 4-1 illustrates price and output determination under conditions of pure competition. The supply curve, labeled S, indicates the quantity that sellers are willing to provide at each price. There is a direct relationship between the amount supplied and the price: the higher the price, the greater the amount supplied. The demand curve, labeled D, indicates the quantity that buyers are willing to purchase at each price. The relationship between the amount demanded and the price is inverse: the higher the price, the lower the amount demanded. Equilibrium is reached when the quantity that sellers are willing to sell is equal to the quantity that buyers are willing to buy. The market price is set by this equilibrium point. At any point above the equilibrium point, supply exceeds demand; at any point below the equilibrium point, demand exceeds supply. In the diagram, the price OP is the market price, and the quantity OA is what is sold.

Competitive prices are explained mainly as the supply and demand for two different periods: first, a short-run period during which sellers

Diagram 4-1 Supply and Demand Analysis

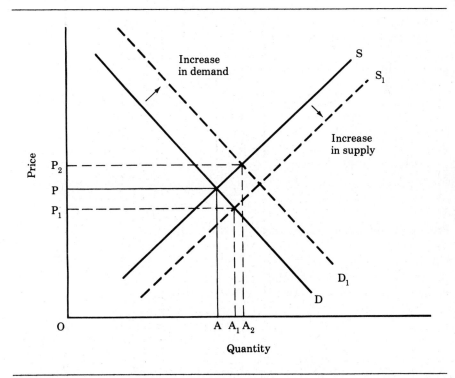

can vary supply only as is possible using existing production facilities and, second, a long-run period during which sellers can freely vary their actual production capacity. In the short run, sellers can sell all they please, but only at the equilibrium price that clears the market. This equilibrium price bears no relation to the cost of production for an individual seller, which may be higher or lower than the price. In the short run, some firms can make profits, and others can sustain losses.

Demand, supply, or both can change in the short run. For instance, an increase in demand means buyers are willing to purchase more at each of a series of prices than they were formerly. In the diagram, the demand line would shift to the right, as indicated by the curve D_1. A decrease in demand means just the opposite. An increase in demand, with supply remaining constant, would result in an increase in both price and quantity; a decrease in demand would have the opposite effect. An increase in supply means sellers are willing to offer more at each of a series of prices than formerly. In the diagram, the supply curve would shift to the right. The result would be a decrease in the equilibrium price and an increase in the quantity bought. A decrease in supply would have the opposite effect.

Demand originates with the consumer. It implies a desire for a good or service that can be expressed, usually through willingness to pay money for it. The demand schedule assumes its shape, first, because individual incomes are limited, and second, because as the quantities of a given commodity increase at a given time, they become less useful to the consumer. In other words, the consumers' desire for a particular product tends to diminish as they acquire more of it. This is the principle of diminishing marginal utility. Marginal utility is the amount by which total utility would be changed with the addition of one unit to a stock of goods. The principle of diminishing marginal utility states that marginal utility varies inversely with the number of units acquired. When expenditures are increased for a given item, successive increments will make smaller and smaller additions to total satisfaction. The basis for the principle is that any physical want is probably satiable.

Price and Output Determination — Short Run

Under conditions of pure competition, the individual firm must accept the price established in the market by market supply and market demand. Since the firm has no effect on or control over price, it must try to maximize profits or minimize losses by adjusting its output to this price. The average revenue curve is a horizontal line, indicating that the firm can sell varying amounts of output at the established price (see Diagram 4-2). Average revenue is the total revenue divided by the number of units of output and is synonymous with the price per unit.

For a competitive firm, average revenue and price are the same. Since the price remains unchanged as more units are sold, each additional unit sold increases the total revenue by an amount equal to the price. This is illustrated in the table below. There is also the economic concept of marginal revenue, the amount by which the total revenue is increased by the sale of one more unit of product. As shown in the table, marginal revenue, average revenue, and selling price are the same.

The firm can sell all it can produce at the selling price of $20, and so we shall figure how much it will produce under conditions of pure competition in the short run. Output is based on the cost of production. In the short run, there are both fixed and variable costs. Fixed costs are those that remain constant regardless of the amount of output. Variable costs are those that vary in amount in accordance with changes in the volume of output. From the standpoint of cost, the firm can adjust its output by changes in variable factors, such as labor, but cannot change its fixed physical factors. The key cost concept, however, is marginal cost, the amount by which the total cost is increased when an additional unit of output is produced. Given these cost concepts, the basic economic principle governing the behavior of the firm in the short run is that output will be adjusted to the point at which marginal cost and marginal revenue are equal. The firm must do this to maximize its profits or, for that matter, to minimize its losses. Whenever marginal revenue is greater than marginal cost, total profit can be increased by expanding production, but whenever marginal cost exceeds marginal revenue, total profit is increased by reducing production.

The table on the next page shows the principle of profit maximization in the short run under conditions of pure competition. The price, as determined in the marketplace by supply and demand, is assumed to be $20, and total fixed costs are assumed to be $10, regardless of the

Output	Selling Price ($)	Average Revenue ($)	Total Revenue ($)	Marginal Revenue ($)
1	20	20	20	20
2	20	20	40	20
3	20	20	60	20
4	20	20	80	20
5	20	20	100	20
6	20	20	120	20

number of units of output produced. Profit maximization occurs at ten units of output. If a firm stopped producing before this point, it could still add more to unit revenue than to unit cost; if it went beyond this point, the cost of producing an additional unit of output would more than offset the addition to revenue.

Reaching the point of equality of marginal cost and marginal revenue does not imply that a firm always makes a profit. Whether or not it does make a profit depends on the relation between total cost and total revenue, or average cost and price. The equality between price and marginal cost guarantees that a position of maximum profit or minimum loss has been attained, but it does not offer any information about the absolute profit or loss position. If a firm has decided what to produce and has constructed a single plant to house a certain quantity of physical resources, its ability to change output is limited. It can change the inputs of its variable factors and thus adjust output somewhat, but it cannot change its overall scale of operations, since that would require changing fixed as well as variable factors. The marginal cost function represents the rate of change in total cost as output is changed within a given plant. Since for the individual seller in a purely competitive market, price does not vary as output varies, the marginal cost function becomes, in the short run, the supply function for the competitive firm, that is, the quantities that will be supplied at all possible prices.

It is also desirable to think in terms of average costs rather than total costs, since this allows costs to be related directly to prices. Corresponding to the concepts of total cost, total variable cost, and total fixed

Output	Fixed Cost ($)	Variable Cost ($)	Total Cost ($)	Marginal Cost ($)	Price ($)	Total Revenue ($)	Marginal Revenue ($)
1	10	15	25	15	20	20	20
2	10	28	38	13	20	40	20
3	10	39	49	11	20	60	20
4	10	50	60	11	20	80	20
5	10	59	69	9	20	100	20
6	10	67	77	8	20	120	20
7	10	81	91	14	20	140	20
8	10	97	107	16	20	160	20
9	10	115	125	18	20	180	20
10	10	135	145	20	20	200	20
11	10	160	170	25	20	220	20

cost, are average total cost, average variable cost, and average fixed cost. The average total cost is the sum of the average variable and the average fixed costs. Average variable cost is derived by dividing total variable costs by output, and average fixed cost is derived by dividing total fixed cost by output. Marginal cost is neither a total nor an average cost but is simply the additional cost incurred as a result of producing an additional unit of output. The marginal and average cost concepts are presented in the table below. Average fixed costs show that fixed costs per unit decline continuously as output increases. Average variable costs decrease, then reach a minimum value, and thereafter increase. The initial decline in average variable cost is because, within limits, the more units of variable factors there are, the more effectively fixed factors are put to use.

The concepts of marginal revenue (MR), average revenue (AR), marginal cost (MC), average variable cost (AVC), and average total cost (ATC) are given in Diagram 4-2. As mentioned earlier, the marginal cost curve is the short-run supply curve for a firm operating in a purely competitive industry. We should qualify this, however: the marginal cost curve represents the supply curve of the firm only above a certain price. A firm that cannot cover its variable costs should shut down. No sensible firm would supply any amount of goods at a price below that which would bring in enough revenue to cover variable costs. This can be shown in the diagram. AVC is the firm's average variable cost curve. No quantity will be supplied at any price below OP_1. If the price falls below this point, the firm should shut down. Thus, the marginal cost curve (MC) becomes the supply curve at all prices above OP_1. As long

Output	Total Fixed Cost ($)	Total Variable Cost ($)	Average Fixed Cost ($)	Average Variable Cost ($)	Marginal Cost ($)
1	10	15	10.00	15.00	15
2	10	28	5.00	14.00	13
3	10	39	3.33	13.00	11
4	10	50	2.50	12.50	11
5	10	59	2.00	11.80	9
6	10	67	1.67	11.16	8
7	10	81	1.43	11.57	14
8	10	97	1.25	12.12	16
9	10	115	1.11	12.77	18
10	10	135	1.00	13.50	20

as the price is above OP_1, the firm will continue to operate even if it is not covering total costs. At prices above this level, it will be more than covering variable cost; it will also be making some return on its fixed investment.

The diagram shows three price levels: OP_1 is the minimum price a firm can receive and remain in business; OP_2 is the break-even point at which the firm would make neither a profit nor a loss; and any point above OP_2 — for instance, OP_3 — is a price at which a firm would make a profit. Using OP_3 as one price, the quantity supplied is OQ_3. At the point L, where MC = MR, profit is maximized and the firm is in short-run equilibrium. At the price OP_3, the average revenue per unit, LQ_3, multiplied by the number of units of output, OQ_3, equals total revenue, which is the area of the large rectangle OP_3LQ_3. Similarly, average total cost, KQ_3, multiplied by the number of units of output, OQ_3, equals total cost, or the area of the rectangle $OJKQ_3$. The net profit rectangle is the total revenue rectangle less the total cost rectangle, or JP_3LK.

Diagram 4-2 Alternative Price Levels, Pure Competition in Short Run

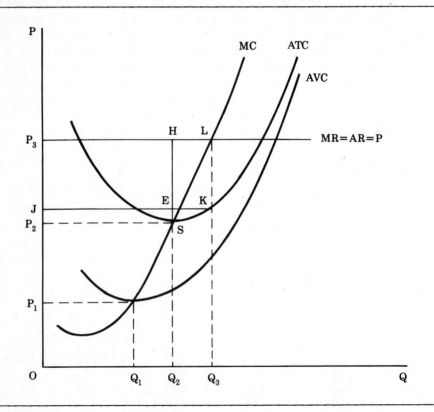

Price and Output Determination — Long Run

In the long run, firms operating under conditions of pure competition can adjust both output and capacity to a given demand and price. In the short run, a firm can adjust output only by changing the amounts of the variable factors of production, but plant capacity remains fixed. In the long run, there may also be a change in the total number of firms in the industry. Assuming firms are free to enter into and depart from a market, new firms will be attracted to a given industry if existing firms are making an above-normal profit. In other words, if the price is above the short-run average cost, there is an incentive for new firms to enter the industry. Inefficient firms, those sustaining losses, will be eliminated. A long-run equilibrium price is then achieved at the point at which marginal revenue equals not only marginal cost but also the average cost of the firms in the industry. This is possible only at the lowest point on the long-run average cost curve, since this is the only point at which marginal cost and average cost are equal.

Diagram 4-3 shows the long-run equilibrium for a firm operating under pure competition. The firm is operating at an output level at which its average total costs (ATC) are lowest, but all of its economic profit has disappeared. Marginal cost (MC), marginal revenue (MR), and price (P) are equal at the equilibrium point. The industry itself is in equilibrium because it has reached a point at which for all the firms in the industry the price just covers their average total cost. There is no incentive for new firms to come into the industry, and each firm will find itself in an equilibrium position. Marginal revenue equals not only each firm's marginal cost but also its average cost. This is possible only at the lowest point on the long-run average cost curve, since this is the only point at which marginal cost and average cost are equal. Under pure competition, each firm will in the long run produce at the lowest point on the long-run average cost curve.

The long-run equilibrium price can be called a normal price that brings sellers a normal profit — that is, enough profit to keep them from leaving the industry, but not enough to entice other sellers to stop producing other things and shift into this industry. Normal profit may be considered a cost of production, a rate of return on the resources a firm owns, including the labor of the owner. It also means that the rate of return on all a firm's resources, including internally owned labor and other factors of production, is no greater than can be obtained elsewhere in the economic system. Excess, or economic profit, which is considered a surplus over and above all costs of production and which can attract new firms into a competitive industry, would be eliminated in the long run under pure competition.

Economic Significance of Pure Competition

From the standpoint of the consumer, the most desirable condition under which a free enterprise market economy can operate is pure competition. Under this condition, different goods are usually supplied at a minimum price. In such a market, the numbers of buyers and sellers are so large that no one of them can influence the price; buyers and sellers are completely aware of market conditions; and firms may move freely in and out of an industry. An individual firm operating within the framework of pure competition, however, is confronted with several limiting factors. Since it is such a small part of the total market, it cannot by any individual action in any way affect prices. It must accept the market price and must adjust its production to this price if it is to maximize its profits. The firm therefore can have no price policy of its own, since price is fixed by market forces. But this protects the consumers, for only impersonal market forces can determine price. The market price presumably also reflects consumer preferences,

Diagram 4-3 Long-Run Equilibrium for Firm Under Pure Competition

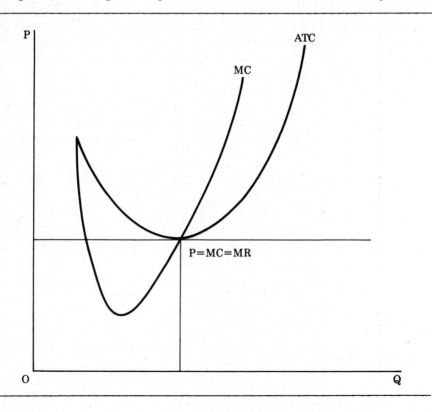

because it measures the marginal utility to the consumer of the final unit of the commodity produced.

In a long-run equilibrium position, price is equal to marginal cost for each firm in a purely competitive industry. An optimum allocation of resources within the industry has been reached. If all industries in the economy were purely competitive, an optimal use of resources in the entire economy would occur; there could not be an excess of profits in any one industry, since new firms would be attracted into it as the margin of profit grew. Wages could not remain higher in any one occupation than in others, for workers would be attracted to the high-paying occupation, with the consequence that the pay level would come more into line with that in other occupations. Therefore, an equality of marginal cost and price in all industries would mean that resources could be used in no better way. No improvement in economic well-being could be obtained by shifting resources from one industry into another. Consumers would be satisfied because their marginal utilities for each of the various products would be approximately equal. In the theoretical equilibrium position, consumers cannot improve their satisfaction by changing any one of their expenditures for goods and services.

The ideal market situation epitomized by pure competition is never achieved, except perhaps approximately in the buying and selling of some farm products. But even in agriculture, farmers have created marketing cooperatives for some crops and have obtained special legislation in the form of price-support and acreage-allotment programs. In retailing, in which pure competition is sometimes approached, retail price maintenance laws, usually referred to as fair-trade laws by their supporters, have prevented price competition. Almost all other markets are characterized by imperfect competition, in which sellers or buyers have some control over price. In such situations, the price policy of one seller depends on the expected reaction of rival sellers. Price wars, the elimination of rival competitors, collusion, and combinations all are possible. Instead of regulating prices, the government may try to enforce competition through prosecution based on antitrust laws.

Pure competition should be regarded as one of several economic models developed both to describe a particular structural arrangement within a market economy and to enable economists to predict the consequences of certain changes in variables within that structure. The other models are monopoly, oligopoly, and monopolistic competition. Pure competition is an ideal that can serve as a frame of reference when it is necessary to evaluate whether or not there is viable competition in a given marketplace situation. Actually many different concepts and subconcepts of competition depart from pure competition; for example, the concept of effective or workable competition has a pragmatic legal-economic orientation. The economic idea underlying effective competition is that no seller or group of sellers acting in concert has the power to choose its level of profits by giving less and charging more. So competition means different things to different people.

MONOPOLY

Pure monopoly, or having only one seller of a commodity for which no close substitutes exist, is a rare market situation. But some of the industries classified by law as public utilities are in approximately this situation, and their prices are regulated by the government. Such monopolies avoid duplication of facilities and achieve the low costs made possible by large-scale production that would not be possible under purely competitive conditions. Whether this regulation is effective is debatable, but it does attest to a deep-seated and well-founded suspicion of the American public of what might happen if it were absent. A monopoly may exist in part because of the decreasing costs resulting from an increased scale of production that reduces the number of sellers in a market or allows a few to agree to avoid price competition. Patents are also the basis for many different monopolies.

A monopolist can fix prices by gaining control of the supply of a given commodity, for the individual firm and the industry are, in effect, identical, and the market demand curve for the industry is the same as the average revenue or sales curve for the monopolist. The demand schedule for the product of a monopolist is the same type as shown in Diagram 4-1. There is no supply schedule, for the monopolist has the entire supply, and there is no substitute for the product, so the monopolist need not be concerned with the possibility of consumers shifting to substitute commodities or rival firms. This could be the result of the monopolist's complete control of some strategic raw material or the possession of a specific franchise or patent. The monopolist is primarily interested in regulating supply so as to obtain a maximum profit. Demand and cost of production form the basis for the amount of output. The maximum profit is tied to the quantity sold and the difference between cost and price per unit of output.

Monopoly prices are frequently higher than the prices that would prevail under competitive conditions because a monopolist can sometimes charge different prices to different customers. The individual firm in a purely competitive market can only react to the price set in the market by supply and demand. It need not consider the effect of variations in its output on price, since it is such a small part of the total market. Its average revenue line is horizontal, and it cannot charge different prices to different customers. But the monopolist must examine the effects of pricing policies, for the demand curve for its product, which is also its average revenue curve, slopes downward to the right. This means that a monopolist must consider the effect on the price of changes in its output. A larger output can be sold only at a lower price, the degree to which it is lower depending on the elasticity of demand. If the price is raised, consumers will reduce the amount of the product they purchase, but they cannot shift to substitute commodities or rival producers.

Price and Output Under Monopoly — Short Run

When the objective is maximization of profit, price and output determination under conditions of monopoly follows basically the same rules as those applying to the firm operating under pure competition. The general rule for maximizing profits is usually stated as the output at which marginal cost equals marginal revenue. Net profit for a monopolist depends on the quantity of output sold and the difference between cost and price per unit of output. Operation at the point of greatest difference between cost and price per unit of output may not yield the monopolist the highest total net profit because added sales beyond that point may more than offset the decline in profit per unit. Demand and the cost of production form the basis for the monopolist's choice of output. In more precise terms, profits are at a maximum when marginal costs equal marginal revenue. When the two amounts become equal, further expansion is not profitable. Up to that point, expansion of output adds more to receipts than to costs; past that point it is the other way around. But when there are finite changes in output, marginal cost will seldom exactly equal marginal revenue.

The monopolist's price and output determination is shown in the table below. Remember that in a monopoly, unlike the conditions

Output	Price ($)	Total Revenue ($)	Marginal Revenue ($)	Fixed Costs ($)	Variable Costs ($)	Marginal Cost ($)	Profit ($)
10	100	1,000		500	483		17
11	99	1,089	89	500	544	61	45
12	98	1,176	87	500	598	54	78
13	96	1,248	72	500	659	61	89
14	94	1,316	68	500	725	66	91
15	90	1,350	34	500	802	77	48
16	85	1,360	10	500	890	88	-30

prevailing under pure competition, the average revenue line is not horizontal; the price declines as the output increases. The demand and average revenue lines are the same, sloping downward from left to right. The average revenue column shows the prices at which various quantities of output can be sold, whereas the marginal revenue column shows the increments to total revenue that result from selling additional units of output. In the short run, some costs are fixed and others are variable. In the table, total fixed costs are assumed to be $500, regardless of the volume of output, and total variable costs have been given assigned values.

At all outputs up to the fourteenth unit, marginal cost is less than marginal revenue. The cutoff point is the fourteenth unit, for the production of this unit will add $2 to net profits. At a volume of fourteen units, marginal revenue is $68, marginal cost is $66, total revenue is $1,316, and total costs are $1,225. The difference, or profits over and above all costs, is $91, which is greater than at any volume of output less than fourteen. Beyond fourteen, marginal cost is greater than marginal revenue. To produce the fifteenth unit, the additional cost is $77 and the additional revenue is $34. Profit declines from $91 to $48. The point of maximum profit is at a price of $94 and at a volume of fourteen units.

The same analysis is presented in Diagram 4-4, which shows the monopolist's average revenue or demand curve (d), marginal revenue curve (MR), short-run marginal cost (MC), and average total cost (ATC) curves. The marginal cost and marginal revenue curves intersect at a volume of OQ. For the monopolist to expand up to this point would be profitable, since at all smaller volumes the marginal cost curve lies below the marginal revenue curve. Beyond this point, however, marginal cost rises above marginal revenue. To determine the price at which this volume can be sold, it is necessary to use the average revenue curve, which is also the monopolist's demand curve. The average revenue is the price column in the table, and the curve shows the prices at which various outputs can be sold, whereas the marginal revenue curve shows the increments to total revenue that result from selling additional units of output. The price that will maximize profits is OP, the total revenue is represented by the rectangle OPAQ, and the total cost is represented by the smaller rectangle OCBQ. The total profit over and above all necessary costs is represented by PABC, the difference between the revenue and cost rectangles.

Monopoly profit is usually higher than that which would prevail under pure competition, since the monopolist has control over supply, whereas the individual firm operating under conditions of pure competition is only one among many and so has no control over total output. The individual firm can only react to the price set in the marketplace by supply and demand, but the monopolist can set price and hunt for the point on the demand curve at which profit is maximized. Monopoly profits over and above all necessary production costs do not call forth the type of corrective adjustment that would be needed under pure competition. In other words, there is no free movement of resources into and out of a monopoly industry. Typically, output would also be at a level lower than that which would prevail under pure competition.

Long-Run Adjustments

In the short run, the price may be below the average total cost, but this cannot continue in the long run because if it did, the firm would cease operation. If the price is above the average total cost, there will be excess profits, and in a monopoly market there is nothing that can correct this automatically because of barriers to the entrance of new firms. In the long run, a monopoly is able to adjust its scale of operation because all costs are variable, whereas in the short run it can determine the most profitable rate of operation only for its existing fixed

Diagram 4-4 Short-Run Price and Output for Firm Under Monopoly

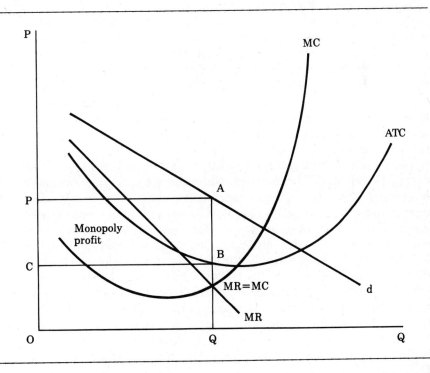

and variable factors of production. The most profitable scale of operation in the long run is the one that equates marginal cost and marginal revenue. The monopoly, like the purely competitive firm, has a U-shaped long-run average cost curve; that is, if the firm is either too small or too large, its production cost per unit will be higher than if it is of optimum size. The actual size of the firm will depend on the expected demand for its product. This size may happen to be that at which the cost per unit is minimal, but because the monopolistic firm does not have to compete, it is more likely that the firm will be either too large or too small to minimize cost.

Economic Significance of Monopoly

Pure monopoly, like pure competition, is a rare market situation and should be regarded as a theoretical framework in which to decide regulatory policies. The main defect in a monopolistic market situation, unlike pure competition, is nothing automatically protects the consumer. The existence of monopolies and their consequent excessive profits obviously would affect the personal distribution of income in the economy and result in a misallocation of resources. Monopoly prices are frequently higher than the prices that would prevail under competitive conditions because a monopolist can charge different prices to different customers. There are no competing sellers to whom buyers may go in case of price discrimination. Moreover, there is less incentive for a monopoly to organize its plant most efficiently because it may make profits that are greater than in competitive industries merely by restricting supply. Modernization of facilities, experimentation with lower prices and larger output, and managerial incentives may be retarded by the lack of competition. In some instances, the monopolist may be unwilling to experiment and expand, even though greater profits are possible.

But in some cases, monopoly prices may be as low as or lower than competitive prices. For instance, when the scale of production is much larger and the level of costs much lower than they would be under competition, a monopoly price may be lower than a competitive price. Furthermore, a greater long-run efficiency of production sometimes may be achieved under monopoly conditions when the economy is highly unstable. A monopoly can operate at a more uniform rate and maintain an inventory to carry it through the changes in demand. Under competition, firms must estimate demand and also their competitors' probable supplies. The accumulation of an inventory is risky; consequently, many firms may operate beyond capacity at one time and below capacity at another time. High prices encourage expansion, which may result in very low prices. And very low prices may bankrupt many firms, which will result in very high prices from the firms that remain in business. The average competitive price may very well exceed the monopoly price.

OLIGOPOLY

Oligopoly refers to a market situation in which there are a few sellers of a differentiated product. Many American industries have oligopolistic qualities, such as the steel, automobile, and cigarette industries. In fact, oligopoly seems to be a characteristic of industries to which modern methods of production are applicable. The pattern of oligopolistic industries is for there to be a few giant firms that account for one-half or more of the total industry output, followed by smaller firms that produce the rest. For example, General Motors and Ford account for at least two-thirds of the automobile sales by American car manufacturers. Typical of most oligopolistic industries is mass merchandising, which means distinguishing a firm's products from those of its competitors by means of branding and trademarks, and creating a preference for the brand by means of advertising. Some industries, however, approach pure oligopoly. Here the firms in the industry produce virtually identical products. Buyers have little reason to prefer the product of one firm to that of another except on the basis of price. Examples of nearly pure oligopolies are the cement, aluminum, and steel industries.

Oligopoly markets have several important characteristics. First, no one firm can profit by adhering to price competition. For example, if a firm raises its price and other firms do not, its sales usually will suffer. Second, prices are identical or almost identical in oligopoly markets. Finally, without price competition, firms reach some sort of agreement, tacitly or otherwise, about what the set price will be. There may be a leader, usually the largest firm in the industry, that sets the price, and the other firms merely follow it. What little competition there is takes the form of product differentiation. The products of all firms in an oligopolistic industry are nearly interchangeable, but each firm's products have their own distinguishing characteristics, either real (as in quality or design) or fancied (as in brand names).

Price and Output Under Oligopoly — Short Run

The basic tools for analyzing price and output under conditions of oligopoly are the same as those used in analyzing pure competition and pure monopoly. If a firm seeks to maximize its short-run profits, price and output will be set at the point at which marginal cost equals marginal revenue. Under oligopoly, the average revenue curve slopes downward from left to right and in general appearance is similar to that under monopoly. The total sales of a product sold under oligopoly, however, are divided among a number of firms. The average revenue curve of each firm, therefore, reflects not only the change in total sales that accompanies a change in price but also the shifts in sales among the various firms resulting from the price change. If one firm reduces its price, this will increase somewhat the industry's total sales, and it will also attract some sales from its competitors. The extent of the shift in sales will depend on the reactions of its rivals to the initial price reduction. Other firms may leave their prices unchanged, reduce their prices by varying amounts, increase sales promotion activities, or introduce product changes. Firms operating under conditions of oligopoly are faced with much uncertainty; instead of a single determinate average revenue curve, as there is under monopoly, there is a family of average revenue curves, each indicating a different reaction by rival firms.

The above reasoning means that the very nature of an oligopoly frequently rules out price competition. Firms in oligopoly know that price competition is unlikely to yield any significant gain in either sales or revenue. So each firm is likely to practice some form of product differentiation, such as advertising, to increase the demand curve for the firm's product. The individual firm's profit will be increased, too, because a shift to the right in the demand curve increases the differential between price and average total cost. Economies of scale would affect the part of the cost curve in which the average total costs are still declining. Since relatively few oligopolistic firms exist, any successful product differentiation by one firm will have significant effects on the sales of its rivals. These rivals will seek to offset this by trying to differentiate their own products. In estimating the effectiveness of a new advertising program, therefore, each firm must gauge the likely reactions of its rivals.

Price and Output — Long Run

In the short run, an oligopolist can make a profit or a loss. If its losses continue, the firm will be forced to leave the industry. In the long run, all the oligopolist's costs can vary, as existing plant facilities can be expanded. Economies of scale can result from decreases in a firm's long-run average total costs as the size of its plant increases. This is, of course, also true of firms operating in the long run under conditions of pure competition or pure monopoly. Those factors that produce economies of scale or decreasing long-run average costs as plant size increases are reduced input unit costs, greater specialization of resources, and more efficient use of equipment. Economies of scale shift all short-run cost curves to a lower level as the scale of operations becomes larger.

In the long run, the excess profits of firms operating in an oligopoly market situation can be maintained if there are restrictions on the entry of new firms into the market. Entry into an oligopolistic industry may be restricted in many ways, large capital requirements being one. The automobile industry is an example. Few companies have the resources to enter the industry, which was demonstrated after the end of World War II when the highly successful Kaiser Industries, the maker of various defense products, attempted to capitalize on an increased demand for automobiles by entering the market. Its effort ended in failure. There may be legal barriers in the form of patents, licenses, tariffs, or franchises, and it also may be difficult to counter the reputations of established firms. If the entry of new firms is restricted, which is likely in a typical oligopolistic situation, the prices may remain permanently above the average total costs, with excess profits both for the individual firms and the industry.

Economic Significance of Oligopoly

The economic and social losses from oligopolists' collusive practices are similar to those connected with monopoly. Output in such industries tends to be restricted; prices are maintained at high levels; and too few resources are employed when compared with the more competitive areas of the economy. Nonetheless, oligopoly itself does not necessarily contradict the social interest, since it may be based on the economies that can be obtained by large-sized firms. These economies may be so great in relation to the market served that they leave room for only a limited number of firms in an industry. When, however, oligopoly results from the exclusion of new, potentially efficient firms by such means as patent holdings, withholding of needed materials, or any form of collusion, the situation is clearly contrary to the public interest. Even when the small number of sellers can be traced to the economies of scale, this efficiency does the public little good if there is no real price competition to ensure that the prices reflect that efficiency.

In summary, in a free enterprise market economy, theoretically the most desirable goal is pure competition because goods purchased by consumers usually are supplied at a minimum price under these conditions. The forms of competition in the real world, however, are far more numerous than the simple price and output adjustments that occur in the classical model of pure competition. In addition to price, real world competition includes, among others, the variables of product quality, product performance, and product financing and marketing. Business firms' planning and controlling activities are efforts to adjust to external economic and market conditions, including the strategies of rival firms. The use of standard costing, target pricing, market share measurements, and similar practices are common to small and large firms and are part of the competitive process rather than evidence of monopoly power. Competition can occur in oligopolistic industries, and large firms can enable society to benefit from important economies of scale.

APPLICATION OF ECONOMIC MODELS
TO ANTITRUST LAWS

Economic models have been developed to help describe our economic structure and to enable economists to predict the consequences of certain changes in variables within that structure. Although very few industries in the United States come close to the market structure of pure competition or monopoly, they provide a frame of reference for policy decisions. They represent opposite extremes. Pure competition represents a desirable market situation which, if it existed, would result in the maximum welfare of consumers. Both price and output would be market determined. In a purely competitive market, there would be no excessive concentration of economic power and no barriers to market entry.

Many American industries can best be described as oligopolies. An important social welfare question that must be asked is whether or not an oligopolistic market is able to allocate resources well enough to meet the wants of consumers and to provide effective competition. Since there are a few firms in oligopolistic industries, they may restrict competition through certain practices, such as agreements to limit output to be able to charge higher prices. Collusion among such companies can be used to lessen or eliminate competition. In this way they act like monopolies. Oligopolies with rather high levels of economic concentration and high entry barriers are more likely to act in a collusive way than are oligopolies with lower levels of economic concentration and low entry barriers.

To understand the purpose of antitrust laws, it is first necessary to examine the subject of industrial concentration in the U.S. economy. By concentration we mean the control of the whole supply of a given class of goods by a small number of business firms. It may result from the growth and extension of a single enterprise, or more likely, from the acquisition of separate firms. Mainly in the field of large corporations is the government faced with the problem of creating and preserving competition. The realization of actual competition depends on the creation and maintenance of competitive conditions through the use of antitrust laws. The subject of industrial concentration will be discussed in detail in Chapter 5.

SUMMARY

There are several types of markets. In a purely competitive market, output prices always tend to be equal to marginal costs of production. This equality between price and marginal cost means the consumer is required to pay for a product an amount equal to the additional costs of producing an additional unit of that product. This cost represents the amount that would have been produced elsewhere in the economy by the resources used in the production process. Output prices in the short run may be above, equal to, or below average costs of production. In the long run, prices tend to equal average costs of production. Furthermore, average costs of production tend to be forced to the minimum level by the pressure on firms to operate at the most efficient scale.

From a social point of view, monopoly, with some exceptions, is the most objectionable type of market structure. A given sum spent on a good produced by a monopoly gives the consumer a smaller amount of productive services than if the same sum had been spent on a good produced in a competitive market. This is because price under pure competition tends to equal marginal cost of production, whereas price under monopoly exceeds marginal cost. However, in some industries the economies of a large firm are so great that monopolies are desirable. Examples are electric power and gas companies. In such cases, it is socially desirable to permit monopolies and regulate rates through publicly appointed commissions.

In oligopolistic markets, the number of firms is small relative to the total output. This type of market best describes the market conditions for many American industries. Pricing policies of firms operating in an oligopolistic industry depend to a large degree on an estimate of what other sellers will do as a result of such action. When one firm is substantially larger than other firms, it is likely to be the price leader. This means it is usually the first to announce a price change, and its rivals will follow. Competition in an oligopolistic industry may take the form of product differentiation, where firms try to capture large shares of the market through brand names and advertising. A good example is the competition between Coca-Cola and Pepsi-Cola in the soft drink industry.

QUESTIONS FOR DISCUSSION

1. Do the economists' models of market structure have any validity in the study of antitrust enforcement?
2. What is the economic rationale for competition in the marketplace?

3. What is the economic significance of pure competition?
4. How are prices determined under conditions of monopoly?
5. Is it possible for monopoly prices to be lower than prices determined under purely competitive conditions? Discuss.
6. Why are oligopolistic industries often characterized by uniform action?
7. Oligopoly seems to be the market type that accurately describes almost all major industries in the United States. Do you agree?
8. Price leadership can take place in oligopolistic markets. What is price leadership?
9. Oligopoly, like monopoly, contradicts the public interest. Do you agree?
10. Prices in oligopolistic markets would always be higher than prices in purely competitive markets. Do you agree?

Chapter 5
Industrial Concentration in the United States

The industrial development of the United States accelerated during the period following the end of the Civil War. There were many contributory factors, one of which was an abundance of natural resources such as coal, oil, iron, lead, and silver. Railroad construction widened the domestic market, opened up new areas for settlement, and was itself a prime mover in stimulating demand for coal and iron. Population growth was accelerated by an influx of immigration, which provided a cheap supply of labor. Technological advances in transportation and industry opened the way to mass production, increased labor productivity, and large-scale economic organization. The institutions and goals of society were uniquely favorable to the individual entrepreneur. Agriculture, too, was undergoing a process of mechanization and expansion; the increasing emphasis on cash crops helped to provide export balances to pay interest and dividends on the imported capital that was furthering economic growth.

A trend toward industrial concentration began in the last century when many industries came to be dominated by a few relatively large firms or even by only one firm. The development of the corporation in the latter part of the century facilitated the concentration of control in many industries because corporations were able to buy the common stock of other corporations. Various anticompetitive business practices also enabled firms to drive their competitors out of business. By 1884, Standard Oil was selling more than 80 percent of the oil that flowed out of American wells. In 1891, the American Tobacco Company controlled 88 percent of the total output of cigarettes, and by 1901, the U.S. Steel Corporation controlled 65 percent of the nation's steel capacity. This concentration continued unabated into the twentieth century. A contributory factor was the rising power of the investment banker, who supplied the funds to finance industrial expansion. In 1914, firms with an annual output valued at a million or more dollars constituted only 2.2 percent of the total number of manufacturing firms, but they employed 35.3 percent of all manufacturing workers and produced, in value, 48.7 percent of all manufactured products.[1]

1. Solomon Fabricant, *The Output of Manufacturing Industries, 1899-1937* (New York: National Bureau of Economic Research, 1940), pp. 84-85.

In the 1920s an extraordinary expansion of industrial concentration occurred. In part this concentration was an inevitable concomitant of a rapidly developing industrial society in which the use of large specialized machines and facilities and assembly-line methods of production necessitated large firms. A case in point is the automobile industry. In 1900, 4,192 automobiles were built in the United States. By 1910, the number of cars produced increased to 181,000, and by 1920, automobile production had increased to 1,900,000.[2] During the 1920s, the automobile industry forged rapidly ahead, bringing along with it such related industries as rubber, oil, glass, steel, and road building. However, a consolidation took place in the automobile industry so that in 1911, Ford and General Motors had 37.7 percent of the automobile market, and by 1923, their share had increased to 66.3 percent. The rewards went to the companies that could turn out the most cars. The higher the volume of production, the lower the cost of turning out each individual automobile. But this required the building or acquisition of vast manufacturing and distribution facilities.

Industrial concentration in the United States was accentuated by events during and immediately after World War II. Large corporations emerged from the war in a much stronger position, whereas small businesses were weakened. War contracts had been given mainly to large firms, most likely because large firms had the capacity to mass-produce the thousands of airplanes and tanks necessary for the war effort. Indeed, the U.S. industrial might was probably the decisive factor in the Allied victory over the Axis powers. War contracts were instruments of economic power that guaranteed their holders markets and sizable profits, gave them priority in obtaining parts and raw materials, and gave them the right to take advantage of favorable depreciation and tax carry-back provisions. During the war, the federal government spent about $600 million a year on industrial research, over one-third of all the research funds going to large corporations. And even when the large firms subcontracted work, three-fourths of their subcontracts went to other large firms. The federal government also financed new production facilities, which also benefited the largest corporations most.

In the 1960s and 1970s, there arose a new form of business combination called the conglomerate, which represents a union of unrelated companies. Conglomerates are multiproduct, multimarket companies that are the result of an amalgam of unlike companies. The conglomerate became the most popular form of business combination when companies hastened to acquire other companies with different products and markets. An example of a conglomerate merger was the acquisition of Columbia Pictures by Coca-Cola. Moreover, conglomerates have

---

2. Motor Vehicle Manufacturers of the United States, *Facts and Figures, 1985,* p. 6.

taken over other conglomerates; for example, the acquisitions in 1985 of Nabisco by Reynolds Industries, and General Foods by Philip Morris. In attempting to diversify their product lines, oil companies have acquired chain retail stores and a copper company, and U.S. Steel acquired an oil company.

MERGERS

Typically, large firms have become larger through mergers. A classic example is General Motors, the largest manufacturing firm in America, which was formed in 1908 by William Durant as a holding company. Buick, Cadillac, and Oldsmobile were joined together in the holding company, which by 1910 controlled ten automobile, three truck-making, and ten parts and accessories firms.[3] The Chevrolet automobile company was acquired in 1915. In 1916, General Motors purchased makers of roller bearings, radiators, horns, and starting, ignition, and lighting systems. General Motors then became a corporation, and the various holding company subsidiaries became divisions. It acquired companies making tires, leather, aluminum, gears, casting, and machine tools. From its original inception in 1908, General Motors acquired more than sixty companies by 1920. The whole strategy of General Motors was predicated on capitalizing on the potential mass market for automobiles by combining the production, assembly, and distribution facilities of many existing companies.

The same conditions of industrial concentration prevail in the United States today as in the past. A case in point was the twenty-fifth anniversary of *Fortune* magazine's annual list of the 500 largest manufacturing corporations in the United States. Of the top 500 companies when the list was first published in 1953, only 262 were still around by 1980.[4] Almost all the departed 238 were acquired by mergers or acquisitions by other large firms; only four of them actually went out of business. Since 1980, there have been many more mergers involving firms in *Fortune*'s 500. One example was DuPont's acquisition of Conoco in 1981. This merger, the largest in the history of the United States up to that time, involved two of the twenty-five largest industrial corporations in America, with combined sales of $32 billion. Two larger mergers were consummated in 1984 when Standard Oil of California (Chevron) acquired Gulf Oil and Texaco acquired Getty Oil.

3. Alfred D. Chandler, *Giant Enterprise: Ford, General Motors, and the Automobile Industry* (New York: Harcourt, Brace and World, Inc., 1964), pp. 44–53.
4. *Fortune*, May 5, 1980, p. 88.

Types of Mergers

On the basis of the economic interrelationship between the firms involved, mergers may be classified into three basic types — horizontal, vertical, and conglomerate. The last one can also be divided into three types of mergers — market extension, product extension, and pure conglomerate.

Horizontal Merger

A horizontal merger involves the merger of two competing firms at the same stage of the production or distribution process. Examples would be the merger of two beer companies or two shoe companies. Of the three kinds of mergers, a horizontal merger has the most immediate effect on competition. The unification of two firms producing the same product will increase concentration within an industry no matter how small the firms are. The merger may be insignificant with respect to its effect on competition, or it may be patently anticompetitive. In a horizontal merger, there is the question of what constitutes an anticompetitive share of the total market. The factors considered are the number of firms, the degree of industry concentration, the conditions of entry, and product characteristics.

Vertical Merger

A vertical merger brings under one ownership, control over firms engaged in different stages of production and distribution. The acquisition of a shoe retail outlet by a shoe manufacturer is an example. A vertical merger may serve to give a firm access to essential raw materials and outlets for its products. It is often based on projected realization of economics in distribution. In other instances, it may be used to ensure sources of supply for a manufacturing firm, particularly in industries in which the availability of essential supplies may vary erratically. A manufacturer having difficulty in obtaining retailers to handle its product line may acquire a retail chain to enable it to directly market its product. A vertical merger may stem from the difficulty of preventing partial excess capacity in multifunctional firms.

Conglomerate Merger

The conglomerate merger unites firms producing diverse and unrelated product lines in which the end products bear no similarity. An example would be the acquisition of a bank by an oil company. The conglomerate merger does not entail firms in direct competition with each other, nor are there usually any extensive vertical relations between the firms. Many large American firms have attained their size through the conglomerate merger. One firm is Reynolds Industries, which has expanded from the production of tobacco products to the production of fried chicken, alcoholic beverages, cookies, Chinese food, and canned fruits and vegetables. Another example is the International Telegraph and Telephone Company (ITT), which originally operated almost exclusively as a telephone, telegraph, cable, and wireless public utility. Through mergers, it acquired companies in such areas as book publishing, baking, hotels, fire insurance, vending machines, and consumer financing.

There are three types of conglomerate mergers:

1. Market extension. A market extension merger is one in which a conglomerate wants to get a toehold in a particular industry through the acquisition of an existing firm in the industry. An example was the acquisition of the Miller Brewing Company by Philip Morris.

2. Product extension. A product extension merger is one firm's acquisition of a second business producing a product closely related to the acquiring firms product line. The classic example of a production extension merger was the attempted takeover of Clorox, a maker of liquid bleach, by Procter and Gamble, the largest manufacturer of household cleaning supplies in the United States.

3. Pure conglomerate. A pure conglomerate merger is a merger of two totally unrelated firms. An example would be the acquisition of Avis, a rental car company, by ITT, a manufacturer of telecommunication equipment.

Development of Mergers

Mergers tend to come in cycles, the first coming around the turn of the century. The Sherman Act had little effect on curbing industrial concentration in the United States in the first decade after its passage. By 1900, after ten years of enforcement of the Sherman Act, the number of industrial combinations in the United States with capital of $1 billion or more had increased from ten to three hundred.[5] The catalyst in the merger movement was an economic depression that occurred between 1893 and 1896. The merger was one way to protect

5. Temporary National Economic Committee, Monograph No. 21, *Competition and Monopoly in American Industry* (Washington, D.C.: U.S. Government Printing Office, 1940), p. 88.

against a decline in economic activity, for if a firm could gain control over competing plants in its principal line of commerce, it would have a better opportunity to fix prices and control output. The mergers consummated at the end of the century were in such industries as petroleum, iron and steel, copper, sugar, lead, and salt.

There was a second cycle of mergers during the prosperous 1920s, with the peak occurring in 1929, when some 1,245 mergers were formed.[6] During that entire decade there were around seven thousand mergers, primarily in the mass production and entertainment industries — automobiles, automobile parts, motion pictures, movie theaters, and appliances. The mass production of the automobile effected certain economies of scale that could be best achieved through mergers. Automobile companies acquired medium-sized firms that could produce such things as parts and components used in the automobile industry. The stock market itself had an influence on the merger movement of the 1920s. This was a period of rapidly rising securities prices, which provided an opportunity for selling new securities to brokerage houses, and mergers were a way of stimulating speculative interest in securities.

A third cycle of mergers began in the middle 1950s and continued up to the latter part of the 1970s. There was a significant increase in the number of conglomerate mergers, a movement that cut across different types of industries — manufacturing, mining, banking, insurance, trade, and service areas. The reasons for the continued growth of mergers were varied and included the desire to meet foreign competition, the need to control the various stages of product flow, to diversify, and to improve access to credit. Certainly a widespread, unstated motive may have been the desire to restrict competition. However, an acquiring firm may also gain from a merger by securing the acquired firm's personnel, marketing facilities, and trade reputation.

A fourth cycle of mergers began in the 1980s. What differentiates this cycle from the others is the size of the firms involved in the mergers. The biggest wave of corporate acquisitions in American history contributed to the rise in stock prices to historic highs, and increased the debt of many corporations so that they could finance their multibillion dollar takeovers of other companies. Table 5-1 presents the value of all mergers and acquisitions completed for each year during the period from 1970 to 1985. A new kind of corporate acquisition developed during this time — an acquisition not for the purpose of expansion or diversification but for liquidating a company and making an immediate profit. The fourth cycle of mergers also reflects the free market policies of the Reagan administration.

In 1985, there were a record 36 mergers and acquisitions valued at $1 billion or more, headed by General Electric's purchase of RCA for

6. Ibid., p. 105.

$6.3 billion in the largest nonoil merger in history. Some of the largest mergers and acquisitions are presented in Table 5-2. Companies and corporate raiders, such as T. Boone Pickens and Carl Icahn, have financed some of these acquisitions through the sale of high-yield junk bonds to wealthy persons and institutional investors. There are companies that make money by acting as an intermediary to the merger of other companies. Some companies are simply in the business of buying companies. An example is the Kohlberg, Kravis, Roberts buyout of Beatrice for $6.2 billion. It is not in the business of running a company

Table 5-1 Value of Mergers and Acquisitions Completed, 1979-1985 (billions of dollars)

Year	Value
1979	$ 34.2
1980	33.6
1981	67.0
1982	62.7
1983	52.2
1984	124.8
1985	125. est.

Source: *The New York Times*, December 29, 1985, Section F, p. 1. Copyright © 1985 by The New York Times Company. Reprinted by permission.

Table 5-2 Major Corporation Acquisitions, 1985 (billions of dollars)

Buyer	Company Bought	Value
General Electric	RCA	$6.3
Kohlberg, Kravis, Roberts	Beatrice Co.	6.2
Philip Morris	General Foods	5.8
General Motors	Hughes Aircraft	5.1
R. J. Reynolds	Nabisco	4.9
Baxter Travenol	American Hospital Supply	3.8
U.S. Steel	Texas Oil and Gas	3.7
Capital Cities Communications	American Broadcasting Co.	3.5
Monsanto	G. D. Searle	2.8
Pantry Pride	Revlon	1.8
Rockwell International	Allen-Bradley	1.7
Procter and Gamble	Richardson-Vicks	1.6

Source: *The New York Times*, December 29, 1985, Section F, p. 6. Copyright © 1985 by The New York Times Company. Reprinted by permission.

on a day-to-day basis; it will either keep management on or hire a management team to run the company. The acquisition of Revlon by Pantry Pride was a "hostile" takeover — that is, even though Revlon opposed the merger, Pantry Pride raised $700 million from the sale of junk bonds and acquired the company.

THE EXTENT OF CONCENTRATION BY INDUSTRY

The extent of concentration in the United States varies considerably by industry. In some industries, one large firm is clearly dominant, in that it contributed 50 percent or more of total output. General Motors, with more than 60 percent of America's domestic output of automobiles is an example. In other industries, a few firms may account for the bulk of sales, with no one firm clearly dominant over the others; for example, the dominance of the tobacco industry by R. J. Reynolds Industries and Philip Morris, and of the soft drink industry by Coca-Cola and PepsiCo. Both industries correspond to an oligopolistic market. There are also industries that have little or no concentration and thus come fairly close to approximating a purely competitive market situation. The shoe, concrete products, and women's clothing industries are examples.

There are several ways of measuring the extent of industrial concentration. One way is concentration by firm size, which divides firms on the basis of such criteria as number of employees, payrolls, and value added by manufacturing. A second way is to measure changes in the share of value added by manufacturing for large companies over various periods. A third way is to compare shares of value added by manufacturing, value of shipment, and other measures of concentration for large companies over different periods. And a fourth way is to measure the extent of concentration for each industry by dividing its market output for the four largest firms. If 80 percent of the output of an industry is contributed by the four largest firms, it can be said that the industry possesses a high degree of industrial concentration.

Concentration by Firm Size

Table 5-3 presents payrolls, value added by manufacturing, and capital expenditures for a distribution of firms based on number of employees. The data are for 1982. Firms employing one thousand or more workers accounted for 0.6 percent of all firms, but accounted for 25.2 percent of total employment in manufacturing, 33.1 percent of total value of payrolls, 31.5 percent of value added by manufacturing, and 34.6

Table 5-3 Distribution of Industry in the United States by Employment Size, 1982 (establishments and employees in thousands; money figures in millions of dollars)

Item	Total	Employment Size				
		Under 20	20–99	100–249	250–999	1,000 and over
Establishments	348	230	84	21	11	2
Employees	17,818	1,405	3,662	3,287	4,977	4,486
Payroll	341,406	20,404	59,103	55,708	93,125	113,068
Value added by manufacturing	824,117	45,997	135,932	134,379	247,729	260,081
New capital expenditures	74,562	3,639	9,469	12,323	23,331	25,800

Source: U.S. Department of Commerce, Bureau of the Census, *1982 Census of Manufacture: General Summary* (Washington; U.S. Government Printing Office, 1986), pp. 1-3.

percent of new capital expenditures. However, these percentages show a decline when compared to statistics for 1977. The respective percentages for 1977 were employment in manufacturing, 28 percent; total value of payrolls, 35.4 percent; value added by manufacturing, 34.2 percent; new capital expenditures, 35.8 percent. However, approximately only 2 percent of all industrial firms in the United States produced about half of the value added by manufacturing and about all new capital expenditures for 1982.

There also has been no discernible long-run trends toward greater concentration of output from a smaller number of firms; in fact, the opposite appears. When 1954 is used as a base year, firms with one thousand or more workers employed 32.6 percent of the labor force in manufacturing compared to 25.2 percent in 1982. The percentage of payrolls provided by these largest firms declined from 37.3 percent of the total in 1954 to 35.4 percent in 1982. The contribution made to total new capital expenditures by the largest firms decreased from 38.3 percent in 1954 to 35.8 percent in 1982, and the contribution of the largest firms to value added by manufacturing declined from 37.0 percent in 1954 to 34.2 percent in 1982. That there has been a decline in the number of workers employed in manufacturing should also be noted.

Concentration Based on Value
Added by Manufacturing

Table 5-4 presents the percentages of the share of total value added by manufacturing of the largest companies over several periods, with 1947 as the base year. The trend during the earlier periods was toward greater concentration of output. The largest 50 companies, as measured by their contribution to value added by manufacturing, contributed 17 percent of value added in 1947 to 24 percent in 1982. But from 1954 to 1982, the percentage share of the 50 largest firms has remained virtually unchanged. The percentage share of the 200 largest firms of total value added by manufacturing was 30 percent in 1947 compared to 43 percent in 1982. However, almost all this increase was during the period from 1947 to 1963, and there has been little change since. A large overall relative gain was made by the second 50 largest firms in the top 100, which increased this share of value added from 6 percent in 1947 to 9 percent in 1982. It is important to note that the largest 50 companies contributed more to the total value added by manufacturing in 1947 and 1982 than the next largest 150 firms did.

Table 5-4 Percent Share of Largest Companies of Total Value Added by Manufacturing, 1947–1982

Company Rank Group Based on Value Added by Manufacturing	1947	1954	1958	1963	1966	1967	1970	1972	1977	1982
50 largest	17	23	23	25	25	25	24	25	24	24
100 largest	23	30	30	33	33	33	33	33	33	33
150 largest	27	34	35	37	38	38	38	39	39	39
200 largest	30	37	38	41	42	42	43	43	44	43

Source: U.S. Bureau of the Census, 1982 Census of Manufacture, *Concentration Ratios in Manufacturing*, Table 1; May 1986, p. 7.

Concentration as Measured by Share of Value Added by Manufacturing and Other Criteria

Table 5-5 compares the shares of value added by manufacturing, employment, value of shipment, and capital expenditures by the 200 largest manufacturing firms for three periods, 1967, 1977, and 1982. The dominance of the 50 largest firms is apparent. In 1982, the 50 largest firms accounted for 24 percent of the total value added by manufacturing; the next largest 50 firms contributed only 9 percent; and the remaining largest 100 firms accounted for 10 percent. The 50 largest firms employed 17 percent of all manufacturing workers in 1982; the next largest 150 firms employed 16 percent. The 50 largest companies accounted for 23 percent of the total value of shipment in 1982 compared to 21 percent for the next largest 150 companies. With regard to new capital expenditures, the 50 largest firms were responsible for 27 percent of the total in 1982 compared with 22 percent for the next largest 150 companies. However, there was very little change in the firms' relative shares in each classification for the three periods, 1967, 1977, and 1982; if anything, there is a slight decline in the shares of the 50 largest companies. In 1982, the 50 largest companies contributed 24 percent of the value added by manufacturing compared to 25 percent in 1967. They employed 17 percent of all manufacturing workers in 1982 compared to 20 percent in 1967, and they contributed 23 percent of the total value of shipments in 1982 compared to 25 percent in 1967.

Concentration Based on Share of Industry Output

A common measure of industrial concentration is the total output of the four largest firms within an industry. Table 5-6 compares the output of the four largest firms in a number of high- and low-concentration industries. The extent of concentration is highest in the production of motor vehicles and car bodies, household laundry equipment, and cereal breakfast foods, and lowest in women's and misses' dresses, concrete products, and fur goods. However, a high degree of concentration does not necessarily indicate a monopoly or a lack of competition. For one thing, the concentration data offered by the Bureau of the Census cover only U.S. production and omit foreign imports. Omitting this foreign competition leads to a significant overstatement of economic concentration in some U.S. markets. A case in point is the U.S. car market. Although the four largest U.S. firms produce more than 90 percent of domestic-made cars, 25 percent of all cars sold in the United States are foreign imports. There are a variety of cars, domestic and foreign, from which consumers are free to choose.

Table 5-5 Share of Value Added, Employment, Payroll, Value of Shipments, and Capital Expenditures Accounted for by the 200 Largest Companies, 1982

Company Rank Group Based on Value Added by Manufacturing		Value Added by Manufacturing	All Employees		Production Workers			Value of Shipments	Capital Expenditures, New
			Number	Payroll	Number	Man-hours	Wages		
50 largest	1982	24	17	24	14	14	20	23	27
	1977	24	16	25	16	17	24	25	28
	1967	25	20	25	18	18	23	25	27
51 to 100 largest	1982	9	7	8	6	6	8	9	10
	1977	9	7	8	6	7	7	9	11
	1967	8	6	7	5	6	6	8	13
101 to 150 largest	1982	6	5	6	4	4	5	7	7
	1977	6	5	5	5	5	5	6	6
	1967	5	4	5	4	4	4	6	6
151 to 200 largest	1982	4	4	4	3	3	4	5	6
	1977	4	4	4	4	4	4	4	5
	1967	4	4	3	3	3	3	4	4
200 largest	1982	43	33	41	28	28	37	44	49
	1977	44	33	42	31	32	40	45	49
	1967	42	34	40	30	31	37	43	51

Sources: U.S. Bureau of the Census, Census of Manufacture, 1982, *Concentration Ratios in Manufacturing*, Table 4, May 1986; Census of Manufacture, 1977, *Concentration Ratios in Manufacturing*, Table 4, May 1981.

Table 5-6 Percentages of Industry Output Produced by the Four Largest Firms in High- and Low-Concentration Industries (output measured by value of shipment)

	Percent of Industry Output Produced by Four Largest Firms
High-concentration Industries	
Motor vehicles and car bodies	92
Household laundry equipment	91
Cereal breakfast foods	86
Cigarettes	84
Organic fibers	77
Malt beverages	77
Photographic equipment	74
Sewing machines	72
Tires	66
Primary aluminum	64
Aircraft	64
Motor vehicle parts and accessories	61
Soap and other detergents	60
Metal cans	50
Low-concentration Industries	
Meat packing	29
Petroleum refining	28
Pharmaceutical products	26
Men's and boys' suits and clothes	25
Millinery	24
Radio and TV equipment	22
Poultry dressing	22
Canned fruits and vegetables	21
Sawmills	17
Fluid milk	16
Wood household furniture	16
Fur goods	12
Concrete products	10
Women's and misses' dresses	6

Source: U.S. Bureau of the Census, 1982 Census of Manufacture, *Concentration Ratios in Manufacturing*, Table 5.

There have been some shifts in concentration ratios by industries over time. For example, in 1967, the four largest tire companies had 73 percent of their industry output compared to 66 percent in 1982. Conversely, the four largest car companies had 52 percent of industry output in 1967 compared to 77 percent in 1982. The four largest cereal breakfast food companies had 90 percent of industry output in 1967 compared to 86 percent in 1982. For less concentrated industries, the four largest meat packing companies contributed 22 percent of total industry output in 1967 compared to 29 percent in 1982. The four largest firms in petroleum refining contributed 24 percent of industry output in 1967 compared to 28 percent in 1982. On the other hand, the share of output of women's and misses' dresses produced by the four largest firms declined from 9 percent in 1967 to 6 percent in 1982.

INDUSTRIAL CONCENTRATION AND GLOBAL MARKETS

Almost all American and foreign industrial corporations do not confine themselves to domestic sales but participate in business activities outside the boundaries of their countries. These corporations are called multinationals because they transcend national boundaries. They have contributed to the internationalization of production. Many foreign companies sell in the United States, and in some markets, they have more than 50 percent of the market share. Realistically, there should be a reappraisal of market definitions because the change to a global economy means that traditional measures of industrial concentration understate the existence of competition. Many U.S. industries appear highly concentrated when measures of concentration are limited only to domestic markets, but fall far short of this concentration when world markets are considered. The U.S. auto industry is a case in point.

The U.S. Automobile Industry

The U.S. automobile industry is highly concentrated when only domestic automobile output is used to measure industrial concentration. In 1984, General Motors, Ford, and Chrysler produced 94 percent of all cars manufactured in the United States.[7] Their shares of domestic auto production were respectively 56 percent, 22 percent, and 16 percent. However, when imports of foreign cars are taken into consideration, the market shares changed. Of the more than 10 million cars

7. Motor Vehicle Manufacturers Association, *Facts & Figures, 1985*, pp. 8-9.

sold in the United States in 1984, General Motors accounted for 42 percent, Ford 16 percent, Chrysler 11 percent, and Toyota 9 percent.[8] Total foreign imports of cars accounted for around 27 percent of automobile sales in the U.S. market, giving American consumers a variety of choices when it came to buying automobiles.

The automobile market has to be viewed in terms of a global market. There are some forty automobile producers in the world, and almost all sell in a number of foreign markets. Ford sells as many cars outside the United States as it does in it. Table 5-7 presents the total number of passenger cars produced for the twelve largest automobile companies in the world. These twelve companies accounted for 84 percent of all automobiles produced in the world in 1983. The four largest automobile producers accounted for around 48 percent of world output. Japan was the world's largest producer of automobiles in 1983; the United States was second, West Germany third, and France fourth. Approximately 60 percent of all cars manufactured in Japan were shipped to foreign markets, with the United States being the largest of them.

Table 5-7 Leading World Automobile Producers and Their Share of Total Output, 1983 (in thousands)

Company	Passenger Cars	Percent of World Production
General Motors — U.S.A.	6,097	21.0
Ford — U.S.A.	3,416	11.8
Toyota — Japan	2,381	8.2
Renault — France	1,983	6.8
Volkswagen — West Germany	1,936	6.7
Nissan — Japan	1,899	6.5
Peugeot — France	1,608	5.5
Fiat — Italy	1,442	5.0
Chrysler — U.S.A.	1,036	3.6
Honda — Japan	913	3.1
Mazda — Japan	861	3.0
Lada — U.S.S.R.	780	2.7
	24,352	83.9
World Output	29,081	100.0

Source: *Facts & Figures, 1985* (Detroit, MI: Motor Vehicle Manufacturers Association), p. 28. Used by permission.

8. Ibid., p. 15.

THE ISSUES IN INDUSTRIAL CONCENTRATION

In some industries, a certain amount of industrial concentration apparently is inevitable, since some types of business organizations lend themselves to large-scale production. For example, there are industries in which the product itself is highly complex and can be constructed only by a large and diversified organization. Automobiles and computers are examples. There are also industries in which the product is large in size, requiring complex equipment for construction and large capital investments, for example, shipbuilding. Then there are industries that require a large capital investment, particularly in plants and equipment. The steel industry is an example of this. Finally, there are industries in which a natural resource is required that is available only in limited amounts and in specific geographic locations. An example is the petroleum industry.

Industrial concentration may also be an inevitable concomitant of advancing technology in all major industrial countries, regardless of their ideologies. For example, data show that for some industries, concentration ratios are generally higher in other Western countries than in the United States; that the foreign industries in which concentration is high are generally the same as those in which concentration is high in the United States; and that the industries that are not highly concentrated in other Western industrial countries are generally the same as those industries that are not concentrated in this country. In Japan and West Germany, the steel, chemical, and rubber industries are more concentrated than they are in the United States.[9] In France, Peugeot and Renault produce 100 percent of all French cars.[10] These data suggest that technological and economic factors determine somewhat the degree of concentration of industry in all market economies.[11]

Advantages of Concentration

There are several advantages to large-scale production. An expansion of a firm's production unit often permits greater specialization in the use of both labor and capital equipment. Overhead cost may be spread over

9. The Report of the President's Commission on Industrial Competitiveness, *Global Competition: The New Reality*, vol. 2 (Washington, D.C.: U.S.Government Printing Office, 1985), p. 190.
10. Motor Vehicle Manufacturers Association, *Facts & Figures, 1985*, p. 29.
11. Industries in the centrally planned economies of the Soviet Union and Eastern Europe are even more concentrated.

a larger output, which results in a lower unit cost. Economies can result from new lower minimum cost combinations of production factors, that is, land, labor, and capital. Specialized labor and capital equipment frequently can be added to a production unit only in large indivisible amounts, and because of the inability of specialized factors to diversify, they cannot be used profitably in small-scale operations. In many industries, smaller business units may well result in higher unit costs, and hence the answer to the problem of monopoly may not necessarily be the breaking up of large firms. Market power can be based on underlying economies of scale and technological or managerial leadership; in some cases, large firms are the price of efficiency and innovation.[12]

Disadvantages of Concentration

In a competitive market economy, the interests of producers and consumers coincide because the way to larger profits for producers is through greater efficiency, price reductions, and increased sales volume, all of which naturally benefit consumers. In a monopolistic or oligopolistic market, profits may be maximized at the expense of consumers by selling a smaller quantity of goods at a higher price than under competitive conditions. There is also evidence that small or medium-sized firms are often more innovative than larger firms. Apple Computer Company, for instance, was created in the 1970s by two men in their twenties who started their operations in a garage. Although the computer-data processing industry was and is dominated by IBM, Apple became the leading exponent of technology for the masses. Finally, industrial concentration can and has resulted in the growth of unfair business practices designed to eliminate competition and exploit consumers.

Market Power and Barriers to Entry

The idea of entry has for a long time been used by economists as an important part of economic theory. In pure competition, freedom of entry and departure bring about the long-run equilibrium of an industry. In the short run, if profits are high in an industry, new firms will enter and compete away profits. In the long run, all firms in the industry will receive a price equal to their average total costs. Conversely,

---

12. In a case involving Alcoa, the Supreme Court was unwilling to split up the company for fear of losing substantial economies of scale in production and research and development.

firms will leave less profitable industries. Market power exists in any industry when there are significant barriers to entry. The extent of this market power varies considerably by industry. In some oligopolistic industries, entry would be extremely difficult, if not impossible — automobile and cigarette industries, for example. There have been no new domestic producers of automobiles in the last forty years. On the other hand, although IBM dominates the computer data processing industry, six new firms entered the market during the 1970s.

There can be several barriers to entry into a market. One barrier is product differentiation. The greater the degree of product differentiation, the higher the barrier to entry. An example is the soft drink industry, which is dominated by Coca-Cola Company and PepsiCo. Coca-Cola and Pepsi-Cola are well-known products. In December 1985 and January 1986, Pepsi-Cola had 19.3 percent of total soft drink sales compared with 14.7 percent for Classic Coke and 3.5 percent for New Coke.[13] Then there are a number of other soft drinks each company makes that are differentiated on the basis of taste, caffeine or calories. Examples are Diet Coke, Cherry Coke, Diet Pepsi, Tab, Pepsi-Free, Slice, Sprite, and so forth. Consumer acceptance of these products makes entry of new soft drink firms very difficult. The same would hold true for other industries where products are differentiated and there is a high degree of consumer acceptance. Examples are the breakfast food, cigarette, and detergent industries.

Another barrier to entry can occur when firms in an industry possess an absolute cost advantage over potential entrants into the market. This advantage can exist in several ways. First, existing firms may already possess the best natural resource — coal, timberland, or iron ore deposits. Second, the existing firms may already have patents on the most popular products. Third, they may have access to capital at lower rates of interest than would be available to new entrants into the market. Fourth, they possess management and marketing advantages over potential rivals who have to hire skilled managers. These advantages would give existing firms a lower average total cost advantage over potential competitors at a whole range of output that could be supplied.

A third barrier to entry is capital requirements. The reason there have been no entrants into the automobile industry in many years is that an enormous amount of money would have to be invested in plants and equipment to compete with the existing automobile companies. In 1985, the assets of General Motors, the world's largest automobile company, amounted to $63 billion.[14] Entry is made difficult because

13. *The Washington Post*, April 26, Section F1.
14. *Fortune*, April 28, 1986, p. 182.

auto company assets are durable and specialized. Moreover, any market entrant would have to achieve a substantial market share to realize economies of scale. The established Japanese and European automobile companies have been able to successfully penetrate the U.S. market because they have existing plant facilities and are able to mass produce cars.

INDUSTRIAL CONCENTRATION — BANKING

The structure of the U.S. banking system is undergoing changes of unprecedented magnitude.[15] To some extent these changes reflect the impact of rapid technological change. They also reflect the passage of laws that have eliminated many of the regulatory constraints on the management of commercial banks, as they have allowed many other institutions to alter the nature of deposit and lending services offered to their customers. For example, Merrill Lynch offers credit for real estate and related purposes and for the purchase of securities. Furthermore, with its Cash Management Account (CMA), Merrill Lynch has created a financial instrument directly competitive with checking accounts offered by commercial banks. Money market mutual funds also provide another example of the growth of nondeposit financial institutions that provide competition to commercial banks. Moreover, many offer a number of convenient services, the most attractive of which is the ability to write checks against the value of the account. The elimination of interest rate ceilings has stimulated the growth of money market funds.

There have also been changes within the banking system itself. One change is the development of branch banking, which means that banks are permitted to branch throughout a state. The advent of automatic teller machines (ATMs) is a second change. They allow a bank to offer deposit and check cashing services without constructing and staffing a branch. Placing ATMs across state lines is economically feasible and, where economic communities or metropolitan areas spread over state lines, desirable. Furthermore, in an effort to provide twenty-four-hour service at minimal cost in many locations, banks have created interbank ATM networks. Because of the strength of market forces, banks anticipate further liberalization of laws governing branch banking and the geographic extension of services. The growing acceptance of regional banking has resulted in a momentum for national banking.

15. Kerry M. Cooper and Donald R. Fraser, *Banking Deregulation and the New Competition in Financial Services* (Cambridge, Mass.: Ballinger Publishing Co., 1984), chapters 1 and 2.

Mergers

Bank mergers have become a common phenomenon in the United States, and the prospect is for these mergers to increase among the larger banks. There are several reasons for the increase in bank mergers.[16] First, branch banking has provided the impetus toward mergers in which large banks create branches by mergers with smaller ones. Second, if a bank wishes to offer a new form of service, a merger can be the easiest way to acquire the facilities. Third, economies of scale provide a motive for bank mergers. Spreading overhead costs over a larger volume of business reduces unit costs. Fourth, mergers allow banks to increase their capitalization and deposits. This is significant because legal limits on the size of loans made to one borrower are based on the size of the bank's capital. With a merger, the newly enlarged bank has a larger capital base and can make larger loans.[17]

Holding Companies

Bank holding companies are an important feature of the banking industry. They have evolved in response to the increasingly competitive operating environment of the banking system and to increasing demands by consumers for varied financial services. The growth of the holding company has been phenomenal. At the end of 1957, there were fifty bank holding companies registered with the Federal Reserve System, and they held 7.5 percent of all bank deposits. By the end of 1982, there were 3,702 bank holding companies, and they held 99 percent of all the deposits in the United States.[18] Bank holding companies can be divided into two categories — multibank holding companies and single-bank holding companies. In 1982, they controlled 38.2 percent of all commercial banks and 72.0 percent of the branch banks in the United States.

Issues of Bank Concentration

There are certain advantages that accrue to large-scale bank operations that can benefit their customers. Their size enables them to afford the

16. Emmanuel N. Roussakis, *Commercial Banking in an Era of Deregulation* (New York: Praeger, 1985), p. 54.
17. Smaller banks may also find it advantageous to be acquired by larger ones. To avoid failure, financially weak banks may agree to acquisition. Another reason for agreeing to be absorbed is the problem of management. Small banks are often at a disadvantage when it comes to attracting skilled management personnel.
18. Roussakis, *Commercial Banking in an Era of Deregulation*, p. 56.

most advanced computer technology that can facilitate the immediate withdrawal of funds by their depositors. They can hire highly specialized experts, such as economists and engineers, whose expertise can be used to advise their clients; management specialists can also provide bank customers with expertise on portfolio management. In addition, large banks often have access to inside information of value to their customers, they can provide capital to their clients at a lower cost, and they are able to offer a variety of consumer services including discount brokerage accounts.

There also can be disadvantages to the public from bank concentration; for instance, trial agreements among banks on such matters as price fixing and terms of service, and unspoken agreements not to encroach on each other's territory. The interest rate spread between bank loans and borrowings reflects a degree of monopoly: interest rate differentials against smaller borrowers exceed the differences in costs and risks. Moreover, interest rates, particularly on credit cards, remain high even though the prime rate and mortgage and other lending rates in early 1986 were at their lowest levels in eight years.[19] Innovation in the banking system has been slow; in fact, most innovations have been introduced by firms outside the banking system. Computer handling was prepackaged by computer firms, and sidewalk push-button transaction units also were an outside innovation.

It is important to point out that many other financial institutions have begun to offer financial services in direct competition with commercial banks. In 1973, commercial banks provided 45.6 percent of all credit in the United States; by 1982, the share had declined to 26.1 percent.[20] Insurance companies, retailers, securities dealers, and savings and loan banks are also in the business of providing credit, although the importance of S&Ls as a source of credit has also declined. Even though the banking industry is getting more concentrated, the market shares of total credit outstanding for both commercial banks and S&Ls has declined.

INDUSTRIAL CONCENTRATION — COMMUNICATIONS

A generation ago, nearly every American city had two or more newspapers. Almost every small town had its weekly newspaper, locally

19. In May, 1986, interest rates on many Mastercard and Visa credit cards ranged from 18 percent to 21 percent. Execu-Charge, a Visa card issued by Citibank, carried an annual interest rate of 21.6 percent, the same as it did in 1984, when interest rates were much higher than they are today.
20. Board of Governors of the Federal Reserve System, *Flow of Funds Accounts*, December 1984.

owned and operated. But today virtually all city newspapers have the same owner and thus no competition, and almost all the daily newspaper circulation is controlled by companies that publish two or more dailies. Weekly newspapers also have become part of the newspaper chains; today, it is rare to find a locally owned, independent weekly newspaper. Newspaper companies own commercial radio and television stations as well. The *Washington Post* owns *Newsweek* magazine, various television stations, and other newspapers. All this means that a single newspaper can have a monopoly of news and information in its circulation area.

Obviously, the communications industry has forms of communication other than newspapers. CBS, the leader in the broadcasting industry, owns Holt, Rinehart, and Winston, a major book publishing company, and ABC, which was acquired by Capital Cities in 1985, also owns movie theaters and publishing companies.[21] Thus, there is much cross-pollination in the communications industry, with newspaper chains owning magazines and television stations, broadcasting companies owning book publishing companies and movie theaters, and book publishing companies owning magazines and television stations. There is also a trend toward concentration in the publishing industry, facilitated by high advertising and publishing costs. In the advertising industry, there have been global mergers of advertising companies.[22] Whether all this is good or bad is a matter of opinion. Economies of scale can result from this concentration, and firms such as General Cinema have been able to revive the once moribund movie theater business by showing as many as ten or twelve pictures under the same roof.

INDUSTRIAL CONCENTRATION — RETAILING

The general store was once the most important retail outlet in America. But as the country became urbanized and living standards increased, the general store was supplanted by more specialized stores — grocery stores, dress shops, shoe stores, drug stores, and so forth. Until the 1930s and early 1940s, the majority of these stores were owned by local merchants who were someone's next-door neighbor. But all this

---

21. Capital Cities is also in the communication business.
22. In May, 1986, **BBDO** International Inc., the sixth-largest U.S. advertising agency, announced that it would merge with the Doyle Dane Bernbach Group, the twelfth-largest U.S. advertising firm, and Needham Harper Worldwide, the sixteenth-largest firm. The combined advertising revenues of $5 billion will make the new advertising firm one of the largest in the world.

has changed: the local drug store is now part of the Peoples Drug chain; the local grocery store is now a Winn-Dixie; and the locally owned department store has gone the way of a Sears Roebuck or a K Mart store. These changes are not necessarily bad; they reflect the continuing change in the evolution of distribution and the transformation of America from a rural to an urban society. Economies of scale can be effected by mass volume sales, and lower prices redound to the consumers' advantage.

There is also concentration in retailing. In 1960, the ten largest retail firms accounted for 56.4 percent of total retail sales of *Fortune*'s fifty largest retail companies. In 1979, the ten largest retail firms accounted for 54.5 percent of total retail sales among *Fortune*'s top fifty. The top twenty retail firms accounted for 74.4 percent of the top fifty's total sales in 1960 and 73.7 percent in 1979.[23] In 1985, the ten largest retail companies accounted for 52.9 percent of total retail sales of the largest fifty companies, and the top twenty firms accounted for 71.1 percent of total sales.[24] The trend from 1960 is toward a little less concentration of retail sales by the largest companies. There were also many shifts in and out of the top ten and top fifty. McDonald's and Eckerd Drugs were not in the top fifty in 1960, but both were in 1985. K Mart was not in the top fifty in 1979, but ranked second in total sales in 1985. Wal-Mart barely made the top fifty in 1979 but was thirteenth in total sales in 1985.

SUMMARY

The U.S. economy is characterized by the control of a large share of the output in particular industries by comparatively few large firms. This control has been typically accomplished by mergers, which are of three types — horizontal, vertical, and conglomerate. Mergers tend to come in cycles, the latest of which has occurred during the 1980s. More large mergers have taken place during this period than at any other time since the merger movement began, with dramatic increases in the total value of all mergers occurring in 1984 and 1985. In part, these mergers can be attributed to the acquirer's desire for speculative gain. Some firms have become specialists on mergers. But mergers have occurred for other reasons, including the desire to expand into a new market or to diversify into a new product line. Since competition has become global, mergers can help firms to better compete in international markets.

Industrial concentration varies considerably by industry, with some industries being far more concentrated than others. In the automobile

23. *Fortune*, July 14, 1980, pp. 154-155.
24. *Fortune*, June 11, 1986, pp. 170-171.

industry, for example, the four largest U.S. auto companies accounted for 92 percent of the domestic output of automobiles in 1984. However, the most current Bureau of the Census data on concentration in manufacturing indicates there has been little change in concentration over the last several decades, and some measures of concentration have actually showed a decline. In the banking industry, deregulation, financial and technological innovations, and economic change have clearly transformed the nature of competition. An increase in outside competition from nondepositor financial institutions and from brokerage firms and insurance companies has contributed to an increase in the number of bank mergers. Concentration also has occurred in a variety of other U.S. industries, including communications and retailing.

There can be problems in industrial concentration, such as barriers to entry of new firms. Large firms can restrict competition and impede the rate of capital investment, and large firms' economies of scale are limited. Large firms also do not necessarily excel in productive efficiency in comparison with medium or small firms. Increasing corporate size can create managerial problems, for the top management of a large firm cannot know all the details of the business and must rely on the support of their subordinates. Finally, large firms in certain situations can exercise discretionary power over prices and entry into markets. This power to engage in restrictive practices forms one of the bases for American antitrust policy, which is the subject of Chapter 6.

QUESTIONS FOR DISCUSSION

1. What is a conglomerate merger? Give examples.
2. What are some of the barriers to entry into markets that are considered concentrated?
3. Discuss the reasons for the number of bank mergers that have taken place.
4. What is meant by economies of scale?
5. What are the advantages and disadvantages of large-scale production?
6. It is argued that industrial concentration is an irreversible trend that is occurring in all industrial societies. Do you agree?
7. Using the various measures of industrial concentration, has there been an increase or a decrease in concentration in recent years?
8. How is the cycle of mergers in the 1980s different from previous cycles?
9. How can individuals, such as T. Boone Pickens, benefit from acquiring companies?
10. Industrial concentration can also be measured in terms of global markets. Discuss.

RECOMMENDED READINGS

Cooper, Kerry, and Donald R. Fraser. *Banking Deregulation and the New Competition in Financial Services.* Cambridge, Mass: Ballinger Publishing Co., 1984.

Herman, Edward S. *Corporate Control, Corporate Power.* Cambridge, England: Cambridge University Press, 1981.

Kennan, Michael, and Lawrence J. White, eds. *Mergers and Acquisitions: Current Problems in Perspective.* Lexington, Mass.: Lexington Books, 1982.

Neal, Alfred C. *Business Power and Public Policy.* New York: Praeger, 1982.

Louis, Arthur M. "The Bottom Line on Ten Big Mergers." *Fortune*, May 3, 1982, pp. 84–89.

Roussakis, Emmanuel N. *Commercial Banking in an Era of Deregulation.* New York: Praeger, 1984.

Scherer, Frederick M. *Industrial Market Structure and Economic Performance.* 2d ed. Boston: Houghton Mifflin, 1980.

Weston, J. Fred. "Industrial Concentration, Mergers and Growth." In *Mergers and Economic Efficiency*, vol. 2. Washington, D.C. U.S. Government Printing Office, 1982.

Chapter 6
Antitrust Laws in the
United States

Antitrust legislation in the United States rests on two premises. The first is the English common law as it evolved through court decisions over a long time. In general, these decisions held that restraint on trade or commerce is not in the public interest. In interpreting the common law, courts in both England and the United States ruled that contracts or agreements to restrain or attempt to restrain trade were illegal. The second premise is the belief that competition is an effective regulator of most markets and, with a few exceptions, that monopolistic practices can be stopped by competition. This premise is based on the economic theory espousing pure or perfect competition as the ideal, since according to the theory, competition forces firms to be efficient, cut costs, and receive no more than normal profits. The theory assumes that in a state of pure or perfect competition, economic decisions would be made on the basis of prices, price changes, and price relationships, all of which are determined by the market-related forces of supply and demand.

Ideal competition of the pure or perfect type does not exist, nor can it, given the impact of modern technology and the economies of scale resulting from this technology. Modern attitudes toward industrial concentration assume that when a few firms dominate an industry they are in a position to set prices higher than would prevail in more competitive pricing situations and are therefore able to gain profits higher than total competition would allow. It is presumed that concentration and competition are inversely related. So some form of competition requiring sellers in a given industry to compete against one another in terms of prices is desired. In addition, there should be no natural or artificial barriers to entry so that there will be a flow of sellers in and out of markets that will reflect market changes. Each seller would then be limited in his or her ability to control prices.

Unfortunately, competition has many facets, and it is likely to mean different things to different people. And as an objective of national economic policy, it may have even more meanings. Thus, many of the federal regulatory laws are concerned with different definitions of competition and may not be totally compatible with one another. The American economy is characterized by its heterogeneity, and no one model or set of normative criteria can be used to explain or evaluate overall economic performance. Therefore, the issue for those responsible for regulatory policymaking must necessarily be to determine whether consumers have realistic alternatives rather than to engage in a quixotic search for perfection in marketplace competition.

A REVIEW OF ANTITRUST LAWS

Although we discussed the major antitrust laws, with the exception of the Celler-Kefauver Act of 1950, in Chapters 2 and 3, our aim then was largely to set them in their historical context. Now we shall review these laws in some detail, for they are complex and constantly subjected to changes in interpretation, but not to changes in principle. These laws contain sweeping provisions directed against private restraints that might threaten a competitive market economy. There has been no meticulous itemization of these restraints by Congress because it is possible for a specific type of conduct to be prohibited in most settings, although it could be in the public interest to permit it in others. For example, defining an illegal monopoly as a firm seeking to control 90 percent of the output of a product might be justified for large producers of basic commodities competing in a national market, but such a determination would be unrealistic for the only movie theater in a small town. To catalogue a list of antisocial restraints invites evasion by ingenious firms, for what is applicable to one industry may not be applicable to another.

The Sherman Act, 1890

The Sherman Act is, of course, the original and most basic of the antitrust laws. Its most important provisions are summarized here.

Section 1 prohibits agreements, expressed or otherwise, conspiracies, or combinations between two or more persons, who may be individuals or corporations, that unreasonably restrain the trade or commerce of the United States. This trade or commerce may be domestic, interstate, or foreign. This section's provisions are relevant only if the facts — when weighed by the courts — reveal either an unduly restraining effect on trade or an intent so to affect it.

The Supreme Court has held that certain types of agreements, conspiracies, or combinations are in and of themselves so restrictive of competition as to be conclusively presumed unreasonable restraints of trade. In other words, the Court has declined to inquire into whether or not such arrangements cause any public injury or are justified for business reasons and has not considered the amount of interstate trade and commerce affected so long as it is clearly beyond a small level. Any of these arrangements is unlawful if it limits the import of products into the United States or the export of products from the United States or if it impedes commerce within the United States. The government need not prove any more than that the parties to such arrangements have in fact entered into them. Among these offenses, called per se violations, are the following:

1. Price fixing — This is any agreement or understanding between two or more competitors to fix, stabilize, or in any way affect the price of a product. The courts are here concerned about the inhibition of price competition. Arrangements that tamper in any way with the price structure have been determined to constitute price fixing.

2. Division of customers, markets, and volume of production — This pertains to agreements or understandings between two or more corporations to divide or allocate the markets in which each will sell a product and to arrangements to divide, limit, or maintain the production of a given product at a certain level. The courts have consistently struck down arrangements between two or more competitors in which they agree to divide customers, allocate markets, or in any way control the output of goods.

3. Boycotts or concerted refusals to deal — An agreement or understanding among competitors to boycott or refuse to deal with any third party is unlawful. Moreover, a single seller may not agree, directly or indirectly, with one or more of its independent distributors to refuse to deal with anyone else desiring to purchase the product for sale.

4. Tie-in sales — Any type of tying arrangement may be a per se violation, for example, when the tied product is patented or the seller has a dominant economic position in the sale of the product. Unlawful tie-in sales usually occur when the seller seeks to force or induce a buyer to purchase one or more less desirable products in order to purchase the desired product over which the seller has significant economic control.

In addition to these per se violations, the courts have applied "a rule of reason" approach to deciding which other types of conduct may be unlawful under Section 1 of the Sherman Act. As a general proposition, this rule results in legalizing certain types of conduct, even though there is some restraint of trade when the restraint is ancillary to the main business purpose of an arrangement. In this situation, a corporation may defend a challenged course of conduct on the ground that there is a sound business justification for it and that any restraint of trade is ancillary or incidental to the main business purpose. Under this rule, the legality of business conduct may be determined on the basis of the duration of the agreement, the percentage of the market affected by it, the relative bargaining power of the parties involved, and the size of the geographic market affected.

Section 2 prohibits any single company from monopolizing, or attempting to monopolize, any part of interstate trade and commerce in any relevant market. A relevant market is defined both by the geographic area in which a product competes and by the products with which the product in question can reasonably be interchanged in its end use. This section also makes it unlawful for two or more competing firms to agree to, or to conspire to, monopolize any part of trade or commerce. No exact minimum percentage of a relevant market has been fixed by the courts as constituting monopoly; the real test is whether a company has the power to control prices or to exclude competition. If that power is proved, the company is a monopolist. Note that Section 2 prohibits even attempts to monopolize; that is, a company could violate the law if it engaged in conduct intended to result in monopoly even if it did not succeed.

Civil Remedies

The enforcement of the Sherman Act is entrusted to the Justice Department, which in 1903, created a special antitrust division for this purpose. The punishments for violating the act are spelled out in Sections 1 and 2. Section 4 provides for the use of civil suits, giving the attorney general the right to enforce the act by using civil proceedings to prevent and restrain violations. Dissolution, divestiture, or divorcement proceedings can be used to prevent combinations and to promote competition. Another civil remedy is to use an injunction, a restraining order used by a judge to prevent unfair business practices. A third method of court action against violators of the act is given in Section 7, which provides for damage suits by private parties injured by other private parties acting in a manner forbidden or declared unlawful by the act. If successful in their suit, the injured parties can recover three times the amount of damages sustained.

Criminal Remedies

All violations of Sections 1 and 2 of the Sherman Act are subject to criminal penalties, and provision is made for punishment by fine, not to exceed $100,000 for each violation, or by imprisonment, not to exceed three years, or by both. Upon conviction, the fine may be levied against each party indicted and for each charge in the complaint. Criminal cases are essentially punitive; they seek to penalize past illegal conduct — mainly conspiracies — and to prevent a repetition of such conduct. In criminal cases, it is possible for a defendant to plead nolo contendere with the consent of the court. This plea means the accused party makes no contention about whether or not he or she is guilty and agrees to accept the decision of the court. If the court accepts the plea, it is in a position to impose criminal penalties according to the provisions of the law.

Two major antitrust acts were passed in 1914, the Clayton Act and the Federal Trade Commission Act. Both were designed to strengthen the Sherman Act by adding teeth to its enforcement provisions. By 1914, the Sherman Act, through judicial interpretation, had lost much of its efficacy. There was no legislation to prevent holding companies, interlocking directorates, price discrimination, or other abuses designed to lessen competition, and the trend toward the concentration of economic power in the hands of a few business firms and investment banks continued unabated. The Sherman Act was surrounded by a cloud of uncertainty because it failed to state precisely which kinds of abuses or actions by business were prohibited. Without being specific, the Sherman Act emphasized the punishment of abuses, whereas the Clayton and Federal Trade Commission acts tried to define and prevent abuses. In particular, these two acts were aimed at the practice of unfair competition, including price discrimination, exclusive and tying agreements, and interlocking directorates.

The Clayton Antitrust Act, 1914

The Clayton Act was passed almost concurrently with the Federal Trade Commission Act. It represented an attempt to modify the Sherman Act by specifying unfair business practices and thus eliminating some of the uncertainty introduced by the concept of the rule of reason. The act dealt with a wide range of activities, most of which can be organized into three categories: (1) provisions prohibiting various forms of business abuses, such as price discrimination and tying agreements; (2) provisions providing various kinds of remedies against these abuses, and (3) provisions relating to labor unions.

Probably the most important provision of the Clayton Act is Section 2, which deals with primary-line price discrimination. This type of price discrimination involves a geographic price differential, that is, the sale of goods at a higher price in one area and a lower price in another area, to the injury of a local seller. However, this kind of discrimination may also occur within the same geographic area. Section 2 prohibits price discrimination in the sale of goods of like grade or quality when the effect is to injure or prevent competition. Price discrimination is identified by considering variations in the net prices charged by a seller and in the selling price of the same class of goods under the same circumstances.

Section 3 of the Clayton Act prohibits tying contracts and exclusive dealing arrangements. The tying contract, as mentioned in Chapter 2, makes the lease or sale of a particular product conditional on the lessee's or purchaser's use of associated products sold by the same manufacturer. In the exclusive dealing arrangement, one firm induces another not to deal with the former's competitors. The prohibition of the tying contract was designed to prevent the extension of a partial monopoly into a wider field. The decision of the Supreme Court in the A. B. Dick case of 1912 made the passage of Section 3 imperative.[1] In this case, the Supreme Court had allowed the A. B. Dick Company to compel purchasers of its patented mimeograph machines to use only ink paper sold by it. Tying contracts and exclusive dealing arrangements have generally been condemned by the courts only when a seller enjoys substantial market power and they result in a lessening of competition.

Section 7, which pertains to mergers and acquisitions, is another important provision of the Clayton Act. A wave of mergers had taken place in the United States during the period 1894-1904. In an effort to stop them, the federal government brought action against the American Sugar Refining Company in 1895, charging it with a violation of Section 2 — the antimonopoly provision of the Sherman Act. This company had gained control of more than 98 percent of the refined sugar capacity of the United States. However, the Supreme Court ruled that manufacturing was not commerce and that industrial monopolies could be prosecuted only by the states.[2] The effect of the case was to give firms seeking monopoly power a new way to bring scores of competitors under control. Since the Sherman Act made the trust form of combination illegal, mergers would serve just as well to control competition. Mergers took place in a wide variety of industries, ranging from petroleum to whiskey. By 1900, companies such as American Tobacco and Standard Oil controlled some 90 percent of the output of their products.

Section 7 prohibits any corporation engaged in commerce from acquiring the stock of another corporation when the effect may be to reduce competition substantially or to create a monopoly in any line of business and in any section of the country. It should be emphasized that Section 7 applies to firms engaged in either interstate or foreign commerce. The acquisition by a U.S. firm of a major interest in a foreign firm that threatens actual or potential competition to firms in the United States would almost certainly be scrutinized, as would any joint venture by a U.S. firm and a competing foreign firm.[3] Section 7

---

1. *Henry* v. *A. B. Dick Co.*, 224 U.S. 1 (1912).
2. *U.S.* v. *E. C. Knight Co.* 156 U.S. 1 (1895).

does not exclude all mergers; it excludes only those that substantially lessen competition. From its application, it exempts those acquisitions in which one of the two parties is an individual or a partnership or in which the acquired firm is not engaged in interstate commerce. It also exempts the acquisition of stock when it is made solely for investment and therefore is not used to restrain trade.

Section 8 pertains to interlocking directorates. The interlocking directorate arrangement was a device commonly used to gain control over the activities of competing corporations. It was associated with investment banks, in particular J. P. Morgan and Company, a major New York investment banking firm. Investment banks would gain control over the financial affairs of corporations as a condition for issuing investment credit. They achieved this control by having one or more of their executives appointed to the board of directors of corporations with which they did business. At the peak of its control, J. P. Morgan and Company held directorates in sixty-three corporations with assets of $74 billion.[4] Section 8 of the Clayton Act provides that no person shall be a director in two or more corporations if they are competitors and if they have capital, surplus, and undivided profits in excess of $1 million. The act does not require the government to find that the interlocking directorate reduces competition. The fact of the interlock itself makes for illegality.[5]

Violations of the Clayton Act are civil offenses. The government can sue defendants for actual damages, and private plaintiffs are entitled to sue for triple damages. In dealing with violations, Section 14 provides that individual directors or officers of a corporation can be fined as much as $5,000, or sentenced to prison for up to one year, or both. The Federal Trade Commission was given joint responsibility with the Justice Department for the enforcement of Sections 2, 3, 7, and 8 of the act. Section 15 invests the U.S. district courts with the power to prevent and restrain violations of the act, and Section 16 permits any

3. Joint ventures involve a partnership arrangement between two firms or between a firm and a government. An example is the General Motors-Toyota arrangement to build subcompact cars in a General Motors plant in California. This arrangement was challenged by both Ford and Chrysler on the grounds that it lessened competition in the automobile industry. However, the joint venture was approved by the Federal Trade Commission by a 3 to 2 vote. Joint ventures between U.S. and foreign firms will increase in importance.
4. National Resources Committee, *The Structure of the American Economy* (Washington, D.C.: U.S. Government Printing Office, 1939), pp. 306–317.
5. Section 8 has not been actively enforced, and the few attempts that have been made to carry out its provisions have resulted in judicial emasculation. The section prohibits interlocks only where two companies produce the same items. It is still possible for competitors to have interlocking directorates and interlocks between sellers and buyers, and between manufacturers and bankers.

person or firm to sue for and have injunctive relief against potential loss or damage by violations of Sections 2, 3, 7, and 8 of the act.

The Federal Trade Commission Act, 1914

The Federal Trade Commission Act was passed in September 1914 to replace the Bureau of Corporations with the Federal Trade Commission, consisting of five members, each holding office for seven years. It was hoped that the commission, which was made independent of the president, would be a specialized body that would aid in law enforcement and supervise and apply guiding rules to the competitive market system. Application of the Sherman Act to specific competitive practices had proved unsatisfactory to business groups and the general public, since victims of predatory business acts felt that the law should intervene before such acts had been committed. Moreover, many business people wanted clearer guidelines about what constituted unfair methods of competition. The premise of the Federal Trade Commission Act is that fair competition should stand as the basic economic policy for the nation, and that unfair competition should be prohibited.

The Federal Trade Commission Act supplements the Sherman and Clayton acts by using sweeping prohibitions of unfair methods, acts, and practices to foster competition. It provides that these prohibitions are to be interpreted and enforced in administrative proceedings brought by and before the Federal Trade Commission, subject to review by the courts. Section 5 of the act empowers the FTC to prevent unfair methods of competition and unfair or deceptive acts or practices in or affecting commerce. Generally, this section is used to stop practices before they develop into other violations of the antitrust laws. As a consequence, the FTC has used it to attack alleged price fixing that would not necessarily be a violation of the Sherman Act, as well as mergers, tie-in sales, exclusive dealing, and other actions that the commission deems are unfair methods of competition. For example, a suit was brought in 1972 against the major cereal companies for alleged price fixing, even though the FTC admitted publicly that there was no charge of agreement or conspiracy, which would be essential to a Sherman Act case. The suit has since been dropped.

It can be said that Section 5 has been interpreted to go further than the other antitrust laws do to reach all unfair business practices, whether or not they have an impact on competition. Section 5 gives to the FTC and the courts the power to prohibit present and potential trade restraints proscribed by the Sherman and Clayton acts and also allows the commission to proceed against other antisocial conduct. The current aim of the commission's enforcement activities under Section 5 is both to protect fair competition and to assure that the consumer is not subjected to unfair or deceptive practices, without regard to their effect on competition. One example of the latter is the commission's attack on false or misleading advertising.

The Robinson-Patman Act, 1936

The Robinson-Patman Act is commonly known as the "Chain Store Act." It is an amendment to the Clayton Act, in particular to Section 2, which had sought, among other things, to outlaw price-cutting practices by large firms that were designed to eliminate competition from smaller firms. But Section 2 had not been widely used, even though the Federal Trade Commission had on occasion attempted to apply it to discriminatory discounts and to geographic discrimination resulting from the use of basing-point price systems, under which uniform delivered prices were charged regardless of the origin of the shipment. In one case, the commission condemned a manufacturer who granted discounts to chains for the combined purchases of their separate stores while refusing to grant a similar privilege to associations of independent stores, even though selling costs did not vary between the two.[6] The commission was rebuffed in its attempt by a circuit court of appeals on the grounds that the Clayton Act applied only to the reduction of competition in the seller's own line of commerce.

The most important provision of the Robinson-Patman Act is Section 2(a); it amends Section 2 of the Clayton Act to prohibit secondary-line price discrimination, that is, the sale of the same good to different buyers in the same geographic area at different prices when there is no cost difference. The impact of this kind of discrimination falls on small buyers who, because of their size, are unable to obtain discount concessions that large buyers are able to obtain from sellers. It does permit a seller to show that lower prices to some buyers are based on cost differences related to different methods or quantities involved in the sale or delivery of the product. Section 2(a) also prohibits any form of price discrimination when the end result is to lessen competition; when it tends to create a monopoly in any line of commerce, or when it injures, destroys, or prevents competition with any person who either grants or knowingly receives the benefits of such discrimination. Not only restraint of competition but also injury to competitors became a test of illegality.

The remaining subsections of the amended Section 2 of the Clayton Act enacted prohibitions not included in the original Clayton Act. For example, the payment of brokerage fees when no independent broker was involved became illegal. It was designed to eliminate the practice

6. *National Biscuit Co.* v. *FTC*, 299 Fed. 733 (1924).

of some chains of demanding the regular brokerage fees as a discount when they purchased directly from the manufacturers. This was compensation that normally went to a broker, traditionally a seller's agent who assembled the output of a number of small producers for shipment to the distributor. Advertising allowances also were prohibited. These, which normally were made for point-of-sale advertising of goods manufactured by the seller and sold at retail by the buyer, could no longer be given unless the allowances were made on equal terms to all competing purchasers. Advertising allowances and the remission of brokerage fees were considered forms of secret rebates secured because a buyer was in a strong position to extract them from a seller. The Standard Oil Trust was thought to owe its rise to a monopoly — and its continuance in that position — in part to its ability to extract secret discounts from the railroads. The authors of the Robinson-Patman Act felt that price discrimination in the form of secret brokerage fees or advertising allowances should be forced into the open, where it would come under Section 2(a).

The Celler-Kefauver Act, 1950

The Celler-Kefauver Act was passed in 1950 to plug a loophole in Section 7 of the Clayton Act. Section 7 specifically forbade the acquisition of one firm's stock by another firm when the end result was to reduce competition substantially in interstate or foreign commerce. But over time, the courts had generally emasculated this provision through judicial interpretation: in 1926 the Supreme Court distinguished between acquisition of stock and acquisition of assets, holding the latter to be beyond the reach of the Federal Trade Commission even if the merger of physical assets had been based on an illegal acquisition of voting stock. Moreover, the Supreme Court in several other cases had held that such mergers were not illegal under the Clayton Act if a corporation used its stock purchases to acquire assets before the FTC issued a complaint or before it issued its final order banning the stock acquisition. Thus the number of mergers based on the acquisition of firm assets steadily increased, and it was not until the late 1940s that federal legislation to plug the loophole was considered seriously. There had been a wave of post–World War II mergers, leading to the fear by Congress that greater industrial concentration would lead to a signifcant decline in competition.

Section 7 of the Clayton Act was amended to make it illegal for one corporation to acquire the stock or assets of another corporation when the end result might be to lessen competition substantially or to tend to create monopoly. Celler-Kefauver also tightened the constraints against business mergers by making a merger illegal if there was a trend toward concentration in an industry, thereby creating a presumption of tendencies toward monopoly. It delineated markets more narrowly by defining them as "a line of commerce" in any section of the nation. The intent of Congress in passing the Celler-Kefauver Act was that competition be maintained. Small firms that merge to improve their competitive position are generally not challenged, but mergers that would ordinarily be allowed in nonconcentrated industries may well be challenged if a large firm acquires a small competitor. For example, Alcoa, which accounted for 27.8 percent of all aluminum conductor production, acquired Rome Cable, whose market share was 1.3 percent.[7] The merger was disallowed in 1964 on the grounds that Alcoa would increase its market share through the acquisition and thus competition would be substantially reduced, since Rome had been an aggressive competitor in the aluminum conductor field. It has been said that Celler-Kefauver has virtually stopped horizontal and vertical mergers between large companies.[8]

The Hart-Scott-Rodino Act, 1976[9]

This act made a number of procedural changes in antitrust law. It gives the Justice Department the authority to issue civil investigative demands to third parties, such as competitors of those companies under investigation, and to compel oral testimony and answers to written questions. It also requires notice to the antitrust division of the Justice Department and to the Federal Trade Commission thirty days in advance of mergers involving large companies. The law covers companies with stock or assets of $100 million or more that plan to merge with companies worth $10 million or more when the transaction involves acquisitions of more than $15 million in stock or assets. This gives the Justice Department or the Federal Trade Commission time in which to challenge the merger. The act also authorizes state attorneys general to bring triple damage suits in federal court on behalf of state citizens injured by violations of the Sherman Act. This provision has had the effect of increasing the amount of antitrust enforcement by state governments.

Before the passage of the act, it was often difficult for the Justice Department or the Federal Trade Commission to stop a merger once it had been consummated. When mergers were contested, decisions often

---

7. *U.S.* v. *Aluminum Co. of America*, 377 U.S. 271 (1964).
8. George J. Stigler, "The Economic Effects of the Antitrust Laws," *Journal of Law and Economics*, 9 (October 1966), 235-236.
9. The full name of the act is the Hart-Scott-Rodino Antitrust Improvements Act of 1976. It is Public Law 94-435.

took time, and firms were able to consolidate their assets. The Hart-Scott-Rodino Act enables the government to act quickly against many proposed mergers. Firms know before the completion of a merger whether or not it will be challenged, thus eliminating from their minds any uncertainty about any future antitrust action after the merger had been consummated. The act requires that firms contemplating a merger provide the government with extensive information pertaining to the merger. The government then decides whether or not to challenge the merger. It may decide to approve the merger subject to certain conditions; for example, it may require the acquiring firm to divest itself of a part of the assets of its new acquisition.

Section 301 of the act amends the Clayton Act to permit parens patriae actions by state attorneys general. Any state attorney general may bring a civil action on behalf of persons residing in the state to secure monetary damages for injuries sustained as a result of any violation of the Sherman Act. The state attorney general may sue in any district court having jurisdiction over the defendant. For example, residents in certain states have had to pay more for a product as a result of a price fixing agreement involving regional distributors. The attorney general of each state can initiate parens patriae action for damages. Section 301 strengthens state antitrust enforcement. A district court will exclude from the amount of monetary relief any amount duplicating an award for the same injury, and it can award a state as monetary relief triple damages for the antitrust violation.

ANTITRUST ENFORCEMENT

The antitrust laws are enforced by the Antitrust Division of the Justice Department and by the Federal Trade Commission. The Antitrust Division, exclusively, is responsible for enforcing the Sherman Act and, with the Federal Trade Commission, is responsible for enforcing the Clayton Act. The FTC has exclusive jurisdiction to enforce the Federal Trade Commission Act and has primary responsibility for enforcing the Robinson-Patman Act. Both public agencies can make use of four basic remedies to enforce the antitrust laws:

1. They may use an injunction to prohibit a specific action such as false advertising.

2. They may use an order for specific performance requiring action on the part of the party against whom the order applies. An example would be divestiture of certain designated firm assets.

3. Criminal sanctions can also be used. Violation of the Sherman Act is a misdemeanor and may result in imprisonment for up to three years.

4. Fines of up to $100,000 per violation are provided for in the Sherman Act.

Table 6-1 Important Antitrust Provisions

Act	Provisions
Sherman Act (1890)	Section 1 — prohibits contracts, combinations, and conspiracies in restraint of trade in interstate or foreign commerce, including price fixing, group boycotts, and tie-in sales. Section 2 — prohibits monopolies and attempts to create monopolies in interstate or foreign commerce.
Clayton Act (1914)	Section 2 — prohibits primary-line price discrimination lessening sellers' level of competition. Section 3 — prohibits exclusive dealing and tying arrangements that substantially lessen competition. Section 7 — prohibits mergers when the effect is to substantially lessen competition or to tend to create a monopoly.
Federal Trade Commission Act (1914)	Section 5 — prohibits unfair methods of competition and defines powers of the FTC.
Robinson-Patman Act (1936)	Amends Section 2 of the Clayton Act to prohibit secondary-line price discrimination.
Celler-Kefauver Act (1950)	Amends Section 7 of the Clayton Act to include the acquisition of assets of one firm by another firm when the result is to substantially lessen competition.
Hart-Scott-Rodino Act (1976)	Section 301 — permits parens patriae actions by state attorneys general to secure monetary relief for any violation of the Sherman Act. It also requires advance notice of proposed mergers.

The majority of antitrust cases initiated by the federal government are settled by an agreement between it and the defendant.[10] This saves the government time and money. After the terms of a proposed settlement have been agreed on, the government must take the proposed settlement to the judge before whom the case was initially filed to obtain approval. This is a second check to ensure the public's interests are being served under the terms of the settlement. If the judge approves, a consent decree is filed with the court. Violations of the terms of a decree will mean the offending party is in contempt of court. There is one major drawback to the use of the consent decree: had the government litigated and won the suit against the defendant, the victory would have constituted prima facie evidence of the antitrust violation and would be used by a private plaintiff in a triple damage suit.

Exemptions from Antitrust Laws

The Sherman Act, as well as other antitrust legislation, is applicable in principle to all forms of private business enterprise carried out in interstate and foreign commerce. The Sherman Act itself makes no exceptions and declares that every restraint of trade and commerce is unlawful. However, certain industries and organizations are exempt from the antitrust laws. The reasons for exemption are as varied as the industries and organizations exempted. Each exemption is supposed to accomplish some specific objective, which, in the minds of a particular group, is necessary to its interests. Over time, moving forces, or interest groups, have demanded relaxation of the antitrust laws. Some of the more important industries and organizations and the reasons for their exemption from antitrust laws are presented below.

Labor Unions

Section 6 of the Clayton Act exempts labor unions from antitrust laws. There were two main reasons for this exemption. First, the Sherman Act had been used on occasion to break up labor unions. In the Danbury Hatters Case of 1908, for example, a labor union was convicted of

10. It is also necessary to point out that companies can bring action against other companies to obtain compensation for injuries they have suffered as a result of violation of the antitrust laws. An example is the Pennzoil suit against Texaco charging it with wrongdoing in acquiring Getty Oil, a company Pennzoil had planned to acquire. A judge awarded Pennzoil $11 billion in damages.

restraint of trade when it organized an interstate boycott against the hat manufacturers of Danbury, Connecticut.[11] The court found the members of the union liable for triple damages of $240,000 for the boycott. The end result of the conviction was the dissolution of the union. Second, it was felt that labor had a bargaining position far inferior to that of business; therefore, collective action by labor was necessary to improve this position. Today, labor unions retain their exempt status as long as they do not combine with nonlabor groups to effect restraint of trade.[12]

Natural Monopolies

The so-called natural monopolies exist in those industries that possess special conditions inherent to the nature of their operations that would make competition self-destructive and hence incompatible with the public interest. Since they provide an indispensable service to the public, however, they are subject to government regulation in the interest of the public. Such industries include transportation, electricity, gas, and broadcasting. A public utility is usually given a monopoly over a particular area. The purpose is in part to prevent the wasteful and duplicating competition that prevailed at one time. During the nineteenth century, the railroads built duplicating lines in a desire to surmount their competition. The end result was cutthroat competition and a great waste of resources.

In return for its control over a given service area, a natural monopoly is subject to the regulation of rates, services, and other functions by federal and state agencies to ensure the protection of the public interest. Regulation is designed to prevent public utilities from making too much profit. Because these industries are so strictly regulated, there is no particular need to subject them to antitrust laws.

Export Trade Associations

The Webb-Pomerene Act of 1918 specifically exempts export trade associations from the Sherman Act. The rationale for this exemption was the existence of cartels and monopolies in other countries actively engaged in international trade. Countries such as Germany and the United Kingdom encouraged the formation of these cartels as a matter of public policy. The purpose of the Webb-Pomerene exemption was to enable U.S. firms to compete more effectively with foreign com-

11. *Loewe* v. *Lawlor*, 208 U.S. 274 (1908).
12. *U.S.* v. *Hutcheson*, 312 U.S. 219 (1941).

panies belonging to cartel arrangements. The act permits the formation of export associations, which are required to file outlines of their organization with the Federal Trade Commission. The commission is then supposed to investigate association activities to see that there is no violation of the law, since the Webb-Pomerene Act was intended to promote competition rather than collusion in the world markets.

Agricultural Cooperatives

Agricultural cooperatives were exempted by the Clayton Act from antitrust laws provided they issued no capital stock and were not run for a profit. The Capper-Volstead Act of 1922 amended the Clayton Act to allow the formation of cooperatives issuing capital stock; it also legalized action by the members of a cooperative marketing association to enhance the prices of their products. The Capper-Volstead Act provides agricultural producers with a substantial exemption from antitrust laws in giving their associations the power to set prices. However, this power has limits, for the price must not be increased unduly. A single cooperative association also may enter into contracts with many farmers that require them to market their products only through the association.

Other Exemptions

There are also other exemptions from antitrust laws. Transoceanic shipping rates established by shipping conferences have for years been exempted from the antitrust laws on certification by the U.S. Maritime Board. Combinations and mergers were sanctioned by Congress in the case of the railroads in 1920, telephone companies in 1921, motor carriers in 1935, and water carriers in 1940. Combinations of marine insurance companies were exempted from the antitrust laws in 1920. There is also an antitrust exemption for small businesses in that the Small Business Act of 1953, as amended, provides that voluntary agreements may be made by small business concerns for joint programs in research and development and for joint participation in national defense contracts. The McCarran Act of 1945 partially exempts insurance companies from the antitrust laws in that it leaves their regulation up to the states. The Reed-Bulwinkle Bill of 1948 specifically authorizes the Interstate Commerce Commission to approve railroad traffic association agreements with respect to rates and fares. The Miller-Tydings Act and the McGuire Act extended antitrust exemptions to retailers so as to maintain resale prices. But the Consumer Goods Pricing Act of 1975 repealed these provisions, mainly because they sanctioned a form of price fixing that was having a perceptibly adverse effect on consumer purchasing power.

State Antitrust Laws

As mentioned in Chapter 2, the first antitrust laws were passed by the states in the latter part of the last century. The development of trusts and other kinds of business combinations created much popular discontent, which was translated into state laws. Kansas enacted the first antitrust law in 1889, and at least thirteen states had antitrust laws before the passage of the Sherman Act in 1890. The first state laws came from the farming states in the Midwest, where populism was influential. In fact, the Sherman Act was intended to supplement, rather than supplant, state power. The federal courts were supposed to cooperate within the limits of their constitutional power with the state courts in curbing and controlling any form of business combination that threatened American commerce.

By 1900, thirty states had antitrust laws that varied in content but, in general, restricted monopolies and combinations in restraint of trade, prohibited specific unfair business practices, and provided criminal penalties and other sanctions. These laws fell into disuse after the turn of the century, however, and the enforcement of antitrust was left almost entirely to the federal government. There were several reasons for the decline in state activity. First, state antitrust law was attacked and often invalidated on the grounds of vagueness. Second, the laws were subjected to a prolonged series of constitutional challenges. State statutes were often attacked on equal protection and due process grounds. Third, the courts set severe restrictions on the extraterritorial jurisdiction of state enforcement efforts. Fourth, the enforcement of state laws was generally haphazard and poorly financed, and it was difficult for the states to deal with national or international economic institutions through their limited jurisdiction.

State antitrust activities picked up during the 1960s and accelerated even more during the 1970s. From 1970 to 1974, twelve states, one territory, and the Commonwealth of Puerto Rico enacted or reenacted antitrust statutes.[13] This resurgence of antitrust enforcement can be attributed to a number of factors: protecting state and local governments from the collusive bidding practices of some business firms, combating the efforts of organized crime to take over legitimate business interests, and protecting the general business community from the predatory actions of a few firms. In some states, organizations of small businesspersons lobbied successfully for the state's enforcing its own

---

13. Unpublished data furnished by the Antitrust Division, Department of Justice.

antitrust laws once again. There was also a growing belief that the federal government could not and should not bear sole responsibility for the enforcement of antitrust. And there was an increasing recognition that the state attorney general, as the people's advocate, must combat abuses of the marketplace through antitrust as well as consumer protection programs. Finally, there had been a great growth in state procurement of goods and services and an accompanying belief that a vigorous antitrust program could save money on government purchases.

Example of State Antitrust Laws

State antitrust laws may differ in terms of form and content, but basic patterns have been followed. The antitrust laws of Connecticut and Virginia can be used as examples. Connecticut was one of the first states to pass an antitrust law. Modeled after the Sherman Act, it prohibits various forms of price fixing, including agreements among competing business firms to fix or lower prices, bid rigging, and resale price maintenance.[14] The antitrust laws of Connecticut also prohibit competing firms from agreeing to divide geographic areas in which each will do business. It prohibits tying arrangements where the seller conditions or ties the sale of a popular product to the purchase of a less popular product when the intent is to lessen competition. The law prohibits group boycotts where business firms conspire to deny a competitor access to supplies or services. Price discrimination is also illegal when the intent is to lessen competition.

The Virginia Antitrust Act was passed in 1974. Its provisions are somewhat similar to those of Connecticut's antitrust law.[15] Any contract in restraint of trade in Virginia is unlawful. Monopolies and combinations that restrain the commerce of Virginia are illegal. Various discriminatory practices are also illegal, including secondary-line price discrimination where a seller discriminates in price between different purchasers of products or services when any of the purchasers are in direct competition with one another. Tying arrangements are also illegal when the intent is to lessen discrimination. Price fixing, including bid rigging, is illegal, as are boycotts. The Virginia antitrust law is considered a fair trade law, and practices that discriminate against trade are illegal.

14. State of Connecticut, Office of Attorney General, *Antitrust Law in Connecticut.*
15. Information provided by the Office of Attorney General, Commonwealth of Virginia.

Importance of State Antitrust Laws

State antitrust law is important because much business is strictly intrastate. In the federal system, the regulation of intrastate or local commerce is left to the state governments, which perform the same kind of economic regulation that the federal government performs at the national level. Moreover, the Department of Justice and the Federal Trade Commission prosecute only a small fraction of the complaints they receive; their efforts are concentrated on the restraints and abuses that are national in scope. This leaves the states with jurisdiction over a wide area of economic activity within interstate commerce; for example, the production and sale of food and beverages, fuel oil, lumber, used cars, hotels and housing facilities, building and road construction, recreational facilities, local transportation, and banking services. The kinds of abuses and anticompetitive business practices that occur nationally can also occur locally. State governments also have such functions as prohibiting false advertising and preventing monopoly and unfair competition.

State antitrust enforcement can be expected to increase in importance in the future for two reasons. First, the Hart-Scott-Rodino Act of 1976 authorizes the attorneys general of the fifty states to bring suits against companies that fix prices or engage in other forms of anticompetitive business practices, and to recover damages for consumers injured by such practices. Second, the Reagan administration has attempted to reduce the role of the federal government in the U.S. economy. Emphasis has been placed on increasing the responsibility of the states in all areas of economic and political activity. That there will be an increase in the role of the state attorneys general when it comes to the enforcement of state antitrust laws can therefore be assumed.

SUMMARY

Antitrust laws are designed to protect and encourage vigorous and open competition — the hallmark of a free enterprise market economy. Competition creates incentives for business firms to reduce costs while improving products or services. Business firms offering the highest quality products or services at the lowest price will thrive in a competitive environment. Because competition leads to higher quality at a lower price, the consumer is the ultimate beneficiary. The benefits of competition disappear when business firms agree on prices or engage in other illegal activities that may unfairly force competitors out of business or discriminate against consumers. However, not every restraint on competition violates antitrust laws; rather, courts have consistently held that only unreasonable restraints on competition violate the antitrust laws.

The antitrust laws of the United States are used to prevent certain business practices considered economically harmful. The laws are designed to maintain a competitive market structure by challenging monopoly power, whether achieved through internal growth or through mergers. The laws also are directed at specific business practices considered anticompetitive. Examples are price fixing, group boycotts, and tying arrangements. These and other practices have been defined by the courts over time and have become an integral part of the legal environment in which the modern business manager has to operate. Obeying the antitrust laws is not always simple. The laws are complex, and there is often a hazy line between legal and nonlegal conduct. In most cases, the marginally illegal acts that a business manager engages in are not likely to be challenged, but there is always the risk that some action will violate federal or state antitrust laws.

QUESTIONS FOR DISCUSSION

1. What is meant by a per se violation of the Sherman Act?
2. What is a tying agreement? When is it illegal?
3. How do state antitrust laws differ from federal antitrust laws?
4. Distinguish between primary-line and secondary-line price discrimination.
5. What is the difference between a civil remedy and a criminal remedy in antitrust enforcement?
6. What is the purpose of the Hart-Scott-Rodino Antitrust Improvements Act?
7. Summarize the methods of enforcing the antitrust laws.
8. What is a consent decree?
9. Company A, located in the northern part of a state, sells office equipment throughout the state. Company B, located in the southern part of the state, also sells office equipment throughout the state. The owners meet at a trade association convention and agree that they each will sell office equipment in three different parts of the state. Does this violate antitrust laws?

RECOMMENDED READINGS

Asch, Peter. *Industrial Organization and Antitrust Policy.* New York: Wiley, 1983.

Bock, Betty. *Continuation and Discontinuation in Antitrust.* New York: The Conference Board, 1982.

Calvani, Terry, and John Siegfried. *Economic Analysis and Antitrust Law.* Boston: Little, Brown, 1980.

Demsetz, Harold. *Economic, Legal and Political Dimensions of Competition.* New York: Elsevier Science Publishing Co., 1982.

Kintner, Earl. *An Antitrust Primer.* 3d ed. New York: Macmillan, 1978.

Singer, Eugene M. *Antitrust Economics and Legal Analysis.* Columbus, Ohio: Grid Publishers, 1983.

Van Cise, Jerrold G. *The Federal Antitrust Laws.* 4th ed. Washington, D.C.: American Enterprise Institute for Public Policy Research, 1983.

Waldman, Don E. *The Economics of Antitrust.* Boston: Little, Brown, 1986.

Chapter 7
Application of Antitrust Laws
to Market Power

On the basis of their economic models, both oligopoly and monopoly can generally be regarded as indicators of market power. Certainly in an oligopolistic industry, the barriers to entry can be formidable. Oligopolistic industry structure, in which four or fewer firms make up 70 percent or more of all sales in a particular product market, accounts for a significant amount of all manufacturing in the U.S. economy. The dominant firms in these industries are usually characterized by uniform pricing practices, which means that if one firm in an oligopolistic industry raises its prices and the others do not, consumers will quickly shift to purchasing the less expensive product; conversely, if one firm lowers prices and the others do not, all the firms not lowering their prices could lose business.[1] The product differentiation, advertising, and vertical integration of dominant firms also provide barriers to entry.

In Chapter 5, we pointed out that large firms in the United States have achieved their growth either through internal growth or, more often, through mergers. This is not necessarily bad. To a considerable extent, industrial growth and concentration is a logical concomitant of an advanced industrial society. Large business size has certain advantages, one of which is the mass production of one or a few products, such as automobiles or rubber tires. In addition, there can be economics of mass production, including division of labor and specialization in particular operations, and economics of large-scale buying and selling. However, large firms can restrict competition and impede the rate of capital formation. In certain situations, they can exercise discretionary power over price and entry into market.

Antitrust laws can be applied to the market power achieved by a particular firm. This dominance can be achieved in a single product market or in a geographic market. One problem that has arisen over time is there has been no set test of market power within a particular relevant competitive market. In applying Section 2 of the Sherman Act, a variety of tests can be used. One is the existence of an intent to monopolize; another is the committing of specific anticompetitive acts;

---

1. This can be theoretically explained by the so-called kinked demand curve.

and a third is the attainment of an illegal absolute or relative size. The last test comes closest to meeting the economic test of a monopoly. However, in applying Section 2 of the Sherman Act, the courts have been unable to rely on the economic model of monopoly because it is based on the concept of one firm being protected from the entry of others into the market and thus, in the absence of competitive products, does not represent a practical legal standard.

ANTITRUST LAWS AS APPLIED TO MONOPOLIES

In applying the antitrust laws, especially Section 2 of the Sherman Act, the courts have not used a clear definition of monopoly based on economic concepts. Generally, they have focused their attention on predatory acts, exclusion of competitors, conspiracies to monopolize, and the impact of mergers on competition. In particular, enforcement of the monopoly provision of the Sherman Act has been based on determining whether or not the industry structure in question rose out of any wrongdoing. Under the act, monopoly and the offense of monopoly have two characteristics: the actual possession of monopoly power in a market and the maintenance of that power or its willful acquisition. The following court cases will illustrate how the courts have applied Section 2 of the Sherman Act to monopoly power.

The Northern Securities Company Case, 1904

The Northern Securities Company was a holding company for three large railroads — the Northern Pacific, the Great Northern, and the Chicago, Burlington, and Quincy. Involved in its formation were some of the nation's largest finance capitalists and railroad tycoons, including J. P. Morgan and Company, the Rockefeller interests, James J. Hill, and E. H. Harriman. To Morgan, the holding company combination represented stability and the removal of wasteful competition. The holding company acquired, by giving its own stock in exchange, more than nine-tenths of the stock of the Northern Pacific and three-fourths of the stock of the Great Northern. The effect of this arrangement would have been to end competition between those two railroads; the former stockholders in the two roads, as common stockholders in the holding company, would have an interest in preventing competition.

The federal government instituted a suit to have the Northern Securities Company dissolved as a combination in restraint of interstate commerce and the railway stock returned. The case reached the U.S. Supreme Court, which by a vote of five to four, ordered the company dissolved.[2] The case was significant because it condemned the holding company as a method of control over previously competing companies and because it included this type of stockholding within the scope of the commerce clause.

The Standard Oil Case, 1911

The Standard Oil Company was a classic example of what President Theodore Roosevelt called a "bad" trust.[3] After the Ohio decision of 1892,[4] it had reorganized itself as a holding company to hold the stock of seventy different corporations engaged in operating oil refineries, oil wells, pipelines, storage plants, and distribution facilities. Almost all the facilities had been united under central control by means of a trust. As early as 1882, the trust had secured control of about 90 percent of the oil refining business, and this control had been maintained in the new organization. Its record of operations was replete with examples of predatory practices designed to injure, eliminate, or buy up competitors to secure monopoly control over oil production. Among other things, it was found that the Standard Oil Company had pursued a policy of cutting prices in areas where there was competition, while maintaining or increasing them in areas where there was no competition.[5] It bribed railway and other employees for information on competitors, and it controlled pipelines to the detriment of competitors.

In 1906, the government initiated action against the Standard Oil Company, charging it with conspiracy to restrain trade and commerce in crude oil, refined oil, and other petroleum products in interstate and foreign commerce. In 1911, the U.S. Supreme Court unanimously affirmed a circuit court decision to dissolve Standard Oil.[6] In its decision, the Supreme Court ordered the holding company to transfer to the original holders the stock that had been turned over to it in exchange for holding company stock. Each owner of one share of stock in Standard Oil of New Jersey received securities in thirty-three companies; in addition, each retained control in the parent company, which continued as a producing concern. Since a few persons owned a large proportion of the stock of Standard Oil of New Jersey, the decree resulted in giving these same persons a controlling interest in all thirty-four companies. The effect of this decree was to divide Standard Oil

2. *U.S.* v. *Northern Securities Co.*, 193 U.S. 197 (1904).
3. The development of the Standard Oil Company was discussed in the special case in Chapter 2.
4. The Ohio decision of 1892 resulted in the dissolution of the Standard Oil Trust.
5. This is primary-line or seller's discrimination.
6. *U.S.* v. *Standard Oil of N.J.*, 221 U.S. 106 (1911).

into a series of companies, each of which was supreme in a given geographic area.

The American Tobacco Case, 1911

The American Tobacco Company was also a "bad" trust. Before 1890, competition existed in all branches of the tobacco trade: snuff, plug, cigarettes, and cigars. The Tobacco Trust differed from its contemporaries in that it was formed to hold property, whereas the others held securities. It exchanged its shares directly for the plants, business, brands, and good will of the five companies that manufactured cigarettes. The trust was originally formed as a horizontal combination, but then it expanded and absorbed the MacAndrews and Forbes Company, which had an almost complete monopoly of the manufacture of licorice, a substance used in processing tobacco. Other concerns that did not process tobacco but made related products were bought by the trust, including those that manufactured tin foil, the cotton bags in which tobacco was packed, and wooden boxes. The trust controlled the companies that made the machinery used in the manufacture of tobacco as well as those that held the patents for these machines.

The American Tobacco Trust was formed to check a decline in the price of tobacco products, and this it set out to do by controlling competition in foreign and domestic markets. To control foreign markets, a cartel was formed, and to eliminate domestic competition, the trust used its financial power. In 1889, it bought and closed thirty competing companies engaged in the manufacture, distribution, and sale of tobacco. Price wars were entered into freely to force the manufacturers of competing cigarette products to agree to terms set by the trust. The trust also required vendors, stockholders, and employees to promise to use only its products. While buying up the tobacco companies, American Tobacco also seized the plug tobacco trade. It approached the leading manufacturers of plug tobacco and sought to bring about a combination of plug tobacco interests. Failing in this, it simply tried to ruin the competition by lowering the price of its plug tobacco to below cost. It was successful.

In 1907, the government initiated a suit against the American Tobacco Company, charging it with violations of Sections 1 and 2 of the Sherman Act. The lower courts dismissed the suit, but the government appealed the case to the Supreme Court. In May 1911, the trust was dissolved by order of the Court.[7] The dissolution did little to promote competition in the tobacco industry because subsidiary com-

7. *U.S.* v. *American Tobacco Co.*, 221 U.S. 106 (1911).

panies of the American Tobacco Company were reorganized into new companies. The American Snuff Company, which had a monopoly on the manufacture of snuff, gave part of its facilities to two new snuff companies, George W. Helme and Weyman-Burton. American Tobacco gave to its common stockholders the stock it held in R. J. Reynolds Company, a manufacturer of plug and pipe tobacco. American Tobacco was then split into three full-line companies making cigarettes, small cigars, plug, pipe, and fine-cut tobacco. These companies were American Tobacco, Liggett and Myers, and P. Lorillard.

Rule of Reason

The Standard Oil and American Tobacco cases represent a landmark in the Court's interpretation of antitrust laws. In these cases, the legal concept of rule of reason, that is, the guidelines by which to distinguish good trusts from bad trusts, was drawn up. In the mind of the Court, the size and power of a combination created only the presumption of an attempt to dominate an industry. Before the Sherman Act could be applied, proof that predatory acts — such as price discrimination, allocation of markets, or other devices designed to achieve market dominance — had been committed was needed. In other words, size could be achieved through the normal methods of industrial development or through the commission of predatory acts designed to eliminate competition. Only the latter, the Court believed, imposed unreasonable restraints on competition.

In deciding these two cases, the Supreme Court essentially distinguished between good and bad trusts. Large firm size in itself was not illegal; illegal was the commission of predatory acts. The Supreme Court adopted the famous rule of reason. Since the Sherman Act did not specifically define those acts that were in restraint of trade, the courts had to do so. Rule of reason meant that in applying a statute condemning restraints on trade, a court could use flexibility and discretion. Two criteria were used to determine the kind of business practice that would be in violation of the Sherman Act. First, there had to be unworthy motives or predatory acts designed to harm competitors, and second, there had to be such overwhelming control of an industry that competition had virtually ceased to exist.

The U.S. Steel Case, 1920

Later, during the 1920s, the Supreme Court, acting under the rule of reason doctrine, held that the existence of monopoly power that was not abused did not violate the Sherman Act. The U.S. Steel case of

1920 is an example of the application of the rule of reason doctrine.[8] U.S. Steel, then the nation's largest industrial enterprise, was a holding company formed in 1901 to merge concerns that were themselves amalgamations of smaller companies. It had been set up to forestall a threat of overexpansion and ruinous competition at a time when other manufacturers of heavier semifinished products had been about to integrate forward into the finished lines, and other manufacturers of finished products had made plans to integrate backward. The U.S. Steel Corporation brought under its control in one financial unit a series of corporations that had already secured control over the principal plants in their respective lines of business in the steel industry. These and other acquisitions gave U.S. Steel control of 65 to 75 percent of all lines of steel manufacturing in the country and also more than 80 percent of the best iron ore reserves, bringing together major companies that were themselves competing with one another.

The Justice Department brought action against U.S. Steel in 1912, accusing it, among other things, of a conspiracy to fix prices in the steel industry. The corporation had made it a practice to meet with its competitors to set prices. These became the official prices for all iron and steel products. When U.S. Steel changed prices, its competitors followed suit. In 1920, the Supreme Court reached a final decision in the case and refused to allow a dissolution of the company.

There were several reasons for the Court's decision. One was that the meetings of U.S. Steel and its competitors had been discontinued before the government suit. In its approach to competition, a majority of the Court emphasized the legal rather than the economic concept. Competition had not been restrained, for U.S. Steel had made no effort to suppress other companies by unfair means. The Court also held that the corporation did not have sufficient power to control prices in the industry and that size in itself did not constitute a violation of the Sherman Act. To violate the act, overt predatory actions were required. The decision of the Supreme Court gave rise to the so-called abuse theory of monopoly. In other words, in the absence of abusive market practices, the Sherman Act did not make mere size an offense.

The Alcoa Case, 1945

The Alcoa case is considered a landmark case in that it broke sharply with antitrust cases of the past.[9] In this case, Judge Learned Hand, speaking for the Supreme Court, declared monopolies illegal per se, thus abandoning the rule of reason. A government suit had been initi-

8. *U.S.* v. *U.S. Steel Corporation,* 251 U.S. 417 (1920).
9. *U.S.* v. *Aluminum Co. of America,* 148 F. 2d, 416 (1945).

ated in 1937 charging that the Aluminum Company of America (Alcoa) had violated Section 2 of the Sherman Act by monopolizing virgin aluminum production. At the time of the suit, Alcoa controlled more than 90 percent of the production of aluminum ingots. It had become a monopoly originally through its exclusive control over patent rights and then by its control over bauxite deposits and generation sites for the hydroelectric power needed in aluminum manufacture. Moreover, Alcoa was able to anticipate and forestall virtually all competition in the production of aluminum ingots by stimulating demand and producing new uses for the metal. Thus, it was difficult for the company to maintain it was a passive beneficiary of a monopoly that had come about from an involuntary elimination of competitors by automatically operating market forces.

The significance of the Alcoa case lies in the identification and condemnation of monopoly in and of itself, without respect to abuses, predatory acts, injuries to competitors, or intent to monopolize. In initiating the suit, the Justice Department asked for the dissolution of Alcoa. A district court ruled in favor of Alcoa, finding no abuse of power. The case was then appealed, and Judge Hand ruled against Alcoa. The test of a monopoly, he emphasized, is the existence of that size that gives a firm the power to fix and manage prices. Alcoa's control of 90 percnt of all aluminum ingots was sufficient in itself to constitute monopoly power. The mere existence of such a monopoly gave the firm as much or more power to fix prices as would an illegal combination or contract among several firms. Monopoly power, even though not abused, was now to be considered a violation of the Sherman Act. The good behavior of the company, which before 1945 would have been acceptable defense to the court, was no longer valid, for Congress, according to the Supreme Court, in passing the Sherman Act, did not condone "good" trusts and condemn "bad" trusts; it forbade all. Therefore, Alcoa was required to divest itself of certain facilities, which were given to other aluminum companies to encourage more competition.[10]

Subsequent court decisions have not reversed the thinking advanced in the Alcoa case. At this time, the judgment of monopoly is based on such factors as the number and strength of the firms in the market, their effective size from the standpoint of technological development, their ability to compete with similar domestic and foreign industries, and the public's interest in lower costs. But the Alcoa case also indicated that the courts would not apply Section 2 of the Sherman Act to

10. There was a second Alcoa case in 1950. The Justice Department accused Alcoa of price fixing and asked that the company be required to divest itself of more facilities. The court decision favored Alcoa this time, however, on the grounds that there was strong competition in the industry.

a firm with overwhelming market power when that position was "thrust upon" the defendant. This meant a firm could achieve market power legitimately in one of several ways: through historical accident, by lawful use of government-granted patent protection, or by uncontrollable factors in the marketplace.

The AT&T Case, 1974–1982

The AT&T case, perhaps the most important antitrust case of all time, was also resolved in January 1982. Not since the breakup of Standard Oil in 1911 has there been a more complex and potentially revolutionary restructuring of an American corporation, which in 1982 happened to be the largest in the world. In 1980, AT&T had total assets of $137 billion, and its total operating revenues amounted to $51 billion.[11] In contrast, the next largest public utility, General Telephone & Electronics, had assets of $21 billion and operating revenues of $10 billion. In fact, AT&T's assets and operating revenues were larger than the nine next largest public utilities combined. The company's stock is owned by more stockholders than any other company in the world, and the stock has always been regarded as the bluest of the blue chips.

In its suit against AT&T, the Justice Department sought to separate ownership of AT&T's local operating phone companies, its long-lines department, and its equipment-manufacturing subsidiary, Western Electric, which by itself ranked nineteenth among the five hundred largest industrial corporations in the United States. This presented the anomaly of a regulated public utility owning an industrial firm not subject to regulation. The Justice Department charged that AT&T's subsidiaries bought equipment from Western Electric even when other companies were developing better and cheaper equipment. It contended that AT&T set unreasonable restrictions on the connection of terminal equipment produced by other companies and that AT&T either refused to deal with competitors of its long-lines department who wanted to connect with local phone networks or subjected them to discriminatory terms and prices. Finally, the Justice Department wanted a realignment of AT&T's research unit, Bell Laboratories.

AT&T, on the other hand, contended that the government was attacking policies the company developed under comprehensive state and federal regulation. The company argued that its policies were reasonable responses to regulation and were subject to change by the regulators and therefore should be immune from antitrust laws. It maintained that restrictions on the connection of some equipment were necessary to protect the telephone network from harm. It defended its opposition

11. *Fortune*, May 31, 1981, p. 124.

to competitors in long-distance service as a way to prevent "cream-skimming" by competitors — that is, taking the most lucrative lines of business and leaving AT&T as a utility, with an obligation to supply the most costly services. AT&T also contended that competition in the communications industry increased dramatically during the 1970s. A side argument, advanced by the Department of Defense, was that fragmentation of AT&T might well prove detrimental to the national defense. The company argued that its telecommunications system produced an important contribution to the nation's missile, defense, space, and scientific programs.

Results of the AT&T Settlement

The results of the AT&T settlement were as follows:

1. AT&T had to divest itself of the local telephone services of its twenty-two Bell Operating Companies. They became a part of seven independent holding companies.

2. Western Electric, Bell Laboratories, and the long-distance division of AT&T were retained by AT&T. All intrastate long-distance service was turned over to AT&T by the local companies.

3. AT&T is no longer barred from offering unregulated nontelephone service, thereby opening the way for the corporation to enter the computer processing and information service business.

4. Local telephone companies divested by AT&T are required to share their facilities with all long-distance telephone companies on the same terms.

5. Local companies are barred from discriminating against AT&T's competitors in buying equipment and planning new facilities.

6. AT&T's stockholders retained stock in AT&T and were issued proportionate shares in the local companies.

Diagram 7-1 presents the organization of AT&T before and after the divestiture of its twenty-two operating companies. The divestiture, the largest in antitrust history, amounted to $87 billion. The settlement leaves AT&T partially regulated (Long-Lines Division) and partially unregulated (Bell Labs, Western Electric). The local telephone companies are regulated. AT&T is also able to enter the highly profitable computer and information industries, such as cable television and electronic newspapers. But working against AT&T is its lack of marketing expertise; as a regulated monopoly, the company never really had to sell anything.

Diagram 7-1 AT&T Before and After the Divestiture

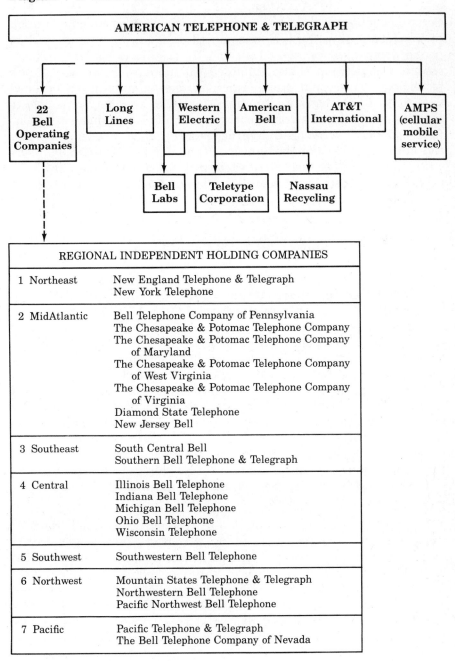

AMERICAN TELEPHONE & TELEGRAPH					
22 Bell Operating Companies	Long Lines	Western Electric	American Bell	AT&T International	AMPS (cellular mobile service)

Bell Labs	Teletype Corporation	Nassau Recycling

REGIONAL INDEPENDENT HOLDING COMPANIES	
1 Northeast	New England Telephone & Telegraph New York Telephone

2 MidAtlantic	Bell Telephone Company of Pennsylvania
	The Chesapeake & Potomac Telephone Company
	The Chesapeake & Potomac Telephone Company
	   of Maryland
	The Chesapeake & Potomac Telephone Company
	   of West Virginia
	The Chesapeake & Potomac Telephone Company
	   of Virginia
	Diamond State Telephone
	New Jersey Bell

3 Southeast	South Central Bell Southern Bell Telephone & Telegraph
4 Central	Illinois Bell Telephone Indiana Bell Telephone Michigan Bell Telephone Ohio Bell Telephone Wisconsin Telephone
5 Southwest	Southwestern Bell Telephone
6 Northwest	Mountain States Telephone & Telegraph Northwestern Bell Telephone Pacific Northwest Bell Telephone
7 Pacific	Pacific Telephone & Telegraph The Bell Telephone Company of Nevada

Benefits of the AT&T Divestiture

Certain benefits are supposed to accrue to the U.S. economy as a result of the AT&T divestiture. New competition is lowering prices paid by phone companies for equipment and by customers for long-distance service. Competition is also supposed to stimulate the growth of new technology. This could prove critical as telecommunications becomes vital to an increasingly information-based U.S. economy. The divestiture has also had some drawbacks: higher costs for equipment installation and service provided by the short-distance phone companies and more customer confusion over telephone bills, for example. Many customers have become dissatisfied with local phone service. They believe that it costs more than it should and that the quality of service is deteriorating.

The Cereal Manufacturers Case, 1974–1982

In May 1972, the Federal Trade Commission initiated antitrust action against the four largest manufacturers of breakfast cereals — Kellogg, General Mills, General Foods, and Quaker Oats.[12] The case was important for several reasons. First, it involved an oligopolistic market situation. In 1972, these four firms accounted for 91 percent of the market in ready-to-eat cereals; Kellogg alone accounted for 45 percent. Second, the FTC was not claiming any conspiracy or predatory acts by the companies; it was trying to prove, instead, that a number of long-standing industry practices were anticompetitive and permitted the companies to share monopolistic power. Third, it was charged that the shared monopoly violated Section 5 of the Federal Trade Commission Act, so the case marked an attempt to attack oligopolistic structures and mergers that occurred before passage of Celler-Kefauver.

The specific anticompetitive business practices the cereal companies were accused of are as follows:

1. Unfair methods of competition in product promotion and advertising. Specifically, statements and representations shown in the cereal companies' advertisements implied to children that the cereals would enable them to perform the physical feats depicted in the ads.

2. Brand proliferation, product differentiation, and trademark promotion. During the period 1950–1970, the four companies introduced around 150, mostly trademarked cereal brands. All were promoted by extensive advertising. Because brand names were so indelibly

12. *FTC* v. *Kellogg et al.*, 711 U.S. 0004 (1972). Quaker Oats was later dropped from the case.

impressed on the minds of consumers, the end result, the FTC claimed, was to create high barriers to the entry of other firms in the ready-to-eat cereal market.

3. Control of shelf space. Kellogg, the leading cereal company, controlled display space for the ready-to-eat cereal sections in many retail grocery outlets. The other major cereal companies, the FTC claimed, acquiesced in and benefited from Kellogg's control of shelf space because it helped them to maintain their market shares through the removal or controlled exposure of other breakfast food products.

In oligopolistic industries, the presence of homogeneous products, such as breakfast foods, may induce two types of anticompetitive business practices — product differentiation based on little except advertising, and consciously parallel pricing policies theoretically explained by the so-called kinked demand curve in the economic model of oligopoly. There is nothing wrong with product differentiation per se. In the cereal suit it was alleged that the large cereal manufacturers came up with so many different forms of essentially similar breakfast foods, differentiated primarily by advertising, that competition was in effect locked out of the cereal market. Smaller firms could not afford the expensive advertising campaigns necessary to break into the market.

Applied to the cereal companies case, the theory of shared monopoly was an untried economic concept with a weak foundation. The theory asserted that a small number of firms may violate the antitrust laws simply by virtue of possessing substantial market shares. Merely the structure of the industry makes out the cause of action, and no collusive or otherwise illegal conduct need to be demonstrated. Moreover, the political likelihood of the shared monopoly concept was small. In the 1980 presidential campaign, both Reagan and Carter expressed opposition to the FTC suit against the cereal companies. Equally significant was the opposition in Congress. Congressman Howard Wolpe of Michigan, whose district includes the Kellogg Company, introduced a bill to place a moratorium on the case, which was to remain in place until Congress defined shared monopolies and suggested remedies. The case was dropped by the Federal Trade Commission in late January 1982 after an FTC judge recommended the suit be dismissed.

The Aspen Skiing Company Case, 1985

Aspen Skiing Company owns three of the four major mountain facilities for downhill skiing in Aspen, Colorado. Aspen Highlands owns the fourth. In earlier years, each company offered its own ticket for daily use of its mountains, and they both offered an interchangeable multiday, all-Aspen ticket. Allocations from the multiday, multiarea ticket were based on samples of the number of skiers on each mountain. However, Aspen Skiing refused to continue offering the multiday, multiarea ticket unless Aspen Highlands accepted a fixed percentage of the revenues. Aspen Highlands accepted but refused to take a lower percentage a year later. Aspen Skiing then tried to eliminate Aspen Highlands from the joint ticket arrangement, and the latter went to court, alleging that Aspen Skiing was monopolizing the market in violation of Section 2 of the Sherman Act.

A jury ruled that Aspen Skiing had used exclusionary means to enhance its monopoly position and awarded the plaintiff triple damages of $7 million. This was affirmed by a circuit court, which held that the multiday, multiarea ticket had become an essential facility of the Aspen downhill skiing market and that Aspen Skiing had a duty to make that essential facility available to its competitor. The U.S. Supreme Court affirmed the decision and also held that Aspen Skiing's refusal to cooperate with its business rival, combined with the absence of any justification of efficiency whatsoever for its conduct, demonstrated an intent to monopolize in violation of Section 2 of the Sherman Act.[13]

ANTITRUST LAWS AS APPLIED TO MERGERS

The foundation of merger law is Section 7 of the Clayton Act, which states a merger is unlawful "when in any line of commerce or in any activity affecting commerce in any section of the country, the effect of such acquisition...may be substantially to lessen competition, or to tend to create a monopoly."[14] By 1950, the original language of Section 7 was considered inadequate. The courts had ruled it inapplicable to mergers by the acquisition of assets, and many people believed that it only proscribed mergers between direct competitors (horizontal mergers) but not between firms in a buyer-seller relationship (vertical mergers). A number of mergers occurred during the period after World War II, and Congress produced the Celler-Kefauver Amendment to Section 7 in 1950 to include asset acquisition. All types of mergers are banned provided it can be shown that the effect may be a substantial lessening of competition or a tendency to create a monopoly. The prohibition of the law turns on market effects.

Economic analysis can be used in the application of Section 7 to specific mergers. This proceeds from the concepts of competition and

13. *Aspen Skiing Co.* v. *Aspen Highland Skiing Corp.*, 53 U.S.L.W. 4818 (June 19, 1985).
14. U.S. House of Representatives, Committee on the Judiciary, *Compilation of Selected Antitrust Acts*, 95th Cong., 2nd sess., 1978, pp. 14-15.

monopoly discussed in Chapter 5. These concepts describe diametrically opposite results that can occur when society allocates limited resources in the free market. Under perfect competition, sellers produce and sell goods in an open market. In the long run, production results in maximum efficiency: goods are produced with the least possible expenditures of resources and the lowest possible cost per unit, and they are sold at the lowest possible price. Conversely, a monopolist has complete control over production of a good and need not produce at the lowest cost or sell at the lowest price. In maximizing profits, the monopolist can sell at a price above that which would have prevailed under perfect competition. Consumer well-being is not maximized, for fewer units of a good will be sold. However, real markets rarely conform to either model, and most industries fall within a continuum of each.

Mergers are of three types: horizontal, vertical, and conglomerate. All have the potential to lessen competition by increasing industrial concentration in the hands of fewer firms and preventing market entry by new firms. Nevertheless, some mergers stimulate competition; therefore, it is necessary to restrain only those mergers that can lessen competition. That judgment depends on the facts and circumstances of each merger within the context of a particular industry and market. In the remainder of this chapter, the antitrust laws will be applied to horizontal, vertical, and conglomerate mergers. But first we will discuss what factors condemn a merger as anticompetitive or monopolistic. These factors determine market power, which enables firms to keep prices above competitive levels. They are barriers to entry and market structure, and they are mostly applicable to horizontal mergers.

In a market characterized by pure competition, there are no barriers to entry. New firms can enter a market and compete against existing firms. Any barrier to entry protects existing firms against increased price competition and increases the possibility of collusion. In a monopolistic market, however, there would be a complete barrier to entry of another firm; in an oligopolistic market there also can be barriers to entry. For example, Coca-Cola and PepsiCo dominate the soft drink industry. In early 1986, PepsiCo announced it intended to buy Seven-Up from Philip Morris; not to be outdone, Coca-Cola announced it would buy Dr. Pepper.* The acquisitions, if consummated would give the two companies 81 percent of the soft drink market. The two companies dominate the soft drink market through advertising, product differentiation, and control over display space. Whether a new firm could enter the soft drink market today is doubtful.

Market structure refers to the number of firms and the degree of concentration in an industry. A basic distinction is made between

*The FTC has disallowed both mergers. Coca-Cola and PepsiCo plan to appeal.

oligopolistic industries and less concentrated industries. Mergers that would ordinarily be allowed in nonconcentrated industries may be challenged in oligopolistic industries. Decisions to challenge a merger may turn primarily on the answers to two questions: how concentrated would the market be after the merger? and how much of that concentration will result from the merger? However, even in concentrated markets, mergers may not be precluded from occurring when it can be demonstrated that economies of scale would be achieved or that competition could in some way be enhanced.

Horizontal Mergers

The horizontal merger is an economic arrangement between companies performing similar functions in the production or distribution of comparable goods. Almost all early mergers in the United States were horizontal, and Section 7 of the Clayton Act had them specifically in mind when it stated that no corporation shall acquire the stock of another corporation when the effect may be to substantially lessen competition. The factors that have been considered over time are the number of firms, the degree of industrial concentration, the product line, the conditions of entry, and the geographic market. The following cases illustrate some of the factors that have been weighed by the courts in arriving at decisions in horizontal merger cases.

The Brown Shoe Case, 1962

The Brown Shoe case was a landmark case with regard to the application of Section 7 of the Clayton Act as amended by Celler-Kefauver.[15] The Justice Department challenged the acquisition of the Kinney Shoe Company by the Brown Shoe Company. At the time of the acquisition, Brown was the third largest shoe retailer and the fourth largest shoe manufacturer in the United States, and Kinney was the eighth largest shoe retailer and the twelfth largest shoe manufacturer. Between them, Brown and Kinney had about sixteen hundred retail outlets but produced only 5 percent of the total national output of shoes. The Justice Department challenged the merger on the grounds that competition would be lessened substantially vertically and horizontally — vertically because Brown Shoe would use the Kinney retail outlets to sell Brown Shoes exclusively, thus excluding independent firms from using the same outlets, and horizontally because the former retail store competition between the two shoe companies would be eliminated.

15. *Brown Shoe Co.* v. *U.S.*, 370 U.S. 294 (1962).

There were also other issues in the Brown Shoe case. An important one, often considered in merger cases, was the determination of the relevant market area. To determine a merger's effect on competition, the relevant market area can be subdivided into a geographic market and a product market. The latter is determined by the reasonable interchange of products or the cross-elasticity of demand between the product itself and the substitutes for it. Within the product market are submarkets whose boundaries may be defined by examining industrial customs and practices. Regarding the vertical arrangement in the case, the relevant geographic market was the United States, and the product market was various lines of shoes. The geographic market involved in the horizontal arrangement was cities with a population of ten thousand or more and their environs in which both Brown and Kinney retailed shoes through their own outlets. The horizontal product market was men's, women's, and children's shoes sold in all retail stores.

We should emphasize that there were both horizontal and vertical aspects to the merger. There was a horizontal combination at both the manufacturing and the retail outlet level. The ruling of the district court, which was upheld by the Supreme Court, was that the merger at the manufacturing level was too insignificant to affect competition adversely. But at the retail level, the ruling was different. It was ruled that as a result of the merger, competition was lessened in those cities in which both Brown and Kinney had retail outlets. In some 118 cities with populations of ten thousand or more, the combined retail outlets exceeded 5 percent of the total market. Even though there was a lack of concentration in the shoe retailing industry, it was felt that a merger resulting in 5 percent market control could have an adverse effect on competition, particularly since future merger efforts by Brown's competitors might be encouraged. It was also ruled that a vertical restraint existed, specifically that Brown would use its control to force its shoes into the Kinney retail stores, thus excluding other manufacturers.

The Von's Grocery Case, 1966

Von's Grocery acquired Shopping Bag Food Stores. At the time of the acquisition, Von's and Shopping Bag were respectively the third and sixth largest retail grocery chains in the Los Angeles area. Their combined share of annual retail grocery sales in the Los Angeles market was 7.5 percent in 1960. Both companies had enjoyed great success before the merger. From 1948 to 1958, the number of Von's stores had increased from fifteen to thirty-four. During the same period, Von's share of the Los Angeles market almost doubled, and Shopping Bag's share of the market tripled. The merger of the two successful supermarket chains created the second largest grocery chain in Los Angeles behind Safeway, which had around 10 percent of the market.

The government brought action in a federal district court alleging that the merger violated Section 7 of the Clayton Act and asking that the merger be enjoined. The district court ruled in favor of the defendants, and the case was appealed to the Supreme Court. The latter, by a vote of six to two, found the merger violated Section 7 and ordered it dissolved.[16] Von's argued that the merger would enable it to compete more effectively against Safeway. However, the Supreme Court found that the number of individual competitors in the Los Angeles market area had decreased. In 1950, there were 5,365 single grocery store owners in the market area; by 1963, the number of stores decreased to 3,590. During the same period, the number of chains with two or more stores doubled, with small stores being absorbed by mergers. This, in the minds of the majority of the justices in the decision, made it necessary to prevent economic concentration in the U.S. economy by keeping a large number of small competitors in business.[17]

Times have changed since the Von's Grocery case, and it is doubtful whether the government would challenge a merger between two small firms today. The total sales of the two grocery chains at the time of their merger was $173 million. Compare this to two horizontal mergers consummated in 1984. Texaco acquired Getty, and Standard Oil of California (Chevron) acquired Gulf Oil. The combined sales of Texaco and Getty after the merger were $50 billion, and the combined sales of Chevron and Gulf were $36 billion. Merger guidelines have changed to reflect a more lenient government attitude. The standards that the antitrust agencies have applied in reaching a prosecutorial determination can be illustrated by presenting the Justice Department's Merger Guidelines for 1968 and 1984.

Merger Guidelines

The Justice Department has emphasized market structure in establishing the boundaries of allowable horizontal mergers. In 1968, it issued its first set of merger guidelines, which were based on the four-firm

16. *U.S.* v. *Von's Grocery*, 348 U.S. 270 (1966).
17. The district court and a minority on the Supreme Court found that there was no increase in market concentration before or after the merger. Entry barriers appeared to be nonexistent, for 173 new retail grocery chains had entered the Los Angeles market between 1953 and 1962. Between 1948 and 1958, the market share of Safeway had fallen from 14 percent to 8 percent. Many of the stores that had gone out of business were small "Mom and Pop" stores, inefficiently run and with prices higher than those charged by the supermarkets.

industrial concentration ratio. Markets were classified as highly concentrated and less highly concentrated depending on the concentration ratio. In new guidelines, first issued in 1982 and revised in 1984, the Justice Department adopted a measure of concentration called the Herfindahl-Hirschman Index. It reflects both the distribution of the market shares of the top four firms and the composition of the market outside the top four firms. It also gives proportionately greater weight to the market shares of the larger firms by the technique of squaring all market shares. A comparison of the two sets of guidelines follows.

1968 Merger Guidelines

The 1968 merger guidelines emphasized market structure in establishing the boundaries of allowable horizontal mergers. A basic distinction was made between oligopolistic industries and less concentrated industries. Mergers that ordinarily would have been allowed in less concentrated industries could have been challenged in oligopolistic industries. The following examples show the postacquisition market shares of horizontal mergers that ordinarily would have been challenged by the Justice Department.

Concentrated Markets (four firms with 75 percent of market)

Acquiring firm	Acquired firm
5%	4%
10%	2%
15% or more	1%

Less Concentrated Markets

Acquiring firm	Acquired firm
5%	5% or more
10%	4% or more
15%	3% or more
20%	2% or more
25% or more	1% or more

A new attitude toward mergers began in the 1970s. Economists and the courts felt that industrial concentration in itself does not necessarily mean a lack of competition. In this view, the notion that increasing the number of competitors in an industry will add to competitive pressures is conjectural. There is nothing to prove that it is the number of competitors that guarantees efficiency or increases the likelihood that decision making will be improved. Bigness cannot be equated with badness, and in the absence of proof to the contrary, why ban it? Bigness is often a result of efficiency, and efficiency contributes to economic growth. Partially as a result of this new attitude, and partially as a result of the conservative Reagan administration, a new set of merger guidelines was introduced.[18]

Herfindahl-Hirschman Index

New horizontal merger guidelines were introduced by the Justice Department in 1982. It departed from traditional concentration ratios and adopted another measure of market power called the Herfindahl-Hirschman Index. The index can take into consideration a larger number of companies and their relative sizes in determining market concentration. The index is obtained by squaring and summing the market shares of a given number of firms. If there is only one firm, the index would attain its maximum value of 100 percent squared, or 10,000 percent, because the firm would be a pure monopoly. If four firms have an equal share of the market, the index would be $25\%^2 + 25\%^2 + 25\%^2 + 25\%^2 = 2,500\%$. By squaring market shares, the index is weighted more heavily in favor of firms with large market shares than firms with smaller market shares. If one firm has a 50 percent market share, and four firms have an equal share of the remaining 50 percent, the index would be $50\%^2 + 12.5\%^2 + 12.5\%^2 + 12.5\%^2 + 12.5\%^2 = 3,130\%$.[19]

The following guidelines are applicable to horizontal mergers.[20]

1. If the postmerger index is below 1,000 percent, the merger will not be challenged by the Justice Department or the Federal Trade Commission. Price fixing and other forms of collusion prohibited by Section 1 of the Sherman Act is unlikely to occur because the market is not concentrated.

2. If the postmerger index is between 1,000 and 1,800, and the increase in the index is less than 100, the merger is not likely to be challenged; if it is more than 100, it is likely to be challenged.

3. If the postmerger index is greater than 1,800, the merger is likely to be challenged if (1) the increase in the index is greater than 50 or

---

18. Industrial concentration is now also looked at in terms of global reality. Japanese car manufacturers now have one-fourth of the U.S. car market. U.S. car manufacturers compete globally. Americans can choose between U.S., Japanese, British, French, German, Italian, South Korean, and Yugoslavian cars.

19. The Herfindahl-Hirschman Index is discussed in more detail in Thomas W. Brunner, Thomas J. Krattenmaker, Robert A. Skitol, and Ann Adams Webster, *Mergers in the New Antitrust Era* (Washington, D.C.: The Bureau of National Affairs, Inc., 1985), pp. 21-24.

20. U.S. Department of Justice Merger Guidelines, July 14, 1984, section 3.11, pp. 9-10.

(2) the merger will substantially lessen competition.[21]

An application of the Herfindahl-Hirschman Index to horizontal mergers is shown below. Assume that the five largest firms in a market have 30 percent, 20 percent, 10 percent, 8 percent, and 5 percent. The third largest firm wants to acquire the fifth largest firm. The premerger and postmerger indexes are computed below.

	Premerger Index				Postmerger Index	
Firm A	$(30\%)^2 =$	900%		Firm A	$(30\%)^2 =$	900%
Firm B	$(20\%)^2 =$	400%		Firm B	$(20\%)^2 =$	400%
Firm C	$(10\%)^2 =$	100%		Firm C	$(15\%)^2 =$	225%
Firm D	$(8\%)^2 =$	64%		Firm D	$(8\%)^2 =$	64%
Firm E	$(5\%)^2 =$	25%				
	Index =	1,489%			Index =	1,614%

The G. Heileman Brewing Company Case, 1983

The U.S. beer industry presents a classic example of industrial concentration that has developed over a relatively short time. As late as 1947, there were some six hundred breweries in the United States; by 1981, there were less than thirty. Almost all the beer companies had been absorbed by other beer companies, but some had discontinued their operations. By 1981, the beer industry was dominated by two companies, Anheuser-Busch, with sales for the year of $3.8 billion out of total industry sales of $10.7 billion, and Miller Beer, which is actually owned by Philip Morris, with sales of $2.1 billion.[22] The combined sales of the two brewers amounted to 55 percent of the market, a classic oligopoly. Table 7-1 presents how much the industry had changed over time.

Schlitz and G. Heileman were moving in opposite directions. Schlitz, with a name identification going back to the last century, was long a leader in the beer industry. However, during the 1970s, the company had fallen on hard times. It began the decade with a 15 percent share

21. The Justice Department is likely to challenge the merger of any firm with a market share of at least 1 percent with the leading firm in the market, providing the leading firm has a market share of at least 35 percent. For example, the index of two firms with market shares of 36 percent and 2 percent would be $(36\%)^2 + (2\%)^2 = 1,300\%$. If the two firms merged, the index would be $(38\%)^2 = 1,440\%$.

22. Data taken from Value Line Investment Survey and Standard & Poor's Industrial Surveys, The Beverage Industry, and the 1982 Census of Manufacturing, *Concentration Ratios in Manufacturing* (Washington, D.C.: U.S. Government Printing Office, 1986), table 5, p. 12.

of the national beer market; by 1980, its share had declined to around 8 percent. With declining sales relative to total market sales, Schlitz found it more difficult to finance advertising to increase its total share of the market. Conversely, Heileman enjoyed considerable success during the 1970s, advancing to fourth place behind Schlitz by the end of the decade. Through a number of acquisitions, including Carling and Falls City, the company became the dominant beer marketer in the Midwest. Because Heileman was an aggressive merchandiser of beer, the company proposed an acquisition of Schlitz, whose stock was selling at around book value, and offered Schlitz stockholders $17 a share for stock selling at $11.

The proposed merger was challenged by the Justice Department, which used the new guidelines concerning mergers and industrial concentration that were established in 1982. The critical test worked this way: a figure corresponding to the market share of one company is multiplied by that of the other, and the result is doubled. If the final total is more than 100 and the market falls within the middle range of concentration, the Justice Department is likely to challenge the merger. In the case of Schlitz and G. Heileman, the decision process worked as follows: based on 1980 industry statistics, Schlitz had 8.3 percent of the industry total, compared to 7.3 percent for G. Heileman. Multiplying 8.3 × 7.3 and doubling the total provides an index of 122. Since the beer industry comes close to being classified as a highly concentrated industry, the total of 122 placed the proposed merger of Schlitz and

Table 7-1 Concentration in the Brewing Industry, 1935–1977 (based on value of shipment for the four largest companies)

Year	Percentage of Shipment
1982	77
1977	64
1972	52
1970	46
1967	40
1963	34
1958	28
1954	27
1947	21
1935	16

Source: U.S. Department of Commerce, Bureau of the Census, 1982 Census of Manufacturing, *Concentration of Ratios in Manufacturing* (Washington, D.C.: U.S. Government Printing Office, 1986), table 5, p. 12.

G. Heileman in the danger zone. Therefore, the proposed merger never materialized.[23]

Vertical Mergers

The basic problem in applying the antitrust laws to vertical mergers is that since direct competition is not involved, it is difficult to apply such criteria as market shares, ease of entry, or concentration indexes. This is true because in a vertical merger the firms operate at different stages of the production or distribution process. Somehow it has to be demonstrated that the merger has an anticompetitive effect. In the Brown Shoe case, the Supreme Court was concerned that independent shoe manufacturers would be denied access to retail shoe store outlets because of the number of retail stores that Brown-Kinney would control after acquisition. Generally, action against vertical mergers is taken when the result is likely either to raise barriers to entry in an industry or to foreclose equal access to potential customers or suppliers.

The Du Pont Case, 1956

A case involving the Du Pont Corporation illustrates the application of Section 7 of the Clayton Act to a vertical merger, even though technically the merger was never consummated.[24] In 1919, when General Motors was just getting a major start in the automobile industry, Du Pont acquired ownership of 23 percent of its stock. The primary issue in the case, which was initiated by the Justice Department in 1949, was whether or not Du Pont had used this stock ownership to ensure a market for many of its products, including automobile finishes, fabrics, and chemicals. Not only was General Motors dominant in the automobile industry, it also was first in sales among all industrial corporations in the United States, so its link with America's largest chemical company was significant with respect to the alleged anticompetitive effects of the stock acquisition. In this case, the complaint was originally issued some thirty years after the stock acquisition, showing that Section 6 can be applied to both past and current mergers.

In 1956, the Supreme Court reversed a ruling by a lower court and ordered that Du Pont divest itself of its General Motors stock. Even though Du Pont and General Motors were not competitors, Du Pont enjoyed a commanding position as a General Motors supplier in a particular line of commerce, namely, automotive finishes and fabrics.

23. Schlitz was eventually acquired by Stroh's.
24. *U.S.* v. *Du Pont and Co.*, 353 U.S. 588 (1956).

In 1946, Du Pont furnished General Motors with 67 percent of its requirements for automotive finishes and, in 1947, 68 percent. In fabrics, Du Pont furnished only 52 percent in 1946 and 38 percent in 1947. The court ruled that anticompetitive effects were created by the stock acquisition because Du Pont was able to use its stock to become the primary supplier of General Motors in these two fields, thus negating the principle of free competition and creating an element of monopoly.

Conglomerate Mergers

Conglomerate mergers do not entail firms in direct competition with each other, nor are there usually any extensive vertical relations between the firms. They do not affect the structure of any market but merely alter the identity of firms already in the market. There are many different types of conglomerate mergers, and thus many different economic effects of them. Because no readily available criteria exist that may simply be applied to determine their legality, the courts have had to analyze each specific merger to evaluate its particular economic effect. This has meant that antitrust law governing conglomerate mergers has had to develop case by case. Case precedents have identified the types of conglomerate mergers most likely to be found in violation of Section 7 of the Clayton Act as amended by Celler-Kefauver.

The Procter & Gamble Case, 1966

A product extension merger is one type of conglomerate merger. It occurs when one firm acquires a second firm producing a product closely related to the acquiring firm's product line. The classic example of a product extension merger, which was not allowed, was when Procter & Gamble, the largest manufacturer of household cleaning supplies in the United States, entered the liquid bleach market through the acquisition of Clorox.[25] At the time of the merger, in 1957, Clorox was the leading manufacturer in the liquid bleach industry, with 48.8 percent of total sales. Its market share had been steadily increasing for the five years before the merger. Its nearest rival was Purex, which accounted for 15.7 percent of the liquid bleach sales in an industry dominated by the two companies. Since liquid bleach is chemically identifiable, Clorox spent around $3.7 million in advertising, almost one-tenth of its total sales in 1957. Heavy expenditures on advertising

25. *FTC* v. *Procter & Gamble Co.*, 386 U.S. 568 (1966).

had enabled Clorox to gain such a large share of the liquid bleach market, even though its product was no different from rival brands.

Clorox fitted into Procter & Gamble's production plans. The products were complementary in use, employed the same methods of distribution and advertising, and were sold to the same customers. The merger was challenged by the Federal Trade Commission on the grounds that it was a violation of Section 7. Competition was lessened for several reasons. First, the acquisition would raise the barriers to entry by new firms wanting to make liquid bleach. Procter & Gamble's advertising budget, which was several times larger than Clorox's yearly sales, would be used to promote Clorox bleach at the expense of Purex and other liquid bleach producers. Second, the acquisition of Clorox by Procter & Gamble eliminated the former as a potential competitor. Liquid bleach was a natural avenue of diversification since it was complementary to Procter & Gamble's products. The company could enter the liquid bleach market and compete against Clorox. The Supreme Court, reversing the decision of a circuit court of appeals, dissolved the merger.

The ITT Case, 1970

In 1969, the Justice Department filed suit against the International Telephone & Telegraph Company (ITT), America's largest corporate conglomerate, to force it to divest itself of the Hartford Fire Insurance Company and two other subsidiaries.[26] The Justice Department initiated action against ITT for two reasons. First, it felt that the ITT acquisition of the Hartford Fire Insurance Company, Sheraton, Avis, and a wide variety of other companies would encourage the existing trend of large corporations to acquire dominant firms in concentrated markets, thereby increasing the concentration of control of manufacturing assets. The ITT acquisition of the Hartford Fire Insurance Company was a case in point. With assets of $1.8 billion, it was one of the five largest fire and casualty insurance companies in the United States.

Three separate acquisitions of ITT were challenged by the Justice Department. The first was the acquisition of the Canteen Corporation; the second was the acquisition of the Grinnell Corporation; and the third was the acquisition of the Hartford Fire Insurance Company. The government's case against these mergers was based on several forms of alleged competitive damage — reciprocity, geographic foreclosure of markets, financial resources, and the combination of the automatic sprinkler (Grinnell) and fire insurance (Hartford) business. The record

26. *U.S.* v. *International Telephone & Telegraph Co.*, 324 F. Supp. 19 (1970).

of the ITT-Canteen case documented how ITT promoted reciprocity with banks. As for geographic foreclosure of markets, it was felt that the acquisition of Grinnell, a major producer of automatic sprinkler systems, would enable ITT to capture an expanding share of the foreign market. Finally, there was the interrelationship between Grinnell and Hartford, for insurance rates are related directly to the presence of automatic sprinkler systems. There was the possibility that Hartford insurance agents would recommend Grinnell sprinkler systems to their customers, thus eliminating competition from a segment of the sprinkler market.

There were three judgments in the ITT case:

1. In the judgment involving the Canteen Corporation, ITT was ordered to divest itself, within two years, of all its interest, direct and indirect, in the company.

2. ITT was ordered to divest itself, within two years, of all its interest, direct and indirect, in the fire protection division of Grinnell.

3. ITT was ordered to divest itself, within three years of the final judgment, of all its interests, direct and indirect, in Levitt, Avis, and Hamilton Life or, alternatively, of all its interests, direct and indirect, in Hartford.

Joint Ventures

Section 7 of the Clayton Act applies to most forms of joint venture, which is broadly defined as a combination of two or more firms for a particular business objective. A joint venture often results in the formation of a new entry, but this is not essential; the parties may simply agree by contract to cooperate. Each party contributes to the venture-production facilities, personnel, technology, and funding. Joint ventures are becoming particularly important in the area of international business. Their advantage, domestic or international, is that they allow companies to combine complementary resources, develop new products, or pool capital and share risks where the project is costly or the likelihood of success small. Projects beyond the individual reach of each company may be feasible through a joint venture. But they also can be anticompetitive because potential entry into the market by other firms can be blocked, and collaboration by the partners in the venture can lead to illegal agreements between them to fix prices or divide markets.

The Penn-Olin Chemical Company Case, 1964

Pennsalt Chemicals Corporation, a producer of industrial salt, and Olin Matheson Chemical Corporation, a manufacturer of industrial chemical products, formed a joint venture, Penn-Olin, to produce and market industrial salt in the growing southeastern market. The product, which is used to bleach wood pulp, was produced in a concentrated market dominated by three firms, including Pennsalt. Before the joint venture with Olin Matheson in 1960, Pennsalt's product was marketed in the southeast through an agreement with Olin. The market at that time was dominated by two of Pennsalt's competitors, Hooker Chemical and American Potash, which together had more than a 90 percent share of the market. Pennsalt formed the joint venture with Olin to enter the market.

The government challenged the joint venture on the grounds that either or both companies could have entered the southeast market independently, or that either could be a potential entrant. In its decision, the Supreme Court, reversing the lower courts, held that they should have considered the ongoing effect of both firms standing on the edge of the market as potential competitors and should have determined whether their decision to enter the southeastern market through the venture could have resulted in a substantial lessening of competition. The case was sent back to a district court for further review, where, because it was found that no reasonable probability existed that either company would have entered the market on its own, it was dismissed.[27]

SUMMARY

Power over a market can be achieved through monopolies and mergers. The latter is the more typical way of gaining market power. By reducing the number of firms in a market and enlarging the merged firms' share of market sales, a merger can result in higher prices for consumers and the reduction of competition. The federal statute that deals with monopolies is Section 2 of the Sherman Act. Tests of market power when applied in monopoly cases have varied. In the 1911 decision that broke up the Standard Oil Company, the Supreme Court established a rule of reason approach, in which it looked for an intent to monopolize and actual instances of predatory conduct representing the exercise of this intent. In the Alcoa case of 1945, market power was measured by Alcoa's share of the market. Size alone became an offense because the

27. *U.S.* v. *Penn-Olin Chemical Co.*, 378 U.S. 158 (1964).

possession of power could not be separated from the abuse of that power.

Mergers come under the jurisdiction of Section 7 of the Clayton Act, which was later amended by the Celler-Kefauver Act. The enforcement of Section 7 is done by the Justice Department through its Antitrust Division as well as by the Federal Trade Commission. Private actions to enforce Section 7 may also be brought in federal district court. Merger enforcement in the United States has gone through shifts in philosophy. Many mergers during the 1950s and 1960s, following the passage of the Celler-Kefauver Act, were excluded between companies that were almost microscopic in competitive terms. The 1980s are different from the 1960s. Mergers are treated more in terms of their potential for desirable effects on the economy. A new measure of industrial concentration called the Herfindahl-Hirschman Index is now used. Focus is being placed on market power, barriers to entry, and enhancement of allocative and productive efficiencies.

QUESTIONS FOR DISCUSSION

1. What was the "thrust upon" defense used by Alcoa?
2. Why are oligopolistic industries often characterized by uniform action?
3. How can a vertical merger be anticompetitive?
4. How can a conglomerate merger be anticompetitive when by definition it involves noncompeting and nonrelated firms?
5. Discuss the "legal concept" of rule of reason.
6. Compare the Herfindahl-Hirschman Index to the old Justice Department guidelines.
7. Is it necessary to keep a large number of small firms in business to prevent economic concentration?
8. Discuss some of the results of the AT&T case.
9. Discuss the concept of shared monopoly as it was applied to the cereal companies.
10. Why is the AT&T settlement one of the most important antitrust decisions of all times?
11. What is a product extension merger? Why was the acquisition of Clorox by Procter & Gamble disallowed?
12. Discuss the issues in the Von's Grocery case.

RECOMMENDED READINGS

Bock, Betty. *Antitrust and The Supreme Court.* New York: The Conference Board, 1981.

Brunner, Thomas W., Thomas G. Krattenmaker, Robert R. Skitol, and Ann Adams
    Webster. *Mergers in the New Antitrust Era.* Washington, D.C.: The Bureau of
    National Affairs, Inc., 1985.
Business Week. "Did It Make Sense to Break Up AT&T," December 3, 1984,
    pp. 86–112.
Dunfee, Thomas W., and Frank F. Gibson. *Antitrust and Trade Regulation.* New
    York: John Wiley & Sons, 1985.
Fortune. "Ma Bell's Kids Fight For Position," June 27, 1983, pp. 61–78.
Katzmann, Robert A. *Regulatory Bureaucracy: The Federal Trade Commission and
    Antitrust Policy.* Cambridge, Mass: MIT Press, 1983.
Stigler, George J. *The Economist and The Problem of Monopoly.* Chicago: The
    University of Chicago Law School, 1983.
Waldmen, Don. *The Economics of Antitrust.* Boston: Little Brown, 1985.

Chapter 8
Antitrust Laws and the Regulation of Anticompetitive Practices

The rationale for American antitrust policies has been to promote competition between business firms in the marketplace by prohibiting monopolies and other activities that result in restraint of trade. The essence of competition is for a business firm to try to take business from its rivals. If it succeeds by virtue of superior efficiency or other legitimate advantages, the rivals have no legal recourse. All too often, however, business firms have tried to gain an advantage over their competitors through various practices that have come to be considered unfair. Over time, laws have been developed to confine competition within the framework of a set of rules. The historical development of public policy to regulate certain unfair or anticompetitive business practices began with common law, which is simply a set of legal precedents that have been established over time.

Certain types of practices were condemned by common law as violating standards of common morality. Unfair competition was defined as representing one's goods as those of another's. By adeptly copying a brand name or a style, one firm could trade on the good will established by a rival. The rival could go to court and seek damages. Similar relief could be obtained when one firm maligned the reputation of, or engaged in commercial espionage against, a rival. Common law also extended the concept of unfair competition to apply to infringements on patents and trademarks. But common law provided poor protection against the infinite variety of anticompetitive business practices that developed with the growth of business combinations in the last century. These practices included attacks on small rivals through local price cutting, tying arrangements, exclusive dealing contracts, and other acts.

Common law was supplemented by the Sherman Act of 1890. Among the unfair practices covered by the act were excessive price cutting and local price discrimination when clearly intended to eliminate competition. The Sherman Act was applied to concerted efforts of distributors to preserve the traditional channels of distribution from manufacturer to wholesaler to retailer. Efforts of wholesalers to boycott manufacturers who sold directly to retailers, or to circulate blacklists with this object in mind, were prohibited, as were concerted efforts of retailers or manufacturers to boycott other retailers or manufacturers. The Sherman Act delegated to the courts broad powers to interpret and apply the proscriptions against certain anticompetitive practices, case by case, in civil and criminal actions brought by the Justice Department and by private persons.

Application of the Sherman Act to specific anticompetitive practices was unsatisfactory to many groups. Victims of predatory actions felt the law should intervene before the practices had taken effect. Others felt the courts had not gone far enough. Tying contracts and exclusive dealing arrangements, for example, were often upheld as legitimate extensions of patent rights. Among localities or different types of customers, the permissible limits of price discrimination were uncertain. The Sherman Act was criticized on the grounds that its provisions against unfair restraint of trade were too general. Some business groups favored the creation of a new commission to review potentially illegal acts, and other groups wanted a clearer definition of what constituted an illegal act.

To satisfy these and other complaints, the Clayton and Federal Trade Commission acts were passed in 1914. Their objectives were to modify the Sherman Act by specifically prohibiting certain types of unfair practices and to create new administrative machinery to aid in law enforcement. However, no set of statutory definitions can ever be drawn to include the infinite range of industrial and commercial practices that can be used to prevent competition. As soon as one set of prohibitions are laid down, new methods, or new variations on old methods, invariably spring up to circumvent them, which is why the courts have had to constantly reinterpret the antitrust laws throughout the years. Because they are ultimately responsible for the interpretation and application of the antitrust laws, the courts have been vested with a wide range of discretion in construing their statutory provisions and in molding their remedies. The remainder of this chapter will be devoted to a discussion of various types of anticompetitive practices and how the courts have dealt with them.

ANTICOMPETITIVE BUSINESS PRACTICES

Anticompetitive business practices cover a multitude of sins — price fixing, reciprocity, exclusive dealing, price discrimination against buyers or sellers, territorial restrictions, tying agreements, interlocking directorates, boycotts, preemptive buying, and other coercive practices. Each device can be used to restrain competition. For example, the aim of a price fixing agreement is to eliminate one form of competition. The power to fix prices, whether or not reasonably exercised, includes the power to control the market. Reciprocity can also be used to restrain trade. When a buyer uses its power to compel sellers to buy from it as a condition for doing business, it is a restraint on free trade. Any restrictive agreement can be regarded by the courts as a conspiracy of firms that results in a restraint of trade among separate companies. Usually the restrictive agreement is understood to entail some direct or indirect, overt or implied, form of price fixing, output control, market sharing, or exclusion of competitors.

The antitrust laws apply to various forms of restrictive agreements. Section 1 of the Sherman Act has been used to prohibit both vertical and horizontal price fixing arrangements. With respect to price fixing, the courts have applied, with few exceptions, an absolute prohibition. Pricing discrimination would generally come under Section 2 of the Clayton Act, as amended by the Robinson-Patman Act. This legislation attempts to foster competition by prohibiting both primary-line and secondary-line price discrimination. Tying arrangements that restrain trade would come under the Clayton and Sherman acts. Exclusive dealing arrangements would come under Section 3 of the Clayton Act, and boycotts or concerted refusal to deal would come under Section 1 of the Sherman Act. Preemptive buying would also come under the Sherman Act.

Price Fixing

Agreements among competing firms to fix, stabilize, raise, or lower prices constitute illegal price fixing. These agreements have always had an allure to business firms because they reduce, perhaps even eliminate, the risks of economic loss. But price fixing destroys the right of each business firm to determine independently the prices of goods and services and often leads to higher prices for consumers. Horizontal price fixing occurs when business firms compete directly against each other. For example, company A and company B are competitors. The presidents of each company, Mr. Smith and Mr. Jones, are friendly and often meet for lunch. At one lunch, Mr. Smith suggests there is enough business for both companies without a need for price competition. Mr. Jones agrees, and both companies decide not to charge less than $75 for their product. Vertical price fixing occurs between firms that operate at different levels in the distribution channels of particular goods.

Bid rigging is a form of price fixing in which business firms interfere with the integrity of the bidding process. State and local governments, as well as many private firms, purchase products by inviting businesses to submit competitive bids. The firm submitting the lowest bid is awarded the contract to sell its product or service to a buyer. When business firms agree on which one will submit the winning bid or agree to submit the same price bid, the process breaks down, and the buyer pays a higher price for the product or service. For example, companies A and B are invited by a city to bid on the sale of stationery. The president of A asks the president of B to submit a high bid so that A can win the contract. The president of B agrees but in return asks the president of A to submit a high bid on stationery bids being solicited by another city. The president of A is agreeable, and both of the businesses win a government contract.

Another form of price fixing is resale price maintenance, in which a manufacturer or distributor of a product enters into an agreement with, or pressures, a retail dealer to sell the product at a specific retail price. This is vertical price fixing because the agreement is made between business firms at two different levels of distribution (wholesale and retail). For example, Sweater Inc., which manufactures sweaters, sells to two retail merchants, Mr. Black and Ms. Brown. To attract more customers, Mr. Black decides to sell sweaters at a 10 percent discount. Ms. Brown is upset because this discount will likely attract some of her customers. She calls Sweater Inc., to complain. The company then calls Mr. Black and tells him to sell at the suggested retail price or else he might not be allowed to sell the company's products at all. Both Sweater Inc. and Ms. Brown have conspired to fix prices by attempting to force Mr. Black to maintain his prices at the suggested retail level.

An effective price fixing agreement permits firms to set a price as if they were one company — a single-firm monopoly. It constitutes a per se violation of Section 1 of the Sherman Act, which states that a contract, combination, or conspiracy in restraint of trade in interstate or foreign commerce is illegal. It is a per se violation because its aim is the elimination of price competition. Price fixing is also illegal under Section 5 of the Federal Trade Commission Act, which is designed to prevent unfair methods of competition in commerce. It may be added that, since collusion or conspiracy to fix prices is illegal under the antitrust laws, firms closely guard any agreements on price that they may make. Price fixing agreements are usually made in secret, and all sorts of subterfuge can be used. The following case involving General Electric, Westinghouse, and other makers of electrical equipment is a good illustration.

The Electrical Equipment Case, 1961

The Electrical Equipment case of 1961 is a good example of a restrictive business practice, specifically price fixing by a number of firms in the electrical equipment industry.[1] Agreements to fix prices violate Section 1 of the Sherman Act and are illegal per se, for they vitiate the essence of competition in the marketplace. The case involved a conspiracy by a number of companies, including General Electric and Westinghouse, to fix prices and rig bids in the sale of heavy electrical equipment to private and public utilities. Markets were also divided up among the companies, with General Electric and Westinghouse getting the biggest shares. The conspiracy had been going on for nearly twenty-five years, and the companies were accused of fixing prices and rigging bids on the sale of $7 billion of heavy electrical equipment between 1953 and 1960.

The conspiracy followed an elaborate pattern. Executives of the various electrical equipment companies would meet at conventions, hotels, and private homes to work out arrangements to divide markets and to rig bids on contracts. The companies would take turns in submitting low bids. The executives used false names and blank stationery to correspond and phases of the moon to determine which company would put in the low bid on a contract. Using the phase of the moon system, each firm knew when to bid high and when to bid low. With twenty-nine different companies, including the two largest, taking part, the conspiracy was about as complete as possible. This meant that over the period of the conspiracy, millions of extra dollars were charged to utilities and their customers. The conspiracy directly or indirectly affected almost every dam built, every power generator installed, and every electrical distribution system set up in the United States. Eventually, the TVA became suspicious of the similarities of a series of bids and notified the Justice Department.

The fines, penalties, and loss of business prestige resulting from the outcome of the suit, which was initiated by the Justice Department, were enormous. Both the Clayton and Sherman acts provide for triple damage suits by private citizens. Both fines and jail sentences are provided for in the Sherman Act. Convictions by a federal court led to the thirty-day imprisonment of seven executives, the greatest number of jail terms ever in an antitrust proceeding, and suspended thirty-day jail sentences for twenty-one other executives. A total of $1.9 million was levied against both the companies and their executives. In addition, by the end of 1967, a series of private triple damage suits filed against the major companies had cost General Electric $225 million and Westinghouse $125 million. Although the victims of this price fixing conspiracy were able to recover hundreds of millions of dollars, the triple damage

1. *U.S.* v. *General Electric et al.*, 209 F. Supp. 197 (1961). For discussions of the case see John G. Fuller, *The Gentlemen Conspirators* (New York: Grove Press, 1962); and Walter Jensen, "The Light of the Moon Formula — Some Whys and Wherefores," *Western Business Review*, 5 (May 1961), 27-33.

remedy generally has not been an effective tool for victimized persons, who often have found antitrust litigation too costly and time-consuming.

The Spray-Rite Case, 1984

Monsanto is a large chemical company. It manufactures many chemical products, including agricultural herbicides. Spray-Rite, an authorized Monsanto distributor, engaged in a discount operation. Following complaints from other Monsanto distributors that Spray-Rite's prices were too low, Monsanto refused to renew Spray-Rite's one-year distributorship term. Spray-Rite brought suit under Section 1 of the Sherman Act, claiming, among other things, that Monsanto and some of its distributors had conspired to fix the retail prices of herbicides and that Spray-Rite was terminated as a result of the conspiracy. The case went to a trial court where the jury was instructed that Monsanto's conduct was illegal per se if it was in furtherance of a vertical conspiracy to fix prices. The jury so found. A court of appeals and the Supreme Court affirmed the decision.

The Supreme Court enunciated a standard of proof required to find the existence of a vertical price fixing conspiracy.[2] It stated that evidence of complaints from other distributors, or even that termination came about in response to these complaints, is not enough to show the existence of a conspiracy. According to the Court, there must be evidence that reasonably tends to prove a producer and others had a conscious commitment to a common scheme designed to achieve an unlawful objective. To clarify its standard, the Court stated that the concept of a common scheme means more than showing the nonterminated distributors conformed to Monsantos' suggested price. It also means showing that the distributor communicated their agreement and that this was sought by the producer. The Spray-Rite case reaffirms the per se illegality of vertical price fixing agreements and raises the burden of proof necessary to show the existence of such agreements.

The Country Stoves Case, 1983

State antitrust laws were discussed in Chapter 6. They are important because there is a significant area of business that is clearly interstate. If a policy of competition is to be maintained in this area, it is up to the states to do it. State antitrust laws prohibit price discrimination where the intent is to lessen competition. The State of Washington charged

2. *Monsanto Co.* v. *Spray-Rite Corp.*, 52 U.S.L.W. 4341 (March 20, 1984).

Country Stoves, a manufacturer of wood stoves, six of its dealers, and eight individuals with conspiring to fix retail prices of wood burning stoves, fireplaces, and related services and equipment.[3] Their alleged objective was to eliminate competition among retailers of wood burning stoves and fireplaces through price fixing and by refusing to deal with retailers who did not agree to fix prices. The state claimed that, as a result of the price fixing, nonconspiring retailers and consumers were denied the benefits of free and open competition. The case was resolved through a consent decree that provided for injunctions and penalties of up to $25,000 for each violation.

The Mid-Atlantic Toyota Case, 1984

State antitrust laws are also important because of the doctrine of concurrent jurisdiction, which means a state government can bring action under its respective laws to reach a business practice that is at once local and interstate in nature. Toyota dealers in Delaware, Maryland, Pennsylvania, Virginia, West Virginia, and the District of Columbia, as well as the Toyota distributor for the Mid-Atlantic region, were charged with conspiring to fix prices. They participated in a new program in which protective sealants were applied to 1980 model Toyota cars. The price of the protective sealants was fixed. The attorneys general for the five states and the general counsel for the District of Columbia filed parens patriae class action suits on behalf of customers who had purchased the 1980 Toyotas.[4] They specifically sought the award of damages sustained by consumers that resulted from price fixing of the sealant.

A settlement was reached in the U.S. District Court for Maryland.[5] It provided buyers of the 1980 Toyotas with the option of receiving either $135 in cash or $250 in goods and services. Of the approximately fifty thousand buyers of 1980 Toyotas, nearly 75 percent were qualified to receive the benefit of the settlement, which amounted to $5.1 million. It was the responsibility of the car dealers to find and inform these customers of their benefits. Moreover, the district court awarded the plaintiffs, including the attorneys general of the five states and the general counsel for the District of Columbia, compensation for the cost of litigating the suit. These costs, calculated at a rate of $50 an hour, were also paid out of the settlement with the car dealers and distributor.

3. *Washington* v. *Country Stoves of Washington, Inc.*, No. 83-2-13283-5, Wash. Super. Ct., King City (September 23, 1983).
4. A state attorney general can file a parens patriae (father of the country) suit. It is designed to protect consumers injured by some particular action.
5. *Mid-Atlantic Toyota Antitrust Litigation*, No. MDL-456 (D. Md., 1984).

Tying Arrangements

When a seller conditions or ties the sale of a popular product or service (the tying item) to a buyer's purchase of another less popular product or service (the tied item), the seller has engaged in a tying arrangement. Such sales are illegal if the seller has economic power in the tying product or is successful in conditioning the sale of the tying item on the purchase of the tied item. A tying arrangement interferes with a competitive marketplace because the seller is able to sell the tied item without regard to its price or quality but solely because the buyer needs to purchase the tying item. By tying, the seller is able to sell a greater quantity of tied items and, thus, take business away from other firms that sell the tied item or a similar product. Tying also directly harms the consumer by forcing the purchase of an unwanted item as a condition of purchasing a desirable item.

An example of a tying arrangement is as follows: A company called Stereco manufactures a popular high-quality stereo record player. All retail stores carry the Stereco brand record player. A retail store not carrying the brand could lose a considerable amount of business to the competition. Stereco also manufactures a tape deck, but it is not nearly as popular as its record player. To sell more of its tape decks, Stereco tells its retail outlets they must buy one tape deck for each record player purchased. By doing this, it has illegally tied the sale of its tape decks to the sale of its record players. This discriminates against both retailers and consumers by denying freedom of choice and limits other sellers of the tied product from competing in that particular market.

Tying arrangements would come under either Section 1 of the Sherman Act or Section 3 of the Clayton Act. Where the tying product is a legal monopoly, such as a patent, the seller is likely to have monopoly control, and the arrangement would constitute a per se violation of Section 1 of the Sherman Act. More likely, the arrangement would come under Section 3 of the Clayton Act, which, whenever there is substantial injury to competition, prohibits the following: the tie-in sale, mentioned in the example above; the exclusive dealership, where goods are sold only on the condition the dealer will not handle the goods of a competitor; and the requirement contract, where the sale of a product is made on the condition the customer will buy subsequent products from the seller. However, tying arrangements are allowed when a seller can prove the tied product or service is necessary to maintain the operation of the tying product or service.

The Chicken Delight Case, 1977

Chicken Delight was a fast-food chicken chain that operated through the use of the franchise arrangement. Franchising is a business approach involving the permission to use a certain product, including a special name or trademark, and often incorporating a specific set of procedures for creating the product. Chicken Delight had several hundred franchises and required its franchisees to buy a specified number of cookers and frying chickens and other supplies and sauces exclusively from the company. This arrangement was challenged by one of the franchisees who argued that the tying agreement interfered with the right to buy supplies from other sources. Chicken Delight argued that its arrangement enabled it to supervise quality and maintain control over the revenue derived from the sale of its food products and other supplies to its fast-food outlets.

A circuit court ruled that the agreement was in violation of Section 3 of the Clayton Act.[6] It held that Chicken Delight could maintain quality standards over the product on which it had a trademark, even if the product were purchased from other suppliers. Trademarks did not immunize a product from antitrust laws. Chicken Delight contended that its income was dependent solely on the revenues it generated from selling its products to its outlets. However, the court ruled that there were other ways in which it could receive money from its franchises. Royalties based on sales volume is a common form of payment in a franchise arrangement, and they do not involve a tying arrangement or have an undesirable effect on competition.

The Marine Operators Case, 1984

Tying arrangements that lessen competition are also subject to state antitrust laws. In two actions in separate state courts, the Virginia attorney general charged that Urbanna Marine and Perico Corporation had engaged in tying arrangements. Urbanna allegedly tied the purchase of boat brokerage services to the rental of marina berths. Perico allegedly tied the purchase of marine supplies and boat brokerage and repair services to the rental of berths. The courts ruled against the companies. Both Urbanna and Perico were prohibited from requiring, as a condition of leasing marine berths, that lessees purchase products or services from them.[7]

Exclusive Dealing Agreements

In an exclusive dealing agreement, one firm induces other firms not to deal with the former's competitors. For example, the American To-

6. *Siegal* v. *Chicken Delight*, 448 F. 2d 43 (1971).
7. *Virginia* v. *Perico Corp.*, No. 3841, Va. Cir. Ct., Gloucester City (January 3, 1984); *Virginia* v. *Urbanna Marine*, No. 2299, Va. Cir. Ct., Middlesex City (January 30, 1984).

bacco Company was able to use its economic power to compel wholesalers and retailers of tobacco products to agree to deal only with it and not with its competitors. The effect on competition was appreciable because American Tobacco was able to foreclose on the tobacco market. In general, exclusive dealing agreements that have the effect of eliminating competitors from a particular market have been held to violate Section 3 of the Clayton Act. At one time, the courts generally enforced the rule of Section 3 against exclusive dealing only when a seller dominated a particular market. Today, less than market dominance is sufficient to indicate that a portion of the market can be foreclosed by an exclusive dealership agreement.

Not all exclusive dealership agreements are illegal. They are illegal only when used to eliminate rivals. In many situations, they are socially and economically beneficial. For instance, a buyer and a seller can enter into an agreement for fuel supplies. This may require the supplier to undertake capital outlays, which it would be unwilling to do unless assured of a long-term contract. The buyer is assured of a long-term fuel supply. An agreement between a buyer and a seller can also ensure price stability. By guaranteeing a market to the supplier and adequate supplies to the consumer, business costs may be reduced. The nature of a product may also require an exclusive dealership agreement. The product may be so specialized that it has to be sold and serviced by dealers trained to represent the company.

The Standard Oil of California Case, 1949

Standard Oil of California was the largest seller of gasoline in the Western part of the United States. In 1946, it had 23 percent of the total gallonage sold in that market, 6.7 percent of which was sold to independent gasoline dealers. Standard Oil had obtained exclusive dealing contracts with 5,397 independent stations, or 16 percent of the total retail gasoline outlets in the Western market area. The exclusive dealer contract required the dealers to buy all of their gasoline and, in some cases, oil, tires, and batteries from Standard Oil. The government obtained an injunction prohibiting Standard Oil from using the exclusive agreement as violative of Section 1 of the Sherman Act and Section 3 of the Clayton Act. The government contended that these contracts foreclosed a substantial amount of the gasoline market and thereby created a barrier to entry for new independent refiners in the gas refining sector.

A district court found that competition was substantially lessened by these tying contracts because they covered a substantial number of retail gas outlets and a substantial number of products. Standard Oil of California appealed the decision to the Supreme Court, which upheld the decision of the district court.[8] It ruled that the validity of contracts under Section 3 of the Clayton Act can be tested by whether a substantial amount of commerce is affected. The sale of 6.7 percent of the total volume of gasoline sold in the relevant trade area was held to be substantial. Therefore, the Court reasoned that a substantial lessening of competition would be an automatic by-product. The very existence of these contracts denies dealers opportunity to deal in the products of competing suppliers and excludes suppliers from access to the outlets controlled by these dealers. The contracts also create a barrier to entry into the gasoline market by new refiners.

Group Boycotts

Group boycotts occur when businesses on the same level of competition agree to deny another business access to business advantages such as supply sources, credit, or advertising. For example, there are three cleaning businesses in a small city. A fourth dry cleaning business plans to open in two weeks. The owners of the three existing businesses meet at a local restaurant and discuss the impending opening of the new cleaning business. All three, worried about the new firm cutting into their business profits, agree to call their supplier of cleaning fluid, the Jones Supply Company, and threaten to stop buying from it if it sells cleaning fluid to the new business. The Jones Supply Company agrees. The three existing businesses and their supplier of cleaning fluid have entered into an illegal group boycott where the intent is to drive the new competitor out of business.

The three cleaning firms possess market power and are able to exert it to the detriment of consumers and the new entrant into the dry cleaning business. The boycott is anticompetitive and represents a per se violation of Section 1 of the Sherman Act. Courts have applied a per se prohibition to this type of activity when carried out in commerce. As in price fixing, a key to the illegality of a boycott is the concerted action of its members. This creates a problem, for in many situations a firm may find that sellers refuse to sell to it, but it is unable to prove there is an agreement not to do so. The following cases illustrate the application of antitrust laws to group boycotts.

The Klor's, Inc. Case, 1959

In this case, it was alleged that a combination of manufacturers, distributors, and retailers had boycotted Klor's, Inc., a small appliance

8. *Standard Oil of California* v. *U.S.*, 337 U.S. 293 (1949).

dealer in San Francisco. The dealer operated near one of the branches of Broadway-Hall Stores, a chain of department stores, and brought a suit against the chain, and ten national manufacturers and their distributors, accusing them of a conspiracy of refusing to sell to it. A district court and an appeals court ruled that there was no injury to the public because there were many other appliance dealers in the San Francisco market area. The case was appealed to the Supreme Court, which ruled that the boycott interfered with the natural flow of commerce and was an effort to drive Klor's out of business as a dealer.[9]

The Tennessee Realtors Case, 1983

The attorney general of Tennessee brought action against a number of real estate brokers, accusing them of trying to shut competitors out of the real estate market through the use of a boycott. The accused realtors refused to show property or let their property be shown with a realtor. Under a consent judgment with the state attorney general, the firms admitted they were engaged in a conspiracy to lessen competition, which is in direct violation of Section 1 of the Sherman Act. The judgment prohibits them from enforcing any agreement that attempts to exclude another real estate firm either from obtaining information about property or from inspecting any property.[10] They are also enjoined from any future group boycotts in which there is a concerted refusal to deal.

Reciprocity

A business practice that can come under the jurisdiction of antitrust law is reciprocity, where a buyer uses its power to compel a seller to buy from it. For example, buyer A, a major customer of seller B, tells seller B that since it is a good customer, seller B should reciprocate by buying from seller A. The implicit threat of coercion or the mere presence of large purchasing power may convince B to buy from A. In many instances, firms dealing in a variety of products have discovered they are both potential buyers from and sellers to each other; thus, they may tend to implicitly agree to purchase from each other. Reciprocity is not illegal unless its use in some way lessens competition.

Reciprocity has come to be associated with conglomerate mergers. Firm A acquires firm B. A reciprocal buying arrangement arises when they both sell products that the other buys. If this lessens competition

9. *Klor's, Inc.* v. *Broadway-Hale Stores, Inc.*, 359 U.S. 207 (1959).
10. *Tennessee* v. *Martin*, No. 4-83-76, ED Tenn. (September 2, 1983).

by giving firm A unfair competitive advantage, there is a violation of antitrust law. For example, Consolidated Foods, a major food processor and retailer, acquired Gentry, a manufacturer of dehydrated onions and garlic. Consolidated Foods was an important purchaser of food products from several food processors, which in turn were large purchasers of dehydrated onions and garlic. Consolidated sent letters to the food processors from which it purchased goods, asking them to buy Gentry products. This action was challenged by the Federal Trade Commission in a court case.[11] The court ruled that the attempt at reciprocity would give Gentry an unfair competitive advantage over other suppliers of dehydrated onions and garlic.

Price Discrimination

If a manufacturer or wholesaler sells a product at different prices to two or more competing buyers, the seller is engaging in price discrimination. The practice is a violation when all the circumstances of the sale are the same, such as grade, quality, and time. Discrimination in price, however, can be justified on the basis of manufacturing or delivery costs, or as a "good faith" attempt by a seller to meet the price of its competitors. For example, oil company A supplies gasoline to several competing retail stations in a major city. It drops its price to retail station B when the owner complains a competitor, not supplied by oil company A, is selling gasoline at a lower price. The oil company agrees to lower its price to retail station B but not to those stations that compete with B. It did not lower the price to meet its competition but rather to meet station B's competition; therefore, it is guilty of price discrimination.

Price discrimination can be exercised by a seller only when it has some degree of monopoly control over the market. In a purely competitive market, price discrimination in any form would be impossible. No one seller would have the power to discriminate against other sellers, for sellers are too numerous. Nor could one seller make buyers pay more than the market-determined price, for they have other alternative suppliers. The market price is one that makes trade advantageous to both sellers and buyers, for it is influenced by supply and demand forces. Price discrimination is the opposite of price competition. It is used by a seller to enhance profits and to limit or injure the competitors.

11. *Federal Trade Commission* v. *Consolidated Foods*, 380 U.S. 592 (1965).

Primary-Line Price Discrimination

There are two main forms of price discrimination — primary line and secondary line. Primary-line discrimination refers to discrimination in the primary line of commerce, namely, the same line of commerce in which the seller practicing discrimination is engaged. One form of primary-line discrimination is whipsawing, which occurs when a seller operates in several geographic areas and cuts prices in one while maintaining them in the others. This gives it an unfair advantage when competing with a seller who operates only in a single geographic area. Unable to maintain its price, the latter has no way to maintain its profits; the former, however, can make up at least a portion of its losses by profits made in other areas. After eliminating one regional competitor by selective price cutting, the seller operating in several areas can turn its attention to another competitor and so on until all regional competitors are eliminated.[12]

An example of primary-line price discrimination is as follows: seller A is located in city X, and seller B is located in city Y. Both sell an identical product. Seller A sells the product for $1 a unit in city X, and seller B sells it for the same price in city Y. The cities are far enough apart to add transportation costs of $.10 per unit to seller A's product if sold in city Y. Seller A goes into city Y and sells its products for $.95. It is undercutting seller B. Given the additional transportation costs of $.10 per unit, seller A should be selling the product for $1.10 instead of $.95. Unless seller A can somehow demonstrate it is actually cheaper for it to sell in city Y than it is for its rival, it is guilty of primary-line price discrimination.

Secondary-Line Price Discrimination

Price discrimination can also be anticompetitive when a seller grants lower prices to some buyers and not to others. Sales to buyers at different prices affect the "secondary" or buyers' level of competition. The pricing abuse most likely to restrain competition at this level is granting rebates or discounts to favored buyers thus giving them a competitive advantage over their rivals. In many cases, buyers are able to exert pressure on sellers to grant them special discounts. This can occur when the buyer is large enough to use its economic leverage to force favored treatment. The retail price charged by the large buyer can then be lower than the prices charged by smaller buyers that lack the economic leverage to gain discounts from the seller. Secondary-line price dis-

12. Primary-line price discrimination can also occur in the same geographic area.

crimination has been associated with chain stores that, able to buy in bulk from sellers, demanded price concessions not made available to small buyers.

An example of secondary-line price discrimination is as follows: seller A has several customers. It sells an identical product to each customer for $1 a unit. One of the customers tells seller A that since it is a large customer, it should be allowed to buy the product for $.90 a unit. Seller A agrees. This is price discrimination in favor of a large buyer and against the other customers. The initial example of price discrimination in which oil company A dropped its gasoline price to one of its retail stations, so that the latter could meet the price of its competitors, is also secondary-line price discrimination. In that example, the oil company gave a price break to one of its customers but not to the others.

Section 2 of the Clayton Act, as amended by the Robinson-Patman Act, applies to both primary-line and secondary-line price discrimination. Sellers may not sell goods to different purchasers at different prices if the result is to injure competitors in either the seller's (primary) or the buyer's (secondary) market. In the seller's market, a seller may lower price to meet competition or where it can demonstrate economies of scale. In a buyer's market, a seller may discriminate between buyers to meet the equally low price of a competitor. A seller can also discriminate between buyers if it can justify the price differential by actual cost savings. However, the Federal Trade Commission, which has the primary responsibility for enforcing the Robinson-Patman Act, does have the right to limit quantity discounts.

The Morton Salt Case, 1948

This case involved secondary-line price discrimination, with injury being sustained by customers who were paying a higher price for salt than their competitors. Morton granted substantial quantity discounts to large-scale buyers of salt. The Federal Trade Commission found that the lower prices granted to grocery chain stores constituted price discrimination, and that its effect was to injure competition between small grocery stores and large chains. The company argued that its quantity discounts were openly available to both small and large stores alike and, therefore, were not discriminatory under the Robinson-Patman Act. Howver, the Federal Trade Commission found that the company had failed to show that the differences in price were justified by cost savings, and an order was issued against the granting of price discounts.

Morton appealed and the case eventually went to the Supreme Court, which held for the FTC. To the argument that the discounts were not discriminatory because they were openly available to all, the Court replied that, in fact, only four or five large buyers were able to use the largest discount. The purpose of the Robinson-Patman Act, it declared, was to deprive a large buyer of any competitive advantage it might secure in lower cost prices, except when the lower prices can be justified by a savings in cost or by a seller's effort to meet a competitor's price.[13] The Morton Salt case established the principle that a seller charged with illegal secondary-line price discrimination must be prepared to justify quantity discounts by showing actual cost savings. This Morton Salt could not do.

The Utah Pie Company Case, 1967

This case involved primary-line, or seller's discrimination. The Utah Pie Company was the leading seller of frozen pies in the Salt Lake City market area. Because of its location, it was able to maintain the lowest prices for pies in the market. During the period from 1957 to 1961, it was challenged at one time or another by three major pie competitors, Pet Milk, Carnation, and Continental, all of which operated in several market areas. Each of these competitors sold pies in the Salt Lake City market at prices lower than what they charged in other markets for pies of like grade and quality. In some cases, pies were sold at below costs. Utah Pie brought an action against each of the three competitors, charging them with a violation of Section 2 of the Clayton Act as amended by the Robinson-Patman Act. The evidence suggested the companies had cut into Utah Pie's share of the market.

In lower court, a jury found price discrimination and judgment was entered for Utah Pie. A court of appeals reversed the decision, holding that the evidence was not sufficient to justify any discrimination to Utah Pie because it still remained the major seller of pies in the Salt Lake City market. The case was appealed to the Supreme Court, which ruled in favor of Utah Pie.[14] The Court cited evidence that lower prices of Pet Milk, Carnation, and Continental could not be justified on the basis of cost. It noted that Pet had sent an industrial spy into the Utah Pie plant and that Continental sold its pies in Salt Lake City at below cost, forcing Utah Pie to lower its price, thus creating some financial damage. In this case, there was evidence of predatory intent by each of the three national competitors to lessen competition.

13. *FTC* v. *Morton Salt Co.*, 334 U.S. (1948).
14. *Utah Pie Company* v. *Continental Baking Company*, 386 U.S. 685 (1967).

The Falls City Beer Case, 1983

A statutory defense to charges of price discrimination provided by the Robinson-Patman Act is that a lower price was made in good faith to meet an equally low price charged by a competitor. The Falls City case involved a claim of price discrimination by an Indiana beer distributor, Vanco, against its former supplier, Falls City, which charged Vanco and other beer distributors in Indiana prices 20 percent higher than those prices paid by the brewer's customers located across the state line in Kentucky. At issue was whether a seller would use the meeting competition defense even though the seller had created the price discrimination by raising prices to a disfavored customer rather than lowering them to a favored customer. It also had used an areawide pricing system instead of adjusting prices on a customer-by-customer basis and had met its Kentucky competitor's lower price in an attempt to gain new customers rather than simply to retain existing customers. The Supreme Court ruled that the meeting competition defense applied to each situation.[15] The decision is important because it provides more flexibility to sellers in attempting to respond to the lower prices of competitors.

The Jefferson County Pharmaceutical Case, 1983

In 1983, the Supreme Court issued a landmark decision on construing the Robinson-Patman Act's prohibition against secondary-line price discrimination. The Court considered whether the sale of pharmaceutical products to state and local government hospitals for resale in competition with private retail pharmacies is subject to the price discrimination restrictions of the Robinson-Patman Act. The evidence showed that drug manufacturers' prices to pharmacies operated by a state university hospital and a county hospital were lower than their prices for the same products to privately owned pharmacies that competed in the same area. A lower court held that because the price-favored pharmacies were government owned, the difference in prices was beyond the intended reach of the Robinson-Patman Act. The decision was appealed to the Supreme Court, which reversed it. It held that sales of products to government-operated facilities that resell in competition with private enterprises are not exempt from restrictions against price discrimination simply because the government is involved.[16]

15. *Falls City Industries* v. *Vanco Beverage Co., Inc.*, 51 U.S.L.W. 4275 (1983).
16. *Jefferson County Pharmaceutical Association, Inc.* v. *Abbott Labs.*, 51 U.S.L.W. 4195 (1983).

ANTITRUST LAWS AND PATENTS, TRADEMARKS, AND COPYRIGHTS

Patents, trademarks, and copyrights convey intellectual property rights to their owners. These rights date back a long time. With the rise of strong nation-states in Europe at the close of the Middle Ages, the kings began the practice of granting patents as a reward to enterprises for introducing new processes and products. As an inducement and reward for developing new inventions, patents were granted to inventors, giving them the right to exclude others from making or using the invention for a number of years. Patent rights are recognized in the U.S. Constitution, which specifies that Congress has power to promote the progress of science by securing for limited times to inventors the exclusive right to discovery. This provision on the making of grants of exclusive rights was implemented by statutes. The Patent Act of 1952 was adopted to codify existing patent statutes, particularly with reference to the conditions for patentability.

Trademarks are also a form of intellectual property. A trademark is a name or symbol used to indicate the source or origin of certain goods. Trademarks, particularly trade names, may be used in a variety of ways. They may be used in advertising that relates to particular products or in institutional advertising that emphasizes the image of a firm. They may be used on product packaging, company letterheads, and even on company buildings. Because of the variety of users and uses possible, effective control of the trademark is difficult. Nevertheless, control is vital to ensure that usage is consistent with the company's image and that the legal rights of the company in its trademark are being protected. Trademarks are registered in the United States Patent and Trademark Office and are issued for a period of twenty years. They come under the jurisdiction of the Lanham Act of 1946, which provides the legal right to register any mark that has become distinctive.

Copyrights are particularly relevant to the publishing and entertainment industries. They vest rights in authors and entertainers that prevent others from using their works without permission. Companies argue that copyright laws are necessary for their survival. They depend on the sale of books or music for their existence. Otherwise, competitors could simply copy best-selling works and participate in their continued sale. With the advent of photocopiers, this would be easy to do. Presumably, firms making photocopies could substantially undercut the original publisher because the former would not have to pay for typesetting or editing, nor would they have to pay royalties. Copyrights are issued by the Copyright Office in the Library of Congress and as of 1978 are protected for the life of the author plus 50 years.

Each of the areas of intellectual property law is important to business firms. Without patent law, successful research would be more difficult. Without the protection granted by trademark law, a business firm could not clearly distinguish its name from those of its competitors. A copyright may be very important in protecting a business firm's interest in certain types of products. However, each area conveys a certain monopoly privilege to its owner; often, they have been used to eliminate competition. Patents have been used to monopolize the sale of a particular line of goods, and patents and trademarks have often involved the use of tying arrangements to lessen competition. Antitrust law is applicable to the use of patents, trademarks, and copyrights when they are used to lessen competition.

Patents

The patent is a seventeen-year monopoly created by statute. It confers on its holder exclusive rights to processes and products, monopoly power that the government deems appropriate as a means of encouraging inventive initiative. The legal monopoly of a patent can protect only the invention claimed in the patent, nothing else. However, patents have formed the basis of various forms of agreements that have had the effect of restricting competition in the marketplace. Attempts to extend the reach of the patent monopoly beyond its proper scope can lead to charges of misuse of the patent, which can prevent the patent owner from enforcing his or her patent against parties injured by the misuse, or to an antitrust violation if the misuse has had or may have the requisite anticompetitive effect. The antitrust laws place the following types of restrictions on a patent monopoly:

1. An arrangement under which the grant of a license is made conditional on the purchase of unpatented supplies from a specified source is merely a form of illegal tie-in sale because the patent is practically a per se violation of Section 1 of the Sherman Act. In rare cases, if there are legitimate technical considerations in using the patented invention, it may be legal to require the licensee to buy special or specially adapted supplies.

2. An attempt by a patent owner to fix the price at which the licensee may sell articles manufactured under the license is narrowly restricted and in practice is almost impossible to justify.

3. The right of the patent owner to license the patent for specified uses may in some circumstances be legal, although as a general rule it is suspect under the antitrust laws. Licenses may be limited geographically in rare situations, but it is almost impossible to do so without running afoul of the law.

4. The practice of package licensing, in which a licensee accepts a license in a package deal, is proper only when the licensee voluntarily accepts the package; otherwise, it is an illegal tie-in situation.

5. The accumulation of patents in a company's portfolio is not in itself illegal, although the purchase of patents may be illegal under the merger provisions of Section 7 of the Clayton Act.

Various sharing devices such as the cross-licensing of patents or the pooling of patents for mutual benefit are not held to be illegal as such, but they generally are declared to be illegal when in the eyes of the courts, they are used as a means of eliminating competition among patent owners and licensees. For example, the Justice Department has challenged long-term agreements between two leading American and Japanese electrical equipment manufacturers, Westinghouse and Mitsubishi, covering both patents and know-how.[17] Each firm has a license to the technology of the other, and each is prevented by the agreement from selling products that use the technology of the other. The broad result has been to keep these two large electrical equipment manufacturers out of each other's home markets — an important consideration for the United States, given the concentrated nature of the electrical equipment market and its history of anticompetitive business practices.

The General Electric Case, 1926

An important case involving the restriction of competition between a company possessing a patent and a license of the patent was the General Electric case of 1926. The defendant in the case, the General Electric Company, owned patents for the use of tungsten filament in electric light bulbs. In 1912, it licensed the Westinghouse Company to make electric light bulbs using its patents. It provided the conditions that Westinghouse sell the bulbs at prices fixed by General Electric and that it follow General Electric's distribution policies. The licensing agreement specifically forbade Westinghouse from selling light bulbs at a price lower than General Electric. Similar agreements were enforced with other licensees of General Electric light bulb patents. The agreements enabled General Electric to maintain around 70 percent of the total light bulb market. It, Westinghouse, and the other licensees of its patents had 93 percent of the market. The government brought suit against General Electric and Westinghouse, charging that the agreement violated Section 1 of the Sherman Act.

The case was dismissed by a district court, and the Supreme Court, in reviewing the case, affirmed the dismissal.[18] The decision in the case looked at the patent licensing arrangement from the standpoint of the patent owner and the licensee. Private advantage rather than the public welfare was made the test of the validity of a license agreement. The

---

17. *U.S.* v. *Westinghouse Electric Corp.*, Cic. No.70-852-SAW (April 22, 1970).
18. *U.S.* v. *General Electric Co.*, 272 U.S. 476 (1926).

Court stated that when a company makes and sells a patented product, it no longer has control over what the purchaser does with it. But it is different when a company licenses its patent to another company to make and sell the product. Should it be able to limit the selling by limiting the method of sale and the price? The Court felt the company (General Electric) could do so, provided the conditions of sale are reasonably adopted to secure financial reward for the holder of the monopoly.

The Gypsum Case, 1948

The Gypsum case, decided in 1948, involved price fixing arrangements among the licensed producers of gypsum wallboard, a product made in accordance with a number of patents. The facts of the case were that the dominant producer, the United States Gypsum Company, entered into a separate patent-licensing and price fixing agreement with each of the principal producers of gypsum wallboard in the United States. U.S. Gypsum had modeled its price fixing activities precisely on the General Electric precedent, fixing both prices and terms of sale for gypsum board. Since each agreement was an individual one, the company maintained that, on the basis of the General Electric case, its license arrangements were legal. The government charged a violation of the Sherman Act and noted the use by the company of a subsidiary to check on the prices of the various licensees to ensure price compliance.

The Supreme Court upheld the government in the Gypsum case. It stated that the formal separateness of the contracts did not alter the reality of a combination to fix prices. Lawful acts may become unlawful when taken in concert. The General Electric case offers no protection for a patent holder, acting in concert with all members of an industry, to issue licenses under the terms of which the industry is regimented, the class of distributors squeezed out, and the prices on unpatented products stabilized.[19] In essence, the case limited the application of the General Electric case in that restrictive powers given a patent holder were narrowed.

Trademarks

Trademarks are also subject to the antitrust laws, particularly when used in restraint of trade. The purpose of a trademark, as originally conceived, was to identify the origin or ownership of a product. They are a vitally important component of the operating marketing mix of

19. *U.S.* v. *U.S. Gypsum Co.*, 333 U.S. 364 (1948).

most successful business firms. Business firms have come to regard trademarks as a strategic device for establishing product differentiation and, through advertising, strong consumer preference. The use of a trade name, a form of trademark, for a wide variety of products will cause the name to become associated intimately with the overall image of the particular business. In this way, firms have sometimes been able to establish a degree of market control that has remained substantially unchallenged for many years. An example is Coca-Cola, which has achieved worldwide recognition. There is nothing wrong with trademarks, provided they are not used to restrict competition in a particular market. There are several types of trademark abuses that can violate the antitrust laws.

1. Tying agreements in which a trademark owner ties the use of the trademark by other parties to the purchase of goods not normally sold or required under the trademark. In the aforementioned Chicken Delight case, the main issue was a tying agreement in which the Chicken Delight franchises had to purchase cooking equipment, dry-mix food items, and other products from the company as a condition for getting the Chicken Delight trademark. It was ruled that the tying product — the license to use the Chicken Delight trademark — possessed sufficient economic power to lessen competition to constitute a violation of the Sherman Act. The tying restrictions imposed by the company were not essential to the protection of its trademark.

2. Exclusive dealing arrangements in which the trademark owner is able to persuade users to use its product to the exclusion of others. For example, General Electric was able to persuade government procurement agencies to establish specifications requiring the use of Mazada light bulbs. It licensed Westinghouse to use the name, but denied its other licensees the same right. Trademarks have also been used to effect a division of markets among the members of an international cartel, with each member of the cartel being given the exclusive right to use the trademark in its own territory.

The Parker Brothers Monopoly Case, 1982

The real estate investment game of "Monopoly" was created during the Depression when people had few jobs, little money, and lots of time on their hands. Paradoxically, the game pertained to making money in real estate when money in any form of activity was hard to make. The creator of the game sold it to Parker Brothers, which obtained a trademark on the name "Monopoly" in 1935. The game went on to become the most popular parlor game of all time, making millions of dollars for Parker Brothers, which was eventually purchased by General Mills.

In 1973, a company called Anti-Monopoly, Inc. began producing and selling a game under the name "Anti-Monopoly." General Mills claimed that "Anti-Monopoly" was an infringement of its trademark rights in "Monopoly." Anti-Monopoly, Inc. then sought a judgment that "Monopoly" was an invalid trademark, and went to court to cancel General Mills federal registration.

The court's decision turned on the factual question of whether "Monopoly" had become a generic term primarily denoting the game itself as distinguished from the game's producer Parker Brothers or General Mills. The court reasoned that if the primary significance of the term "Monopoly" was not the product's but the producer's, then the trademark is valid. On the other hand, when a trademark primarily denotes a product, not the product's producer, the trademark is lost. Applying this set of reasoning, the court concluded that Parker Brothers and General Mills had promoted "Monopoly" so successfully as the name of the game that its source identifying function had been lost. Accordingly, the court found that "Monopoly" had become generic and that its registration as a trademark was no longer valid.[20]

The Supreme Court declined to hear the lower court's invalidation of "Monopoly" as a trademark for the famed real estate investment game. As a consequence, "Monopoly" joins aspirin, linoleum, zipper, and thermos as a generic name unprotected by the federal trademark laws. This case illustrates an important principle of trademark law: a trademark is valid only when it is recognized by the public, not as an identification of the product alone, but as the identification of some particular producer's version of that product. Thus, trademarks are not necessarily forever.

Copyrights

Copyrights have a far more circumscribed use than patents and trademarks in that they are limited primarily to publishing and entertainment. The use of copyrights as an anticompetitive business practice would most likely take the form of a tying agreement. For example, a motion picture company might tie the use of a copyrighted film on television to the purchase of other products from the company. However, the enormous advances in photocopying and other forms of reproduction have increased the importance of copyright laws. In response to new technological changes, Congress enacted the 1976 Copyright Act. Among the rights provided for in the 1976 Copyright Act is that the copyright holder is to be the only person to reproduce

20. *Anti-Monopoly, Inc.* v. *General Mills Fun Group, Inc.*, 684F 2d 1316 (9th Cir. 1982), cert. denied, 51 U.S.L.W. 3613 (February 22, 1983).

the copyrighted work or to authorize such reproduction. However, there are exemptions and exceptions to this general grant of monopoly rights. One exception would be where progress and learning are adversely affected by a lack of access to copyrighted work. This exception involves fair use, which is reasonable but unconsented use of copyrighted works despite the owner's exclusive rights.

The Betamax Case, 1984

In 1976, Universal City Studios and Walt Disney Productions sued Sony, the manufacturer of Betamax, for copyright infringement, alleging that Betamax owners had used their machines unlawfully to copy commercially sponsored television programs exhibited by Universal and Disney. The plaintiffs sought monetary damages and an accounting of profits from Sony, as well as an injunction against the manufacture and sale of the Betamax recorders. As such, the case was an attempt to impose copyright liability on a manufacturer of copying equipment and was a direct threat to the viability of the electronic recording industry. The case also posed an indirect threat to the manufacture and sale of other products capable of being used for copying, such as photocopiers and audio tape recorders.

A circuit court of appeals held as a matter of law that home use of video recorders was not a fair use because it was not productive in that it was not undertaken for any purpose other than to record copyrighted material. Moreover, the court distinguished between video recorders, which are sold for the primary purpose of reproducing copyrighted television progams, and audio recorders and photocopiers, which as stable articles of commerce, do not create copyright problems. The court then held that Sony was liable for contributory copyright infringement because it was aware of the fact that owners of the Betamax machine would use it to reproduce copyrighted materials on television. Sony, ordered to pay damages to Universal and Walt Disney, appealed the case to the Supreme Court.

The Supreme Court ruled that Sony's sale of video recorders to the general public did not constitute infringement under federal copyright laws.[21] The Court held that the sale of a video recorder did not constitute an infringement since it is capable of other uses. The Court stated that many copyright owners, including sports, religious, and educational broadcasters, had encouraged copying of their programs for noncommercial home entertainment. Its decision is important for two reasons. First, it makes clear that private noncommercial taping of

21. *Sony Corporation of America* v. *Universal City Studios, Inc.*, 52 U.S.L.W. 4090 (January 17, 1984).

television programs for later home viewing is a legitimate use of copy-righted materials and, therefore, does not violate copyright laws. Second, and more important, it rejects the proposition that a manufac-turer may be held liable for violating copyright law simply by selling a product, capable of a noninfringement use, to a customer who uses the product in a manner that could constitute an infringement.

SUMMARY

Competition is a hallmark of a free enterprise market economy. It requires, among other things, freedom of entry into a market, and open noncollusive pricing based on market factors. Competition creates incentives for business firms to reduce costs while improving products or services. The benefits of competition disappear when business firms agree on prices or engage in other illegal activity that may unfairly force competitors out of business. Antitrust laws generally prohibit business firms from interfering or restricting free and open competition. Not every restraint on competition violates antitrust laws; rather courts have consistently held that only reasonble restrictions on competition are illegal. The courts have identified a number of different business practices as anticompetitive. Price fixing is one practice, and price discrimination against sellers or buyers is another. Exclusive dealing, tying arrangements, reciprocity, and group boycotts can also be used to lessen competition. Intellectual property, such as patents, also is subject to antitrust law if used to reduce or eliminate competition.

QUESTIONS FOR DISCUSSION

1. What economic injury is likely to result from a group boycott?
2. Give an example of a specific cost justification that can be offered for price discrimination under the Robinson-Patman Act.
3. What is a vertical price fixing agreement? Is it applicable to the Spray-Rite case?
4. What types of unfair business practices were condemned by com-mon law?
5. Why did common law provide no protection against many types of anticompetitive business practices?
6. What is the difference between horizontal and vertical price fixing?
7. Discuss the Morton Salt case of 1948.
8. What is secondary-line price discrimination?
9. Discuss the Utah Pie case of 1967.
10. Why is the Jefferson County Pharmaceutical case important?

Chapter 9
Antitrust Laws and International Trade

Almost all large, and many small, U.S. corporations participate in business outside the United States, with trade and investments in many countries. These corporations now have the power to act as agents of change on societies, economics, and cultures. In particular, the multinational corporation has emerged as the most sophisticated type of organization yet developed to globally integrate economic activity. Some multinationals have sales volumes larger than the gross national product of most countries. But size is only one component of their power; they also control the means of creating wealth and make decisions that touch hundreds of millions of people. They have contributed to the internationalization of production, and in this process, their investment decisions determine the world's allocation of resources and welfare.

However, the global influence of business is by no means limited to U.S. corporations. European and Japanese business firms also operate all over the world, and have invested in plants and equipment in the United States. These firms operate on an ideological basis quite different from our own. American attitudes toward competition, particularly during the 1980s, will have to be reevaluated in light of increased world competition. Given the dynamic nature of international business, the domestic government regulation of business has become much more complex. In regard to the United States, it has become more difficult to apply antitrust laws written during the last century or the early part of this one to corporations that operate throughout the world. Moreover, countries' varying antitrust policies create conflicts of natural interest because international commerce is subject to overlapping jurisdictions.

Although a number of other Western countries have antitrust laws, they are generally not as far reaching as U.S. law. As a consequence, actions taken by a multinational operating in a foreign country may be legal under the laws of its home nation but illegal in the United States. The American view that a freely competitive economic system is the most efficient, most desirable form of society is not necessarily the view held by other major industrial powers. To compete more successfully with U.S. enterprises, the Western European countries and Japan have permitted the use of combinations and cartels of domestic enterprises. One result is that the extent of industrial concentration is greater in many industries in Japan and West Germany than in similar industries in the United States.

APPLICATION OF U.S. ANTITRUST LAWS TO U.S. MULTINATIONALS

American antitrust policy is applicable to any U.S. firm engaged in international business. In regard to foreign commerce in general, U.S. antitrust policy has three separate objectives: to eliminate unreasonable restraints on American exports and imports, to encourage foreign firms to enter the American market, and to prevent American or foreign firms from restraining commerce in the United States through their foreign operations. These objectives are governed primarily by four laws: the Sherman Antitrust Act, the Clayton Antitrust Act, the Federal Trade Commission Act, and the Webb-Pomerene Act. Of these, the Sherman and Clayton acts have had the greatest impact on the multinationals' operations. Through judicial interpretation, the Sherman Act has been extended to apply to both U.S. firms and foreign firms operating in the United States, which permits American courts to govern parties and acts both inside and outside the United States.

Two important concepts pertain to the application of U.S. antitrust laws. One is extraterritorial reach, which is defined as the employment of U.S. domestic antitrust statutes in considering business operations outside American territorial limits. Extraterritorial reach is also the legal basis for controlling the actions of corporations operating outside the United States, thus subjecting worldwide actions to national control. The second concept is the effects test, which means that any action, no matter when or where committed, is subject to U.S. antitrust law if it affects American commerce. This gives the U.S. courts a potentially limitless charter of jurisdiction, because an act committed anywhere in the world conceivably can affect U.S. commerce.

The Sherman Act

The Sherman Act aims primarily at maintaining and promoting interstate and foreign trade or commerce. Both Sections 1 and 2 are applicable to U.S. corporations operating in other countries. Section 1 provides that any contract or combination in the form of a trust or otherwise, or any conspiracy in restraint of trade or commerce among states or with foreign nations, is illegal. Section 2 makes it a crime to monopolize or attempt to monopolize, or combine or conspire with anyone to monopolize, any part of trade or commerce among the states or with foreign nations. To invoke the Sherman Act, involvement in either interstate or foreign commerce is enough. Foreign commerce normally refers to U.S. exports and imports, but the act may also apply to transactions whose impact is entirely outside the limits of the United States if American interests are involved. In the 1968 Pacific Seafarers case, the act set up restraints used solely in shipping between foreign ports, in which any shipments financed by the U.S. government were limited by law to transportation in U.S. ships.[1]

The American Tobacco Case, 1911

The first major international application of the Sherman Act came in the landmark American Tobacco case of 1911.[2] The American Tobacco Company and the Imperial Tobacco Company of Great Britain had agreed to divide markets, with Imperial agreeing not to sell tobacco in the United States except through the American Tobacco Company.[3] The two companies then formed a third corporation, the British-American Tobacco Company, which took over all the foreign business of American and Imperial, though British-American Tobacco could not export to the United States. As a part of its overall decision, the Supreme Court ruled that this allocation of markets illegally restrained trade under the provisions of the Sherman Act. All parties to the agreement, including Imperial Tobacco, were held to have violated the act. The pooling agreement under which the American Tobacco Company and the Imperial Tobacco Company had combined to form the British-American Company was canceled. The Court held that the Sherman Act applied to restraints, including contracts or combinations, that operated to the prejudice of the public by unduly restricting competition.

The Sherman Act has been applied outside the United States by reasons of market power, intent, and effect, although until World War II, the courts required that for an act to be considered a violation of the Sherman Act, it had to be committed within the United States.

In 1927, in a case involving the Sisal Sales Corporation, the Supreme Court declared a conspiracy to monopolize U.S. foreign commerce to be illegal.[4] The Court emphasized the aspect of unlawful results within the United States and asserted that for an act to be illegal it had to be

1. *Pacific Seafarers, Inc.* v. *Pacific Far East Lines, Inc.*, 404 F.2d 804 (D.D.C. 1968).
2. *U.S.* v. *American Tobacco Co.*, 221 U.S. 10C, 31 Sup. Ct. 632 (1911).
3. This was only a part of the American Tobacco Case.
4. *U.S.* v. *Sisal Sales Corporation*, 247 U.S. 268 (1927).

committed by both domestic and foreign firms within the country. After World War II, however, the courts shifted their position to include acts committed outside the United States. The landmark Alcoa case of 1945 established the principle that the U.S. courts could regulate actions conducted outside the United States that have direct and foreseeable economic consequences inside the United States.[5] In the National Lead case of 1947, American and foreign companies were found to have participated in an international restraint of trade in the production of titanium pigments.[6] A majority of the Supreme Court ruled that the Sherman Act was applicable because the restraint affected U.S. commerce. In the Timken Roller Bearing case of 1951, the Supreme Court ruled that a joint venture between Timken and British and French roller-bearing firms created a cartel arrangement to allocate world markets and restrict imports to the United States.[7] In addition, Timken held 30 percent of the British company's common stock and 50 percent of the French company's common stock.

The test of the applicability of the Sherman Act in both the National Lead and Timken cases came to be known as the effects test and enabled an almost unlimited extraterritorial application of the Sherman Act, for almost any commercial enterprise anywhere in the world conceivably could have an effect on U.S. domestic commerce. Agreements made on foreign soil do not relieve an American defendant from the responsibility for restraint of trade. So, at present, proven effects on American commerce may bring totally foreign conduct under the purview of the Sherman Act. No longer is the place where the act occurs the key; rather, when an act or agreement can be shown to have a direct effect on markets within the United States, the Sherman Act will cover it. Of course, it is necessary to have jurisdiction over the party or parties committing the act for this to have any effect. This normally presents no problem with a subsidiary of a U.S. corporation, let alone with the corporation itself.

The Timberlane Lumber Company Case, 1983

Timberlane was a U.S. firm seeking to develop sources of lumber for delivery to the United States from Honduras. Bank of America, which had interests in competing lumber mills, allegedly tried to protect those interests by driving Timberlane out of the Honduran lumber market.

5. The Alcoa case was discussed in Chapter 7.
6. *U.S.* v. *National Lead Co.*, 63F, Supp. 513 (S.D.N.Y. 1945) modified 332 U.S. 319 (1947).
7. *U.S.* v. *Timken Roller Bearing Co.*, 83F, Suppl. 284 (N.D. Ohio 1949) modified 341 U.S. 593 (1951).

The actions of the bank were said to have resulted in attempts to foreclose on mortgages, in the placement of an embargo on the company's property, and in the use of Honduran guards to shut down Timberlane's milling operation. The company's claim relating to the mortage foreclosure was resolved in the Honduran court system, but it also filed an antitrust action in the United States seeking more than $5 million in damages from Bank of America and its Honduran subsidiaries. The case involved a test of the extraterritorial application of U.S. antitrust law.

A U.S. court decided that jurisdiction over this claim would be based on three points: the determination of the effect or intended effect on the foreign commerce of the United States, the type and magnitude of the alleged illegal behavior, and the appropriateness of exercising extraterritorial jurisdiction over an action committed in another country. The court, stating that the first two points were satisfied in terms of U.S. legal jurisdiction, focused on the last part, the extraterritorial jurisdiction, and came to the following conclusions:[8]

1. Applying the U.S. antitrust laws would potentially conflict with the efforts of Honduras to foster a particular type of business climate.

2. Any judgment against Bank of America could be enforced in a U.S. court.

3. Bank of America's acts were directed primarily toward securing a greater rate of return on its investment in Honduras and were consistent with Honduran customs and practices.

4. The insignificance of the effect on U.S. foreign commerce when compared to the substantial effect in Honduras suggested that U.S. jurisdiction not be exercised.

5. That virtually all the illegal activity occurred in Honduras weighed against the exercise of U.S. antitrust authority.

The suit of Timberlane against Bank of America was dismissed by the court.

The Japanese Electronic Products Case, 1983

Dumping is a practice associated with foreign trade where companies faced with overcapacity will unload their products in foreign markets at prices below the cost of production. Two American companies, Zenith and National Union Electric Corporation, filed an antitrust suit against the major Japanese television manufacturers accusing them of a

8. *Timberlane Lumber Co.* v. *Bank of America National Trust & Saving Association*, 574 F. Supp. 1453 (N.D. Cal. 1983); also *Timberlane Lumber Co.* v. *Bank of America*, 549 F. 2d. 597 (9th Cir. 1976).

conspiracy to keep prices high for TV sets sold in Japan, while keeping prices of Japanese TV sets sold in the United States low, causing financial injury to the American companies. A U.S. district court ruled that much of the evidence offered by the two companies was inadmissible, and that the remaining evidence purporting to show the existence of a price conspiracy among the Japanese firms did not sufficiently show proof of a need for antitrust action.

However, a court of appeals reversed the judgment granted by the district court.[9] It concluded that there was sufficient evidence of a price fixing conspiracy. It accepted as evidence the findings of the Japanese Fair Trade Commission on the subject of the conspiracy, despite the differences between U.S. and Japanese antitrust procedures. It was also willing to accept as evidence reports prepared by various experts and the diaries of Japanese company executives — evidence that had been dismissed by the district court as hearsay, based on hearsay, or otherwise unreliable and inadmissible. The judgment of the court of appeals opened the case for further antitrust litigation.

The judgment of the court is important because it provides an example of the ability of the Sherman Act to reach conduct in foreign markets that has sufficient effects on U.S. commerce. Following the well-established rule that the Sherman Act reaches conduct abroad that is intended to and does have an effect on U.S. commerce, the court of appeals acknowledged that a conspiracy among the Japanese companies to fix prices in their home market would in and of itself be beyond the reach of U.S. antitrust law. The court concluded, however, that the Sherman Act does apply if the effect of such an action is to make it possible for the Japanese companies to sell at prices in the U.S. market below production costs. This fact, the court said, is sufficient to justify an antitrust claim, since the collusive setting of dumping prices supports an inference of collective predatory intention to harm U.S. companies.

Almost all international violations of the Sherman Act are per se violations, which are in and of themselves illegal because they impose an unreasonable restraint on trade. Included in these violations are price fixing, division of customers and markets, boycotts or concerted refusals to deal, and tie-in sales. Any of these arrangements is illegal if it affects the flow of imports into the United States, or if it affects the flow of exports out of the United States, or if it has an adverse effect on the domestic commerce of the United States. Both the National Lead and the Timken Roller Bearing cases involved per se violations of the Sherman Act in that there was an attempt either to fix prices or to divide markets.

9. Japanese Electronic Products Antitrust Litigation, GCH Trade Regulation Report, No. 626, 1984.

The Clayton Act

The Clayton Act, particularly Sections 1 and 7, also can be applied to U.S. firms operating abroad. Section 1 includes trade with other nations in its definition of commerce, and Section 7 prohibits one firm from acquiring the stock or assets of another firm when the result may substantially lessen competition or create a monopoly. Section 7 applies to the acquisition of foreign firms by U.S. firms only if the latter are engaged in the foreign commerce of the United States and if the acquisition lessens competition in any part of the country. A transaction that reduces competition does not have to occur within the continental limits of the United States. For example, an American firm could acquire a foreign firm in Argentina that resulted in its controlling the market for a given product in that country. If this restricted American exports to this market, with adverse effects being felt by a particular part of the United States, then Section 7 would apply. The key is whether or not the acquisition will lessen competition in U.S. markets or among U.S. firms engaged in foreign commerce. Thus, the Clayton Act could be used to promote greater competition in a foreign market if the business activities in some way reduced competition in the United States.

A merger between a U.S. firm and a foreign firm not operating in the United States can be challenged by Section 7 of the Clayton Act when the consequence is to reduce competition. In fact, foreign acquisitions can also be challenged under the doctrine of potential competition. In *U.S.* v. *Joseph Schlitz Brewing Company*, Schlitz's proposed acquisition of John Labatt, Ltd., a Canadian brewery, was challenged on the grounds that a small California brewer owned by Labatt was a competitor of Schlitz and that Labatt was a potential entrant on a larger scale in the U.S. market.[10] This doctrine was also applied to the Gillette case.

The Gillette Case, 1975

In this case, resolved in December 1975, the acquistion of Braun, a major European electric razor firm, by Gillette, the leading American manufacturer of razors, was challenged on the grounds that potential competition would be eliminated.[11] The rationale behind this challenge was that a potential entrant, while standing at the periphery of the market, may significantly affect the performance of an oligopolistic

10. *U.S.* v. *Joseph Schlitz Brewing Company*, 253F, Supp. 129 (1966) and 385 U.S. 37 (1966).
11. *U.S.* v. *Gillette Co.*, Civ. No. 68-141 (D.C. Mass., 1975).

industry.[12] This is true whether the potential entrant is domestic or foreign. Gillette, given the nature of its product, does operate in an oligopolistic industry and probably dominates it. That Braun had not entered the U.S. market was not a deterrent to the merger challenge since the company had the ability to enter the market and provide competition. Thus, the merger was not allowed, and Gillette was ordered to create a new company to market Braun's products in the United States.

The Clayton Act requires only that anticompetitive effects be felt in any line of commerce in any section of the United States. The transaction that causes the effects does not have to occur within the geographic limits of the United States, nor do transgressors have to be U.S. firms. Section 7 of the Clayton Act was amended in 1980 to extend to all transactions affecting the interstate or foreign commerce of the United States; previously, it had reached companies only directly involved in such commerce.[13] The amendment provides a firmer basis for the assertion of the broadest possible jurisdiction over international as well as domestic transactions. A merger between two foreign-based companies meets the same statutory standard if it affects competition within the United States.

The Rockwell International Case, 1980

The Justice Department brought an antitrust suit in 1980 against Rockwell International and one of its wholly owned subsidiaries.[14] Rockwell, the largest producer of lubricated tapered plug valves in the United States, and its subsidiary had acquired a stock interest in a British firm that was a principal international competitor of Rockwell's and was also a potential entrant into the U.S. plug valve market. Rockwell and its subsidiary were ultimately required by a consent decree to divest themselves of a 29.7 percent stock interest in the British firm. Pending the divestiture of the stock, the U.S. companies were barred from voting their shares, from attempting to influence the British firm, and from increasing their equity in it. In addition, any acquisition of the assets of the British firm was subject to court approval.

The Pilkington Brothers Case, 1983

Pilkington Brothers, a British company, is the largest float glass producer in the world. It was challenged by the Federal Trade Commission

12. Trade Reg. Rep. 4.345.19.
13. H.R. Rep. No. 871, 96th Cong., 2d sess., 1980, pp. 6-7.
14. *U.S.* v. *Rockwell International Corp.*, No. 80-1401 (W.D. Pa., 1980).

in 1983 for its acquisition of assets in competing Canadian and Mexican firms.[15] The FTC took the position that the acquisitions lessened competition in the manufacture and sale of float glass in the North American market. Pilkington entered into a consent order requiring divestiture of its shares in the Canadian firm within five years and removal of its representatives from the boards of directors of the Mexican firms it had acquired. Although Pilkington was allowed to retain its shares in one Mexican firm, any attempt to amend its charter was subjected to prior FTC approval. Although Pilkington is a British firm, its activities had an effect on competition within the United States.

Tying Arrangements and Exclusive Dealing

Tying arrangements and exclusive dealing prohibited by Section 3 of the Clayton Act are rarely applied to the foreign activities of U.S. business firms. Congress was concerned that extending prohibitions to sales overseas would hinder the ability of U.S. firms to compete in overseas markets with foreign firms. In *Reisner* v. *General Motors*, a New York court ruled that Section 3 was not applicable to the plaintiff's claim that General Motors engaged in tie-in sales of automobile engines and components for sale in Europe for automobiles that were to be sold for European consumption.[16] Likewise, Section 2 of the Clayton Act, which prohibits primary-line or "sellers" price discrimination, would have little application to the foreign commerce of the United States.

The Robinson-Patman Act

Section 2 of the Clayton Act, as amended by the Robinson-Patman Act, prohibits the sale of goods of like grade and quality within the United States at discriminatory prices to two or more purchasers, where at least one of the transactions is in interstate commerce. This is secondary-line or "buyers" discrimination. Unless it can be demonstrated that somehow there is injury to competition within the United States, this provision is not likely to involve foreign commerce.

The Federal Trade Commission and Webb-Pomerene Acts

The Federal Trade Commission Act and the Webb-Pomerene Act also can be applied to multinational corporations. The Federal Trade Com-

---

15. Trade Req. Rep. (CCH) 22, 167 (FTC June 22, 1984).
16. *Reisner* v. *General Motors Corp.*, 511 F. Supp. 1167, (S.D.N.Y. 1981).

mission has concurrent jurisdiction with the Justice Department in dealing with acts that are illegal under antitrust laws. Moreover, Section 5 of the Federal Trade Commission Act supplements the power of Section 7 of the Clayton Act. The Webb-Pomerene Act exempts U.S. firms from the antitrust laws for cooperative participation in export associations. Its purpose is to ensure free access to foreign markets for domestic exports on a basis that will be competitive with foreign exporters. But the act does prohibit the formation of associations when the result is to restrain trade in the United States or to restrain exports of domestic competitors. Section 4 of the Webb-Pomerene Act expands the jurisdiction of the Federal Trade Commission to include unfair methods of competition outside the United States, and Section 5 provides for the registration of all export associations with the Federal Trade Commission.

The Webb-Pomerene Act does not automatically immunize every type of joint export venture from the Sherman Act. There are prohibitions against acts in foreign trade that substantially reduce competition in the United States. In the Minnesota Mining and Manufacturing case of 1950, which involved a joint venture by nine American abrasive manufacturers to establish an export association and create a joint subsidiary in Europe, the Supreme Court ruled that the move would restrict exports from the United States.[17] The Court reasoned that the association would reduce the firms' zeal for competition in the American market. In general, then, the rule for applying Webb-Pomerene is that participating companies in an export association may agree among themselves on prices and allocate world markets for exports, as long as competition within the United States is not affected. In practice, Webb-Pomerene has proved to be of little practical importance because most joint export arrangements may be carried on under the Sherman Act and because U.S. firms selling highly differentiated products have generally not wanted to merge with their competitors.

The Foreign Trade Antitrust Improvements Act, 1982

This act amends the Sherman and Federal Trade Commission acts to exempt from their application export activities that do not have a direct, substantial, and reasonably foreseeable effect on U.S. trade or commerce. The act applies to all U.S. firms engaged in exporting and is supposed to remove antitrust uncertainties by codifying the views of the Antitrust Division of the Justice Department on the proper scope of the Sherman Act with regard to foreign trade. It does not change the fundamental principles that the Sherman Act applies to U.S. export

17. *U.S.* v. *Minnesota Mining and Mfg. Co.*, 92 F. Supp. 947, 1958 (D. Mass. 1950).

and import trade, as well as purely domestic commerce, and to business conduct outside the United States. Basically, the act requires courts to pay closer attention to antitrust claims than they have in the past to better ascertain their effect on the U.S. economy.

Criticism of U.S. Antitrust Laws

Many U.S. business firms claim that American antitrust laws place them at a disadvantage with foreign firms at a time when competition is becoming increasingly global. They argue that investment and sales opportunities are often avoided in the world marketplace for fear they would attract the attention of the Justice Department or the Federal Trade Commission. They also feel the U.S. antitrust laws are more punitive and restrictive than those used by Japan and other competitors. The latter view is reinforced by a study made by the President's Commission on Industrial Competitiveness which, among other things, compared the antitrust policies of the major industrial countries.[18] Although the primary goal underlying U.S. antitrust policy is the promotion of free competition, other countries have other goals of equal or paramount importance, such as the rationalization of industry and the promotion of the public interest in terms of national goals. In the policy area, the United States is unusual in taking a prohibitory, as opposed to a regulatory, approach in applying per se rules of illegality and a structural test for mergers.

In February 1986, the Reagan administration sent to Congress five legislative proposals for improving U.S. antitrust laws. The proposals deal with mergers, triple damages, interlocking directorates, extra-territorial reach, and U.S. industries adversely affected by foreign import competition. The objectives of each proposal are as follows:

1. The proposal dealing with mergers is called the Merger Modernization Act of 1986. It would amend Section 7 of the Clayton Act to distinguish between mergers that enhance competition and mergers that are likely to increase prices to consumers.

2. The proposal dealing with triple damages is called the Antitrust Remedies Improvement Act of 1986. It would permit, for the first time, the recovery of triple damages by the United States when it has been overcharged by antitrust conspirators.

3. The interlocking directorate proposal would remove restrictions on permissible corporate directorships. Currently, a person may not serve on the boards of two or more corporations that compete with

18. The Report of the President's Commission on Industrial Competitiveness, *Global Competition: The New Reality*, vol. 2 (Washington, D.C.: U.S. Government Printing Office, 1985), pp. 188-192.

each other, even if that competition is minimal. The proposal, called the Interlocking Directorate Act of 1986, would permit interlocking directorates where overlaps in the firms' business are small and do not pose any risk in competition.

4. The extraterritorial reach proposal is called the Foreign Trade Antitrust Improvements Act of 1986. It would amend both the Sherman and Clayton Acts to require courts to determine jurisdiction in international commerce cases. It would instruct courts to dismiss such antitrust cases when the exercise of jurisdiction would be unreasonable. Factors to consider would be the presence or absence of a purpose to affect U.S. consumers or competitors and the significance of the effects of the conduct on the United States as compared to the effects abroad.

5. The proposal to help U.S. industries adversely affected by foreign competition is called the Promoting Competition in Distressed Areas Act of 1986. It would provide antitrust relief for industries in that mergers and acquisitions would be less likely to be challenged.

FOREIGN ANTITRUST LAWS AND THE MULTINATIONALS

The attitudes of the United States and of other countries toward the role of antitrust laws in regulating various forms of industrial concentration differ. U.S. antitrust law is based on the principle that competition per se is good. The Western European and Japanese governments do not agree, particularly with respect to foreign trade, feeling that industrial concentration and anticompetitive agreements are beneficial, as long as they lead to increased productivity, economic growth, and the advance of technology. European and Japanese antitrust laws are not directed toward breaking up cartels and combinations, but toward regulating and guiding them in the national interest. This is to be expected, since government is more directive in most European countries and in Japan than in the United States. Several European countries not only permit but encourage agreements, combinations, and mergers among companies for the purpose of rationalizing production. They have encouraged joint research and joint marketing, have permitted pricing agreements, and also have allowed the formation of export cartels.

The United States is often faced with foreign competitors that are allowed to grow much larger relative to their domestic markets than U.S. firms. For example, when concentration is measured by country using the Herfindahl-Hirschman Index, many U.S. industries are less concentrated than those of other major industrial countries.[19] For example, applied to the chemical industry in the United States, the

19. Ibid., p. 189.

Herfindahl-Hirschman Index for the four largest firms in the industry is 682. However, it is 946 for the four largest firms in Japan's chemical industry, 2,246 for the four largest firms in West Germany's chemical industry and 6,566 for the four largest firms in the United Kingdom's chemical industry. The index for the four largest firms in the U.S. steel industry is 937, compared to an index of 1,734 for the four largest Japanese steel firms and an index of 1,442 for the four largest West German steel firms.

Antitrust Laws in Japan

The cartel arrangement has been synonymous with the growth of the modern Japanese economy. In 1880, the first Japanese combines, called *zaibatsu*, were formed. These combines dominated the economy to the point that by the beginning of World War II five family-owned *zaibatsu* produced more than one-half of the Japanese gross national product and controlled 80 percent of the total private overseas investment.[20] After the end of the war, American occupation authorities passed an antimonopoly act to dissolve the *zaibatsu* and to create a free market economy. Later, however, the Japanese government enacted various laws to exempt certain industries from the antimonopoly act. Generally, these laws permitted exemptions for three types of cartels — cartels to prevent excessive competition among smaller enterprises, cartels for export and import industries, and cartels for special rationalization in which economies of scale are involved. These exemptions were designed to improve Japan's position as a world exporter, to stimulate its rate of economic growth, and to enable it to compete effectively with American multinationals. Indeed, the present Japanese antimonopoly legislation permits the development of cartels and other forms of combinations to a far greater extent than is permitted by U.S. antitrust laws.

Japanese government policy, however, has stressed consumer protection against such practices as price fixing. The Japanese Fair Trade Commission has taken action against internal price fixing agreements in such areas as automobile tires, synthetic fibers, petroleum, and household electrical appliances. The commission also has initiated action against false or misleading advertising. With regard to unfair business practices, Japanese antitrust law is as stringent as American law, but with regard to mergers, corporate interlocking directorates, and stockholdings, Japanese law is far more lenient, particularly when international trade is involved. In one merger case, the merger of three firms, each dominant in its field, was allowed on the grounds that it

20. Corwin Edwards, "The Dissolution of Zaibatsu Continues," *Pacific Affairs* (September 1946), 8-24.

was necessary to meet international competition. But mergers that account for more than 30 percent of a given market may be challenged unless it can be demonstrated that foreign competition must be met or that a company is failing. Almost all mergers in Japan have been between competing enterprises; that is, they have been horizontal mergers.

Antitrust Laws in West Germany

West German multinationals also compete with U.S. corporations. In the area of antimonopoly legislation, West Germany passed a law called the "Law Against Restraints of Competition."[21] With respect to cartels and combinations, the law prohibited horizontal and vertical restrictive agreements among groups, including price fixing and market sharing. The law also created a Federal Cartel Authority. One function of the authority is the supervision of cartels, all of which have to register with it. For individual enterprises that have no competition or no substantial competition for a particular category of goods, the authority can initiate court action if an enterprise abuses its position. In addition, all mergers in which the participating firms employed ten thousand or more persons at any time during the previous year, had a turnover of DM 500 million or more, or maintained a balance of DM 2 billion or more in the last completed business year have to register with the authority. Details of horizontal and vertical mergers of business firms also have to be filed with the authority.

The stated purpose of the West German antimonopoly legislation is to improve the functioning of a competitive market system — something to which the Germans historically have been unaccustomed. The government is somewhat ambivalent toward the legislation. For example, mergers are allowed if they are deemed good for the economy as a whole or if they promote the public welfare. The same holds true for cartels. There are exceptions to the prohibition of vertical agreements, particularly with respect to resale price maintenance for branded goods, as long as the products concerned are open to some form of price competition. The German position is that it would be disadvantageous to unilaterally control mergers and concentrations as well as restrictive practices if elsewhere in the same economic area other governments are encouraging them. Indeed, to prevent concentration in certain areas may be to preclude the economies of scale that is one of the chief advantages of the Common Market.

21. Gesetz gegen Wettbewerbsbeschränkungen.

International Antitrust Laws

The antitrust laws of the United States, Japan, and West Germany are national laws that reflect differences in attitudes toward cartels and combinations. In the United States, business practices are illegal if they are prohibited by any of the antitrust laws. In Japan and West Germany, there is an attempt to differentiate between those restrictive practices that may have a harmful effect on a given market situation and those firms operating within the Common Market. A practice is restrictive if it affects trade among member countries or has as its objective the prevention, restriction, or distortion of trade in the Common Market. However, certain transactions are exempt from Article 85 sanctions if they are found to stimulate the general economy and strengthen the position of member states. Article 86 prohibits the abuse of a dominant position within the Common Market or a part of it. The Rome Treaty also created the European Economic Community Commission (Article 60) as the antitrust governing body of the Common Market. Articles 85 and 86 are directed, respectively, at agreements in restraint of trade and abuses of dominant market position, but they contain no provision that deals expressly with mergers and acquisitions.

Significance for U.S. Multinationals

As mentioned earlier, Europe is one of the main areas for investment by U.S. multinationals, and much of the expansion in the Common Market has been through mergers or acquisitions. Both American and European multinationals are free from antimerger prohibitions, for the policy of the Economic Communities has been to promote the integration of firms in the Common Market in order to achieve enterprises of larger scale, and national governments have encouraged economic integration in order to forestall a supposed American takeover of European business enterprises.[22] But it is possible to apply Article 86 to mergers in that it prohibits abuses of a dominant position in the Common Market. The focus is not on the acquisition of one firm by another, but on an abuse that may result from a dominant position achieved by a firm either before or after the merger.

22. Howard Adler and Murray J. Belman, "Antitrust Enforcement in Europe — Trends and Prospects," *Journal of International Law and Economics*, 17 (1974), 31–41.

The Continental Can Case, 1971

The Continental Can case of 1971 illustrates the application of Article 86 to the abuse of a dominant market position.[23] Continental Can, an American manufacturer of metal containers and paper and plastic packaging materials, acquired through its European subsidiary, Europenballage Corporation, a controlling interest in German and Dutch container companies. The European Economic Community Commission initiated action against Continental Can, contending that its acquisitions virtually eliminated competition in light metal containers for canned meats, metal lids, and so on, for a substantial part of the Common Market.

Continental Can appealed to the Court of Justice of the Economic Community, which overruled the commission on the grounds that Article 86 was applicable only to an abuse of a dominant position in a market. It also ruled that an increase in market dominance at the expense of competition could be an abuse but that the ultimate test was whether competition was affected so substantially that any remaining competitors no longer could provide sufficient counterbalance. In this respect, the court found the commission's decision wanting.

The Effects Test

A U.S. company is alleged to have participated in a cartel with a number of other suppliers from the United States and other countries to fix the price of wood pulp sold in the European Economic Community (EEC).[24] Virtually all the conduct alleged to have given rise to the complaint took place outside Europe. Moreover, almost all the U.S. participants and many of the foreign participants in the alleged cartel have little or no corporate presence in the EEC. Rather, they sell through independent agents or distributors or have salesmen in the United States visit European customers from time to time. Nonetheless, the Commission of the EEC has asserted the right to assess substantial fines against the participants in the alleged cartel on the basis of the purportedly adverse effects of the cartel on pulp prices in the EEC. This so-called "effects" test for jurisdiction, which is followed in and to a large extent originated in the United States, is widely accepted in international antitrust law.

23. U.S., Congress, Senate, Committee on Foreign Relations, *Multinational Corporations and United States Foreign Policy: Hearings Before the Subcommittee on Multinational Corporations* (Washington, D.C.: U.S. Government Printing Office, 1975), pt. 10.
24. Information provided by a law firm.

Table 9-1 presents a comparison of antitrust policy in the United States, the European Economic Community, and Japan. There are five areas of comparison — approach, exemptions, enforcement, goals, and structure. The United States is different in its approach to antitrust in that it applies per se rules of illegality and a structural test for mergers. In the area of enforcement, the United States has both rigorous government and private enforcement; for instance, it is the only country to permit triple damages in private antitrust actions. Other countries can grant exemptions from antitrust actions, particularly with respect to mergers, to increase the level of employment or to strengthen domestic enterprises that compete in international markets. It would appear that companies in these countries are able to take advantage of arrangements that would be illegal in the United States.

Table 9-1 Comparative Antitrust Policies

	United States	European Economic Community	Japan
Approach			
Theory	Prohibitory	Regulatory	Regulatory
Practice	Mixed	Regulatory	Regulatory
Exemptions			
Economic/technical	Limited	Yes	Yes
Promote international competitiveness	Limited	Yes	Yes
Enforcement			
Government	Stringent	Mixed	Mixed
Private	Rigorous	Rare	Rare
Damages	Triple	Single	Single
Goals			
Promote competition	Yes	Yes	Yes
Rationalization	No	Yes	Yes
Public good	No	Yes	Yes
Structure			
Degree of enforcement authority independence	High	Low	Low

Source: Report of the President's Commission on Industrial Competitiveness, *Global Competition: The New Reality*, vol. 2 (Washington, D.C.: U.S. Government Printing Office, 1985), p. 191.

Application of U.S. Antitrust Laws to Foreign Multinationals

Antitrust laws are applied equally to U.S. and foreign corporations to preserve competitive market structures and to forbid specific anticompetitive business practices. It is argued that by maintaining a competitive market, such laws do not discourage foreign investment in the United States, but rather make it more attractive than other countries to the foreign investor. In fact, foreign competition has proved to be particularly important to U.S. consumers in two situations. The first is when all or almost all the goods originate abroad, and the second is an oligopolistic situation in which outside competition is needed. As a result, such products as small cars and stainless steel razor blades have become available in the United States largely because of the pressure of the foreign firms selling them here. It is an important goal of antitrust policy to preserve this kind of foreign competition in the American market.

Section 7 of the Clayton Act is the principal statute safeguarding against further industrial concentration in the United States. It prohibits any merger or acquisition that may substantially reduce competition or create a monopoly in any line of commerce in any section of the United States. Foreign direct investment is subject to antitrust scrutiny when such investment involves a purchase, merger, or joint venture with an existing U.S. firm. The antitrust laws are applicable in the following situations: the merger of actual competitors in the U.S. market, the merger of potential competitors in the U.S. market, and joint ventures between potential competitors in the U.S. market. The acquisition of a U.S. company may be the easiest way to enter the U.S. market, but the antitrust laws may prevent the particular acquisition because of its effect on actual or potential competition. A merger between an important exporter to the United States and a significant domestic company will be treated in much the same way as would the merger of two U.S. companies with corresponding shares of the market.

The British Petroleum Case, 1968

In one such case, British Petroleum (BP), already a major petroleum distributor on the East Coast, in 1968 acquired Standard Oil of Ohio (Sohio), which controlled about 30 percent of the Ohio market.[25] The Justice Department objected to the merger on the grounds that BP was a potential entrant into Ohio, Sohio's primary market, and that the merger would foreclose an independent entry into that market. The

---

25. *U.S.* v. *British Petroleum Co.*, Civ. No. 69-954 (N.O. Ohio, 1969), settled by consent decree, 1970 Trade Cases Par. 72, 988.

case was settled by a consent decree under which the merger was allowed to proceed, provided that Sohio divested itself, by sale or exchange for stations in other parts of the country, of stations handling a total of 400 million gallons of fuel per year in the Ohio market. This case is important because it indicates that the Justice Department will challenge acquisitions when a major foreign firm, an actual or potential competitor in the U.S. market, merges or enters into a joint venture with a major U.S. firm in a concentrated market and the effect is to foreclose independent entry or expansion of the foreign firm.

General Motors–Toyota Joint Venture, 1984

In March 1983, General Motors and Toyota, the first and third large automobile companies in the world, announced plans to establish a joint venture to build a four-passenger subcompact car in the United States. Under the agreement, which was approved by the Federal Trade Commission in late 1984, the firms will begin producing 200,000 cars annually at an idle General Motors plant in Fremont, California. The design and engineering of the subcompact is based largely on Toyota's successful compact car. Toyota is to contribute $150 million to the venture, and General Motors is to contribute $120 million and the plant. For each company, there are potential gains. General Motors gains in two ways: it can learn how the Japanese produce subcompacts with such a big cost advantage, estimated at $1,500 to $2,000 over comparable American cars, and it can learn the subtleties of management style that has contributed to the Japanese edge in the world automobile market. Toyota gains in that it establishes a beachhead in the United States at a time when protectionist sentiment against Japanese imports is high.

Any foreign entity that chooses to do business in the United States must do so in accordance with U.S. law, including the U.S. antitrust laws. The General Motors–Toyota joint venture is a good example of the global nature of competition in many industries. The rationale for prohibiting the joint venture on antitrust grounds would be that it would have a significant adverse effect on competition in the U.S. automobile market by decreasing competition between General Motors and Toyota. By the same token, approval of the joint venture would be premised on the market's remaining competitive notwithstanding the combination of the joint venture partners, or indeed, being made more competitive as a result of the better products produced by the joint venture. In the automobile industry, a joint venture between General Motors and Toyota could be permissible and an antitrust matter because of the presence of a number of other foreign competitors, for example, Nissan, Honda, Renault, and others.

Opponents of the joint venture argued that competition would be lessened in the relevant geographic market, that is, in the United States and Canada. General Motors is by far the largest car manufacturer in the United States. At the time of the proposed joint venture, it had 44 percent of total U.S. and Canadian sales. It was also the largest seller of small cars in the United States, with a 27 percent market share, and the third largest seller of subcompact cars in the United States and Canada. Toyota was the second largest seller of subcompact cars in the U.S. and Canada, the fourth largest seller of small cars in the United States, and the fourth largest seller of all cars in the United States and Canada. When the United States and Canada are viewed as a geographic market, and all new cars as a product market, the market can be considered highly concentrated. Moreover, the automobile market has high barriers to entry. The joint venture, its opponents argued, would simply reinforce this concentration.

A second argument against the joint venture was that the U.S. automobile industry, until the 1970s, was a complacent oligopoly. Product innovation was low, prices were high, and management and labor inefficiencies became entrenched. The development that undercut this oligopoly, and eventually made the U.S. automobile companies become more competitive, was an increase in the imports of foreign, particularly Japanese, cars. However, in the 1980s, quotas on Japanese cars imported into the United States were reduced, which created a step backward toward the preservation of the oligopoly, and increased the power of General Motors to set prices in the automobile industry. Cooperation between General Motors and Toyota, opponents argued, would reduce competition in both the United States and Canada, without showing any benefits to consumers.

Supporters of the joint venture argued it was needed to help General Motors, and presumably other U.S. car companies, produce and sell small cars that could compete on an equal footing with the Japanese. It provides competitive benefits because it allows Toyota to avoid any import restrictions on Japanese cars. The venture would also provide a transfer of Japanese management techniques, to which the success of the Japanese auto industry is attributed, to American managers. Furthermore, it provides the Americans with access to superior Japanese technology. The venture will increase the number of small cars in America, allowing American consumers greater choice at lower prices. Finally, the small size of the venture, which has a nominal production of 200,000 cars annually, poses no problem to traditional concentration analysis, whether expressed through the Herfindahl-Hirschman Index or through other measures.

The joint venture was approved by the Federal Trade Commission by a three to two vote.[26]

SUMMARY

U.S. antitrust laws cover much ground. Multinational companies seeking to expand through foreign mergers or acquisitions must be increasingly wary of possible antimerger enforcement. For example, if a U.S. company acquires abroad, or if a foreign company acquires a U.S. competitor, Section 7 of the Clayton Act may be applied. The scope of Section 7 is broad and has been extended to include acquisitions that eliminate potential competition in U.S. markets. Section 1 of the Sherman Act also has widened its application to multinationals. It declares illegal every contract, combination, or conspiracy in restraint of interstate or foreign commerce. The act has been expanded through judicial interpretation to cover parties and acts outside the confines of the United States, which has permitted domestic courts to exercise jurisdiction over foreign nationals and corporations and over U.S. corporations domiciled overseas. The Supreme Court has broadened the interpretation of the Sherman Act to include certain types of conduct regarded as illegal per se. Price fixing agreements, agreements among competitors dividing geographic markets or classes of customers, tying agreements, concerted refusals to deal, and certain kinds of reciprocity agreements are included.

A new dimension has been added to the scope of the multinational corporations. In recent years, the United States has become more attractive as a repository for foreign investment, both direct and portfolio. Both European and Japanese multinationals have acquired U.S. firms and have established branch plants in this country. The impact on the U.S. economy can be regarded as favorable, at least in the short run, since jobs are created and the tax base is expanded. These multinationals also are subject to U.S. antitrust laws. In general foreign firms will be welcomed as long as they provide competition for U.S. firms. But a merger between a foreign and a U.S. firm would be treated the same way as a merger between two U.S. firms. If competition is reduced, the Clayton Act is applicable. If the foreign corporation restrains trade in interstate or foreign commerce, the Sherman Act can be applied.

26. For an analysis of the General Motors–Toyota joint venture see Federal Register, "General Motors Corp. and Toyota Motor Corp.: Proposed Consent Agreement With Analysis to Aid Public Comment," vol. 48, no. 250, December 28, 1983, pp. 57246–57257.

QUESTIONS FOR DISCUSSION

1. Discuss the international application of the Sherman Act in the American Tobacco case of 1911.
2. What is the effects test? Discuss its application to the Timken Roller Bearing case.
3. What is meant by the concept of extraterritorial reach?
4. What is the significance of the Timberlane case?
5. What is the significance of the Japanese Electronics Product case?
6. How do foreign antitrust laws differ from those of the United States?
7. What is the relationship between U.S. antitrust laws and mergers consummated in the United States?
8. What is the significance of *Reisner* v. *General Motors*?
9. What is the significance of the Gillette case?
10. What were some of the issues in the General Motors–Toyota joint venture?

RECOMMENDED READINGS

Brunner, Thomas W., Thomas G. Krattenmaker, Robert A. Skitol, and Ann Adams Webster. *Mergers in the New Antitrust Era.* Washington, D.C.: The Bureau of National Affairs, 1985.

Dunfee, Thomas W., and Frank F. Gibson. *Antitrust and Trade Regulation.* New York: John Wiley and Sons, 1985.

Garson, John R. *Codes of Conduct for Multinational Corporations.* New York: Praeger, 1982.

Neale, A. D., and D. C. Goyder. *The Antitrust Laws of the United States.* 3d. ed. Cambridge, England: Cambridge University Press, 1982.

Rahl, James A. "American Antitrust Policy and Foreign Operations: What is Covered?" *Cornell International Law Journal*, 8 (December 1974), 1–15.

Townsend, James B. *Extraterritorial Antitrust: The Sherman Act & U.S. Business Abroad.* Boulder, Colo.: Westview Press, 1982.

PART IV
SOCIAL REGULATION OF BUSINESS

The point was made in Part II that there have been three major cycles in the government's regulation of business. The first cycle occurred in the last century and involved the passage of antitrust laws to control monopolies and railroad laws to regulate anticompetitive railroad practices. This cycle continued into the early part of this century and culminated in the passage of additional antitrust laws (Clayton Act) and laws to regulate the sale of electric power. The second cycle came during the Depression of the 1930s and was mainly reformative, including reforms of the banking system and the securities market to prevent abuses that had contributed to the collapse of the stock market and the banking systems. The legal environment for the labor unions was thus greatly improved, and the unions then became a countervailing force to business. The third cycle of regulation began in the late 1960s and early 1970s and was social in nature. We are currently digesting this social regulation, which includes the protection of the environment, consumer protection, and the safety and health of the labor force.

Social regulation, unlike the traditional rate-setting regulation for public utilities, is not subject to the market forces and public opinion that can limit costs. The public reaction to rising utility rates, for example, has been an important constraint on public utility commissions. The disparity between intrastate and interstate airline tariffs increased the pressure to deregulate the interstate airlines. Because the price of such regulation is visible, it invites a political response. Furthermore when prices are set above the cost of production, many customers will shop for alternative sources of supply. Thus a decision of the Interstate Commerce Commission to allow value-of-service pricing for interstate trucking and generally to permit interstate truck rates to exceed the cost of service led shippers to find other, unregulated forms of transportation. Similarly, improperly set toll rates induced large users of communications to establish their own microwave systems or to obtain them from non-Bell carriers.

The corrective forces of the market and public opinion do not exist in most areas of social regulation. A businessperson has no alternative but to comply with a mandatory standard if the regulatory agency has sufficient enforcement tools. The cost of health, safety, and environmental standards is not directly observable; therefore, the public cannot separate the mandatory costs from the other costs incurred in producing a pound of aluminum or a ton of paper. Social regulation often entails some aspect of human health or safety that can be used by a regulatory agency to incite strong emotional support for its actions, no matter how extreme or costly they may be. After all, who could be so callous as to be opposed to protecting workers from exposure to a cancer-producing agent? What all this means is that much social regulation cannot be subject to rational economic analysis, even though it is costly and inefficient. A peripheral example is the national social security program, which is in some danger of running out of funds in the near future. Revising it, as President Reagan has attempted to do in order to make the fund more solvent, is tantamount to defiling the holy places in Mecca.

During the 1970s, the federal government extended its involvement in the market system, directing more and more of its effort toward cushioning individual risks and regulating personal and institutional conduct. The cumulative impact of its actions have strongly affected business. In some cases, this was necessary because business was not responsive to public demands for such measures as safer working conditions; in other cases, actions were taken because business became an easy target for the discontent of many special interest groups. There was a conflict between a political system that emphasized public well-being and economic equality and a business system that adhered to a utilitarian goal of efficiency. Government social regulation proved to be quite costly, and people came to believe that somehow costs were never taken into consideration and little attention was paid to finding alternative ways of achieving the same social goals. The Carter administration did try to apply sunset measures to regulation of all types and to new procedures that would require federal agencies to show that their rules were beneficial to the economy and society as a whole. The Reagan administration appeared to increase those efforts.

Many regulatory changes were expected from the Reagan administration, particularly in those rules and regulations that do not help business. An unfettered business, like Prometheus unbound, is supposed to save the economy, solve all social problems, restore the virtue of hard work, and create a new "Golden Age." But earlier business indifference and inaction contributed to many social problems that government then had to try to solve. President Calvin Coolidge once said "The business of America is business," and many business firms still accept this as an article of faith. How business will respond to such problems as protecting the environment and employing minorities without some form of coercion like the threat of losing government contracts is still not known. Also, as was evident in the Chrysler bail out, in restrictions on Japanese autos, and in import quotas to protect the steel industry, business is not at all hesitant to ask for government help when its own ox is being gored.

Chapter 10
Issues of Social Regulation

Broad based in its objectives and enforcement, social regulation encompasses such areas as occupational health and safety, equal employment opportunity, consumer product safety, and environmental protection, areas that have specific social goals — a cleaner environment, safer consumer products, employment of minorities, and so forth. A number of important regulatory commissions, nearly all of which were created during the 1970s, function to enforce the laws designed to achieve these social goals. The most important commissions are the Consumer Product Safety Commission, the Occupational Safety and Health Administration, the Equal Employment Opportunity Commission, and the Environmental Protection Agency. The jurisdiction of each of these relative newcomers extends mostly to the private sector and at times to productive activities in the public sector. Each of these agencies and commissions has a rather narrow range of responsibility, however. For example, the Equal Employment Opportunity Commission is responsible only for employment policies in a given firm or industry. With deregulation, no agency has the complete responsibility it once had.

Social regulation has an enormous impact on business firms, both large and small. Not much more than a decade ago, most business firms were unregulated private enterprises. They were free to design and produce the products they pleased, subject only to consumer acceptance. Marketing practices were subject to management and control, and pricing policies were devised to yield a rate of return on capital based on a standard volume concept. Antitrust laws did not apply to these business firms except as a deterrent to engaging in certain practices. Public utility regulation ruled only public utilities, and about the most interference any business firm could expect from Washington was with respect to bookkeeping involving social security and payroll taxes. Business leaders, of course, complained about Washington, thinking even this amount of interference was excessive, but by and large they were free to manage with few constraints. A businessman could even hire and promote his mother-in-law if he saw fit.

But times have changed, and in instance after instance business firms, both large and small, have been made accountable to the public through legislative or court action, rather than through voluntary action. In great part, the fault was that of business in failing to recognize the changes in American society or, more often, in recognizing the changes but not responding. Another reason was the rise of special interest groups that did not hesitate to alter the political decision-making process to achieve their own goals. The end result was that business firms have become subject to a wide variety of social regulations in a short time. By 1980, they were ruled by detailed government regulations under which almost all phases of their operation were affected. No longer do business firms have complete control over personnel practices: government affirmative action policies have to be considered. Marketing policies have to take into account the possibility of product recall. Today, each auto company now publicly recalls hundreds of thousands of automobiles if serious defects have to be corrected. In many companies, each division has a counterpart agency in Washington with which it must deal — personnel and the EEOC, production and OSHA.

REASONS FOR SOCIAL REGULATION

Justification for social regulation is based partly on the belief that imperfections in the market system are responsible for various social problems. In a market economy, the price mechanism gives people no opportunity to bid against the production and sale of certain commodities and services that they regard as undesirable. There may be many people who would be happier if they could prevent the production and sale of, for instance, alcoholic beverages or the emission of noxious fumes from a chemical plant, and who would gladly pay the price if given the opportunity to do so. But there seems to be no way the market-price mechanism can take these negative preferences into account. The only way this can be done is through government action that places controls on the output of both public and private goods deemed deleterious to the public interest.

A second reason for the onset of social regulation is the externalities created by technological advances. Pollution is an externality because one person can impose a cost on another without having to pay compensation.[1] This other person then demands government protection in the form of regulation prohibiting or limiting the actions of the first person. As our society has become more technologically advanced and congested, one group's meat becomes another group's poison. Airports are necessary to facilitate rapid transportation, but airplane noise damages the environment of those who live near them. Thus these

1. Lester C. Thurow, *The Zero-Sum Society* (New York: Basic Books, 1980), p. 124.

persons will coalesce into a group demanding noise abatement measures. Coal is an important, and often the cheapest, source of fuel in the United States, but there are externalities involved in the mining of it — black-lung disease for the miners plus the despoliation of the environment, particularly after strip mining. Competitive markets are no solution at all to these externalities: a competitive firm will generate as much, or more, smoke than a noncompetitive one does.[2]

A third reason is the preoccupation with the quality of life. Following World War II, the main concern of most Americans was getting a job and buying a car and a house. Memories of the 1930s' Depression were still fresh, and so their requirements were few. But as money supply and real incomes rose, these basic wants were satisifed, and they turned their interest to the quality as opposed to the quantity of life. By the late 1960s, many persons had achieved a level of real income at which they could afford to be concerned about such issues as a clean environment. What fun was it to go to the beach for a vacation if the beach was polluted? This concern about the quality of life extended into other areas as well. Unlike the consumers of the past, who were interested more in the quantity of production to fulfill basic needs, consumers now have come to expect goods and services of better quality and at lower prices; thus laws have been passed in such consumer areas as product warranty and product safety.

A fourth reason for social regulation was a general disenchantment with the American system, resulting from the new social concerns that developed during the latter part of the 1960s. This disenchantment was manifested in several issues. Environmentalists and other groups accused business firms of neglecting their social responsibility to the poor and disadvantaged. Business was also the target of individual crusades, such as Ralph Nader's highly publicized efforts to spearhead improvements in such areas as automobile safety. The criticism of existing institutions, including business, permeated all sections of society. The discontent of the late 1960s did indeed facilitate the passage of social regulation: almost all the major social regulatory commissions, such as the EPA and OSHA, were created in the 1970s, and the principal environmental laws also were passed then. Important consumer laws were also enacted in the early and middle 1970s, the Consumer Product Safety Act of 1972 and the Consumer Product Warranty Act of 1975.

Entitlement was a fifth reason, reflecting the changes in social values. The increase in economic growth during the 1950s and 1960s created what Daniel Bell has called a "revolution of rising expectations."[3]

2. Ibid., p. 125.
3. Daniel Bell, *The Cultural Contradictions of Capitalism* (New York: Basic Books, 1976), p. 275.

Translated into entitlement, it means that anyone who wants to work should be entitled to a job, even under government auspices if necessary. Anyone who is sick is entitled to medical care, and anyone who wants an education should have it. But, more important, entitlement has come to be expressed on a group basis, particularly in the areas of civil rights and social rights. To put it simply, entitlement has come to mean some form of compensation for a particular group. Because society over time deprived particular groups of their rights, those groups are now entitled to higher incomes and equal representation at all levels of the decision-making process, and there are demands that these disadvantaged groups — blacks, women, and specified national minorities — be given quotas or preferential treatment in hiring. Only in that fashion, it is argued, can these historical injustices be redressed. Attention to merit is regarded with suspicion; proportional representation is more important.

To some extent, entitlement is linked to the egalitarian movement that has long been popular in the United States, particularly in the late 1960s. The concept of equality has meant different things throughout American history. The Jeffersonian concept of equality was more attuned to the relationships among a particular group of people, namely, property owners. In other words, there was an equality of the elect. The Jacksonian idea of equality was somewhat simpler. In essence it was that any person was just as good as the next one, that no one should put on airs, for that would be emulating the effete aristocracy in England. In fact, spitting on the floor was probably as good a way as any to demonstrate one's democratic and egalitarian instincts. On the positive side, this kind of equality came to mean the opportunity to get ahead regardless of one's origins. The egalitarianism of the late 1960s also was antielitist; in fact, *elitism* became a pejorative term for any social philosophy opposed to the notion that rigorous egalitarianism was a democratic imperative. Equality was defined in terms of equity; hence the emphasis on equality of result.

THE ADMINISTRATIVE AGENCIES

Almost every type of American business enterprise falls within at least the indirect influence of a number of administrative agencies. It is important to study these agencies and their functions, though first some general points should be made. Administrative agencies, regardless of responsibility, acquire their authority to act from the legislative branch of government. Because they do most of the day-to-day work of government, they make many significant policy decisions. Administrative agencies can be divided into two categories: independent regulatory commissions and agencies that are part of the executive branch of government. In many areas of domestic policy formulation, independent agencies exercise more control, although different economic and political needs have produced administrative agencies exercising vast legislative and adjudicative powers that cannot be classified as independent regulatory agencies. Many executive agencies perform regulatory functions as part of their broader responsibility. Administrative functions can be divided into legislative, judicial, and executive categories and are performed by all types of agencies, although the agencies themselves may differ in the reasons for their creation, principal goals, and organizational structures.

Most regulatory agencies that function within the executive departments possess both quasi-legislative and quasi-judicial powers, just as the independent regulatory commissions do. The power to make rules and regulations has been delegated to these agencies by legislative fiat. The only important difference between an agency rule and a law enacted by a legislative body is that the rule may be slightly more susceptible to attack because it was not made by elected officials. Administrative agencies can also implement policy or legislation through a process of initiating and settling specific cases. They also engage in administrative adjudication, which includes procedures used in deciding cases. For many types of cases, the procedures are carefully outlined: hearings are frequently prescribed, records are required, and so on. Furthermore, there often are elaborate provisions for judicial review, which suggests that if the agencies overstep the boundaries of legitimate authority, redress can always be secured in the courts. However, the scope of the judicial review of particular administrative agency decisions is limited, the logic being that the agency rather than the court is supposed to be the expert in the field in which it has been empowered to act.

Administrative agencies, as agents of Congress, reflect group demands for positive action. They are not supposed to be arbiters like the courts, but rather, they should be activists and initiate policy in accordance with their policy interests. For example, when the Federal Trade Commission (FTC) ferrets out deceptive business practices, either through its own investigation or through information gained from an outside source, it initiates action in the name of the FTC against the party involved. It then adjudicates the very case it initiates. If the case reaches a formal hearing and goes to a hearing examiner for an initial decision, it is not at that point subject to commission control. But after the examiner renders the decision, the commission may reverse it. The result is that the FTC can control the decisions rendered in almost all the cases it initiates.

Sanctions

Government intervention in business carries with it the threat and the actual application of sanctions to achieve desired economic and social outcomes. When industry survival, industrial externalities such as pollution, or both, are of concern, sanctions may often be positive, taking the form of subsidies, tariffs, and tax incentives. When the target is the undesirable behavior of firms or groups of firms within an industry, negative sanctions are often used to induce compliance. These negative sanctions can designate noncompliance either as a criminal offense requiring the imposition of fines, imprisonment, or both, or as a civil offense involving the deprivation of the right or privilege to engage in economic transaction through the loss of licenses, permits, and franchises. For example, the Clean Air Act of 1970, which is administered by the Environmental Protection Agency, subjects willful polluters to fines of up to $50,000 a day and jail sentences of up to two years. Plants can be shut down and permits to operate canceled if pollution continues. Citizens and interest groups have the right to sue in federal court to force polluters, including the federal government, to cease and desist pollution practices.

In applying negative sanctions, the intent is to use the coercive powers of the state to obtain compliance. This is done by announcing to society or its components, including business, that various actions are not to be carried out and to ensure that fewer of them are. Business firms have no choice other than to comply with a mandatory standard if the regulatory agency has sufficient enforcement tools. In addition, the regulatory agencies are expected to amass facts, to apply the law to these facts, and to impose the appropriate sanctions when noncompliance is found. Thus, the intent and process of regulation is more like adjudication than other types of political action. It can be said that violators of economic regulation differ from violators of criminal law only in the degree of responsibilty for societal harm that is attributed to them by policy makers, regulators, and the community as a whole. Firm owners and managers are generally held responsible only for their actions, which are often technical and morally neutral.

The Major Social Regulatory Agencies

The following social regulatory agencies stand in the forefront: the Consumer Product Safety Commission (CPSC), the Environmental Protection Agency (EPA), the Equal Employment Opportunity Commission (EEOC), and the Occupational Safety and Health Administration (OSHA). These and several others of the alphabet-soup variety, in particular the Federal Trade Commission (FTC), are authorized to make rules that have the force of law; in other words, they have quasi-legislative powers. They also possess quasi-judicial power in that they settle disputes and hear and decide on violations of statutes of their own rules. Finally, much of the work of these agencies is administrative, including investigating firms in a particular industry, determining if formal action should be taken, and negotiating settlements.

The Consumer Product Safety Commission (CPSC)

The Consumer Product Safety Act of 1972 created the five-member CPSC, which functions as an independent regulatory commission. The commission is regarded by its critics as the most powerful regulatory agency in Washington.[4] It has jurisdiction over more than ten thousand consumer products and has the power to inspect facilities where consumer goods are manufactured, stored, or transported. The commission can also require all manufacturers, private labelers, and distributors to establish and maintain books and records and to make available additional information as it deems necessary. It can require the use of specific labels that set forth the results of product testing. The greatest impact that this requirement has is in the production process, in which the design of numerous products must conform to federal standards. Since safety standards are formulated at various governmental and independent testing stations, a manufacturer may find that a finished product no longer meets federal standards, and product lines may have to be altered drastically.

The Environmental Protection Agency (EPA)

In July 1970, President Richard Nixon submitted to Congress a reorganization plan to create an independent environmental protection agency. The organization was approved, and the EPA was created in the executive branch. Functions that formerly belonged to the Department of the Interior relating to studies on the effects of insecticides and pesticides in the United States were transferred to this agency. Also transferred were functions originally belonging to the Department of Health, Education and Welfare (now the Department of Health and Human Services), including the creation of tolerance norms for pesticide chemicals under the Food, Drug, and Cosmetics Act. The EPA was given supervision over air pollution standards as set forth in the Clean Air Act of 1970 and its subsequent amendments. The EPA also

4. U.S., Congress, Joint Economic Committee, *Hearings on the 1979 Economic Report of the President*, 96th Cong., 1st sess., 1979, p. 32.

was given jurisdiction over water pollution control programs, particularly those set forth in the Water Pollution Control Act of 1972, including the setting of water quality standards. The jurisdiction of the EPA was later extended to apply to the Noise Control Act of 1972, and it became responsible for setting noise emission standards for products identified as major sources of noise. The EPA has jurisdiction over all the major federal environmental laws passed during the last decade.

The Equal Employment Opportunity Commission (EEOC)

The EEOC was created by the Civil Rights Act of 1964 as an independent commission, and its enforcement authority was greatly increased by the Equal Employment Opportunity Act of 1972. The EEOC now has the power to investigate and act on a charge of a pattern or practice of discrimination, whether filed by or on behalf of the person or group claiming to be aggrieved or by a member of the commission. The EEOC has the right to initiate civil suits against employers, labor unions, and any group accused of practicing employment discrimination. What is more, private individuals and groups have the right to sue under Title VII of the Civil Rights Act of 1964. The EEOC also can investigate company records to see whether a pattern of discrimination exists and to subpoena company records if necessary. Every employer, labor union, and organization subject to the Civil Rights Act and subsequent executive orders must keep records that can determine whether unlawful practices have been committed, and they must furnish to the EEOC a detailed description of how persons are selected to participate in job-training programs.

The Federal Trade Commission (FTC)

Few regulatory agencies have had more effect on business than the FTC has. It was created by the Federal Trade Commission Act of 1914 with the intent of preventing unfair business methods of competition. It was given the power to prevent persons or corporations, except banks and common carriers subject to the various acts that regulate interstate commerce, from using unfair methods of competition in commerce. It was also given the power to investigate the practices of business combinations and to conduct hearings. The FTC was authorized to issue cease-and-desist orders and to apply to a circuit court of appeals to enforce them. A violation is punishable by contempt of court. In addition to cease-and-desist orders, the commission was given the power to negotiate terms of agreement, known as consent decrees, violations of which are cause for court action. The commission was also given joint responsibility with the Justice Department for enforcing certain prohibitions that pertain to various forms of price discrimination.[5]

The FTC has come to be an all-purpose agency. It administers not only the antitrust laws of the United States but a wide variety of other laws as well. The Wheeler-Lea Act of 1938 authorizes the FTC to protect the public by preventing the dissemination of false or misleading food and drug advertisements. Also under the FTC's jurisdiction are various labeling acts such as the Wool Products Labeling Act and the Fur Products Labeling Act. The McCarran Insurance Act of 1948 gives the commission partial jurisdiction over the insurance industry. This responsibility is complex because it varies according to the differences in state law. Then there is the Consumer Credit Protection Act of 1968 or, as it is more commonly called, the Truth-in-Lending Act, which requires that borrowers be made aware of basic information about the cost and terms of credit. Finally, the Consumer Product Warranty Act of 1975 provides minimum disclosure standards for written consumer product warranties and defines federal content standards for these warranties. The act also extended the FTC's consumer protection powers to cover local consumer abuses when state or local protection programs are inadequate.

The Occupational Safety and Health Administration (OSHA)

OSHA was created as an agency of the Department of Labor to administer the Occupational Safety and Health Act of 1970. The purpose of the act is "to assure safe and healthful working conditions for working men and women."[6] It requires employers to comply with safety and health standards promulgated by OSHA. In addition, every employer is required to furnish for each of his or her employees a job "free from recognized hazards that are causing or are likely to cause death or serious physical harm."[7] Although this "general duty" clause might appear to be an all-encompassing requirement for the provision of safety, it was clearly Congress's intent that the clause be limited in scope and relied on infrequently. "Recognized hazards" were defined in the congressional debate as those that can be detected by the common human senses, unaided by testing devices, and that are

5. The FTC has jurisdiction over Section 2 of the Clayton Act, which covers primary-line price discrimination, and over the Robinson-Patman Act, which amended Section 2 to prohibit secondary-line price discrimination. This refers to the sale of the same good to different buyers in the same geographic area at different prices when there is no cost difference.
6. Robert Stewart Smith, *Occupational Safety and Health Act* (Washington, D.C.: American Enterprise Institute for Public Policy Research, 1976).
7. Occupational Safety and Health Act, Section 5a.

generally known in the industry as hazards.[8] Further, a firm can be penalized under the general duty clause only if the unsafe condition has been cited by an inspector and the employer has refused to correct it in the specified time.

Other Social Regulatory Agencies

Several other federal government agencies also have responsibility for social regulation. One is the Food and Drug Administration (FDA), which was created in 1906. It is responsible for the safety, effectiveness, and labeling of drugs, foods, food additives, cosmetics, and medical devices. The National Highway Traffic Safety Administration (NHTSA) was created in 1970. It is responsible for establishing safety standards for trucks and automobiles and certifies compliance with emission standards for pollution control.[9] The Mine Safety and Health Administration (MSHA) was created in 1973 and is responsible for setting and enforcing mining health and safety standards. Then there are a number of government agencies that enforce rules that may have an indirect effect on social regulation. An example would be the meat and poultry inspection programs of the U.S. Department of Agriculture (USDA).

It is also important to realize that state and local governments have their counterparts of the federal regulatory agencies. For example, federal laws pertaining to employment practices are not the only laws that affect business; state and local government laws also exist. The degree of state and local laws varies; some state and local governments provide agencies to enforce the laws, whereas others have voluntary enforcement. State and local governments also have environmental regulations. The first consumer protection laws were passed by state and local governments long before consumer protection laws were introduced by the federal government.[10] Regulations governing occupational safety and health and the sale of food and drug products are also among state and local laws.[11]

IMPACT OF SOCIAL REGULATION

There is more to social regulation than the creation of a number of new federal government agencies. The laws creating these agencies also

8. U.S., Congress, Senate, Committe on Labor and Public Welfare, *Legislative History of the Occupational Safety and Health Act of 1970*, 92nd Cong., 1st sess., 1971.
9. There is also the National Transportation Safety Board (NTSB) that sets rules on needed improvements in transportation safety.
10. State laws date back to before the Civil War.
11. State and local laws also would cover the sale of alcoholic beverages to minors.

defined ambitious health, safety, and equity goals and in some cases established strict deadlines for attaining them nationally. Frequently, the laws restricted agency discretion to moderate regulatory standards in view of economic or other social considerations. They empowered citizen complainants and advocacy groups to sue business firms for damages and government agency officials for failure to promulgate strict rules of enforcement. Business firms were required to undertake extensive recording and reporting of their compliance efforts and of the social and environmental consequences of their operations. Local governments and school districts that failed to meet federally pre-scribed regulatory requirements concerning affirmative action and other goals were threatened with debarment from federal grants-in-aid and contracts.

Social regulation affects society in three ways. First, income is re-distributed; resources are transferred from one income group to another. Second, there are compliance costs, which include the costs of filling out a number of required government reports, adding facilities for handicapped workers, buying equipment to make the environment cleaner, training for minority workers, and making the workplace safer. Finally, social regulation influences business organization. Management must be responsible for the internal monitoring of company operations, including the hiring and promotion of personnel, product evaluation, and other areas. It is also subject to liabilities and restrictions; for example, management has to be responsible for product safety.

Income Redistribution Effects

Environmental protection offers one example of how social regulation results in the redistribution of income. Although most Americans favor a clean environment, the issue itself has been primarily the preserve of the upper-middle classes.[12] Lower-income groups do not rank a clean environment high on their list of priorities because it often threatens their income-earning opportunities, the loss of jobs if plants close. For the lower-income groups, basic needs have to be satisfied; the quality of life does not become important until real incomes rise. For those Americans who can afford boats, summer homes, and leisure time at the beaches, a clean environment ranks as a desideratum; for those Americans who cannot afford these, a clean environment is of less importance.

A transferral of income from society as a whole to a small number of beneficiaries can also occur. For example, OSHA's coke-oven standards protect fewer than thirty thousand workers, but they are paid for by everyone who consumes a product containing steel, that is, nearly all

12. Thurow, *The Zero-Sum Society*, pp. 104-105.

of us. Mine safety standards protect miners but at the expense of the general population. These goals, although desirable, may have few tradeoffs because special interest groups are often able to lobby effectively for particular objectives without considering their overall cost, which is borne by the general public.[13] Rather than impose costs on a group that can organize political pressure, regulators often impose them on the general public.

Costs to Business

Social regulation of business involves direct monetary costs. One cost involves the paperwork required for compliance with federal and state rules and regulations. One company, Goodyear Tire and Rubber, in one year produced 345,000 pages of paper, weighing 3,200 pounds, to meet various OSHA regulations.[14] Paperwork adds to the cost of doing business. Another cost is the cost of installing new machinery and equipment. Emission control devices to control pollution, such as smokestack screens and scrubbers, are expensive to install. New hiring and training facilities for handicapped workers have to be provided by the employer. Recruitment of women and minorities is also a business cost. Then there are government administrative costs in social regulation that are paid out of taxes. These costs have increased over the years.[15]

Opportunity costs also have to be considered in measuring the cost of social regulation to business. Since resources are scarce, the decision to use them means something else has to be given up. When resources are used in a certain way, there is a simultaneous choice not to use them another way. The opportunity cost then can be defined as the value of the benefit lost as a result of choosing one alternative over another. It is an important concept because the real cost of any activity is measured by its opportunity cost, not by its outlay cost. Thus, if resources are used to control pollution, society gives up all the other goods and services that might have been obtained from these resources; for example, resources devoted to the production of pollution control equipment might have been used to produce houses instead.

Obviously many benefits are to be derived from social regulation — cleaner air and water, less noise, safer products, safer working conditions, and better employment opportunities for women and minorities.

13. Robert W. Crandall, "Curbing the Costs of Social Regulation," *Brookings Bulletin*, No. 15 (Winter 1979), pp. 1-3.
14. *Wall Street Journal*, October 28, 1980, p. 1.
15. For example, total U.S. Budget outlays for the Enviromental Protection Agency amounted to $4.5 billion in 1985 compared to $700 million in 1977.

Few would argue for the complete elimination of all forms of social regulation and a return to the old status quo. However, there are costs involved in achieving various social goals. Every benefit has a cost, and some sort of tradeoff is often necessary to balance economic and social goals. For example, the social goal of clean air and water can lead to closing down a marginal plant and lost jobs.[16] The economic goal of national independence from foreign sources of energy can lead to mining more coal in the United States, which can result in strip mining and the despoliation of the environment.

Impact of Social Regulation on Business Organization

The former chairman of the Council of Economic Advisers, Murray Weidenbaum, identified a "second managerial revolution."[17] The first was noted by Adolphe Berle and Gardiner Means more than four decades ago.[18] These observers of the U.S. corporate scene were referring to the divorce of the modern corporation's formal ownership from its actual management, which occurred when the corporate form of management superseded the Carnegies, Fords, and Rockefellers of the world and became the dominant business unit by the end of the last century. In the corporate system, the owner of industrial wealth was left with only a symbol of ownership, and the power, responsibility, and substance that had been an integral part of ownership were transferred to a separate management group. In other words, Standard Oil was no longer both owned and operated by the Rockefellers; rather, it was operated by a managerial class, completing the separation of ownership from management.

The second managerial revolution, according to Weidenbaum, came when the decision-making process shifted to Washington. This shift was particularly pronounced in the early 1970s when the federal government took on the unprecedented tasks of coordination and setting priorities. A vast cadre of government regulators can influence and often control the key decisions of the managers of business firms.

16. Several years ago, CBS News broadcast a story about the impact that water pollution control had on the logging industry of western Maine. After the trees were cut down, they were floated down the rivers and lakes by loggers to the sawmills to be cut into lumber. However, bark from the trees would peel off and clog the waterways. EPA then required that the logs be carried by trucks to the sawmills. The loggers, most of whom had little formal education and depended on logging for their livelihood, became unemployed.
17. Murray L. Weidenbaum, *Government Mandated Price Increases* (Washington, D.C.: American Enterprise Institute, 1975), p. 82.
18. Adolphe A. Berle and Gardiner C. Means. *The Modern Corporation and Private Property*, rev. ed. (New York: Harcourt Brace Jovanovich, 1968).

For example, management has had to accept responsibility for the internal monitoring of company operations, including the hiring and promotion of personnel, personnel safety, product evaluation and safety, and so forth. Government regulation has changed the process of production, one reason being that an increased share of investment became unproductive. Distribution has had to be geared to the possibility of product recalls, and labeling and advertising have had to be reconsidered. Affirmative action has had an impact on employment policies that call for special recruitment, training, and facilities for the benefit of women, minorities, and handicapped persons.

Cost-Benefit Analysis

Interest has risen in efforts to determine more precisely the costs and the benefits of government regulation. The motive for incorporating cost-benefit analysis into the regulatory decision-making process is to achieve a more efficient allocation of government resources. In making an investment decision, for example, business executives compare the costs to be incurred with the expected benefits, namely, revenues. Very likely the investment will be pursued only if the expected costs are less than the expected revenues. If an investment will yield $20 and the cost of the investment is $10, the benefits obtained will be $10. Cost-benefit analysis can also be applied to opportunity costs. For example, suppose a business firm has $10 that it wishes to spend on some benefits. Its rational response would be to examine a number of possible uses of the money and ask which of them would yield the greatest net benefit.

Government agencies do not face the same array of benefits and costs. If the cost of an agency action exceeds the benefits, the result may not have an immediate adverse effect on the agency. Because analytical information on economic costs has rarely existed in the public sector, decision makers have largely been unaware of approving a cost-inefficient regulation. An objective of requiring government agencies to perform cost-benefit analyses is to make the regulatory process more efficient and to eliminate actions that, on balance, generate more costs than benefits. This result is not assured by cost-benefit analyses, since political and social considerations often dominate the decision-making process; however, even in those cases cost-benefit analyses can provide valuable assistance.

Cost-benefit analyses has to be put in a proper perspective. It is only one tool that can be used to reach a decision concerning a socially desirable action. Critics of cost-benefit analyses contend that, even though costs may outweigh benefits, a project may still be socially desirable. Helping the poor and disadvantaged is an example. The effects of regulatory decisions are distributed unevenly, which inevitably involves the imposition of values and ideology. Nevertheless, with cost-benefit analyses, the question of how much additional cost should be incurred to achieve a specific goal can be more precisely answered.

REFORMING GOVERNMENT REGULATION

Discontent with government social regulation of business developed in the late 1970s and early 1980s. There were several reasons for this discontent. One was the cost of social regulation. A study prepared for Congress's Joint Economic Committee estimated that in the fiscal year 1979 the cost to the public of federal regulations was $102.7 billion — $4.8 billion for the administrative costs of the regulatory agencies and $97.9 billion for the compliance costs by the private sector of the U.S. economy.[19] Another study, done by Paul Sommers of Yale University, determined the annual cost of regulation in 1977 was between $58 billion and $73 billion.[20] He also estimated regulatory costs for eleven sectors of the economy, which were grouped into three categories — economic, environmental, and health, safety, and product quality. By far the largest cost to society, set at between $30 billion and $45 billion, came from the regulation of health, safety, and product quality.

Another source of discontent with regulation was less tangible than costs. Many persons disliked the government's specifying for them the means of achieving protective objectives and requiring constant assurances, in reports and other forms of paperwork, that compliance was taking place. Alienation also occurred when government officials appeared to be overbearing and highhanded. Public discussion of regulation was dominated by horror stories about antagonistic regulatory officials who were out to get business. For example, the Consumer Product Safety Commission did not exactly help its image with business when its chairman was quoted as saying, "If a company violates our statutes, we will not concern ourselves with its middle-level executives; we will put the chief executive in jail. Once we put a top executive behind bars, I am sure that we will get a higher degree of cooperation."[21]

19. U.S. Congress, Joint Economic Committee, Subcommittee on Economic Growth and Stabilization, *The Cost of Government Regulation of Business*, 95th Cong., 2nd sess., 1978.
20. Paul Sommers, "The Economic Costs of Regulation: Report for the American Bar Association" (New Haven, Conn.: Yale University, Department of Economics, 1978).
21. Gerald R. Rosen, "We're Going for Companies 'Throats,'" *Dun's Review* (January 1973), p. 36.

Regulatory Reform Under President Carter

President Carter's Executive Order 12044 on Improving Government Regulations was issued in March 1978. It marked an attempt to bring better management to the regulatory process. It contained requirements for economic impact analysis and set criteria for identifying significant regulations that necessitated regulatory analyses. The requirements covered those regulations that cost the economy $100 million or more annually or that produced a noticable increase in costs or prices for individual industries, levels of government, or geographic regions. As an adjunct to the executive order, President Carter also created an interagency Regulatory Analysis Review Group (RARG) to assist agencies in improving regulations. Composed primarily of representatives from the executive branch agencies with regulatory responsibilities, it was supposed to concentrate on those regulations that imposed especially large costs or that promised to set precedents. The Council on Wages and Price Stability (COWPS) was given statutory authority to intervene on its own behalf in regulatory proceedings.

Regulatory Reform Under President Reagan

In 1980, Ronald Reagan promised to get the government off people's backs. In this he had widespread support from business and from the population as a whole. That the regulatory pendulum had swung too far and had reached a point of diminishing returns was the feeling of many. It had to be pushed back, and that Reagan promised to do if he were elected. But President Carter also proclaimed the regulatory reforms implemented during his presidency.[22] The unanimity with which both candidates attacked overregulation signaled an important change in public philosophy.

Regulatory reform was a key element of President Reagan's economic recovery program of the early 1980s, along with government expenditure restraints, tax cuts, and monetary stability. Executive Order 12291, issued on February 17, 1981, directed government agencies to use cost-benefit analysis when promulgating new regulations, reviewing existing regulations, or developing legislative proposals concerning regulation. Administrative decisions on regulations were to be based on adequate information about their need and their economic consequences. Not only did the benefit from regulation have to exceed

---

22. Regulation is used in a broader sense. During the Carter administration, the airline, trucking, and railroad industries were deregulated. However, they had been regulated as natural monopolies by the Civil Aeronautics Board and the Interstate Commerce Commission.

the cost, but the approach chosen had to maximize net benefits. Regarding major regulation, government agencies were required to publish Regulatory Impact Analyses (RIAs) that set forth conclusions about the cost-benefit balance of feasible alternatives.[23] RIAs had to include a description of the potential costs and benefits of the proposed regulation, as well as a description of feasible cheaper alternatives with an explanation of the legal reasons why such alternatives, if proposed, could not be adopted.

President Reagan also created the Task Force on Regulatory Relief, whose responsibility was to review proposed regulations, using the guidelines established by Executive Order 12291. During 1981, the task force earmarked one hundred existing rules and paperwork requirements for review, and more than a third of those reviews resulted in action to eliminate or revise the rules and programs involved.[24] Executive Order 12291 also created a new Office of Information and Regulatory Affairs (OIRA) in the Office of Management and Budget (OMB). In effect, OIRA was to become the gate through which all important regulations had to twice pass on their way to becoming law. It must receive all RIAs at least sixty days before an agency's publication of a Notice of Proposed Rule Making (NPRM) and, if unhappy with an agency's draft, it can delay publication of that notice until the agency has responded to its concerns.

The accomplishments of the Reagan administration in reducing regulation, in particular, social regulation, have been mixed. Although the American public may say it wants government off its back, it is ambivalent about what is does want from government.[25] Opinion polls continue to show high levels of public support for various forms of social regulation. An overwhelming majority of Americans support cleaning up the environment even though a lower rate of economic growth results. In a technologically dynamic society, new chemical hazards and new varieties of social injustice will inevitably emerge from time to time. Catastrophic environmental accidents, such as the ones at Bhopal and Chernobyl, fill the evening news and remind people of the need to protect the environment in which they live. Environmentalists and consumer protection groups watch government agencies for signs of ineffectiveness or flagging regulatory zeal, and business firms

23. Majority rules and regulations consisted of those that had any of the three following effects: an annual effect of $100 million or more; a major increase in costs or prices; or a significant adverse effect on a specific industry or on the economy in general.
24. *Economic Report of the President* (February 1982), p. 142.
25. George C. Eads, "White House Oversight of Executive Branch Regulation" in Eugene Bardach and Robert A. Kagan, eds., *Social Regulation: Strategies for Reform* (San Francisco, CA.: Institute for Contemporary Studies, 1982), pp. 177-184.

have shown opposition to attempts by the Reagan Justice Department to modify affirmative action.

SUMMARY

Social regulation came into being because society's first line of defense — the market mechanism — had not been effective in eliminating certain social problems. The market mechanism had not prevented air and water pollution, high death rates in highway accidents, unsafe or shoddy consumer products, or the improvement of the economic lot of minorities and women. During the late 1960s and early 1970s, social regulation expanded rapidly. A number of major regulatory laws were passed by Congress, each imposing some kind of limitation on business. Several new federal regulatory agencies were created, including the Consumer Product Safety Commission, the Environmental Protection Agency, and the Occupational Safety and Health Administration. These agencies have the right to regulate certain business activities. This regulation creates compliance costs for business, such as the cost of paperwork and the cost of installing pollution control machinery. The direct costs of running the regulatory agencies are paid out of taxes or from government borrowing.

QUESTIONS FOR DISCUSSION

1. Discuss the reasons for social regulation of business.
2. How does social regulation differ from economic regulation?
3. What is opportunity cost?
4. What is meant by entitlement and egalitarianism?
5. Discuss the two types of administrative agencies.
6. Discuss how sanctions can be used to control business activities.
7. What is cost-benefit analysis?
8. What impact does social regulation have on business organization.
9. How do federal regulatory activites affect the U.S. economy?
10. Discuss some of the regulatory reforms established by the Reagan administration.

RECOMMENDED READINGS

Bardach, Eugene, and Robert A. Kagan. *Social Regulation: Strategies for Reform.* San Francisco, Calif.: Institute for Contemporary Studies, 1982.
Breyer, Stephen. *Regulation and Its Reform.* Cambridge, Mass.: Harvard University Press, 1982.

Cegler, Allen J., and Burdett A. Loomes, eds. *Interest Group Politics.* Washington, D.C.: Congressional Quarterly Press, 1983.

Lindblum, Charles. *Politics and Markets.* New York: Basic Books, 1977.

Love, Lester B. *The Strategy of Social Regulation: Decision Frameworks for Policy.* Washington, D.C.: Brookings Institution, 1981.

Noll, Roger G., and Bruce M. Owen. *The Political Economy of Deregulation: Interest Groups in the Regulatory Process.* Washington, D.C.: American Enterprise Institute, 1983.

Stone, Alan. *Regulation and Its Alternatives.* Washington, D.C.: Congressional Quarterly Press, 1983.

Zeckhauser, Richard J., and Derek Leebaert, eds. *What Role for Government? Lessons from Policy Research.* Durham, N.C.: Duke University Press, 1983.

Chapter 11
Equal Employment Opportunity Policies and Their Impact on Business

As mentioned earlier, the newer type of government control differs from the older, more formal type of government regulation of business. It is directed more toward achieving the various social goals of particular interest groups. More important to business is that these controls cut across virtually every kind of private industry. Thus, the Environmental Protection Agency or the Consumer Product Safety Commission has a much broader area to regulate than did the Civil Aeronautics Board, which governed only one industry. The impact of these newer agencies is extensive. Environmental controls apply to all companies, as do requirements for consumer product safety. Moreover, these and other agencies have attempted to bring about social change through the government procurement process — a leverage that few business firms can resist.

A third area of the government's social control of business is affirmative action, the federal Equal Employment Opportunity Commission's term for hiring and promoting women and nonwhites. Because business firms are required to meet affirmative action goals, the federal government has intervened in their personnel practices. The purpose of affirmative action is to ensure equal employment opportunities for all people, regardless of race, sex, religion, or national origin. To put it another way, sex, color, and age cannot be used as criteria to deny hiring or promotion. Noncompliance by employers with affirmative action goals can lead to severe penalties; for example, American Telephone and Telegraph had to pay $75 million in 1973 to employees who charged that discrimination had deprived them of past promotions and raises.

To a considerable degree, affirmative action policies are linked to what Daniel Bell has called a "revolution of entitlement."[1] It used to be that economic growth brought rising expectations, which meant simply the desire for higher material living standards. But modern society has come to believe that each person is entitled to at least a

1. Daniel Bell, *The Cultural Contradictions of Capitalism* (New York: Basic Books, 1976), pp. 232-236.

minimum and decent standard of living, including the right to a job, protection against the various vicissitudes of life — unemployment, sickness, accidents, and old age — and the right to certain social amenities, such as decent housing. This revolution of rising entitlement has also spread to the areas of civil rights, political rights, and social rights. Disadvantaged groups — blacks, women, and others — demand preferential treatment, arguing that only in this way can historical injustices be redressed. Equality of opportunity is no longer sufficient in itself; equality of representation is the desired goal.

DISCRIMINATION AND THE DISTRIBUTION OF INCOME

The rationale for government intervention in employment policy and education is that equal opportunity is a desideratum of the American democratic system — everyone should have the same opportunity to achieve material success, the usual goal. When opportunity is equal, competition and market forces determine one's worth in the marketplace. The idea behind equality of opportunity is that if everyone is given the same, or substantially the same, starting position in a race, the winners will have achieved their rewards through merit rather than through any favored position. Reward will be based on merit, and the result will be a society based on the principle of meritocracy.[2] Logically if everyone is given the same opportunity and there is no discrimination based on sex, age, or other factors, the rewards should be distributed fairly uniformly, without much difference between sexes or among races.

Equality of opportunity has worked better in theory than in practice, however, though the United States has probably done a better overall job of encouraging this equality, particularly by offering mass education, than has any other country. The problem is there are a number of impediments to achieving true equality of opportunity. Clearly, if there is discrimination — on the basis of sex, color, religion, or any criterion outside professional qualifications — there is no genuine equality of opportunity. And equality of opportunity is only part of the picture, for in the United States, it is linked to the distribution of income. In part, income inequality is based on differences in people's abilities; sometimes, however, it is based on sex, race, and age, which have little or no relation to ability. First, therefore, it is necessary to discuss the distribution of income in the United States.

2. Daniel Bell, "On Meritocracy and Equality," *The Public Interest*, 29 (Fall 1972), pp. 18-21.

Trends in Income Distribution

Recent decades have witnessed no real movement toward greater equality in the distribution of income in the United States. There is an apparent conflict between the goals of an egalitarian society and the existence of marked income inequality. However, in a market economy there is bound to be inequality because income distribution is based on institutional arrangements, such as the pricing process, that are associated with this type of system. High prices are set on scarce agents of production and low prices on plentiful agents. In terms of rewards to labor, those persons whose skills are scarce relative to demand enjoy a high level of income, whereas those whose skills are not scarce do not. In a market economy, people are supposedly rewarded on the basis of their contribution to marketable output, which, in turn, reflects consumer preferences and income.

Table 11-1 presents income distribution in the United States for a thirty-five-year period. The frame of reference is personal income, which includes that part of national income actually received by persons or households and income transfers from government and business. Wages and salaries, income from rental properties, interest, and dividends are part of personal income. The table indicates little change has occurred in the distribution of family income based on quintiles. The lowest fifth of family income recipients received around 5 percent of total personal income during the period, and the highest fifth received around 42 percent.[3] There was also little movement of the in-between groups. For those families in the second quintile, there

Table 11-1 Distribution of Family Income in the United States, 1947–1983 (percent)

	1947	1960	1971	1979	1983
Lowest Quintile	5.0	4.9	5.5	5.3	4.7
Second Quintile	11.9	12.0	11.9	11.7	11.2
Third Quintile	17.0	17.5	17.3	17.2	17.1
Fourth Quintile	12.1	23.6	23.7	24.4	24.3
Highest Quintile	43.0	42.0	41.6	41.4	42.7

Source: U.S. Department of Commerce, Bureau of the Census, *Current Population Reports*, "Consumer Income, 1983," March 1985, table 17, p. 47.

3. For perfect equality in income distribution to exist, each quintile would have to receive exactly 20 percent of personal income. Perfect income inequality would exist if the highest quintile got 100 percent of personal income.

was a slight decrease in personal income, for those families in the fourth quintile, some increase.

Demographic Characteristics of Income Distribution

Political and economic traditions in the United States have been focused on the rights of the individual — equality of opportunity, voting rights, and support for those people who in some sense have fallen below society's norm of acceptability. However, the United States has become a pluralistic society, and a group consciousness has developed, with each group wanting a larger share of the national economic pie. Therefore, a more complete analysis of income based on the demographic characteristics of sex, race, and age is necessary. Disparities in income distribution related to each of these characteristics exist. Affirmative action and comparable worth policies represent a demand for government economic policies that focus attention on eliminating differences based on these characteristics.

Sex

In 1983, the median income of households headed by a male was $23,104, and the median income of households headed by a female was $8,510.[4] The median income of single men was $15,510, and the median income of single women was $10,000. There were several reasons for these differences in income. A greater percentage of males were in the labor force, and a greater percentage worked full time. Another reason was a greater concentration of males in the higher-paying occupations. Well over one-half of all women in the labor force were concentrated in relatively low-paying clerical and service occupations. On the other hand, men outnumbered women by three to one in management, professional, and technical jobs. In such high-paying occupations as engineering, accounting, and medicine, men outnumbered women more than four to one.

Moreover, women have not substantially lowered the earnings gap between them and men. In 1947, the median income of women employed outside the home was 47 percent of the median income of men; the 1983 figure was 59 percent.[5] Despite large structural changes in the economy and major antidiscrimination legislation, the economic

4. U.S. Department of Commerce, Bureau of the Census, Current Population Reports, *Monthly Income of Households in the United States: 1983*, March 1985, pp. 1-4.
5. Ibid., p. 3.

well-being of women in comparison with that of men also did not improve much in terms of average income. In 1959, women earned on the average 62 cents for every dollar men earned; in 1983, they earned 69 cents for every dollar earned by males. Although the gap was narrowed during the period 1979–1983 and will continue to be narrowed in the future as women increase their participation in the work force, there is an offset in that women have more financial responsibility for children today than in 1959 because many more of them are single heads of families.[6]

Race

In 1983, white mean household income was $29,875, whereas black mean household income was $18,317, or around 60 percent of white mean income.[7] Hispanic mean household income was $21,020, or around 73 percent of that of white households. The much lower black household income can be explained in part by the high concentration of households headed by women. About 47 percent of black households were headed by women, compared to 25 percent for white and Hispanic households. In 1984, 51.7 percent of households headed by a black female had an income below the poverty level.[8] There is also a difference in income between white and black workers who are single. Single blacks had a mean income of $9,729 in 1983 compared to a mean income of $14,282 for single whites.[9] The difference in income can be explained by a greater percentage of blacks in part-time employment and by their concentration in low-paying jobs.

Age

Both men's and women's income increases in the early years and peaks between the ages of forty-five and fifty-four.[10] For example, the highest average annual income for males with a college education is reached at age 49, after which it declines. This pattern also holds true for college-educated females, for both males and females with high school educations, and for all occupational categories except unskilled workers. This in itself does not prove age discrimination, for a number

6. Victor R. Fuchs, "Sex Differences in Economic Well-Being," *Science*, April 25, 1986, pp. 459–464.
7. Current Population Reports, p. 5.
8. *Economic Report of the President 1986* (Washington, D.C.: February, 1986), Table B-29, p. 286.
9. Current Population Reports, p. 6.
10. Ibid., p. 10.

of factors are at work. As family income needs decrease, many men wish to increase their leisure time and are less willing to work overtime. Many women have not participated in the labor force for an extended time, and many break the continuity of their employment to bear children.

Causes of Income Differences

Differences in the distribution of personal income do not prove discrimination, owing to differences in people's ability, motivation, education, work experience during a given year, and even lifelong work experience. How much income differential, for instance, between men and women, is due to differences in experience or performance on the job, which may be difficult to measure, or due to discrimination is a hard question to answer. The income differential almost disappears when men's and women's earnings are compared within detailed job classifications and within the same plant. In the narrow sense of equal pay for the same job in the same plant, little difference between men and women may exist. But the focus of the problem is only shifted, not eliminated, for then it is necessary to explain why women have a job structure so different from that of men and why they are employed in different types of establishments. This point is made clear in Table 11-2.

Sex Stereotyping

Beliefs about differences between the sexes play an important role in the organization of any society. They are a part of a society's cultural norms and have existed since time immemorial. In the United States, these beliefs can be divided into three categories.[11] First, the traditional belief about the role of women is that their place is in the home. This assumption is held by employers, parents, men, and women in varying degrees. It is invidiously implied that when women work it must be for pin money or for diversion from the chores of domestic life. Second, there are beliefs about the gender differences relevant to male-female relationships. For example, women are more governed by emotions than men, which underlies in part the belief that women should be subordinate to men in the workplace. Third, there are beliefs that assume innate differences between the sexes, that women lack aggressiveness and a capacity for abstract thought, for example.

11. Barbara F. Reskin and Heidi I. Hartmann, eds., *Women's Work, Men's Work: Sex Segregation on the Job* (Washington, D.C.: National Academy Press, 1986), pp. 37-41.

Race Discrimination

In the case of blacks and minorities, income differences can be explained in part by overt discrimination. Over an extended time, blacks have been systematically denied the same educational opportunities as whites, which is reflected in the occupations of blacks. A majority are in the low-pay, low-skill jobs. There has also been discrimination in hiring and promotion policies toward minority groups. Often the discrimination is indirect, as in testing, which although it can be a legitimate device to find out something about employee aptitudes and qualifications, may be culturally biased in favor of certain types of job

Table 11-2 Employment in the Ten Largest Occupations for Men and Women, 1980

Ten Largest Occupations for Men	Percentage Male	Percentage Female
Managers	73.1	26.9
Truckdrivers	97.7	2.3
Janitors	76.6	23.4
Supervisors, production	85.0	15.0
Carpenters	98.4	1.6
Supervisors, sales	71.8	28.2
Laborers	80.6	19.4
Sales representatives	85.1	14.9
Farmers	90.2	9.8
Auto mechanics	98.7	1.3
Ten Largest Occupations for Women		
Secretaries	1.2	98.8
Teachers, elementary	24.6	75.4
Bookkeepers	10.3	89.7
Cashiers	16.5	83.5
Office clerks	17.9	82.1
Managers	73.1	26.9
Waitresses and waiters	12.0	88.0
Sales clerks	27.3	72.7
Registered nurses	4.1	95.9
Nurses aides	12.2	87.8

Source: Barbara F. Reskin and Heidi I. Hartmann, eds., *Women's Work, Men's Work: Sex Segregation on the Job* (Washington, D.C.: National Academy Press, 1986), p. 21. Used by permission.

applicants. Blacks and other minorities have been unable to obtain jobs commensurate with their training.

Age Discrimination

The poet Byron once wrote: "The days of our youth are the days of our glory."[12] No society believes that more than Americans, who are firmly committed to the pusuit of youth. Aging is something to be avoided at all cost, for age carries with it certain stereotypes. That older persons lose their mental faculties and are unable to perform as well as younger workers is a not uncommon belief in the workplace where employers have often discriminated against older workers. Employers have also often refused to hire workers because of their age. Older workers have been denied promotions and have been eased out of their jobs so that employers can hire younger, presumably more productive, workers.

Antidiscrimination Laws

There exists a massive legal and regulatory apparatus to protect workers against most forms of discrimination in private firms and government. As Table 11-3 indicates, this apparatus is relatively new. Although the more important laws will be discussed in some detail later, it is important to differentiate between equal employment opportunity and affirmative action. Equal employment opportunity, which stems from the Civil Rights Act of 1964, is a policy ensuring that all applicants for employment, as well as current employees, are treated equally and are not discriminated against on the basis of sex, race, or national origin. Affirmative action is a policy by which employment opportunities for women, minorities, and the handicapped are enhanced. Affirmative action goes beyond equal employment opportunity from the standpoint of hiring and promotion; it is specifically associated with Executive Order 11246 and Executive Order 4.

AFFIRMATIVE ACTION

Affirmative action means active efforts by employers to correct any racial, sexual, or other minority imbalances that may exist in a work force. The general principle behind affirmative action is that a court order to cease and desist from some harmful activity may not be suffi-

12. *Stanzas Written on the Road Between Florence and Pisa*, stanza 1.

Table 11-3 Summary of the Most Common Federal Rules and Regulations

---

Civil Rights Act of 1964 — prohibits discrimination on the basis of race, color, religion, and national origin regarding civil rights

Title VI — prohibits discrimination on the basis of race, color, religion, or national origin under educational programs receiving federal financial assistance. Applies primarily to the student

Title VII — prohibits discrimination in employment on the basis of race, color, religion, sex, or national origin

Pregnancy Discrimination Act — prohibits discrimination in employment on the basis of pregnancy, childbirth, or related medical condition

Rehabilitation Act of 1973 — designed to ensure equal opportunities in employment for qualified handicapped persons

Section 503 — requires government contractors to take affirmative action to employ and advance in employment qualified handicapped persons. Applies to employment only

Section 504 — prohibits discrimination against the handicapped in federally funded programs or activities. Covers employment and students

Disabled and Vietnam Era Veterans Readjustment Act of 1974, Section 402 — requires government contractors to take affirmative action to employ and advance in employment qualified disabled and Vietnam era veterans

Title IX of the Education Amendments of 1972 — prohibits discrimination on the basis of sex in any educational programs receiving federal financial assistance

Age Discrimination in Employment Act, as Amended 1967 — prohibits discrimination on the basis of age (forty to seventy) in employment

Age Discrimination Act of 1975, as Amended — designed to prohibit discrimination on the basis of age in programs or activities receiving federal financial assistance. Excludes from its coverage most employment practices

Equal Pay Act of 1963 — prohibits discrimination in salaries on the basis of sex

Executive Order 11246 of 1965 — prohibits discrimination in employment on the basis of race, color, religion, national origin, or sex in institutions with federal contracts over $10,000

Executive Order 4 of 1971 — requires affirmative action from employers who hold government contracts

---

cient to undo the harm already done or even to prevent additional harm as a result of a pattern of events set in motion by the previous illegality. For example, racial discrimination is one area in which an order to cease and desist may not be enough to prevent continued discrimination. If a firm has engaged in racial discrimination for years and has an all-white work force as a result, simply to stop explicit discrimination will mean little as long as the firm continues to hire its current employees' friends and relatives through word-of-mouth referral. Clearly, the area of racial discrimination is one in which positive or affirmative steps of some kind appear reasonable — which is not to say the particular policies actually followed make sense.

Affirmative action is far more comprehensive than simple employment discrimination, which may entail only one person over some issue such as age or sex. It requires employers with a federal contract to evaluate their work forces, to analyze their employment needs, and to solicit actively to obtain more minority employees. Affirmative action programs must meet certain minimal requirements in which the burden is on the employer. A primary requirement is a written description of the efforts being made to achieve equal employment opportunity. A program must contain certain basic information. For example, the work force must be analyzed to determine where minorities are being underutilized, why they are being underutilized, and how this can be corrected. Goals and timetables must be actual commitments. Additionally, an employer must inform all recruiting sources of this affirmative action policy and of the firm's desire to recruit more minority employees, in keeping with its goals and timetables. There also must be a specific objective with regard to promotions; for a firm just to state that it will attempt to promote women or blacks to responsible positions is insufficient.

The Development of Affirmative Action

The principle of affirmative action goes back much further than the civil rights legislation of the 1960s and extends well beyond questions regarding ethnic minorities or women. In 1935, the Wagner Act prescribed affirmative action as well as cease-and-desist remedies against employers whose antiunion activities had violated the law. Thus, in the landmark Jones and Laughlin steel case, which established the constitutionality of the act, the National Labor Relations Board ordered the company not only to stop discriminating against employees who were union members but also to post notices in conspicuous places announcing they would reinstate back pay to unlawfully discharged workers.[13] Had the company been ordered merely to cease and desist from economic retaliation against union members, the effect of its past intimidation would have continued to inhibit the free-choice election guaranteed by the National Labor Relations Act.

The Civil Rights Act of 1964

The Civil Rights Act of 1964 was an attempt to eliminate all forms of discrimination in employment. Its genesis was in the Civil Rights Acts of 1866 and 1870, both of which were designed to preclude employment discrimination on the basis of race and color.[14] Section 703 of Title VII of the Civil Rights Act of 1964 obligates employers, labor unions, and government agencies not to discriminate on the basis of race, color, religion, sex, or national origin. Section 704 of Title VII provided for the creation of the Equal Employment Opportunity Commission (EEOC), which consists of a five-member board appointed by the president with the approval of the Senate for a term of five years. Section 701 defines an employer subject to the act as a person engaged in an industry affecting commerce who has fifteen or more employees for each working day in each of ten or more calendar weeks in the current or calendar year. The section also puts employment agencies and labor unions under the jurisdiction of the act. Title VI of the act precludes discrimination on the basis of race, color, sex, or national origin in federally aided employment programs.

The Civil Rights Act of 1964 has been criticized on the grounds that it requires compensatory or preferential treatment of minority groups to compensate for past discrimination. In other words, is anything more than equality of treatment justified under the Fourteenth Amendment's corollary statutes? But the intent of Congress in passing the act was reasonably explicit. Senator Hubert Humphrey of Minnesota, one of the drafters of the legislation, pointed out that it did not force employers to achieve any kind of racial balance in their work forces by giving any kind of preferential treatment to any individual or group.[15] He went on to say there must be an intention to discriminate before an employer can be considered in violation of the law. In fact, Section 703 of the Civil Rights Act states that employers, employment agencies,

13. Harry A. Millis and Emily Clark Brown, *From the Wagner Act to Taft-Hartley* (Chicago: University of Chicago Press, 1950), p. 97.
14. U.S. Equal Employment Opportunity Commission, *Laws and Rules You Should Know* (Washington, D.C.: U.S. Government Printing Office, 1975), p. 91.
15. U.S. Equal Employment Opportunity Commission, *Legislative History of Titles VII and XI of Civil Rights Act of 1964* (Washington, D.C.: U.S. Government Printing Office, 1969), p. 3005.

and labor unions are not required to grant preferential treatment to any individual or any group because of race, color, sex, religion, or national origin on account of any imbalance that may exist with respect to the number or percentage of persons of any race, sex, religion, or national origin.

Executive Orders

Subsequent executive orders declared it a matter of public policy that affirmative action must be taken to rectify the discrimination against minorities. The policy of affirmative action was first proclaimed by President Lyndon Johnson in an executive order in 1965.[16] It states that in all federal contracts or in any employment situation that uses federal funds, employers have to prove they have sought out qualified applicants from disadvantaged groups, have to provide special training when necessary if qualified applicants cannot be found immediately, and have to hire preferentially from minority group members when their qualifications are roughly equal to those of other applicants. This executive order also applies to women. Another executive order banned discrimination by contractors on the basis of age, and an executive order in 1967 banned discrimination in federal employment on the basis of race, sex, color, and national origin.[17] Directors of federal agencies are required to draw up a positive program of equal employment opportunity for all employees, and to hire more women and minority members at all levels. In the early 1970s, affirmative action was extended to universities, and each school with federal contracts was asked to provide data on the number of women and minority persons in each position, academic and nonacademic, and to set specific goals for increasing the number of women and minority members in each classification.

Executive Order 4   Executive Order 4 of 1971 is the basis of most affirmative action programs. Under this order, affirmative action is required from all employers who hold federal contracts. The type of affirmative action employers must take is determined by the nature of the federal contract they hold. A written affirmative action program, demanded by the Office of Federal Contract Compliance (OFCC) regulations, applies to all nonconstruction contractors and subcontractors of the federal government and to agencies of the federal government that employ fifty or more employees and have a contract in excess of $50,000 a year. All business firms or government agencies

16. Executive Order 11246.
17. Executive Order 11375.

that meet these criteria must file a written affirmative action program that contains a statement of good-faith efforts to achieve equal employment opportunity. Such efforts must include an analysis of deficiencies in the use of minorities, a timetable for correcting such deficiencies, and a plan for achieving these goals. In addition, an employer must include an analysis of all major job categories to determine where women and minorities are being underutilized and an explanation of why they are being underutilized.

Sanctions can be used to enforce compliance with Executive Order 4. Failure to develop an affirmative action program can lead to possible cancellation of existing contracts and elimination from consideration for future contracts. If a contractor has set up an affirmative action program at each of his or her plants, the OFCC will grant a precontract award conference during which every effort must be made to develop an acceptable affirmative action program. If the contractor has no program at all or an unacceptable one, the agency can issue notice, giving the contractor thirty days to show cause why enforcement proceedings under the executive order should not be instituted. If the situation is not remedied within this period, the OFCC will commence formal proceedings leading to the cancellation of all existing contracts or subcontracts the firm may have. It is also possible for the OFCC to initiate lawsuits against contractors who fail to live up to their affirmative action policies.

Revised Order 14 In July 1974, the Department of Labor gave final approval to its own Revised Order 14 on the procedures that federal agencies must use in evaluating government contractors' affirmative action programs. Among other things, contractors must list each job title as it appears in their union agreements or payroll records, rather than listing only job group, as was formerly required. The job titles must be ranked from the lowest paid to the highest paid within each department or other similar organizational unit. Further, if there are separate work units or lines of progression within a department, separate lists must be provided for each unit or line, including unit supervisors. For lines of progression, the order of jobs in the line through which an employee can move to the job must be indicated. If there are no formal progression lines or usual promotional sequences, job titles must be listed by departments, job families, or disciplines, and in order of wage rates or salary ranges. For each job title, two breakdowns are required. Besides the total number of male and female incumbents, it is also necessary to have the total number of male and female incumbents in each of the following groups: black, Chicanos, American Indians, and Asians.

Other Antidiscrimination Laws

There also are laws that deal with particular forms of discrimination. The Age Discrimination in Employment Act of 1967 forbids any form of discrimination based on age. Particularly mentioned are those workers between the ages of forty and seventy. Employers cannot discharge or refuse to hire any person on the basis of age, nor can they segregate or classify persons on the basis of age when this criterion would deprive them of opportunities for promotion. The Equal Pay Act of 1963 precludes differences in wages based on sex and is applicable to employers with public contracts. The Vocational Rehabilitation Act of 1973 requires federal contractors to take affirmative action in hiring the handicapped. The Equal Employment Opportunity Act amended the Civil Rights Act of 1964 to vest more power in the federal enforcement agencies, particularly the Equal Employment Opportunity Commission (EEOC). The EEOC can initiate lawsuits against employers believed to be guilty of violating the antidiscrimination laws.

Enforcement of Affirmative Action

The enforcement of affirmative action programs is concentrated in a number of federal agencies, including the Office of Federal Contract Compliance, which is responsible for direct government contracts with business firms, and the Equal Employment Opportunity Commission, which was created by the Civil Rights Act of 1964. Jurisdictions overlap among the Department of Labor, the Department of Health and Human Services, the Department of Justice, the EEOC, and the federal courts. All these agencies also have regional offices, which vary significantly in their practices. Moreover, even though one federal agency approves or requires a given course of action, following such an approved course of action in no way protects the employer from being sued by another federal agency or by private individuals because of these very actions. Indeed, federal agencies have sued one another under the Civil Rights Act.

The Equal Employment Opportunity Commission was created by the Civil Rights Act of 1964 and its enforcement authority was greatly expanded by the Equal Employment Opportunity Act of 1972. The EEOC is empowered to investigate and act on a charge of a pattern or practice of discrimination, whether filed by or on behalf of a person claiming to be aggrieved or by a member of the commission. The commission has the right to initiate civil suits against employers, labor unions, or any group accused of practicing employment discrimination. Private individuals also have the right to sue under Title VII of the Civil

Rights Act of 1964. In addition, the commission can investigate company records to see whether a pattern of discrimination exists and to subpoena company records if necessary. Every employer, labor union, or organization subject to the Civil Rights Act and the executive orders must keep records enabling the determination of whether unlawful practices have been committed and must furnish to the commission a detailed description of the manner in which persons are selected to participate in job training programs. Employers and labor unions have to keep posted in conspicuous places on their premises notices approved by the commission setting forth excerpts from or summaries of the pertinent provisions of the Civil Rights Act and information pertinent to the filing of a complaint.

Title VII of the Civil Rights Act of 1964, as amended by the Equal Employment Opportunity Act of 1972, allows a person who thinks he or she has been discriminated against to file a complaint, called a charge, with the EEOC. The charge has to be filed within 180 days after the alleged discriminatory practice has taken place. The EEOC defers to a state or local agency when such an agency exists. After deferring for the required period, or when the state or local agency completes its process, the EEOC assumes jurisdiction of the charge and notifies the employer or labor union accused of discrimination. Because there has been a backlog of approximately sixty thousand charges, it can be a long time before the EEOC begins investigating the charge. The burden of proving no discrimination is on the employer or union. Because records and witnesses have to be provided, this can be time-consuming and costly. If the EEOC decides that the charge of discrimination is accurate, it can require that corrective measures be taken.

Legal remedies under the Civil Rights Act and related presidential executive orders range from cease-and-desist orders through individual reinstatement and group preferential hiring to cutting off all federal contracts to the offending employer. Lawsuits also may be filed under the provisions of the Equal Employment Opportunity Act of 1972. The federal government's most effective means of enforcing compliance with affirmative action goals is the money it spends. One way or another, most business firms derive some part of their revenue from government spending, and the loss of a contract means a loss of revenue. The latter is a virtual sentence of death to a research firm or a university, for they depend on federal money to maintain their competitive standing. Of course, employers also want to avoid lawsuits of the type that led to AT&T's $75 million settlement in 1973 on employees who had charged that discrimination had deprived them of past promotion and raises. The impact of this lawsuit on all firms and, for that matter, on unions, has been enormous.

Application of Affirmative Action

From the Civil Rights Act and the executive orders has come the principle of disparate or unequal treatment. There is disparate treatment when members of a minority or sex group have been denied the same employment, promotion, transfer, or membership opportunities as have been made available to other employees or applicants. These people must at least be afforded the same opportunities as had existed for other employees or applicants during the period of discrimination. The result of the principle of disparate treatment has been a series of lawsuits involving affirmative action. The impact of these lawsuits on business firms' personnel practices or, for that matter, on all employers, including educational institutions, is considerable. Some of the more important suits are discussed below.

The AT&T Case, 1970

In 1970, the American Telephone and Telegraph Company asked the Federal Communications Commission for a 9 percent increase in long-distance telephone rates. Lawyers from the Equal Employment Opportunity Commission persuaded the FCC not to act on the request until the company changed its policies with regard to women and minority employees. The EEOC took the position that discrimination had been institutionalized in the company's employment policy and moved to change it to provide more jobs at all levels for women and minority groups. In addition, the commission asked for restitution to compensate workers for past discrimination, according to the principle that payment must be made to certain females and minority group employees, even though they had never applied for better-paying jobs because they knew it was company policy not to give them those jobs.

The results of this case had far-reaching implications for business. AT&T agreed to promote 50,000 women and 6,600 minority group workers and to hire 4,000 men to fill such jobs as operators and clerks, jobs traditionally held by females.[18] By 1974, AT&T had also agreed to pay $75 million in compensation to groups that the government said had been victims of discrimination. Some 1,500 female college graduates who held management jobs between 1965 and 1971 but who were, according to the government, kept out of certain training programs received $850,000; 500 switchroom helpers at Michigan Bell received $500,000; and 3,000 women in craft jobs received to $10,000 each.[19]

18. See U.S. District Court, Eastern District of Pennsylvania, Civil Action No. 73-149, Consent Decree, 1973.
19. Diane Crothers, "The AT&T Settlement," *Women's Rights Law Reporter,* vol. 1 (Summer 1973), pp. 8-12.

AT&T also agreed to use an elaborate system of goals and timetables to ensure fair representation in the employment of women and minority groups in the future. A planned utilization of female and minority groups had to be specified for fifteen affirmative action job classifications covering all the Bell System's subsidiaries.

The Weber Case, 1979

The United Steelworkers Union and Kaiser Aluminum entered into an agreement covering an affirmative action plan designed to eliminate racial imbalance in the Kaiser Aluminum plants. Black hiring goals were set for each plant equal to the percentage of blacks in the respective local labor forces. To enable plants to meet these goals, on-the-job training programs were established to teach unskilled workers the skills necessary to become craft workers. For black employees, the plan reserved 50 percent of the openings in these newly created in-plant training programs. Selection of craft trainees was made on the basis of seniority with the provision that at least 50 percent of the new trainees were to be black until the percentage of black skilled craft workers in the plant in question approximated the percentage of blacks in the local labor force.

The Kaiser plant in Gramercy, Louisiana, initiated a program to train workers for skilled craft positions. Twenty white workers and twenty black workers were selected to participate in the program. Brian Weber ranked twenty-first among the white workers. Arguing that he was discriminated against on the basis of race and that he had more seniority than some of the black workers selected for the program, he filed suit under Title VII of the Civil Rights Act of 1964. A district court ruled for Weber, holding that the plan violated Title VII, and enjoined Kaiser from denying whites access to on-the-job training based on their race. A court of appeals affirmed the decision, holding that employment preference based on race violated Title VII prohibitions against racial discrimination in employment.

The decision was appealed to the Supreme Court, which by a vote of five to two, overruled the lower court and upheld the quota system for the training program.[20] As to Title VII of the Civil Rights Act of 1964, the Court found that Congress's primary concern in enacting the prohibition against racial discrimination was with the plight of the blacks. The crux of the problem was to open employment opportunities for blacks in occupations traditionally denied to them. The Court opined that had Congress meant to prohibit all race-conscious affirmative action, it would have provided that Title VII not permit racially pre-

20. *U.S. Steelworkers* v. *Brian Weber*, 61 U.S. 480 (1979).

ferential integration efforts; instead, it merely prohibited requiring such efforts. The Court found it significant that the plan was only temporary and was not intended to maintain racial balance, but rather to eliminate racial imbalance. It also held that the company was making a good-faith effort to correct past discrimination.

The Stotts Case, 1984

Carl W. Stotts, a black member of the Memphis Fire Department, filed a class action suit in a federal district court charging that the department and city officials were basing hiring and promotion decisions on race in violation of Title VII of the Civil Rights Act of 1964. A consent decree was entered with the purpose of remedying the department's hiring and promotion policies with respect to blacks. However, when the city announced that projected budget deficits would require the layoff of some firefighters, the district court enjoined the fire department from following the seniority system in determining who would be laid off. A layoff plan, designed to protect black employees who had less seniority than white employees, was presented by the city and approved by the court, and layoffs were carried out. White employees with more seniority were then laid off. The decision was appealed and the case went to the Supreme Court, which overturned it.[21]

The decision of the Supreme Court upheld the seniority system. There was no finding that any of the blacks protected from the layoff had been a victim of discrimination, nor had there been any award of competitive seniority to any of them. Title VII of the Civil Rights Act protects bona fide seniority systems, and it is inappropriate to deny an innocent employee the benefits of his seniority. Moreover, the lower court ignored an agreement between the union representing the firefighters and the City of Memphis concerning seniority. The Supreme Court also stated that there was no merit to the argument the district court ordered nor to that which the city could have done by way of adopting an affirmative action program. The case indicated that the Court would look with disfavor on affirmative action remedies for past discrimination where whites were victims of reverse discrimination.

The Jackson School Board Case, 1986

In a case that can be interpreted in many ways, the Supreme Court ruled that broad affirmative action plans that include hiring goals are permissible as long as they are carefully tailored to remedy past dis-

---

21. *Firefighters Local Union No. 1784* v. *Stotts*, U.S. No. 82-206 (1984).

crimination.[22] The case was a reverse discrimination case. At issue was a voluntary arrangement between a teacher's union in Jackson, Michigan, and the local school board to lay off white teachers before laying off black teachers with less seniority. The Court said that the Jackson plan was unacceptable because school officials failed to provide evidence of past discrimination in the school system. However, the importance of the ruling stems from the language of the individual justices on the Court. Justice Sandra Day O'Connor stated that the Court agreed that public employers could have affirmative action plans to remedy past discrimination as long as the rights of innocent persons were not trampeled on. This means that broad hiring goals or quotas tend to provide job opportunities for whole classes of minorities, whether individually victimized by discrimination or not.

Justice Lewis F. Powell, writing for the majority of the Court, said that the Jackson plan was invalid because school officials did not justify it with careful findings of past discrimination and because layoffs of white teachers were too drastic to be used in affirmative action plans. The Jackson plan could not be justified by generalized claims of societal discrimination. In cases involving valid affirmative action goals, the burden borne by innocent persons is considerably diffused among society. In contrast, layoffs impose the entire burden of achieving racial equality on particular persons. The Jackson case reaffirmed affirmative action on terms of the adoption of hiring goals, but opposed layoff plans that discriminate against innocent people. However, Justice O'Connor, who voted with the majority in most of the ruling, disagreed that layoffs would never be permissible under an affirmative action plan.

The Cleveland Firefighters Case, 1986

On July 2, 1986, the Supreme Court ruled on two more affirmative action cases.[23] In the Cleveland Firefighters Case, the justices upheld by a 6 to 3 vote a lower court approved settlement between the city of Cleveland and minority firefighters that initially called for the promotion of one minority for one white, with the goal of increasing to a certain percentage the number of black officers in each rank. The plan, agreed to by the city to settle a lawsuit brought by black firefighters, was opposed by the majority white firefighters union. They argued that the plan amounted to reverse discrimination and was put into effect over their objections. Justice William Brennan, writing for the majority, said Title VII of the Civil Rights Act of 1964 does not prohibit voluntary agreements ratified in court consent decrees. He stated that it was

---

22. *Wygant* v. *Jackson Board of Education.* 54VSLW 3339 (1986).
23. *The Washington Post*, July 3, 1986, pp. 1, 11, and 14.

the intent of Congress for voluntary compliance to be the preferred means of achieving the objectives of Title VII.[24]

The New York Sheetmetal Union Case, 1986

In this July 2, 1986 case, the justices upheld by a 5 to 4 vote a federal court order for a local sheetmetal workers union in New York to meet specific minority hiring targets of 29.23 percent. This case involved a twenty-two year battle to integrate the sheetmetal workers union in the New York area. Justice Brennan stated that a federal judge correctly ordered a 29 percent minority hiring goal to rectify what he called pervasive and egregious discrimination by the union. The union, joined by the Justice Department, argued that the precise percentage hiring formula was a forbidden quota. Brennan, speaking for the majority, said it was not. Justice Sandra Day O'Connor viewed the hiring percentage differently, saying it was not a goal but a racial quota and therefore impermissible under Title VII of the Civil Rights Act. She stated that even racial preferences short of quotas should be used only when clearly necessary, but not if they benefitted victims of discrimination at the expense of innocent nonminority workers.[25]

The Reagan Administration and Affirmative Action

The Reagan Administration is generally opposed to affirmative action, in particular to what it calls "hiring by the numbers." Its position is that employers can achieve true fairness in hiring workers only by ignoring race and sex altogether. It argues that preference of any kind is illegal except for people who have been discriminated against as individuals. It bases its argument in part on the decision in the Stotts case where the Supreme Court ruled that racial quotas do not supersede seniority as a basis for who gets laid off. However, these three major affirmative action cases may be viewed as a defeat for the Reagan Administration's civil rights policies for several reasons. The Supreme Court in the Jackson case did not forbid the voluntary use of numerical goals in affirmative action. In the two subsequent cases, the Court said federal judges may set goals and timetables requiring employers who have acted in a discriminatory manner to hire and promote specific numbers of minorities. It also gave states and cities broad discretion to agree to similar racial quotas for their work force. It rejected the Administration's arguments that federal civil rights laws and the Constitution prohibit the use of affirmative action remedies based on race or color.

24. *IAFF* v. *Cleveland*, 54 USLW 3573 (1986).
25. *Sheetmetal Workers of N.Y. Local 28* v. *EEOC*, 54 USLW 3596 (1986).

Impact of Affirmative Action on Business

As the above cases demonstrate, the impact of affirmative action programs on the personnel practices of employers is considerable. The cost of compliance for an employer begins with paperwork. A document of employer affirmative action policies has to be sent to the EEOC, and other forms have to be sent to other federal agencies. There is also the cost of litigation, for at any one time, a large company may have several discrimination suits filed against it. Training costs also can be expensive, and so can facilities that have to be installed for handicapped workers. The point is not that affirmative action is in itself undesirable but that costs are involved. In a very real sense, federally mandated rules governing personnel practices can add to the employer's cost of labor, and this cost is then reflected in the selling price of the goods the firm provides or is shifted backward to the employees in the form of lower wages.

However, this does not mean all employers are opposed to affirmative action. One survey of corporations listed in *Fortune*'s 500, indicated an overwhelming majority of chief executive officers supported affirmative action as a part of company objectives.[26] There are practical reasons why companies may support affirmative action. It can enlarge the pool of talent that employers draw on and it has practical value in terms of customer relations with women and minorities. For some companies, almost all of their customers are women. Moreover, once a company has an affirmative action program in force, it is less likely to stir grievances and impair morale among women and minorities on the payroll. The problem of litigation is also reduced. If affirmative action were voluntary, there likely would be an increase in the number of lawsuits brought by impatient employees.

RECRUITMENT AND SELECTION OF EMPLOYEES

Affirmative action is only a part of equal employment opportunity. Employers also are affected by laws concerning the recruitment and testing of employees. In advertising for workers, it is unlawful for an employer to print or publish an advertisement relating to employment that expresses a preference based on sex, except where sex is a necessary qualification for employment. Somewhat similar requirements have been applied to application forms with respect to race, though it quickly became apparent that if there were no records concerning race, there would be insufficient statistical data on which to prove discrimination or the lack of it. Thus, the EEOC has had to grapple with

---

26. Anne B. Fisher, "Businessmen Like to Hire by the Numbers," *Fortune*, September 16, 1985, pp. 26-30.

the fact that the logical time and place to gather certain significant information about a person's qualifications is also the time when there is the greatest likelihood of discrimination in recruitment and hiring at the preemployment stage. Nevertheless, almost all data that employers requested routinely in the past now either are scrutinized by the EEOC or are denied as permissible questions.

Sexual Harassment

Sexual harassment is a violation of Title IX of the Educational Amendments Act of 1972; in the work environment, it is a violation of Title VII of the Civil Rights Act of 1964. It can occur under two conditions. First, if employment decisions hinge on sexual favors between a supervisor and a subordinate, there is sexual harassment. Second, employers who allow employees to make jokes of a sexual nature may be found guilty of condoning harassment. Sexist remarks about a person's clothing, body, or sexual activity and leering or ogling at a person's body are examples of sexual harassment. Employers can be held liable for these, particularly if complaints of harassment have been ignored. Settlement of claims has cost employers hundreds of thousands of dollars, to say nothing of the cost of litigation itself.

Employment Interviews

In the process of hiring workers, business firms can run afoul of Title VII of the 1964 Civil Rights Act or other legislation regulating employment practices. One of the greatest areas of potential problems is in the employment interview, since virtually all business firms use it. There are basically three types of questions that are illegal. First, it is illegal to ask questions about race, sex, or age in the employment interview unless they are relevant to the job. Second, questions asked of one group but not another are generally illegal; for example, asking a woman applicant how many children she has without asking the same question of male applicants is usually illegal. Third, questions that would have an adverse effect on employment should not be asked unless they are job related. Illegal employment questions have resulted in large numbers of lawsuits against employers.

Testing

Certain personnel problems confronting business are quite subtle. The entire area of testing is an excellent example of how genuine efforts at compliance with civil rights laws can still be construed as noncompliance. The courts have held that inquiries into a prospective employee's criminal record would be racially discriminatory unless the inquiry and the answer it was designed to elicit were somehow directly related to the total assessment of the employee. The same is true of all other types of preemployment testing and standards, such as aptitutde tests, IQ tests, and educational achievement tests. That there was no intent to discriminate does not matter. If the effect is discriminatory, it will be disallowed.

Griggs v. *Duke Power*

In the landmark Griggs case the plaintiffs attacked the use of the Wonderlic and Bennett tests.[27] The company justified the use of the tests on the basis of increasing business complexity. In the lower court case, it was held that a test developed by professional psychologists need not have a demonstrable relationship between testing and job performance so long as there was no intent to discriminate and there was a genuine business purpose for the test. Finding no intent to discriminate, the court relied on the employer's contention of genuine business purpose. But the Supreme Court reversed the decision on the grounds that there was no satisfactory relationship between the tests and job performance and concluded that if there was no such relationship, then the tests were discriminatory if their effects were discriminatory, regardless of their intent. The Supreme Court included the company's past record of racial discrimination as a reason it could not use tests that eliminated more black job applicants than white job applicants, that is, tests that had no demonstrated relationship to actual job performance. The decision is particularly noteworthy in view of the findings by the Educational Testing Service that carefully administered preemployment tests can fairly gauge the ability of prospective employees. These findings came from a six-year study conducted in cooperation with the Civil Service Commission. The study concluded that persons who do poorly on job-related tests, regardless of race, do not do well at work either.

Under the general guidelines of *Griggs* v. *Duke Power*, no question that does not have a clear business necessity may be asked either in a preemployment application or of a prospective applicant. It is also forbidden to ask questions not related to the job, even without discriminatory intent, when the inquiry might enable discrimination on the basis of race, color, sex, age, or national origin. Thus, questions dealing with infant children, number of dependent children, willingness

27. *Griggs* v. *Duke Power Co.*, 401 U.S. 424 (1971).

to relocate, and whether or not one is now or plans to become pregnant can get an employer into trouble. Employers also are required to prove that hiring, promotion, or assignment criteria for jobs are job-related. Physical requirements are no exception. If physical strength is required for the performance of a job, all prospective employees must be given an opportunity to prove they have this capability. Educational requirements also are governed by the Griggs case. For example, educational requirements such as the possession of a business or technical degree may discriminate against women or blacks. It is incumbent on the employer to demonstrate the necessity of the requirement, that is, that persons possessing this type of degree are more successful than others in the performance of the job for which it is required.

STATE FAIR EMPLOYMENT LAWS

Federal laws pertaining to employment practices are not the only laws that affect business; there also are state laws. In fact, federal laws are often designed to stimulate activity by the states under their existing laws. The Civil Rights Act of 1964 directs the EEOC to defer to the states for a reasonable time when there is a charge of discrimination. A number of local governments also have antidiscrimination laws. Both state and local laws vary in their effect and enforcement. Almost all state laws provide for an administrative hearing and the judicial enforcement of orders of an administrative agency or official and carry penalties for violating the laws. Some states do not provide for any type of administrative agency or judicial enforcement of orders but do make discrimination in employment a misdemeanor. Other states have voluntary statutes and no enforcement provisions. State laws are applied to all employers, unions, and employment agencies located within a state without being restricted to those engaged solely in intrastate operations. This application of the state laws to interstate employees has been upheld by the Supreme Court.

State laws vary in their coverage but generally prohibit discrimination on the basis of race, sex, color, and religion, unless a necessary occupational requirement.[28] Some states forbid job discrimination based on age, and sex discrimination laws may collide with other state laws prohibiting the employment of women in certain types of work and regulating the hours of work. For example, an employer may reject a qualified applicant for a job that requires overtime solely because a state law says that women may not work more then eight hours a day in such jobs. However, the EEOC has ruled that protective laws conflict

28. Bureau of National Affairs, *Key Provisions in State Fair Employment Practice Laws*, No. 274, 1975.

with Title VII of the Civil Rights Act. Apart from laws governing the employment practices of business firms, many states have separate equal-pay laws requiring equal pay for equal work by male and female employees. These laws are limited to eliminating discrimination in wage differentials and do not touch other forms of job discrimination. In addition to the equal pay laws, discrimination in compensation based on sex also is barred, either specifically or by implication, in states that include sex bias in their employment practice laws.

COMPARABLE WORTH

Comparable worth is one of the most controversial subjects to appear in a long time. It is a compensation policy whereby employers pay equally for jobs of comparable worth or equal value, regardless of market wage rates and other factors. Is, for example, the work of nurses as valuable as the work of truck drivers? Nurses, as a group, make less than truck drivers. The great majority of nurses are female, and the great majority of truck drivers are male. Comparable worth is not the same thing as equal pay for females and males who are doing the same job as is required in the Equal Pay Act of 1963. However, although the Equal Pay Act required equal pay for equal work, men and women seldom did the same work. That men and women are frequently employed in sex-segregated occupations (e.g., nurses and truck drivers) and that they are paid different wages for this different work were not situations addressed by the Equal Pay Act.

The concept of comparable worth rests on several principles. First, workers should be paid in proportion to the worth of their jobs. Second, nonmarket methods exist or can be developed for determining the worth of jobs. Third, these nonmarket methods for evaluating jobs are preferable to the market, can be based exclusively on measures of worth, and can exclude the effects of sex discrimination. The most commonly used nonmarket measure relies on professional job evaluation systems that assign different points to different jobs based on the measurement of factors thought to be generic standards for any job — factors such as skill, effort, responsibility, and working conditions. These methods involve subjective judgments. Someone decides what factors are relevant to an evaluation of job worth, the weight to be attached to those factors, and the wages to be assigned to the various jobs after they are rated.

Before proceeding to discuss comparable worth in more detail, it is necessary to discuss the operation of a market economy. Resources, including labor, are allocated on the basis of the price mechanism. Prices are determined by supply and demand. Resources that are scarce relative to demand should command a high price in the marketplace;

resources that are not scarce relative to demand should command a low price in the marketplace. Resources flow into markets where prices are high, and away from markets where prices are low. The market is supposed to be an impersonal allocation of resources. As to the distribution of income, it is necessary to discuss the marginal productivity theory of income distribution.

The Marginal Productivity Theory of Income Distribution

The most basic concept underlying income distribution in a market economy is the marginal productivity concept.[29] This concept can be applied to the distribution of both labor and property incomes. Accordingly, the income received by the owner of a productive resource is determined by supply and demand under competitive conditions, thus equaling the marginal contribution that the resource is able to make to the exchange value of goods and services. With respect to labor income, it is best for employers to hire the number of workers that makes their marginal revenue product equal to their wage. Marginal revenue product, to put it simply, is the revenue added to the total firm revenue by each additional unit of labor, which in turn determines the demand for labor. A firm will hire that number of persons at which the addition made to total revenue by a one-unit increment of labor equals the addition made to total cost by that same increment.

The marginal productivity concept is based on the law of diminishing returns, which holds that an increased amount of a resource applied to a fixed quantity of other resources will yield a diminished marginal product. Thus if employers were to hire so many workers that their marginal revenue product was not worth the wage that had to be paid, they would soon find that number to be excessive. The number of workers that any employer would want to take on is the number that maximizes profit, and that number is determined by the equality of wages to the marginal revenue of the last worker employed. Below this point, an employer would be reducing revenue more than costs and so diminish profits; above this point, profit is not being maximized. Each unit of labor is worth to its employer what the last unit produces.

From the standpoint of the individual business firm, costs are the key determinant of the supply function. The most important cost element in the short run is marginal cost, defined as the cost of producing an additional unit of output. Since marginal cost represents costs associated with changes in output, it is apparent that the behavior of marginal costs is crucial to the understanding of the behavior of

29. See John M. Hicks, *The Theory of Wages* (New York: Peter Smith, 1948), chap. 1.

prices in response to changes in output. In the short run, with fixed plant capacity, marginal cost is the same thing as a change in variable costs, which are costs that vary directly with changes in output. The most important variable costs are the wages of labor and the cost of materials.

Criticisms of Marginal Productivity Theory

The marginal productivity theory of income distribution can be debated. It assumes that there is a truly competitive market economy and that all units of an economic resource are basically alike and so may be interchanged in production and may contribute to the output of a number of goods and services with different exchange values. Actually, much of the labor market is characterized by imperfect rather than perfect competition. Thus, labor tends to be relatively immobile, and in some markets, one or a few firms, rather than several, may be buying labor inputs. Marginal productivity theory assumes that there is equality of bargaining power between the suppliers and demanders of any productive agent such as labor and that there is no outside interference in the distribution process. If this assumption holds, the price for all the factors of production, including labor, is determined exclusively by the market forces of supply and demand.

However, in a complicated market economy, it is inconceivable that marginal productivity analysis is sufficient to explain the distribution of income. Moreover, there may not be a close correlation between the income received by resource owners and the value of marginal revenue product of the resources they provide. If the resource they provide is scarce relative to demand, their marginal revenue product should be high, as should their income. Discrimination can circumvent their reward. For example, in comparison with other occupations, nurses and secretaries are usually in short supply. Nurses and secretaries are usually females, and the income they receive is often lower than in comparable worth occupations dominated by males. Given a limited supply and a high demand for nurses, their income is not commensurate with their marginal revenue product.

Nevertheless, a business firm has to make some comparisons between what a worker contributes to total output and what it costs to employ the worker. No employer will pay more for a unit of output, regardless of whether it is labor, land, or capital, than it is worth to the firm. An employer will continue to employ an input as long as each unit purchased adds more to total revenue than to total cost; otherwise, the opportunity for profit would not be maximized. In general, a firm's demand for labor is a derived demand based on the productivity of labor, the price of the final product, and the price of labor relative to the price of other factors.

The AFSCME Case, 1983

In 1974, the State of Washington commissioned a management study to determine whether or not a wage disparity existed between employees in jobs held predominantly by men and jobs held predominantly by women. The study examined sixty-two job classifications in which at least 70 percent of the employees were women, and fifty-nine classifications in which at least 70 percent of the employees were men. For jobs considered of comparable worth, it found a wage disparity of about 20 percent against employees in jobs held mostly by women. Comparable worth was calculated by evaluating jobs under four criteria: knowledge and skills, mental demands, accountability, and working conditions. To each category, a maximum number of points was assigned: 280 for knowledge and skills, 140 for mental demands, 160 for accountability, and 20 for working conditions. Every job was assigned a numerical value under each of the four criteria.

In July 1982, two unions, the American Federation of State, County, & Municipal Employees (AFSCME) and the Washington Federation of State Employees (SFSE), initiated a class action suit against the State of Washington on behalf of some 15,000 workers in jobs held primarily by females. In December 1983, the Federal District Court for the State of Washington awarded damages of $800 million to $1 billion to female state employees.[30] This ruling, decided under the theory of comparable worth, represented the largest damage award ever handed down under the equal employment laws. In this case, decided under Title VII of the Civil Rights Act of 1964, the court found that the state had underpaid women in female-dominated state jobs compared to what they were paid in male-dominated state jobs. The damages assessed by the court represented the amount it thought necessary to correct the effects of past discrimination in the state's pay system. In addition, the state was required to adjust women's salaries upward by as much as 30 percent to eliminate the possibility of future discrimination.

In September 1985, a federal appeals court reversed the district court order. In overturning the decision, the appeals court noted that basing salaries on the market is not in itself a proof of unintentional discrimination. The appeals court said that market pricing is a method too complex even to prove discriminatory, and that employees must

30. *AFSCME* v. *State of Washington*, No. C-82-465T (W.D. Wash. 1983).

challenge more clearly delineated practices. Further, the court said that AFSCME failed to prove the state was guilty of intentional discrimination because it did not create the market disparity, and that Congress did not mean Title VII to abrogate fundamental economic principles to prevent employees from competing in the labor market.[31] Because AFSCME and the other plaintiffs never testified to specific incidents of discrimination, the court deemed the evidence too little to prove that the core principle of the state's market-based compensation system was adopted or maintained with a discriminatory purpose.[32]

Impact on Employers

That employers, both public and private, will face increased pressure from unions and other groups to develop comparable worth plans or to negotiate the inclusion of pay comparability in labor agreements cannot be doubted. For example, AFSCME and the state of Minnesota ratified an agreement including a comparable worth provision, and other state legislatures have taken similar actions. Private employers, too, have to be concerned with the issue of comparable worth or some variation of it. Pay disparity between the sexes will continue to be an issue for several reasons. First, women's already large presence in the labor force will continue to rise. Women accounted for the majority of the growth in the U.S. labor force between 1975 and 1985, and the Bureau of Labor Statistics projects they will make up two-thirds of the new entrants between 1985 and 1995.[33] Second, women's earnings continue to lag behind those of men, even though they account for an increasing share of the labor market. This earnings gap is cited by advocates of women's equality as continued existence of wage discrimination.

SUMMARY

In recent years, the focus of government regulation has been on social goals. An example is regulation pertaining to the employment of women and members of minority groups. In 1964, the Civil Rights Act was passed to prevent discrimination based on race, color, sex, religion, or national origin. Other acts also were passed to prevent discrimination

31. In a 1984 decision, that was upheld by the U.S. Supreme Court, the appeals court had ruled that basing salaries on the market does not prove discrimination. See *Spaulding* v. *University of Washington* (740F.2d C8C).
32. The State of Washington has already implemented a revision of its pay system.
33. *The Washington Post*, April 18, 1986, p. 10.

based on age and to provide equal pay for equal work. Executive orders in 1965 and 1967 introduced the idea of affirmative action, which has come to be identified with the hiring and promotion of certain numbers of women and nonwhites. An affirmative action program now is required of all employers with federal contracts. Thus, even without any complaint of prior discrimination, an employer must analyze the composition of each department and compare it with the relevant available pool of women and designated minority groups. If the department's composition reveals a significant underutilization of the pool of women and minority groups, the employer is required to establish certain goals, usually expressed as statistical changes in the composition of the work force reflecting an increase in the percentage of female or minority employees.

The impact of affirmative action on an employer can be considerable, and noncompliance can lead to severe penalties, including the probable loss of federal contracts, on which many business firms and universities depend. Employers also want to avoid lawsuits that demand payment of restitution to employees who charge that discrimination has deprived them of past promotions and raises. But there also is the problem of paperwork. The sheer volume of resources required to gather and process data, formulate policies, make huge reports, and conduct interminable communications with a variety of federal officials is a large, direct, and unavoidable cost to any employer — whether or not the employer is guilty of anything and whether or not any legal sanction is ever imposed. The hiring has been changed by outside pressures so that it now generates much more paperwork as evidence of "good faith."

QUESTIONS FOR DISCUSSION

1. What is meant by affirmative action? What is the difference between affirmative action and equal employment opportunity?
2. Explain some of the reasons for the differences in income between men and women and between whites and blacks.
3. What are the functions of the Equal Employment Opportunity Commission?
4. Discuss the Weber case.
5. When is testing illegal as an employment practice?
6. Discuss the Jackson School Board case. Why is it important?
7. Discuss *Griggs* v. *Duke Power*.
8. In what ways do affirmative action policies directly affect business?
9. Affirmative action can benefit business firms in several ways. Discuss.

10. Discuss the Stotts case.
11. What is comparable worth?
12. Discuss *AFSCME* v. *State of Washington.*

RECOMMENDED READINGS

Aaron, Henry J., and Cameron Lougy. *Comparable Worth: Less than Meets the Eye.* Washington, D.C.: Brookings Institution, 1986.
Bielby, William T., and James N. Baron. "Men and Women at Work: Sex Segregation and Statistical Discrimination." *American Journal of Sociology*, 91 (January 1986), pp. 4-13.
Fisher, Anne B. "Businessmen Like to Hire by the Numbers." *Fortune*, September 16, 1985, pp. 26-30.
Fuchs, Victor. Sex Differences in Economic Well-Being. *Science*, 232, April 25, 1986, pp. 459-464.
Olson, Craig, and Brian E. Becker. "Sex Discrimination in the Promotion Process." *Industrial and Labor Relations Review*, 36 (July 1983), pp. 624-641.
Sape, George P. "Coping With Comparable Worth." *Harvard Business Review*, 63, (May-June 1985), pp. 145-152.
Sindler, Allan P. *Equal Opportunity: On the Policy and Politics of Compensatory Racial Preferences.* Washington, D.C.: American Enterprise Institute, 1984.
Reskin, Barbara F., and Heidi I. Hartmann, eds. *Women's Work: Men's Work: Sex Segregation on the Job.* Washington, D.C.: National Academy Press, 1986.

Chapter 12
Government and the Consumer

Consumerism as a political movement can be divided into three distinct cycles. The first cycle began around the turn of this century and was concerned with pure food and drug laws. The second cycle began in the 1930s and included the passage of several disclosure laws designed to protect consumers against fraudulent advertising, mislabeling, and so forth. The third cycle began in the late 1960s when product safety laws were passed to protect consumers. But the term *consumer movement* is used rather loosely here, for unlike other movements of the past such as the Grange movement, which pertained only to farming, the consumer movement has been a conglomerate of rather disparate interest groups, each with its own set of concerns but able to coalesce and form temporary alliances on particular issues. This coalition of interest groups is expressed from time to time in efforts to bring pressure on government to pass consumer laws.

Consumer protection covers a rather broad category of laws that must be separated on the basis of objectives. Each law in its own way has had an effect on business. Take, for example, the U.S. automobile industry. Before the 1960s, it was largely unregulated by the federal government and pretty much free to do as it pleased as long as consumers were willing to buy its cars. By the end of the 1960s, however, a series of product safety laws were passed that imposed requirements on the automobile industry. Before discussing these and other laws, we must first discuss the reasons for government protection of the consumer.

CONSUMER SOVEREIGNTY AND FREEDOM OF CHOICE

In a capitalistic market economy, consumer sovereignty is an important institution because consumption is supposed to be the basic rationale of economic activity. As Adam Smith said, "Consumption is the sole end and purpose of all production; and the interest of the producer ought to be attended to only as far as it is necessary for promoting that of the consumer." Consumer sovereignty assumes, of course, there is a competitive market economy in which consumers are able to "vote" with their money by offering more of it for products in demand and less of it for products not in demand. There will be shifts in supply and demand in response to the way in which consumers spend their money. In competing for the consumers' dollars, the producers will produce more of those products in demand, for the price will be higher, and fewer of those products not in demand, for the price will be lower. Production is the means; consumption is the end. Those producers that effectively satisfy the wants of the consumers are rewarded by large monetary returns, which in turn enable them to purchase the goods and services they require in their operations. On the other hand, those producers that do not respond to the wants of the consumers will not remain in business long.

Freedom of choice is linked to consumer sovereignty. In fact, one defense of the market mechanism is the freedom of choice it offers consumers in a capitalistic economy. Consumers are free to accept or reject whatever is produced in the marketplace; thus, they are paramount since production ultimately is oriented toward fulfilling their desires. Freedom of choice is consistent with a laissez-faire economy. It is assumed that consumers are capable of making rational decisions, and in an economy dominated by a large number of buyers and sellers, this assumption has some merit. Since the role of the government is minimal, the principle of caveat emptor, or "let the buyer beware," governs consumer decisions to buy.

These statements, however, should be qualified in regard to the position of the consumer in today's marketplace. First, the statements assume some sort of parity between consumers and producers, at least with respect to product knowledge. They also assume that consumers are capable of making rational, dispassionate choices in the marketplace based on information about a particular product. True consumer choice, taking into account that the buyer must be wary, is all very well in a society in which consumers are generally equipped with at least the minimum of technical information necessary for enlightened choice. Indeed, in a far less complex time than now, it was possible for consumers to be relatively well informed about products and markets. In the last century, the range of products from which consumers had to choose was small. The products were generally simple and were in everyday use. Intelligent buyers had the expertise to make a reasonable evaluation of the products, and if they needed credit, the sources to which they could turn, although limited, were at least well known. Consumers in the last century were faced with few choices not within their range of personal experience.

Today the situation is different. Consumers are confronted with many products and not enough information to make the most rational or optimum choice. The average person, in fact even the most intelligent, has neither the ability nor the time, nor probably the inclination to be an expert in the intricacies of the many products industry provides. To many consumers, differences in the qualities of goods are a mystery. If consumers do recognize differences in the quality of certain goods, they face the almost impossible task of determining whether or not a given item is sufficiently superior to another article to justify a higher price. The relation of price to quality is further complicated when retailers sell the same article at different prices or when merchants offer at so-called bargain prices articles that are in reality set at their regular price or even higher. Even in purchasing relatively simple products, such as food, consumers are confronted with added considerations such as weight, color, and chemical substances.

Probably the most important qualification is that producers influence the choice of consumers. First, producers take the initiative in changing the techniques of production that increase the variety and volume of consumer goods. Second, producers use skilled marketing methods, including advertising, that influence the consumer's choice of goods. It can be argued that the purpose of advertising is to provide product information for the consumer, but it also can be argued that the purpose of advertising is to entice consumers into buying products they, for the most part, do not need. The so-called educational benefit of advertising may be designed merely to stimulate conspicuous consumption, such as a new car every year or the emulation of certain living standards. Consumers are goaded into maintaining superficial appearances at the expense of more fundamental needs. The overall effect of the producers' influence on consumers cannot be determined accurately; to consumers, there are both gains and losses.

Cigarette advertisements are a case in point. They suggest sex, youthfulness, virility and elegance. The theme of the Marlboro cigarette commercial is virility as epitomized by the Marlboro Man, a rugged outdoorsman. There is no question but that this commercial has made Marlboro cigarettes the world's most popular brand. Then there is the Virginia Slims cigarette with its theme of the liberated woman who has come a long way from the days when an outraged father or husband would threaten to horsewhip her for smoking. Some cigarette brands, Newport and Parliament, for example, promote popularity or escape. The best way to maintain the smoking population or encourage new persons, particularly teen-agers, to smoke is to reinforce the reason to smoke. With nearly $3 billion in annual advertising, cigarettes are promoted twice as much as automobiles or alcohol, the two next most advertised products.

The market and price mechanism never asks consumers to specify for which commodities and services they would like the scarce resources of society used. The most important choices are made by business managers who decide what commodities and services should be placed on the market, and consumers can choose among only those options offered to them. Consumers are not totally passive, however; they can exercise a considerable degree of selectivity despite the persistent advertising aimed at them. So some freedom of choice exists, but it is related to the alternatives available. Different market structures may determine the degree of choice. For example, the responsiveness of the market to consumer demands will be less than ideal when monopolistic elements are present, whereas a competitive market structure necessarily has to be more responsive to consumer demands. The consumer, although less sovereign than capitalist theory would have it, does have more freedom of choice than in a centrally planned economy, such as in the Soviet Union. There the state reduces choice to a minimum by presenting only a narrow and biased range of alternatives.

GOVERNMENT AND THE CONSUMER

The laws protecting the consumer are of infinite variety, but it is possible to divide them into several categories. The first includes laws designed to protect consumers from the adulteration, misbranding, or mislabeling of food, drugs, and cosmetics. In fact, the original focus of government consumer regulation was in this area. Its first piece of consumer legislation, the Food, Drug, and Cosmetics Act of 1906, was passed in response to public demands to curb these abuses. The second category includes laws to protect consumers from unfair competition, such as false or misleading advertising or various forms of product misrepresentation. Of particular importance in this category is the Wheeler-Lea Amendment to the Federal Trade Commission Act. The third category of consumer protection laws is product safety, which has become even more important in recent years. In essence, the purpose of product safety legislation is to protect consumers from themselves. Implicit in product safety legislation is that the concept of consumer sovereignty is inadequate if there are external costs in a product's consumption or production, or both, that the consumer does not account for in the consumption decision. As a result of this market failure, the government has intervened to control product quality standards and regulations so as to upgrade product quality and repairability.

Both the federal and state governments participate in consumer protection. The Federal Trade Commission Act of 1914 created the Federal Trade Commission to protect both business and consumers against unfair competition. The commission has since expanded its responsibilities so that it is now the primary regulatory agency concerned with consumer protection. Some of the acts that the FTC administers are the Wheeler-Lea Act of 1938, the Wool Products Labeling Act of 1939, the Fur Products Labeling Act of 1951, the

Textile Fiber Labeling Act of 1958, the Cigarette Labeling and Advertising Act of 1965, the Fair Packaging and Labeling Act of 1966, and the Consumer Product Warranty Act of 1975. The FTC also has jurisdiction over certain provisions of the Packers and Stockyard Act, as amended in 1958. In addition, Section 6 of the FTC Act gives the commission the right to collect and make available to the public factual data about various business practices. The FTC has investigated the meat-packing, cereal, oil, and telephone industries, chain stores, and farm implements.

Pure Food, Drugs, and Cosmetics Legislation

The passage of pure food and drug laws was related directly to the consumers' welfare. In the last century, hygienic standards were very low, and many sellers, particularly in the cities, sold goods unfit for human consumption. Adulteration of foodstuffs was a common practice among the bakers and grocers of the 1880s, who met the growing demands of an increasing population by diluting their raw materials with a variety of additives.[1] Milk was often diluted with water, and to improve the color of milk from diseased cattle, dealers often added chalk or plaster of paris. Meat and other perishable goods were displayed on unrefrigerated racks, subject to the vagaries of the weather. Spoilage was common, but the meat was still sold to the public. Fruit was not covered by inspection laws and rotted on the counters. *Harper's Weekly* in 1872 stated that in the markets of New York City there were cartloads of decayed fruit, which, if eaten, would almost certainly cause death.[2] Even the growth of the food canning industry did not necessarily reduce the danger of spoilage, for chemicals often were used to mask the signs of food decay. In fact, many American soldiers died during the Spanish-American War from eating decayed meat packaged in tin cans.

State and local governments were the first to pass laws to protect the consumers' interest. Sanitary regulations, inspection of weights and measures, and the like were established public functions at the beginning of the nation's history. State laws to protect consumers against the adulteration of food and drugs were first passed in Virginia in 1848 and in Ohio in 1853. As production methods became more sophisticated, leading to the development of large-scale food and drug enterprises, state regulation did not work as efficiently. Products sold in interstate commerce were difficult to subject to state regulation, and

1. Cited in Otto L. Bettman, *The Good Old Days — They Were Terrible* (New York: Random House, 1974), pp. 77-85.
2. Ibid., p. 88.

as the problem of consumer protection became more complex, federal action became inevitable. One catalyst for this action was *The Jungle*, written by Upton Sinclair in 1906, which described conditions in the meat-packing industry. Here is one of its more graphic descriptions:[3]

It was only when the whole ham was spoiled that it came into the department of Elzbieta. Cut up by the two-thousand-revolutions-a-minute flyers, and mixed with half a ton of other meat, no odor that ever was in a ham could make any difference. There was never the least attention paid to what was cut up for sausage; there would come all the way back from Europe old sausage that had been rejected, and that was mouldy and white — it would be dosed with borax and glycerine, and dumped into the hoppers, and made over again for home consumption. There would be meat that had tumbled out on the floor, in the dirt and sawdust, where the workers had tramped and spit uncounted billions of consumption germs. There would be meat stored in great piles in rooms; and the water from leaky roofs would drip over it, and thousands of rats would race about on it. It was too dark in these storage places to see well, but a man could run his hand over these piles of meat and sweep off handfuls of the dried dung of rats. These rats were nuisances, and the packers would put poisoned bread out for them, they would die, and then rats, bread, and meat would go into the hoppers together.

The Pure Food and Drug Act of 1906

There is no question but that *The Jungle* was one of the reasons for the passage of the Pure Food and Drug Act. Theodore Roosevelt read the book and was as aroused by its disclosures as was the general public. He immediately ordered an investigation of the meat-packing industry, and a pure food bill that had been bottled up in Congress took a new lease on life and was passed with only a few opposing votes. The Pure Food and Drug Act is considered the first significant piece of consumer protection legislation in the nation's history. Its main provisions were:

1. The federal Food and Drug Administration was formed to administer and enforce the provisions of the act.
2. The law prohibited interstate commerce in adulterated or misbranded foods and drugs. Adulteration was defined as the hiding of damage or inferiority through artificial color or coating, the addition of poisonous or other deleterious ingredients injurious to health, and the inclusion of decomposed or diseased animal or vegetable substances.

3. Upton Sinclair, *The Jungle* (New York: Doubleday & Page, 1906), p. 321.

Foods and drugs were declared to be misbranded if their packages or labels bore statements that were "false or misleading in any particular" or if one were sold under the label of another. Food also was considered misbranded if its weight or measure was not plainly shown, as were drugs if their packages or labels bore false claims of their curative effects.

The Food, Drug, and Cosmetics Act of 1938

The Food, Drug, and Cosmetics Act of 1938 strengthened the Pure Food and Drug Act of 1906. It expanded consumer protection by enlarging the range of affected commodities, broadening the definitions of adulteration and misbranding, increasing penalties, and making special provisions for particularly dangerous substances. Cosmetics and therapeutic devices also were included in its terms. Food was defined as adulterated if it contained any poisonous or deleterious substances; if it was colored with coal tars not approved by the Food and Drug Administration; if it was prepared under conditions that might result in contamination with filth or injury to health; or if it was packed in containers composed of substances that might make it injurious. The definition of adulterated cosmetics was similar to that for food, with special provisions for coal-tar hair dyes. However, no provision was made for the establishment of standards for cosmetics, and the disclosure of ingredients was not required.

Other provisions of the Food, Drug, and Cosmetics Act of 1938 were

1. A food sold under the name of another had to be marked clearly as an imitation, and foods bearing proprietary names had to be labeled with the common or usual name of the food and with each ingredient.

2. The Food and Drug Administration was authorized to inspect factories producing food, drugs, and cosmetics and was empowered to license manufacturers and establish standards of sanitation for granting licenses when the processing of foodstuffs might involve a risk of contamination that would make it a menace to public health.

3. Drug firms developing new drugs were required to obtain approval from the Food and Drug Administration before putting them on the market, and the FDA was authorized to deny approval of drugs that had not been tested or that had been found to be unsafe.

Drug Amendments of 1962

The Food, Drug, and Cosmetics Act of 1938 was amended in 1962 to extend the authority of the Food and Drug Administration, particularly in the area of drugs. The initial impetus for changing the 1938 law came from hearings begun in 1959 by Senator Estes Kefauver's Antitrust and Monopoly Subcommittee.[4] Underlying these hearings was a belief that the prevailing regulation permitted the introduction of new drugs of dubious efficacy that were sold at high prices. This was said to result from a combination of patent protection for new chemical formulas, consumer and physician ignorance, and weak incentives for physicians to minimize the cost of drugs for patients. It was argued that drug companies devoted inordinate time and research to the development of patented new drugs that represented only a minor modification of existing formulas. The companies would then exploit the patent protection through expensive promotion campaigns in which extravagant claims for the effectiveness of the new drug were impressed on doctors. Even when patent protection was weak, as for new products that were combinations or duplicates of existing chemical formulas, consumer ignorance and weak cost-minimization incentives made artificial product differentiation an attractive market strategy.

The hearings characterized much drug innovation as socially wasteful. The waste was said to arise from product-differentiation expenditures in an imperfectly competitive market permeated by physician and consumer ignorance. Product-differentiation expenditures were incorporated in prices that therefore did not reflect the "true value" of the drug to the consumer. It was argued that only in hindsight would doctors or patients discover that claims for new drugs were exaggerated and that consumers would have been better off if they had used the low-priced old drugs instead of the high-priced new ones. It was apparent that accurate information about new drugs would be provided only if the federal government regulated the manufacturers' claims of effectiveness. Thus, the primary feature of the 1962 amendments to the 1938 act is that a manufacturer must prove to the satisfaction of the FDA that a drug has the curative powers the manufacturer claims for it. No drug can be put on the market unless it is approved by the FDA, which also can remove a drug from the market if it has evidence that it carries a threat to health.

Other Food and Drug Laws

The Meat Inspection Act of 1907 was a companion to the Food and Drug Act of 1906. It provided that a veterinarian from the Department of Agriculture must inspect the slaughtering, packing, and canning

4. Sam Peltzman, *Regulation of Pharmaceutical Innovation: The 1962 Amendments* (Washington, D.C.: American Enterprise Institute for Public Policy Research, 1974), pp. 8–27.

plants that ship meat in interstate commerce. The use of adulterates to hide meat decay or to color the meat was prohibited. Animals had to be inspected before slaughter and the carcasses after slaughter. The Wholesome Meat Act of 1967 amended the 1907 act. It is designed to force states to raise their inspection standards to those of the federal government. If the states failed to meet federal standards within two years after the passage of the act, the Department of Agriculture had the right to impose federal standards. The Poultry Products Inspection Act of 1957 gave the Department of Agriculture the right to inspect poultry sold in interstate commerce. In addition, the department was to supervise the sanitation and processing of poultry for sale in interstate commerce. The Wholesome Poultry Act of 1968 offers federal aid to the states so that they can establish their own inspection programs for intrastate poultry plants and meet federal inspection standards. States were given two years to comply with federal standards. Those intrastate poultry-processing plants that posed a health problem were to be cleaned up or shut down.

There are some weaknesses in enforcing the existing pure food and drug laws. One is that the FDA is given far less money than are those agencies with smaller responsibilities but greater political support. The FDA, like many older, well-established agencies, has been accused by consumer interest groups of being more concerned with maintaining the status quo than with protecting the consumer. The increased use of chemicals in many foods and cosmetics has raised some hazards to health and has strained the capacity of the FDA. Chemicals may be added to foods without prior tests: only when the FDA has investigated and found the chemical to be unsafe may its use be banned. Only a small fraction of all the establishments processing or storing foods, drugs, and cosmetics can be inspected in any one year, and an even smaller fraction of their products can be tested. In many cases, gross adulteration of food, such as visible filth or decay, goes undetected until noticed by the consumer.

Advertising and Other Forms of Disclosure

A second area of government involvement in consumer protection is the various forms of disclosure such as advertising and warranties. This area is rather broad, but generally the practices that come under its purview are covered by Section 5 of the Federal Trade Commission Act of 1914, which gives the FTC the right to prevent unfair competitive practices, including those that affect consumers adversely. A rather common practice over the years has been false or misleading advertising. But a study of advertising by no means takes in the entire subject of disclosure. First, there are various product labeling requirements designed to protect consumers against misrepresentation and fraud. There also are laws designed to protect consumers against excessive credit charges. Since 1969, federal law has required that creditors disclose to borrowers basic information about the cost and terms of credit. Finally, there are consumer product warranties. Consumers usually are not aware of the warranty coverage on purchased products until after the sale is consummated and some defect or problem with the product directs their attention to the terms of the warranty.

The rationale for advertising is that for markets to work effectively, buyers must have accurate information about the quality and other characteristics of products offered for sale. Otherwise, the market is unlikely to enable consumers to make purchases maximizing their welfare within the limits of their resources. The provision of information about products is of fundamental importance to a market system. Without individuals or firms producing and selling product information to consumers, almost all information about products would have to be generated by the sellers and, to a lesser extent, by the consumers. As a result of the increases in the complexity and variety of products and in the value of people's time, there has been a major shift from consumer to seller in the comparative advantages of supplying consumer product information. But this increased reliance on sellers for information about products does not mean the information disseminated will be truthful. A seller's general purpose is to provide information that, if believed, will induce consumers to buy this product in preference to other sellers' products.

Several market situations can predispose a seller to use false or misleading information about a product.[5]

1. The first situation is monopoly. This market arrangement is conducive to the use of false or misleading advertising for two reasons. First, there is little likelihood of effective consumer retaliation when the deception is discovered, for consumers have no close substitutes they can turn to. Second, the incentive of other sellers to correct false advertising is weak, for the false claim is unlikely to have much effect on them. By definition there is no close substitute for a monopolized product, and so any sales loss will be a small one distributed among the producers of a variety of distant substitutes.

2. Another market situation is oligopoly, in which a few sellers practice product differentiation through advertising. One seller, in an attempt to gain a competitive advantage over rivals, may make false claims about his or her products. False claims aside, a certain level of industrial concentration is necessary before it becomes profitable for a

5. Richard A. Posner, *Regulation of Advertising by the FTC* (Washington, D.C.: American Enterprise Institute for Public Policy Research, 1974), pp. 22-24.

firm to engage in large-scale product promotion. By and large, only the largest firms in an industry can afford the high costs of advertising, particularly on television. A good example of concentration is the cereal industry, with the three largest firms — Kellogg, General Foods, and General Mills — together accounting for about 85 percent of total industry sales. Advertising is a way of life to the cereal industry, for some form of product differentiation is necessary to facilitate consumer choice among a myriad of products. Thus, each company is compelled to make exaggerated claims for its cereals to maintain its market position and to achieve some payoff on advertising expenses, which amount to around fifteen cents out of every sales dollar.

3. A third market situation is created when the performance of a product is highly uncertain, making false claims difficult to challenge, or when the seller can terminate business quickly and at low cost. The first category covers many restorative services, ranging from automobile repair to medicine, and the second includes various "fly-by-night" operations in which the seller does not have a substantial investment that would be jeopardized if customers, having discovered the falseness of the seller's claim, ceased to deal with him or her.

The Federal Trade Commission Act and False Advertising

The first demands for the control of advertising came at the turn of this century, as a result of the false claims made by the many charlatans who populated the food and drug industries. Although the early postal laws were meant to deal with the wholesale distribution of false advertising by mail, it was not until 1914, when the Federal Trade Commission Act was passed, that broad federal legal weapons against false or misleading advertising came into existence. As mentioned earlier, Section 5 of the act declared that unfair methods of competition in commerce were unlawful and gave the Federal Trade Commission the authority to prevent persons or corporations from using unfair methods of competition in commerce. So preoccupied were the framers of the act with the commission's role in supplementing antitrust enforcement that the intended role of the commission as an agency for protecting consumers against fraud was left wholly undefined. The intention of Section 5, however, went deep, for it authorized the commission to proceed against various forms of antisocial business conduct over and above the unfair practices proscribed by the Sherman and Clayton acts, for example, price fixing and boycotts.

The FTC did attempt to prosecute consumer fraud cases. To circumvent objections that a mandate to prevent unfair methods of competition did not include efforts to protect consumers, the commission claimed that the fraudulent practice harmed the honest competitors of the defendant by diverting sales from them. In 1931, the Supreme Court overturned an FTC ruling that Raladam, the manufacturer of Marmola, cease and desist from representing its product as a remedy for obesity.[6] The Court found misrepresentation common among vendors of such nostrums and concluded that no damage had been done to Raladam's competitors. The Court held that in the absence of proof of such an effect, the FTC could not act against consumer fraud. This decision led to proposals to amend the original Federal Trade Commission Act.

The Wheeler-Lea Amendment

In 1938, the Wheeler-Lea Amendment to the Federal Trade Commission Act changed Section 5 to direct the FTC to prevent "unfair or deceptive acts or practices" as well as "unfair methods of competition," thereby making it the commission's explicit duty to protect consumers against fraud in the form of false or misleading advertising when no harmful effect on other sellers can be established. The amendment also forbids specifically false or misleading advertisements for food, drugs, cosmetics, and therapeutic devices sold in interstate commerce. The term *false advertising* means an advertisement, other than labeling, that is false or misleading in a material sense. When injuries to health ensue from customary or advertised uses of the commodity being falsely advertised, the advertiser becomes subject to the same criminal penalties as those under the Food, Drug, and Cosmetics Act of 1938. The importance of Wheeler-Lea is that it made of equal concern before the law the consumer who may be injured by an unfair trade practice and the merchant or manufacturer injured by the unfair methods of a dishonest competitor.

With Wheeler-Lea, it has become possible to prosecute for deceptive advertising without having to show that competition has been restrained. The amendment, however, has failed to define what is "unfair" or "deceptive" with respect to a practice, nor does it have any provisions for monetary damages, compensatory or punitive. The commission's inability to award monetary reparations to victimized consumers has had two effects. First, it has weakened the consumer's incentive to lodge complaints of deception with the commission, and second, it has weakened the seller's incentive to comply with the statutes enforced by the commission. The only consequence of violation is that if apprehended and successfully prosecuted, a fraudulent seller will be prevented from continuing, or repeating, the violation.

6. *FTC* v. *Raladam Co.*, 283 U.S. 643 (1931).

But the seller is permitted to keep any of the profits obtained during the period of violation.

Enforcement Proceedings

As mentioned earlier, there is only one standard procedure by which the FTC can act to prevent deceptive practices such as false advertising although it can encourage and promote voluntary compliance. That is, the commission will, in certain instances, settle cases by accepting adequate assurance that a given business practice has been discontinued and will not be resumed. The FTC also can make a formal complaint against a business firm engaged in deceptive acts and practices. The business firm, which is the respondent, or accused party, is given an opportunity to enter into a consent settlement without formal litigation. If the respondent decides to contest the complaint, the matter is set for trial before an administrative law judge, or hearing examiner, appointed by the FTC. The commission and the respondent each are represented by their own attorneys. At the conclusion of the hearings, the judge issues his or her findings and an initial decision, which, if it goes against the prosecution, can be appealed to the full commission. The respondent can also appeal if the decision goes against him or her. A judicial review of the commission's decision is available only to the respondent.

The Wheeler-Lea Amendment provides that if a respondent plans to appeal an order of the commission, he or she must do so within sixty days, or the order becomes final and binding. If the respondent is judged guilty, either by the administrative law judge or the full commission, an order is entered directing him or her to cease and desist from the unlawful conduct. Like an injunction, it need not be wholly negative in its terms: it may spell out particular requirements that the respondent must follow. Once the cease-and-desist order has become final, either because the court of appeals has affirmed the commission or because the respondent has not sought a judicial review, any subsequent violation of the order subjects the respondent to contempt proceedings and a civil penalty of up to $5,000 for each day of continuing violation or for each separate offense. This fine — technically a civil rather than a criminal penalty — is enforced through federal court actions brought by the Department of Justice.

Deceptive Advertising

A Supreme Court justice once said about pornography that he couldn't define it, but he would know it when he saw it. The same can be said of deceptive advertising. The legal definitions of deceptive advertising are rather abstruse. The Federal Trade Commission Act contains a general prohibition of deceptive advertising and a definition of false advertising that makes clear that false representations are illegal and that failure to disclose material facts can be illegal. The Federal Trade Commission has used the following criteria in determining whether an advertisement is illegal:[7] An advertisement is illegal (1) if it decreases a significant number of customers, (2) if a false representation or mission relates to facts important to consumers in their purchasing decisions, and (3) when a false implication relates to facts that consumers use in their purchasing decisions.

Deceptive advertising can be considered antithetical to the public interest for two reasons.[8] First, it harms consumers by causing them to have false beliefs about the nature of the products being advertised and thereby causes some consumers to make different purchasing decisions than they otherwise would have. For example, a consumer may select product A because it promises to make him or her a more skillful athlete, even though product B is the better product. Second, it can be argued that, apart from its immediate bad consequences, deceptive advertising can lower the general level of trust essential to the proper functioning of a free market economy. There is, because of this, a strong presumption against deception even when it does no immediate harm.

Deceptive advertising takes many forms. One example is a Rise Shaving Cream commercial of more than a decade ago, in which the manufacturer, Colgate-Palmolive, claimed that the cream had such a softening effect that even the toughest beards could be shaved. To prove this point, Rise was applied to sandpaper, and then a razor was used to "shave" the sandpaper. The lesson to be learned was that if Rise could soften sandpaper, it could surely soften any beard. What the public did not know, however, was that the sandpaper had been soaked in water for a number of hours before the "test" was made. Naturally, the sand did not adhere to the paper after the soaking, and the razor would have taken it off without the Rise.

Labeling

Advertising is by no means the only problem in the area of disclosure. In fact, the FTC is responsible for administering several laws regulating

7. Lewis W. Stern, and Thomas L. Eovaldi, *Legal Aspects of Marketing Strategy: Antitrust and Consumer Protection Issues* (Englewood Cliffs, N.J.: Prentice-Hall, 1984), pp. 371–372.
8. Thomas L. Carson, Richard E. Wokutch, and James E. Cox, Jr., "An Ethical Analysis of Deceptive Advertising," *Journal of Business Ethics*, 4 (1985), pp. 99–101.

various types of disclosure. The Wool Products Labeling Act of 1939 is an example. The purpose of the act is to protect merchants and consumers against deception and unfair competition with regard to articles made from wool. Many abuses prompted the passage of this act. Reused wool was sold as new wool, and products sold as "all wool" often contained less than 5 percent wool. The act of 1939 provided that all-wool garments must disclose on a label attached to the merchandise the percentage of each fiber contained in the product. The Fur Products Labeling Act of 1951 was passed to protect consumers from the mislabeling of furs, such as rabbit fur being called mink. Manufacturers are required to attach labels to a garment showing the true name of the animal that produced the fur and indicating whether the fur is bleached or dyed. The Textile Fiber Products Identification Act of 1958, which covers the labeling of textiles and fibers, protects consumers by requiring a disclosure on the label and in advertising of the exact fiber content of all textile fibers other than wool marketed in interstate commerce. All products must have a label that shows the exact fiber content, the identity of the product, and the name of the product's manufacturer.

Then there is the Cigarette Labeling and Advertising Act of 1965, which requires that cigarettes sold in interstate commerce be packaged and labeled with the warning that cigarette smoking may be hazardous to health.[9] Certain drug products, such as aspirin, are required to carry on the label the warning that the product should be kept out of the reach of children. Some drugs may also be required to carry the notice that their use may be habit forming. Still other drugs may state on their label that they ought not to be taken by pregnant women without first consulting a physician.

Truth in Lending

The Consumer Credit Protection Act of 1968 or, as it is more commonly called, the Truth-in-Lending Act, requires that creditors disclose to borrowers basic information about the cost and terms of credit. The purpose of these disclosures is to encourage competition in financing by making debtors aware of specific charges and other relevant credit information, thus encouraging them to shop for the most favorable terms of credit.[10] Before the act was passed, borrowers had no way of knowing the true percentage rate they were being charged

9. The subsequent Public Health Smoking Act of 1969 required the warning on cigarette packages to read "Warning: The Surgeon General Has Determined That Cigarette Smoking Is Dangerous To Your Health."

10. U.S. Congress, House Committee on Banking and Currency, *Report on the Consumer Protection Credit Act*, 90th Cong., 1st sess., 1967.

for credit. Often they believed the interest rate was less than what they actually paid, for creditors had ways to obfuscate the issue by using a variety of methods in quoting rates. The effect of using a variety of methods was to make it impossible to compare the rates of competing creditors. The act restricts the garnishment of wages by creditors and provides penalties for exorbitant credit charges.

Warranties

A warranty is a promise, either expressed or implied, that affirms a fact or makes an affirmation related to the goods sold. There often have been problems confronting a consumer attempting to have a product repaired under a warranty; for example, the warranty may fail to cover a particular part, or it may not cover the cost of labor. State laws on warranties have conformed to the Uniform Commercial Code (UCC), which follows the theory of the common law that a product when sold carries with it the promise that it is fit for ordinary use. The UCC provides that a sale by a merchant is accompanied by an implied warranty of title and an implied warranty of merchantability together with any expressed warranties, oral or written, that the seller makes as part of the law. The UCC has followed the theory of the common law that a buyer and seller may bargain freely over the terms of the warranty and sale.

The Consumer Product Warranty Act, passed by Congress in 1975, is important for two reasons: (1) it provides minimum disclosure standards for written consumer product warranties, and (2) it strengthens the capabilities of the Federal Trade Commission to function as the protector of consumer rights when deceptive warranties and other unfair acts and practices are found to exist. The act came about because consumers had become increasingly dissatisfied with product warranties and had resorted to the courts for redress. Generally this dissatisfaction centered on such problems as the purchase of a product that turned out to be a "lemon," delay in making repairs, excessive labor charges, failure of companies to honor guarantees, unscrupulous service operators, and the consumer's lack of power to compel performance.

The act's major provisions can be divided into two categories. The first category pertains to consumer warranty provisions. To increase the product information available to purchasers, prevent deception, and promote competition in the marketplace, any warrantor offering a written warranty for a consumer product must disclose the terms of the warranty in simple and easily understood language. The FTC is directed to require that the terms and conditions of warranties be made available to consumers before the product is sold. The second category extended the FTC's consumer protection powers to prescribe rules regulating unfair or deceptive practices to apply to national banks. It was given the authority to move against local consumer abuses when state or local consumer protection agencies are ineffective. With respect to defective warranties, the FTC was given the power to seek injunctions against offenders and to represent itself in litigation. In addition, the FTC can initiate civil suits against offenders that knowingly engage in an act or practice determined to be unfair or deceptive.

Product Safety

Until recently, national product safety legislation consisted of a series of isolated statutes designed to remedy specific hazards existing in a narrow range of product categories. Moreover, enforcement authority was divided among a number of federal agencies. For example, the Flammable Fabrics Act of 1953 was passed after serious injuries and deaths had resulted from the ignition of clothes made from synthetic fibers. The act prohibits the sale of highly flammable apparel and empowers the FTC to issue appropriate rules and regulations, to conduct tests, and to make investigations and reports. Enforcement measures include cease-and-desist orders, seizure of offending goods, and criminal penalties of a year's imprisonment or fines of up to $5,000 for willful violations. Tests of flammability are established by the Bureau of Standards. The act was amended in 1967 to cover interior furnishings, fabrics, and materials.

There is also the Federal Hazardous Substances Labeling Act of 1960, which mandates warnings on the labels of potentially hazardous substances such as cleaning agents and paint removers and which is administered by the Food and Drug Administration. The Child Protection Act of 1966, also administered by the FDA, prevents the marketing of potentially harmful toys and other articles intended for children. The FDA is supposed to remove the potentially dangerous products. The National Traffic and Motor Vehicle Safety Act of 1966 is related specifically to automobiles. Under its provisions, safety standards were set for new automboiles, which include such features as an impact-absorbing steering wheel and column, safety door latches and hinges, safety glass, dual braking system, and impact-resistant gasoline tanks and connections. Tires must be labeled with the name of the manufacturer or retreader and with certain safety information, including the maximum permissible load for the tire. The Public Health Smoking Act of 1970 extends warnings about the hazards of cigarette smoking, and the Poison Prevention Packaging Act of the same year authorizes the establishment of standards for child-resistant packaging of hazardous substances. In 1971, the Lead-Based Paint Elimination Act was passed to assist in developing and administering programs to eliminate lead-based paints.

The Consumer Product Safety Act of 1972

One of the most important laws with a direct impact on business to be passed in a long time is the Consumer Product Safety Act. Fragmentation of legislation and generally ineffective controls over product hazards prompted the federal government to introduce new product safety legislation to protect the consumer. The act was a result of congressional findings that unsafe consumer products are widely distributed, and hence, consumers are frequently unable to anticipate and guard against the risks entailed in their use. Findings presented before the Senate Committee on Commerce indicated more than 20 million Americans are injured by consumer products annually.[11] Of this total, 110,000 persons are permanently disabled, and 30,000 lose their lives. The annual cost to consumers is around $5.5 billion. It has been estimated that 20 percent of these injuries could have been prevented if the manufacturers had produced safe, well-designed products.

The origins of the Consumer Product Safety Act are in the common law in that the manufacturer or seller is liable for injuries to a buyer or others caused by a defective or hazardous product. The common law imposed liability on a broad group of persons involved in the marketing process, including suppliers, wholesalers, and retailers. Many product liability cases have been based on the landmark case of *MacPherson* v. *Buick Motor Company*, which held that the manufacturer of an automobile with a defective wheel is liable for negligence, even though the customer had no direct contact with the manufacturer.[12] Liability is assumed for injuries to the consumer when the results of such injury are reasonably foreseeable, regardless of whether the product itself is dangerous or harmful. A consumer need not have to prove that a manufacturer was guilty of negligence.

Provisions of the Act

The Consumer Product Safety Act is broad in scope and affects those consumer products not already regulated by the federal government. When compared with earlier consumer-oriented legislation, the act not only possesses more effective legal and administrative sanctions but also allows an application of safety standards. Its basic provisions are as follows:

1. It created a five-member Consumer Product Safety Commission, which functions as an independent regulatory agency. A major function

11. U.S. Senate Committee on Commerce, *Hearing of National Commission on Product Safety*, 91st Cong., 2d sess., 1972, p. 37.
12. *MacPherson* v. *Buick Motor Company*, 217 N.Y. 382, 111 N.E. 1050 (1916).

of the commission is the gathering and dissemination of information related to product injuries. In addition, the commission is empowered to create an advisory council of fifteen members to provide expert information on product safety.

2. Section 14 of the act requires manufacturers to conduct a testing program to assure their products conform to established safety standards. After the products are tested, a manufacturer must provide distributors or retailers with a certificate stating that all applicable consumer product safety standards have been met. Section 14 also holds the manufacturer accountable for knowing all safety criteria applicable to the product and requires that safety standards be described in detail. The manufacturer also is obligated to maintain technical data relating to the performance and safety of a product. This information may have to be given to the consumer when purchasing the product.

3. The Consumer Product Safety Commission also can require the use of specific labels that set forth the results of product testing. This requirement will have its most significant impact on the production process, in which the design of numerous products must conform to new federal standards. Since safety standards will be formulated at various governmental and independent testing stations, a manufacturer may find a finished product no longer meets federal standards, and product lines may have to be altered drastically.

4. Section 15 requires a manufacturer to take corrective steps if he or she becomes aware that a product either fails to comply with an applicable consumer product safety rule or contains a defect that could create a substantial product hazard. The manufacturer has to inform the Consumer Product Safety Commission of the defect. If, after investigation, the commission determines a product hazard exists, the manufacturer, or distributor or retailer for that matter, may be required to publicize the information to consumers. The commission can compel a manufacturer to refund the purchase price of the product, less a reasonable allowance for use, or to replace the product with a like or equivalent product that complies with the consumer product safety rule.

DECLINE OF CONSUMERISM

The last cycle of consumerism reached its apogee around 1975 with the passage of the Consumer Product Warranty Act. More consumer protection laws were passed between 1965 and 1975 than between 1890 and 1965. Consumer groups also lobbied for a federal consumer protection agency that would have had the authority to represent and advocate consumer interests before federal agencies and courts, and a bill to create such an agency was introduced in Congress. In 1975, the legislation to create an independent consumer agency within the executive branch of government, designed to represent consumers' interests, was passed by both the House and the Senate but was vetoed by President Gerald Ford. When Jimmy Carter was elected president in 1976, he promised to create a consumer protection agency along the lines proposed by Congress. But the legislation introduced to create the agency failed to clear Congress, showing that consumerism as a viable political factor had already begun to lose its force.

There were several reasons for the decline of consumer regulation. First, a mood favoring deregulation had begun to develop in Congress, a feeling that there was already too much regulation and less, not more, was needed. In 1978, measures designed to deregulate the airline and natural gas industries cleared Congress and were approved by President Carter. Second, consumerism lacked an effective spokesperson. Ralph Nader, the self-appointed advocate of consumerism, began to lose the influence he once had had, when he took on other social issues. He also lost his influence with Congress when he published his own ratings (mostly bad) of its members. Third, many, including the respected late senator from North Carolina, Sam Ervin, felt that consumers could be overprotected. They believed consumers had to assume some responsibility for their actions and were intelligent enough to make rational choices. Fourth, and most important, was the ability of business to organize and lobby effectively against any proposed legislation it did not like. There is no question but that effective business lobbying was the catalyst that killed the consumer protection agency, even though impartial observers considered it unnecessary.

Business has traditionally disdained government, being preoccupied with its own affairs. As special interest groups began to organize and lobby effectively for legislation they wanted, business decided it could no longer remain aloof.

Consumerism and the Reagan Administration

The Consumer Product Safety Commission faced an uncertain future when Ronald Reagan was elected to his first term in office, particularly since he had stressed in his campaign that he was going to reduce the role of government. Opponents of consumer protection regulation had raised some valid arguments. They claimed that regulation increased the cost of goods to consumers, limited their freedom to make significant choices by themselves, and led to bigger and more restrictive government. There were those in the Reagan administration who proposed the outright elimination of the commission, but that did not happen. Changes were made in that it has been required to use cost-benefit analysis in setting industry regulations and to encourage industry-imposed standards.

The new federalism of the Reagan administration has placed more reliance on state agencies to protect consumer interests. This does not mean a return to the principle of caveat emptor, which was relevant in the last century when consumers could be expected to know more about a product. Consumerism is far from dead. It is represented by a conglomerate of disparate interest groups, each with its own set of concerns. Included are senior citizen groups, credit unions, consumer education organizations (such as Consumers Union), and other organizations with related interests. These groups may form a coalition to bring pressure on business and government. However, the action is now more at the state level of government, and consumer groups that once lobbied Congress to take action on specific consumer measures, have now focused their attention on lobbying activities before state legislatures.[13]

Consumer expectations have risen over the years and can be expected to continue to rise. People's standards about the products they consume are higher than ever. They are in favor of regulation that promotes safety and protection. High prices, high interest rates on credit cards, and the poor quality of products are common consumer complaints. The failure of many companies to live up to their advertising claims is also a complaint. Product safety, such as the installation of air bags in cars, has become an issue. Credit availability is also a consumer concern. Deregulation of banks has made it easier to move capital from one area to another. Advances in telecommunications have also made worldwide capital transfer easier. Another issue of concern to consumer groups is customer service, particularly error resolution.[14]

CONSUMER PROTECTION AND ITS IMPACT ON BUSINESS

The impact of consumer protection requirements on business is considerable. One has only to read the daily newspapers to be aware of this. For example, in the June 16, 1986, issue of *The Roanoke Times & World News*, it was announced that Volkswagen was recalling 132,000 Audi 5000s, in the 1984–1986 model years, to reposition the vehicles' brake and accelerator pedals.[15] General Motors recalled 98,000 cars to

---

13. In government, there are 390 state, county, and municipal consumer protection offices. In business, there are hundreds of consumer affairs departments. The society of Consumer Affairs Professionals in Business (SOCAP) has more than 1,500 members. There are 150 Better Business Bureaus who provide consumer information and report on the reliability of companies.
14. Meredith M. Fernstrom, *Consumerism: Implications and Opportunities for Financial Services*, Office of Public Responsibility, American Express Company, 1986.
15. *The Roanoke Times & World News*, Monday, June 16, 1986, p. C-6.

inspect headlight switches for defects. The Consumer Product Safety Commission moved to recall 1.6 million crib toys sold by Johnson & Johnson, claiming that the toys are a strangulation hazard. The toys, Soft Triplets, Piglet Crib Gym, and Triplets Marching Band, consist of three soft figures holding hands in a line held together by elastic. The CPSC claimed that two babies were strangled on the string used to tie the toys across baby cribs. The company, which plans to fight the recall, claimed that the parents of both babies did not follow the instructions included with the toys.

Automobile safety regulation provides an example of the impact of consumer protection regulation on business. Federal safety standards promulgated in the 1960s involved accident avoidance, crash protection, and postcrash survivability.[16] Accident avoidance standards were set for braking systems, tires, windshields, lamps, and transmission controls. Occupant protection standards included requirements for seat belts; head restraints; and high-penetration, resistant windshield glass. Exterior protection standards included the absorption capacity of front and rear bumpers. These and other standards for automobiles are presented in Table 12-1.

Table 12-1 Safety Standards for Passenger Cars

Standard	Effective Date
Occupant protection in interior impact	1968
Head restraints	1969
Impact protection for driver from steering control	1968
Door locks	1968
Seat-belt assemblies	1968
Windshield wiping system	1968
Child seating system	1971
Sidedoor strength	1973
Roof crash resistance	1973
Flammability of interior material	1972

Source: Robert W. Crandall, Howard K. Gruenspecht, Theodore E. Keeler, and Lester B. Lave, *Regulating the Automobile* (Washington, D.C.: Brookings Institution, 1986), p. 48. Used by permission.

16. Robert W. Crandall, Howard K. Gruenspecht, Theodore E. Keeler, and Lester B. Lave, *Regulating the Automobile* (Washington, D.C.: Brookings Institution, 1986), p. 47.

Costs and Benefits of Safety Standards

Using the automobile industry as an example, there are both costs and benefits of safety standards. The costs of safety standards are the original cost of meeting them as well as the costs of complying with them after the companies have had sufficient time to redesign the vehicles to accommodate the standards at the lowest cost. There is the cost of variable inputs required to produce such safety devices as seat belts, padded dashboards, and other interior protection devices. There is also the cost of external production devices including the installation of safer, more durable bumpers. An important part of safety standards cost is the fuel penalty that motorists have to pay as a result of the weight added to cars, which is due in part to bumper standards.[17] There also may be a loss in the driving quality of cars imposed by tight regulatory deadlines.

Benefits also accrue to persons and to society as a whole as a result of safety standards. One obvious benefit is the reduction in the number of injuries and fatalities caused by automobile, and other forms of, accidents. There has been a reduction in the number of highway deaths per 100 million vehicle miles driven. In 1965, the highway deaths were 5.52 per 100 million vehicle miles driven; in 1983, there were 2.70 highway deaths per 100 million vehicle miles driven.[18] In 1965, the highway deaths for passenger-car occupants were 4.58 per 100 million vehicle miles driven; in 1983, the highway deaths were 1.92 per 100 million vehicle miles driven.[19] These reductions can be attributed in part to improved safety standards for automobiles but also in part to other factors such as driver education and the 55 mile-per-hour speed limit.

Table 12–2 on the following page presents an estimate of the costs and benefits of automobile safety regulation. The costs include the various forms of safety devices that have to be installed in automobiles. The benefits include a reduction in premature deaths, a large portion of which occurs among teen-agers and young adults. There is a problem in assigning values to the reduction in early fatalities. The estimates range from $300,000 to $1,000,000. As the table indicates, the benefits far outweigh the costs of safety regulation, regardless of the estimate used.

17. Ibid., p. 47.
18. Ibid., p. 46.
19. In 1965, there were 32,500 highway deaths in passenger cars compared to 27,730 in 1983.

PRODUCT LIABILITY

America is a litigious society, which explains why it has more lawyers than the rest of the world combined. One area of litigation is product liability. Each year between 60,000 and 70,000 Americans sue manufacturers in a broad array of industries, alleging they were injured by unreasonably dangerous products, including asbestos, drugs, medical devices, cars and trucks, toxic chemicals, and toys. Almost all plaintiffs settle out of court. Of the small proportion who go to trial, more than half win damage awards — multimillion dollar sums in a few cases. Two companies, A. H. Robins, manufacturer of the Dalkon Shield, and Johns-Manville, maker of building supplies including asbestos products, have been forced into or are in the process of filing for, bankruptcy as a result of product liability suits against them.

Product liability is a part of tort law, a set of principles developed by judges as part of the common law. This field of the law is concerned with compensating one person for harm caused by the wrongful conduct of another. Courts impose monetary liability on firms whose products have caused personal injury. Liability originally depended on showing that a firm had acted negligently, which meant a firm had failed to exercise that degree of due care as would be reasonably expected in similar circumstances. However, liability has become stricter in that the fault or negligence of the manufacturer is irrelevant;

Table 12-2 Estimates of the Benefits and Costs of Automobile Safety Regulation

Benefits	
Reductions in premature deaths	23,400
Reductions in all deaths	35,100
Value at $1 million per fatality avoided ($ billions)	35.1
Value at $300,000 per fatality avoided ($ billions)	10.5
Costs	
Cost per car (1981 dollars)	$671
Annual cost ($ billions)	7.0
Annual cost without bumper standards ($ billions)	4.9
Benefits less costs — first estimate = 35.1 less 7.0 =	28.1
Benefits less costs — second estimate = 10.5 less 7.0 =	3.5

Source: Robert W. Crandall, Howard K. Gruenspecht, Theodore E. Keeler, and Lester B. Lave, *Regulating the Automobile* (Washington, D.C.: Brookings Institution, 1986), p. 77. Used by permission.

liability is now imposed if the product is defective and the defect is unexpected by the consumer and causes injury. Moreover, product liability has been extended to apply to any purchaser of a product, to members of the purchaser's family, and even to persons having no relation to the purchaser.

In the aforementioned *MacPherson* v. *Buick* case, the company was held liable when a defective wooden spoke in a wheel collapsed and MacPherson was injured as a result.[20] He sued the company, but it claimed that he had bought the car from a dealer, and that it was no longer liable. A judge ruled otherwise, holding the company liable for the defect because it was negligent when it had not properly inspected the wheel before it put it on the car. The significance of *MacPherson* v. *Buick* is that plaintiffs in a suit can go directly to the producer and bypass any intermediary such as a retailer or wholesaler. Before *MacPherson*, a person injured by a defective product could sue only the dealer from whom he or she had bought the product. Then the dealer could sue the wholesaler, and the wholesaler the producer.

The Cigarette Industry and Product Liability

Not one smoker who has sued a cigarette manufacturer has been paid a penny in damages, despite estimates by the U.S. Surgeon General that smoking kills 350,000 Americans annually, mainly from lung cancer, emphysema, and heart disease.[21] Although many of these persons started smoking before cigarette packages were required to carry a warning label, others started after the label first appeared in 1966. The latter group will have to show that the "Dangerous to Your Health" warning was not adequate to warn them of addiction. The warning, it is argued, warned only of the physical danger of smoking; it failed to mention the additional dangers of dependency in that a vast majority of smokers became rapidly addicted to cigarettes. Numerous health and psychiatric associations have also recognized the dependency-producing characteristics of cigarettes; some equal to the dependency produced from using addictive drugs.[22] In *Hudson* v. *R. J. Reynolds Tobacco Co.*, the plaintiff failed to prove that the risk of cigarette-induced lung cancer was foreseeable by the defendant tobacco company at the time the cigarettes were sold.[23] In *Green* v. *American*

20. *MacPherson* v. *Buick Motor Company*.
21. Tobacco companies have been held civilly liable when their products contained foreign objects such as human toes, mice, small snails, nails, and firecrackers, none of which are related to tobacco smoke.
22. See, for example, *1979 Surgeon General's Report*, chapter 12, p. 6.
23. *Hudson* v. *R. J. Reynolds Tobacco Co.*, 427 F. 2d 541 (5th Cir. 1970).

Tobacco, the jury found that Green's lung cancer and subsequent death was caused by smoking Lucky Strikes.[24] However, a federal court of appeals found in favor of the American Tobacco Company, ruling that the plaintiff (Green's widow) had to prove that Lucky Strikes killed more smokers than just Edwin Green.[25] In *Pritchard* v. *Liggett & Myers Tobacco Co.*, the jury determined that Pritchard's lung cancer was caused by smoking but also found he had assumed the risk.[26]

Royston Case

Two product liability cases, both involving the R. J. Reynolds Tobacco Co., were resolved in late 1985 in favor of the company. In the first case, plaintiff Floyd Royston contended that a lifetime of smoking the company's Camel and Winston cigarettes had caused problems with his circulatory system that led to the amputation of his left leg in 1983. He filed a $55 million liability suit against the company. However, a federal judge in Knoxville, Tennessee, dismissed the suit before a jury had reached a verdict. The judge stated that the issue in the case is not what the plaintiff knew or did not know about the dangers of smoking but what an ordinary consumer would be expected to know.[27] Tobacco has been used for more than four hundred years, and its characteristics and qualities are well known. Therefore, there was no way an average consumer would not know the potential risks of smoking cigarettes.

Galbraith Case

A second product liability case was brought by the survivors of John Mark Galbraith, who died at the age of 69 after smoking an average of two packages a day for fifty years. The plaintiffs argued that Galbraith was so addicted to cigarettes that he could not give them up. Galbraith, who suffered from emphysema, would smoke cigarettes when he was not on an inhalator. In December 1985, a jury in Santa Barbara, California, decided that Reynolds was not liable for the death of Galbraith.[28] The jury indicated that although it felt cigarette smoking was harmful, the evidence did not prove it was responsible for his

24. *Green* v. *American Tobacco Co.*, 154So. 2d 169 (Fla. 1963).
25. *Green* v. *American Tobacco Co.*, 391 F. 2d. 97 (Fth Cir. 1968).
26. *Pritchard* v. *Liggett & Myers Tobacco Co.*, 295 F.2d 292 (3d Cir. 1961).
27. *The Roanoke Times & World News*, Monday, December 6, 1985, p. 1.
28. *The Roanoke Times & World News*, Tuesday, December 24, p. 1. This case attracted considerable attention. It was mentioned on CBS Nightly News and on the MacNeil-Lehrer Report. The decision was also covered in *Time* and *Newsweek*.

death. The attorney for R. J. Reynolds argued that Galbraith smoked because he loved it, that he knew the risks involved and took them. The issue, he argued, was freedom of choice. Moreover, millions of Americans have quit smoking; a person has only to do so.

Plaintiffs in cigarette manufacturer liability suits advance several arguments. The first is misleading advertising. Most smokers begin smoking in high school because it is the thing to do or because of peer pressure. This is reinforced by seductive multimillion dollar cigarette advertising campaigns that suggest smoking is sophisticated. A second argument is that cigarette smoking is addictive and creates a dependency not easily broken. When the dependent smoker attempts to stop smoking, a variety of unpleasant things may happen.[29] In addition to experiencing a craving for tobacco, the dependent smoker may become irritable and restless, with accompanying sleeplessness and gastrointestinal disturbances.[30] Concentration and judgment may be impaired as well. Third, it is argued that when warning labels first appeared on cigarette packages, they did not go far enough but should have included an explicit, unequivocal warning of addiction.

The tobacco companies advance the following counterarguments.[31] One is freedom of choice, which is a basic consumer right in a free market economy. As consumers, we are free to smoke or not to smoke. Second, the defendants can argue that Congress has preempted the entire field of cigarette information under the 1965 Cigarette Labeling and Advertising Act and the subsequent Public Health Smoking Act of 1970. The label requires a cigarette warning, but it requires no specific statement relating to health. A third defense is that of comparable fault in product liability.[32] Comparable fault looks at the plaintiff's conduct in determining the extent to which he or she has caused his or her own harm. It is expected that a consumer notice or be aware of a risk. For example, many young smokers understand when they first begin to smoke that certain risks may be involved. Comparable fault permits a jury to hold the plaintiff responsible for some degree of risk conduct.

SUMMARY

One of the fundamental tenets supporting a market economy is consumer sovereignty, which is based on the idea that ultimate decisions as

29. The cigarette liability suits, including the two discussed above, involved smokers who started smoking before there was a ban on cigarette advertising on television and before the warning labels appeared on packages.
30. *1979 Surgeon General's Report*, chapter 16, p. 14.
31. Garner, pp. 1448–1454.
32. *Butaud* v. *Suburban Marine and Sporting Goods*, 555P.2d42 (Alaska 1976).

to what will be produced rest with the consumer. This presupposes that consumers have the information necessary to make rational choices in the marketplace. If this is true, consumer expenditures guide resource allocation into chosen products. But in a complex industrial society, it is difficult for consumers to have the expertise necessary to distinguish among the many products. In addition, consumers are subject to the external pressures of advertising. It can be argued that consumers are led by advertising to make product choices on the basis of subjective factors — conspicuous consumption, envy, and emulating one's peer group, for example. Therefore, laws have been passed to protect consumers against those practices considered deleterious to their interests.

Consumer protection reached a new peak in the late 1960s and early 1970s when the federal government began to increase its support of consumer welfare. This reflected the mood of the times, with consumer interests coalescing into group pressure for the passage of new laws. Business firms often have lacked innovation or have been slow to respond to consumers' needs. But in the minds of many, regulation in the consumer area was carried too far and proved to be costly and inefficient. The basic issue before the public today is whether consumers can be better protected by relying on voluntary standards set by business, transferring responsibility to state consumer protection agencies, relying on existing federal agencies such as the Food and Drug Administration, or allowing consumers to act for themselves.

QUESTIONS FOR DISCUSSION

1. What is meant by consumer sovereignty? Are consumers really sovereign?
2. What is considered false or deceptive advertising?
3. What control does the Federal Trade Commission have over false or deceptive advertising?
4. Discuss the main provisions of the Consumer Product Safety Act of 1972.
5. Discuss the main objectives of the Consumer Product Warranty Act of 1975.
6. What philosophy did Congress adopt for controlling rates of credit in the Truth-in-Lending Act of 1969?
7. There are costs as well as benefits in consumer protection legislation, but the costs are often overlooked. Discuss.
8. What is product liability? Should the tobacco companies be held liable for deaths and injuries that occur from the consumption of tobacco?
9. Discuss the impact of the consumer movement on business.
10. What is the future of the consumer movement?

RECOMMENDED READINGS

Baily, Mary Ann, and Warren I. Gikins, eds. *The Effects of Litigation on Health Care Costs.* Washington, D.C.: Brookings Institution, 1985.

Bloom, Paul N., and Stephen A. Greyser. "The Maturing of Consumerism." *Harvard Business Review*, 59 (November–December 1981), pp. 130–139.

Carson, Thomas L., Richard E. Wokutch, and James E. Cox, Jr. "An Ethical Analysis of Deceptive Advertising." *Journal of Business Ethics.* 4 (1985), pp. 93–104.

Crandall, Robert W., Howard K. Gruenspecht, Theodore E. Keeler, and Lester B. Lave. *Regulating the Automobile.* Washington, D.C.: Brookings Institution, 1986.

Fernstrom, Meredith. *Consumerism: Implications and Opportunities for Financial Services.* New York: American Express, 1986.

Grabowski, Henry G., and John M. Vernon. *The Regulation of Pharmaceuticals: Measuring the Risks.* Washington, D.C.: American Enterprise Institute, 1983.

Pertschuk, Michael. *Revolt Against Regulation: The Rise and Pause of the Consumer Movement.* Berkeley, Cal.: University of California Press, 1982.

Viscusi, W. Kip. *Regulating Consumer Product Safety.* Washington, D.C.: American Enterprise Institute, 1984.

Chapter 13
Environmental Policies and Their Impact on Business

Pollution is a dramatic and controversial subject, made so by the fear that humankind may permanently damage the balance of nature. It is common to all industrial countries, regardless of their ideologies. In May 1986, a major disaster occurred at a nuclear power plant in Chernobyl in the Soviet Union. The potential nuclear fallout for the disaster became a major concern of the entire world. In the United States, a two-year study of the Chesapeake Bay, which was done by the *Washington Post*, concluded that waste from various factories, military bases, and sewage disposal plants has destroyed much of the water life despite federal and state environmental laws.[1] In West Germany, the Black Forest is in danger of being destroyed by automobile fumes from the autobahns. Japan, given its small land area and crowded cities, has the worst pollution problem. Pollution became an end result of the Japanese emphasis on economic growth.

Pollution is by no means a recent phenomenon. In one form or another, pollution probably has existed throughout recorded times. In the United States, pollution as we know it today is a by-product of industrialization, which was stimulated by the Civil War. Industrial cities, such as Chicago and Pittsburgh, were cited by foreign visitors to the United States early in this century as being particularly foul.[2] The largest assemblage of stockyards in the world added a mephitic flavor to Chicago's air, as if a poisonous or foul-smelling gas were being emitted from the earth. Natural drainage was nonexistent, flooding was habitual, and the surface of the Chicago River so thick with grease it looked like a liquid rainbow.[3] If anything, Pittsburgh was worse. The steel mills along the Monongahela River constantly poured a residue of waste into it, which washed down into the Ohio and other rivers, while soot from the mills presented a cleaning problem to residents.[4]

1. *The Washington Post*, Sunday, June 1, 1986, p. 1.
2. Rudyard Kip'ing, *Actions & Reactions* (New York: Doubleday & Page, 1909).
3. Louis Mumford, *The City in History* (New York: Harcourt, Brace, & World, 1961), p. 469.
4. Ibid., p. 474.

PROBLEMS AND CAUSES OF POLLUTION

Modern civilization's capacity for manipulating and modifying nature and the rapidity with which new means and methods of production are being discovered and implemented make it necessary to look for national and global solutions for environmental problems. But before solutions can be identified, the problems and causes of pollution must be explored. The subject of pollution is complex and cuts across many disciplines — biology, geology, chemistry, sociology, and economics. Attempts to alleviate one environmental problem sometimes have created others even more troublesome. What is more, since the quality of the environment is not subject to market forces, allocational efficiency is difficult to attain.

Problems of Pollution

Like almost all economic problems, the problem of the environment is primarily one of choice. Air and water, as commodities, generally have been free because supply has far exceeded demand. And since they have been free, there has been no need to establish property rights or other procedures for deciding on their use. Resource allocation presented no problem of who would get what, for there was no scarcity of these particular resources. As demand has grown, however, the supply of clean air and water has become inadequate, and it is necessary to find ways of allocating these scarce resources among different uses, that is, ways to use them more efficiently. Because of their mobility, it is much more difficult to attach property rights to air and water than to land. Indeed, even in the case of land, the mere establishment of property rights is not necessarily enough to guarantee the best use.

Clean air and water can be considered a public good, and patterns of using them have evolved in the absence of clearly defined and enforced property rights. It is difficult for a private person to lay claim to a particular level of quality in a given lake or air stream. In such cases, a person usually cannot identify his or her water or air, nor can that person purchase identifiable packages of these goods. Though one person's activities affect another's enjoyment of these resources, no recourse exists through property rights for protecting these assets. Thus, in the absence of property rights, other forms of control over the use of air and water have to be imposed. The form of these controls determines their effectiveness and also influences the operations of business firms. The main purpose of these controls is to keep air and water reasonably clean so that nobody will be affected adversely, either by being exposed to harmful substances or by having to incur unreasonable costs to render air and water sufficiently clean for consumption.

One problem of pollution is that it entails social costs that are not measured in terms of prices. In a market economy, resources are allocated on the basis of the price mechanism. These resources, land, labor, and capital are reflected in the money costs to producers of goods and in turn are incorporated in the sales price of the goods. There can be certain adverse side effects generated in the process of production that are not reflected in the money cost of production but, nevertheless, become real costs to society. Pollution is a social cost of production that the market system does not indicate and that may include noneconomic as well as economic costs. The problem, therefore, is to develop mechanisms for protecting resources when internal or private costs to firms differ substantially from their costs to society at large. In the absence of a price mechanism, this can be settled only through the political process.

Reasons for Pollution

The reasons for pollution are varied and cannot be attributed solely to the operations of business firms, as some critics of American society contend. One reason is the concentration of population in the United States and in other industrial countries into urban areas. The geographic distribution of population densities and the volume of pollution have an important relationship to each other. More than half the people in the United States live in 1 percent of the total land area; two thirds live in 9 percent of the area. On this basis, the United States is one of the most overpopulated countries in the world. Such clustering of population greatly intensifies the problem of pollution: the very process of living generates wastes — wastes that, for the most part, nature can cope with efficiently until population density becomes quite high. Thus, at least part of the pollution problem can be attributed to the concentration of a large population in a relatively small land area. The larger the population is, the greater the volume of waste it will create — all other things being equal.

A second reason for pollution is the widespread affluence of Western industrial society. This affluence has created effluence, since many people have the money to demand a wide variety of goods and services, while discarding articles that often are still usable. In the United States and other advanced countries, millions of cars and billions of bottles and cans are junked annually. Demand patterns have shifted to require more convenience goods and services. Parents who themselves walked to school transport their children by auto day after day. In the past, one automobile was enough for most families; today, two cars per family is common. The increased demand for creature comforts is also a part of the changing lifestyles. Few churches today would expect their congregations to keep cool on a summer's day with paper fans from the local funeral parlors as in the past, even though the generation of electricity to operate air conditioning may add to the pollution of the environment.

A third reason for pollution is industry itself. Undeniably, dramatic examples of industrial pollution can readily be found, in part because much of this pollution is highly visible. One has only to look at the effluvia dumped into the rivers and lakes near any industrial city. Lake Erie is an excellent example, for it is one of the most polluted water areas in the world, polluted by industrial wastes from Cleveland's steel mills as well as industries in other cities. Moreover, today's rapidly advancing technology constantly creates new problems of pollution; the very processes that improve the ordinary person's lot as a consumer may have the reverse effect on the ecological balance. As an example, when most steelmakers changed from open hearth methods to the more efficient oxygen process, the demand for scrap metal dropped, since the oxygen process mainly uses iron ore and taconite pellets. Consequently, the incentive for junk dealers to salvage old cars became so low that some dealers actually insisted on being paid for accepting the vehicles. The inevitable result of this was that cities began to face the expensive chore of disposing of old automobiles. This raises the question of who the polluter is: the steelmaker who changed to a new process, the auto manufacturer who builds a car that fails to disintegrate readily, or the auto owner who behaves in an antisocial way by abandoning the car.

Government is the fourth source of pollution.[5] Localities must contend with two major kinds of potential pollutants: sewage and solid wastes such as garbage, sometimes on an incredibly large scale. All too often, localities have taken the most economical approach, letting raw sewage pour into the nearest river and dumping the garbage at the city dump and then burning it, thus polluting the air. In addition, cities that operate their own public utilities and conduct other quasi-business activities are often as guilty of polluting the environment as their counterparts in private industry are. A city that operates a public utility is going to use the same fuels and emit the same fumes as does a privately owned public utility. Federal government facilities also have contributed to pollution.[6]

5. Pollution may also emanate from other sources. One source is agriculture, which adds to pollution through wastes from feedlots, pesticides, and sediments carried by erosion.
6. The Aberdeen Proving Ground, a federal military facility, is a major pollutant of the Chesapeake Bay. (*The Washington Post*, Sunday, June 1, 1986, p. 15.)

GOVERNMENT ROLE IN POLLUTION CONTROL

Several public policy approaches can be used to control pollution — direct regulation; charges for emissions, including taxes; subsidies; and other government activities. Combinations of these approaches also can be used. Each approach has advantages and disadvantages, and because there are different kinds and sources of pollution, many of which are not well understood, it is impossible to say which is best. Hence, a method of control that might effectively curb air or water pollution might not be suitable for reducing noise levels or the misuse of land.

Regulation

Legislation can be used to establish appropriate standards for air, water, noise, and land use: the Clean Air Act of 1970 sets standards for air quality, and there is similar legislation for water. In addition, regulation can require licenses, permits, zoning regulation, and registration. The formulation of air and water standards implies a value judgment about the reasonable degree of control that can be achieved through regulation. A rationale for regulation is that similar standards are established for all business firms. Requiring every steel mill to meet similar effluent standards is deemed to be fair not only among individual firms but also among communities. Proponents of uniform or similar standards contend that unless these standards are applied everywhere, the rules will be neither fair nor effective in reducing pollution. Firms polluting in one area would move to locations where standards are lower, and firms in areas with high standards would be treated unfairly. Communities with high standards also would be at a disadvantage in attracting and holding industry, and pollution would continue to come from communities with low standards.

An objection to regulation is that it leads to rigidities and, in many cases, unwieldy and inefficient forms of control. For example, if uniform emission standards are used, certain problems can result. One is that there are differences among firms in the same industry and differences in environmental conditions among geographic areas. Different firms have different requirements in the use of the environment. The discharge of waste into a river is an example. Some firms want to discharge more waste because their cost of waste treatment is higher; other firms may have lower costs. A firm might be permitted to discharge more waste if the damage done by such waste is lower because few or no people live downstream from the point of discharge. Environmental conditions also may vary considerably among geographic areas, and these differences will be reflected in the prices of the goods produced. An area with natural resources that absorb waste discharges may be prevented from using this absorptive capacity because of uniform national standards for environmental quality. Thus, a law that sets a standard on pollution levels may cause a misallocation of resources.

Emission Charges

Another method of controlling pollution is to levy emission charges in the form of taxes or fees against polluters. For example, in copper smelting, sulphur oxides are among the principal pollutants produced. Rather than requiring copper companies to reduce the sulphur oxides by a given percentage, they could be taxed according to the amount of sulphur oxide they actually do release into the atmosphere. Each polluting firm could then decide for itself how much control it wants to provide. A firm that, for one reason or another, has higher costs for control presumably would release more pollutants than a firm with relatively low control costs. Emission charges would become part of a firm's costs of operation and would cause the firm to calculate both the costs of waste and the costs and benefits of pollution abatement. Since emission charges would take advantage of differences in control costs among polluters, it would be possible to reach an average air standard at a lower cost to society than would be possible by applying a uniform emission standard through law. Another advantage of emission charges is that the government could charge lower emission fees in sparsely populated areas and higher fees in more densely populated areas, thus spreading pollution more evenly throughout the country and encouraging industrial dispersion. This would have the net effect of decreasing total pollution. Furthermore, the fees would provide revenue that could be used for various social purposes, including the construction of waste treatment facilities or research on pollution abatement.

The implementation of a tax or any form of use charge requires an evaluation of the damage done by the emission of an incremental quality of pollution at any given time or place. After this evaluation, an emission charge is assessed to the responsible parties based on the amount of damage. Presumably, those firms with the capabilities to reduce emissions at a cost less than the pollution charge will do so, and the proper amount of abatement will be obtained by the least costly means. If the tax or charge is too low, it will not be an adequate inducement to reduce the wastes disposed; if the price is too high, it will impose more control than necessary and will be uneconomic in its effect. The experience gained through using some sort of charge might resolve this problem; however, charges have yet to be tried extensively, event though numerous task forces and studies have specifically recommended their experimental use.

Subsidies

A third public approach to pollution control would be to award subsidies to business firms to defray the cost of compliance with pollution control standards. A rationale for such subsidies is that business firms are being forced to treat their effluents at least in part so that others may benefit, and therefore, they should be compensated for the benefit. Subsidies could take several forms. First, a tax credit might be given to compensate for the cost of acquiring pollution abatement equipment. This credit would be deducted from the tax a firm would pay on net income after total business deductions. Thus, a $100 tax credit for pollution control equipment would reduce by $100 the amount of tax due. Second, outright cash payments could be made to reduce the level of pollution. Third, accelerated depreciation allowances could be used to reduce the cost of pollution control equipment. Specifically, accelerated depreciation would permit business firms to write off the cost of equipment in a shorter time than would standard depreciation provisions, increasing the cash flow of these firms in the process. Fourth, state and local governments could allow property tax exemptions on pollution control equipment.

Subsidies do have disadvantages.[7] If firms are given aid for their cost of waste treatment or for the purchase of pollution abatement equipment, less pressure is on them to find alternative ways of dealing with the pollution problem. Subsidies in the form of tax relief based on the purchase of abatement equipment favor waste treatment that is capital intensive. A firm must respond to varying consumer tastes, which means manufacturing different products that in turn give rise to different forms of waste. Subsidies for capital equipment reduce its cost to the firm and encourage the firm to substitute fixed for variable costs, and economic inefficiency in waste treatment may result. It also can be argued that subsidies, particularly if they are financed out of general tax revenues, violate the benefit principle of equity. According to this principle, the cost of pollution control should be part of the cost of production, and consumers who buy products should pay the antipollution costs just as they pay for labor, capital, and other inputs.

Other Government Activities

There are several government activities regarding the protection of the environment. Both the federal and state governments have become regulators, establishing laws, setting standards, and monitoring and

---

7. Tax Foundation, *Pollution Control: Perspective on the Government Role* (New York: Tax Foundation, 1971), pp. 11–25.

supervising compliance. Thus, the Clean Air Act as amended in 1970 provides standards of air quality; there is similar legislation for water. The government also offers special tax assistance and subsidies by underwriting or engaging directly in research related to environmental problems. Virtually all the states now have enacted legislation that establishes a legal basis for controlling the sources of pollution. Besides writing laws to regulate pollution and provide subsidies, the government has also had to cope with its own harmful by-products.

Federal legislation for pollution control dates back as far as the turn of the century, when the Refuse Act of 1899 prohibited the discharge of waste materials into navigable waters. The Oil Pollution Act of 1924 forbade the discharge of oil into coastal waters, and in 1948 the Water Pollution Control Act was passed. Asserting that pollution problems were better handled at the local level, the act nonetheless authorized the Public Health Service to coordinate research, provide technical information, and on request from the states involved, provide limited supervision of interstate waterways. The Water Pollution Control Act of 1956, along with amendments of 1961, 1965, 1966, and 1970, considerably extended federal involvement, both regulatory and financial, in water pollution control. The Water Quality Act of 1965 created the Water Pollution Control Administration, which almost immediately was transferred to the Department of the Interior. Responsibility for air pollution, however, remained with the Department of Health, Education and Welfare (now the Department of Health and Human Services).

Federal laws concerned with air pollution were first instituted in 1955, when Congress authorized technical assistance to states and localities, as well as a research program. In 1963, the Clean Air Act was passed to give states grants both to improve pollution control programs and to provide for federal enforcement in interstate pollution cases. The 1963 act also expanded federal research, particularly in connection with pollution from motor vehicles and from the burning of coal and fuel oil, and emphasized the need for controlling pollution from facilities operated by the federal government. A 1965 amendment authorized federal regulation of motor vehicles through standards that became effective in 1968. In 1966, an amendment broadened the federal aid program, making grants available for state and local control programs. The Air Quality Act of 1967 directed the Department of Health, Education and Welfare to delineate broad atmospheric areas for the entire country, as well as air quality control regions. The act continued and strengthened most of the provisions of the earliest legislation and provided for special studies of jet aircraft emissions, the need for national emission standards, and labor and training problems. The 1967 law also established the Presidential Air Quality Advisory Board.

The Clean Air Act of 1970

Probably the most important of all federal laws governing pollution is the Clean Air Act of 1970, which contains a series of provisions that have a direct impact on the operations of business firms. The more important provisions are

1. The act required that by 1975 new cars be virtually pollution-free and specified that emissions of hydrocarbons and carbon monoxide gases had to be 90 percent less than levels permissible in 1970. At the insistence of the automobile manufacturers, who contend that compliance is a costly proposition, the date was extended to 1981. The act also requires manufacturers to offer a fifty-thousand-mile warranty on automobile emission control devices and establishes strict controls for fuel additives.[8]

2. The 1970 act also sets national standards for air pollution, with the states required to establish and enforce programs that meet national standards within four to six years. The federal government has the right to establish minimum ambient air standards for the entire country.

The Clean Air Act directed the Environmental Protection Agency to set national ambient air quality standards for pollutants covered in the act. It also authorized the EPA to set two types of standards, primary and secondary, without considering the cost of compliance.[9] Primary standards were to protect human health with an added margin of safety for vulnerable segments of the population, such as the elderly and infants. Secondary standards were to prevent damage to such things as crops, visibility, buildings, water, and materials. The EPA was also directed to determine maximum emission limits for plants and factories, called new source performance standards. These standards were to be set on an industry-by-industry basis for states to use as a guideline in deciding on more specific emission restrictions for individual factories. Regions that violated standards for any of the pollutants covered by the act were designated as nonattainment areas for those pollutants, and the states had to limit new construction of pollution sources until the air in these regions was brought up to federal standards. Companies wanting to build plants in these regions were required to install equipment that limited pollution to the least amount emitted by any similar factory elsewhere in the country.

---

8. It should be noted that compliance dates and emission standards were amended in 1977. The original hydrocarbon and carbon monoxide standards were put off until the 1980 model year.

9. The functions of the EPA were discussed in Chapter 10.

The Water Pollution Control Act of 1972

The Water Pollution Control Act amends previous acts pertaining to water pollution, including the Water Quality Act of 1970, which extended federal control standards to oil and hazardous substance discharges from onshore and offshore vessel facilities. The Water Pollution Control Act is divided into five categories: research and related programs, grants for construction of treatment works, standards of enforcement, permits and licenses, and general provisions. Responsibility for the enforcement of the act is vested in the EPA and in state governments. Some of the more important provisions of the act are

1. Manufacturers are required to monitor discharges at point sources of pollution and to keep records of the results of their efforts to reduce water pollution. The EPA or the state is authorized to inspect records to determine whether or not the act is being violated.

2. The act extended federal water pollution control to all navigable waters. When there is a violation, EPA can issue an order requiring compliance or notify the appropriate state of the alleged violation. If the state does not begin an appropriate enforcement within thirty days, the EPA can issue a compliance order requiring the violator to comply with a conditional or limited permit, or it can bring a civil action or begin criminal proceedings.

3. Both the Clean Air Act and the Water Pollution Control Act give citizens the right to bring suits to enforce standards set under the acts. Anyone having an interest that is or may be adversely affected by pollution may sue in the judicial district in which the offending source is located, and the U.S. district courts are given jurisdiction without regard to citizenship or amount in controversy.

The Noise Control Act of 1972

Although air and water pollution have been the targets of corrective legislation for a long time, recent efforts have been directed at abating noise to create a quieter environment. The Noise Control Act of 1972 places noise in the formal category of a pollutant. Congressional findings indicated that inadequately controlled noise presented a danger to the health and welfare of the nation's population, particularly in the urban areas. Noise adversely affects human blood pressure and heartbeat and causes other detrimental physiological changes.[10] Although its immediate consequences are usually transitory, sustained noise can accumulate in an almost imperceptible manner, causing

10. Robert A. Baron, *The Tyranny of Noise* (New York: St. Martin's Press, 1970).

permanent injury to the human body. Harmful noise is often difficult to isolate, since the degree of annoyance depends on the person's response to the source of irritation.

The Noise Control Act offers federal regulatory guidelines for controlling noise pollution. Though primary responsibility for control of noise rests with state and local governments, federal action provides national uniformity of treatment. The act is intended to facilitate the establishment of federal noise emission standards for commercial and consumer-oriented products and to allow the federal government to preempt the field of noise control, though not depriving the states of local control and autonomy. The provisions of the act are basically as follows:

1. The act's most important provision is noise emission standards for a wide variety of product categories. The act is designed to control and abate aircraft noise and sonic boom as well as establish railroad, aircraft, and motor carrier emission standards. The EPA is required to establish noise emission standards for newly manufactured products that have been identified as being major sources of noise. Such standards will limit the noise emissions from each product, as is necessary to protect the public health, safety, and welfare. Effective noise emission standards have to be established for all products identified as major noise sources within eighteen months after the passage of the act.

2. Criminal sanctions under the act parallel those of the Clean Air and Water Pollution Control acts. Fines of up to $25,000 per day of violation or imprisonment for up to one year, or both, are authorized for the first offense. Subsequent offenders are liable for fines of up to $50,000 for each day of violation or for imprisonment of up to two years, or both. Each additional day of violation constitutes a separate offense.

3. The act also authorizes citizens to sue in the federal district courts for any violations of noise control requirements. Citizens are also permitted to sue the administrator of the EPA for an alleged failure to perform his or her duties under the act and also the administrator of the Federal Aviation Administration for similar reasons.

4. Technical assistance can be given to state and local governments to develop and enforce ambient noise standards.

5. The act authorizes labeling requirements for any product that emits noise capable of adversely affecting the public health and welfare or that is sold on the basis of its effectiveness in reducing noise. When a product is labeled, purchasers or users must be informed of the level of noise the product emits or its effectiveness in reducing noise, whichever the case may be.

Other Environmental Legislation

The Toxic Substances Control Act of 1976 gives the EPA broad regulatory authority over chemical substances during all phases of their life cycles, from before their manufacture to their disposal. It directs the EPA to make an inventory of the approximately 55,000 chemical substances in commerce; to require premanufacture notice to the EPA of all new chemical substances; and to enforce record-keeping, testing, and reporting requirements so that the EPA can assess the relative risks of chemicals and regulate them. In December 1980, the Comprehensive Environmental Response, Compensation, and Liability Act became law. This legislation created a $1.6 billion fund for the cleanup of both spills of hazardous substances and inactive hazardous waste disposal sites. The Resource Conservation and Recovery Act of 1976 requires the safe disposal of hazardous wastes. Regulations define hazardous waste and establish standards for generators and transporters of hazardous wastes, as well as permit requirements for owners and operators of facilities that treat, store, or dispose of hazardous wastes. A waste generator has to prepare a manifest for hazardous wastes that is to track movement of the wastes from the point of generation to the point of disposal. If a waste is hazardous, it must be properly packaged and labeled.

The Hazardous and Solid Waste Amendments of 1984 provide for the protection of ground water, which is increasingly seen as a vulnerable source because it is used so widely for drinking water. The amendments place restrictions on the treatment, storage, and disposal of hazardous waste in land-management facilities. They provide new regulations for underground tanks that store liquid petroleum and chemical products. They also create new and more stringent requirements for land disposal facilities that now exist and for those that will be created. Land disposal of hazardous wastes contaminate ground and surface waters, thus resulting in adverse human health effects. The amendments require the EPA to develop standards before November 1986 governing the burning of hazardous waste-fuel mixtures. They also require producers and distributors of hazardous waste fuels to place a warning label on the invoice or bill of sale.

COSTS AND BENEFITS OF POLLUTION ABATEMENT

The subject of the environment is very controversial although to argue against a clean environment is almost impossible. Suggestions that environmental laws should be modified to make them less costly to business or perhaps that more public land should be opened up for mineral exploration elicit the wrath of environmental groups and their supporters. If there is a complaint that a certain environmental requirement may cost a firm $10,000 a year per worker, the response may be that the possibility of cancer is reduced or the length of life of the worker is increased. The response does not address the wisdom of the rule, nor does it consider more viable alternatives, but it is virtually impossible to argue against it in any public forum. To make prudent choices about resource allocation, costs need to be weighed against benefits.

Costs of Pollution Abatement

Few things come free in this world, and cleaning up the environment is certainly not one of them. For example, emission control standards, as required by the Clean Air Act, decrease the economy of a car because they require the operation of auxiliary devices, such as air pumps, and the returning of the engine to less than optimal fuel efficiency. Emission controls can also reduce the reliability of a car and thereby increase total repair costs. Therefore, it is necessary to examine some of the costs involved in pollution abatement regulations. These costs can be divided into several categories: opportunity costs, economic costs, and the actual monetary outlays involved in cleaning up the environment.

Opportunity Costs

Opportunity cost can be considered a part of environmental regulation. The money spent for cleaning up the environment could have been spent in modernizing industrial plants to better meet foreign competition. As Table 13-1 indicates, the total pollution abatement expenditures for 1983 amounted to $62.7 billion. In this case, opportunity cost can be applied to the whole economy because it is limited in what it can do with its resources, including its technological ability. Tradeoffs are involved in terms of how much of one good or service must be given up to gain a certain quantity of another good or service. In the case of the $62.7 billion expenditure on pollution abatement, there are many alternative combinations of uses involving expenditures on other goods or services. There may be an alternative combination that better uses the $62.7 billion.

Economic Costs

An example of an economic cost is when a plant shuts down as a result of environmental compliance costs and jobs are lost. This has happened.

EPA records kept from 1971 through early 1977 showed that 107 plants employing 20,318 workers were closed by companies that considered pollution control costs too high to merit keeping the plants open.[11] Plants have been closed down since that time also; for example, Youngstown Sheet and Tube, a steel mill in Youngstown, Ohio. Almost all the plants shut down were marginal in terms of profitability and may have been eventually shut down anyway. However, economic costs transcend the closing down of a plant. The tax base of the community decreases and the quality of social services it can provide declines.

Monetary Costs

In addition to opportunity costs and economic and social tradeoffs, there are the actual monetary outlays related to pollution control. Table 13-1 presents the costs of pollution control for the two main categories of pollution, air pollution and water pollution for the period 1972-1983. This spending includes only federally mandated pollution control requirements. There are also expenditures made in response to state and local regulations, as well as voluntary expenditures. Air pollution expenditures have accounted for almost one half of total national

Table 13-1 National Expenditures for Pollution Abatement and Control, 1972-1983 (billions of dollars)

Year	Air	Water	Total
1972	$6.4	$8.7	$18.4
1973	8.3	10.1	21.9
1974	10.4	11.6	26.3
1975	12.8	13.6	30.9
1976	14.2	15.5	34.7
1977	15.6	16.8	38.0
1978	17.3	19.9	43.4
1979	21.0	21.8	49.9
1980	24.9	22.4	55.4
1981	28.1	21.8	58.9
1982	27.4	22.1	58.9
1983	29.2	23.6	62.7

Source: Council on Economic Quality, *Environmental Quality 1984* (Washington, D.C.: U.S. Government Printing Office, 1984), pp. 614-617.

11. See annual reports of the Council on Environmental Quality for 1975 and 1977.

expenditures for pollution abatement and control during the 1972–1983 period.

Benefits of Pollution Abatement

Benefits also accrue to the individual and to society from cleaning up the environment. The benefit of any environmental improvement can be defined as the sum of the monetary values assigned to the effects of that improvement by all people directly or indirectly affected by the action. These monetary values can be defined in terms of the willingness of people to pay to obtain the effects of the environmental improvement or in terms of the sums people would have to receive to induce them to accept voluntarily the adverse effects of pollution.[12] Benefits can be divided into several categories, the first of which is human health. There are also economic and aesthetic benefits that can accrue to people and to society as a result of a clean environment.

Health Benefits

Air, water, and other forms of pollution can have an adverse effect on health. Exposure to some form of air pollution has been associated with an increase in the mortality rate and also with respiratory ailments, particularly among older people. Outbreaks of infectious diseases have been traced to contaminants in municipal water supplies. Certain chemicals in water supplies have been linked with increased rates of cancer, and there is also a relationship between air pollution and the incidence of lung cancer. Health, then, can be improved by a reduction in the amount of pollution. One study estimated that approximately 25 percent of mortality from lung cancer could be saved by a 50 percent reduction in air pollution.[13] Several measures can be used to place a value on the premature loss of life. One measure uses an opportunity cost approach that values a life lost as the present value of the expected stream of future earnings for that person had his or her death been avoided.

Economic Benefits

Pollution can have an adverse effect on such economic activities as agriculture and commercial fishing. Agricultural production can be

12. A. Myrick Freeman, *Air and Water Pollution Control* (New York: John Wiley & Sons, 1982), pp. 3–5.
13. Lester B. Lave, and Eugene P. Seskin, "Air Pollution and Human Health," *Science*, 169, August 21, 1970, pp. 722–733.

affected by rising acidity in the soil. It might be added that the environmental fallout from the Chernobyl nuclear plant disaster has had an adverse effect on agricultural production in Eastern Europe. Sale of agricultural products to the West has been banned by a number of Western countries, with a resultant loss of revenue to Poland and other Eastern countries. In our country, lowered water control standards have had an adverse effect on commercial fishing production. Pollution in the Chesapeake Bay has reduced or destroyed almost all the fish supply and has put many commercial fishermen out of business.[14] Shellfish beds have been closed to commercial harvesting because of both bacteria and chemical contents, and rockfish, considered a delicacy, has all but disappeared.

Aesthetic Benefits

Aesthetic benefits, though less tangible than health and economic benefits, are also important to personal welfare. Air and water pollution can cause odors and tastes that affect people's ability to function well; the smell of a paper mill is a good example. Both forms of pollution can also be unsightly. Oil slicks on a beach or the presence of dead fish caused by a chemical spill creates a loss of amenities. Noise pollution is also offensive to the senses. Visibly unpleasant pollutants can have an adverse effect on property values in that they can reflect price differentials. In sum, the aesthetic benefits of location increase as air, water, and noise pollution decreases.

Cost-Benefit Analysis: Lead in Gasoline

An example of cost-benefit analysis can be applied to leaded gasoline.[15] Lead in gasoline has been regulated by the EPA since the Clean Air Act of 1970, with a reduction in lead required through various rulings. A new rule, issued in 1984, required that lead in gasoline be reduced from 1.1 grams per leaded gallon to 0.5 grams per leaded gallon by July 1985, and to 0.1 grams by January 1986. The benefits to be derived from the reduction of lead in gasoline included improvement in the health of children and a reduction in high blood pressure for adults. Lead results in the emission of various forms of air pollutants — hydrocarbons, nitrogen oxides, and carbon monoxide. There is a relation of gasoline lead to blood lead, which is linked to blood pressure. Lead also

14. *The Washington Post*, June 1, 1986, p. 14.
15. Council on Environmental Quality, *Fifteenth Annual Report* (Washington, D.C.: U.S. Government Printing Office, 1985), pp. 231-237.

corrodes engines and exhaust systems, which causes excess emissions of pollutants from misfueled vehicles.

There is also a cost involved in reducing the lead content of gasoline. Since the 1920s, refineries have added lead to gasoline as an inexpensive way of boosting octane. To meet octane requirements with little or no lead, refineries must engage in additional processing, which raises costs, or use other additives, which are more expensive than lead. The EPA estimated the cost of reducing lead by specifying the cost of the 1984 lead limit of 1.10 grams per leaded gallon. Then it computed the cost of specifying a tighter lead limit. Based on its analyses, the EPA estimated the rule would cost less than $100 million in the second half of 1985, when the standard was 0.5 grams per leaded gallon, and just over $600 million in 1986, when the standard became 0.1 gram.

Table 13-2 presents the monetary estimates of costs and benefits for the period 1985-1987. Excluded from the table are benefits that cannot be monetarily quantified; for example, there are blood pressure benefits. Since gasoline lead is linked to blood lead, which is linked to blood pressure, it would follow that reduced lead in gasoline would reduce blood pressure levels. This would cause a decline in cardiovascular diseases, with a reduction in the number of heart attacks, strokes, and deaths related to high blood pressure. Monetary benefits in the table were limited to the health effect on children that will accrue from a decline in lead in gasoline. These benefits are based on EPA estimates of the reduction of blood lead and the increased health effects on children.

Table 13-2 Costs and Benefits of Decreased Lead in Gasoline (millions of dollars)

	1985	1986	1987
Benefits	$223	$ 600	$ 547
Children's health effects	$223	$ 600	$ 547
Conventional pollutants	0	222	222
Maintenance	102	914	859
Fuel economy	35	187	170
Total benefits	360	1,924	1,799
Total cost	96	608	558
Net benefits	264	1,316	1,241

Source: Council on Environmental Quality, *Fifteenth Annual Report* (Washington, D.C.: U.S. Government Printing Office, 1985), p. 235.

POLLUTION CONTROL AND ITS IMPACT ON BUSINESS

Pollution control costs are by far the most important regulatory costs imposed on business. There is the incremental cost, that is, the cost of anything that has to be done to comply with a regulation that would not have been done without that regulation. Emission control devices, such as smokestack screens, are an example. Paperwork costs are also part of the incremental costs. In addition to the incremental costs of regulation, there are also secondary effects that incur costs to business and society. These costs may exceed the incremental cost of compliance. Examples of secondary effects are opportunity costs, changes in productivity, and costs of regulatory-imposed delays. One example of a regulatory-imposed delay is the Trans-Alaska Pipeline, which was delayed more than four years. In those four years, the cost of construction was estimated to have increased by 3.4 billion.[16]

The Environmental Protection Agency has made some efforts to decrease the cost of environmental regulation. It introduced the "bubble concept," which is based on the idea that it is often possible to reduce emissions of a given pollutant from one source far less expensively than from another. Thus, instead of compelling each source to meet a certain standard, a "bubble" is placed over the plant or geographic area, and private decision makers are allowed to decide the standard for the area at the lowest cost. For example, a number of smokestacks or even plants could be grouped together and treated as though they were enclosed by one large bubble. Thus, instead of being concerned with emissions from each smokestack, one can deal with the cumulative emissions from that bubble. This allows firms to undercontrol those stacks where control is expensive while overcontrolling stacks where control is cheap.[17]

Cost Shifting

Business firms will regard the cost of pollution control as a part of the total cost of doing business and will attempt to shift it forward to consumers via price increases, backward to stockholders in the form of lower dividends, or to workers in the form of lower wages. The actual extent to which prices change in a given market as a result of the inclu-

16. Arthur Andersen and Company, *Cost of Government Regulation Study: Project for the Business Roundtable* (New York: Business Roundtable, 1979), p. 27.

17. Council on Environmental Quality, *Fifteenth Annual Report* (Washington, D.C.: U.S. Government Printing Office, 1985), p. 60.

sion of pollution control costs in production will depend on a complex set of variables, including the price elasticities of demand and supply and the degree of competition in a given market. When a business firm has to purchase pollution abatement equipment, this represents an addition to total fixed costs and average fixed costs at all levels of output. Marginal costs also will increase. Firms with sharp increments in costs associated with small increases in output are less likely to shift pollution costs forward because profit will decline on incremental amounts sold.

Elasticity of Demand

If the demand for a product is absolutely or relatively inelastic, consumers will purchase the same or similar quantities at a higher price than the original market equilibrium price. There is an inelastic demand for a product when there are few, if any, close substitutes and the product is inexpensive — the smaller the fraction of total expenditures consumers allocate for a good is, the more inelastic the demand for it is likely to be. Thus, all other things being equal, firms confronted with an inelastic demand for their product would be able to incorporate pollution abatement costs into a higher price for the product, and with the quantity demanded decreasing at a rate slower than that of the increase in price, consumers would incur the cost of pollution control. On the other hand, if the demand for the product is elastic, an increase in price to cover the pollution control cost will be accompanied by a more than proportionate decrease in demand, and revenue will fall.

The Nature of the Market

In general, the more competitive a market is, the more difficult it will be for firms to pass pollution abatement costs on to consumers. Under pure competition, this would be impossible, for sellers have no control over the price of their product. The price is determined in the market by supply and demand, and sellers can only react to it. In the short run, a firm can vary its output, but not its plant capacity and hence will have some variable and some fixed costs. Firms will have to absorb the pollution control costs themselves, and some will go out of business. In the long run, a firm can vary not only its output but also its plant capacity and therefore has no fixed costs.

In industries characterized by oligopoly, the market situation is somewhat different. In other market situations, including monopoly, price is determined by how firms react to their cost situation in light of the individual firm's demand curve. The sum of these reactions gives the supply response, which, in combination with total market demand, sets the price. In oligopoly, however, the situation is not so simple, primarily because the individual firm cannot act without considering the reactions of its rivals. Thus, demand, as seen by the individual firm, is not independent of the reactions of rival firms, as it is in other market situations. The precarious position of the individual firm under oligopoly gives it an incentive to move in concert with other oligopolistic firms or to follow a price leader.

There are not many monopolies in the United States, primarily because there are few commodities or services for which there are absolutely no close substitutes. But local or regional monopolies of various kinds are relatively common. A monopolist tends, under any given condition of demand and productive capacity, to limit output to the volume at which the marginal cost of producing the good is equal to the marginal revenue derived from its sales. Since such an output is ordinarily well short of that at which the price just covers the average cost of production per unit of output, it follows that the productive results of operations under conditions of monopoly are quite different from those prevailing under competitive conditions. The monopolist has more leverage and more opportunity to push the cost of pollution control onto the consumer by simply readjusting output to a different point on the demand curve for the product and charging a higher price.[18]

The market mechanism through which changes in prices tend to reflect the inclusion of pollution cost can be illustrated with a simple diagram of market price determination. (See Diagram 13-1.) A business firm will treat the pollution abatement cost the same as it would any other cost of its operations and include it in the final price of its product.

In the diagram, DD and SS represent the respective demand and supply curves before the imposition of pollution cost. Market price is at P_1 and output at Q_1. After the cost, the supply curve shifts to S_1S_1, the vertical distance between SS and S_1S_1 representing the cost of installing pollution control devices. Since demand (DD) is less than perfectly elastic, the price in the marketplace has risen by less than the full cost of pollution control, in other words, the distance P_1P_2. This means that the cost is borne partly by the consumer and partly by the producer; the exact manner in which the cost is divided depends on the relative elasticities of demand and supply.

18. In the case of natural monopolies, such as electric power companies, the cost of air and water pollution control equipment is considerable. But for the most part, pollution control costs to power companies are reflected in higher rates to consumers, who thus pay the major part of the cost of cleaning up its environment.

Environmental Regulation and the Automobile Industry

In a relatively short period, the automobile industry has become one of the most regulated industries in the United States. Federal regulation of the automobile began in the 1960s when the government imposed safety and emission standards on new vehicles. The Clean Air Act of 1970 imposed additional emission standards on the industry, which contributed to the cost of producing automobiles. The Energy Policy and Conservation Act Amendments of 1975 provided a set of corporate average fuel economy (CAFE) standards for new cars produced in the United States, which required car companies to achieve a sales-weighted, fleet-average fuel economy of 27.5 miles in the 1985 model year. These federal laws resulted in increased investments in the auto industry on emission control equipment. Emission costs per auto-

Diagram 13-1 Market Price Determination of Inclusion of Pollution Control Cost

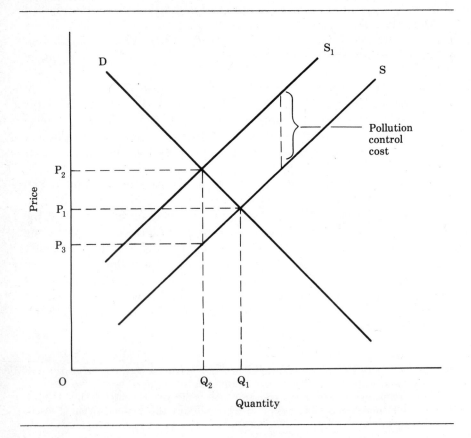

mobile, which can be divided into emissions equipment costs and other costs, including fuel penalties, are presented in Table 13-3 for the period 1968-1984.

Effects on Business

The costs to business of compliance with pollution control requirements may be overemphasized, since there also are benefits to business aside from the aesthetic value of a clean environment. Fulfilling pollution control requirements does increase business's expenditures. Installing and maintaining pollution control equipment necessitate additional bricklayers, electricians, iron workers, operating engineers, carpenters, and plumbers. Additional off-site labor is required to produce or transport the materials and equipment used in the actual construction of a project, as well as the engineering and technical labor needed to design, plan, and evaluate the operational performance of the pollution control systems. Jobs also are created in the pollution abate-

Table 13-3 The Cost Per Automobile of Emissions Regulations, Model Years 1968-1984 (current dollars)

Year	Cost
1968	$ 14
1969	15
1970	24
1971	25
1972	195
1973	532
1974	590
1975	306
1976	323
1977	466
1978	502
1979	559
1980	906
1981	1,551
1982	1,582
1983	1,607
1984	1,601

Source: Robert W. Crandall, Howard K. Gruenspecht, Theodore E. Keeler, and Lester B. Lave, *Regulating the Automobile* (Washington, D.C.: Brookings Institution, 1986), pp. 30, 38. Used by permission.

ment industry. All this can stimulate employment. Nonetheless, this increased employment also can be offset by the closing down of plants that cannot comply with the cost of cleaning up the environment.

Apart from the cost of pollution control, other problems confront business firms. One problem is the regulatory infrastructure that has been built up at the federal and state levels of government to administer pollution control laws. To conform to pollution abatement requirements, business firms have to deal directly with these regulatory agencies. But there is more to regulation of the environment than conformance to required standards of abatement. Government also is making an effort to control other areas that are in some way related to environmental pollution — land use, energy, and urban transportation; all encroach directly on business operations. Land use in particular has an impact on business location. Local governments have adopted controls over the use of land that require the dispersion or isolation of new factories and power facilities from centers of population. Local control over urban transportation designed to meet air quality standards would also affect industrial dispersion and business costs. Even the energy crisis is unlikely to alter materially the total impact of clean air requirements on industry.

THE ENVIRONMENT AND ECONOMIC TRADEOFFS

There is a conflict between the need to find new energy sources and the desire to clean up the environment. The energy shortage in the United States, coupled with its dependence on foreign sources of oil, made the discovery of new fuels mandatory. Another problem is the belief that pollution can be attributed directly to the society's preoccupation with economic growth. It is argued that the level of pollution is indeed linked to an increase in real gross national product: more goods result in more pollution. As a solution, some persons advocate zero economic growth. Conversely, other groups feel an increase in the rate of economic growth is necessary to reduce inflation and to increase job opportunities for minorities. Environmentalism is an economic issue in which one group wants a particular type of goods and services that may be different from what another group wants, and thus there are tradeoffs between them.

Economic Growth and the Environment

Another problem is the apparent conflict between economic growth and the environment. Economic growth is generally defined as the rate of increase in an economy's real output or income over time. Environmentalists contend that economic growth must be curtailed in the name of ecological sanity. They feel that the level of pollution is a direct concomitant of economic growth — as real gross national product increases, so does pollution. The social costs of pollution have been high, as affluence associated with a rising gross national product has increased. Environmentalists regard the world as an ecosystem whose natural resources are not infinite and which it is possible for humans to waste or despoil through imprudent actions. Therefore, environmentalists argue that it is necessary to de-emphasize economic growth. Since population is a variable that influences the rate of economic growth, environmentalists feel it is necessary to introduce worldwide birth control measures to lower the birth rate. Otherwise, the world will not be able to support the billions of people projected to be born during the coming decades.

Energy and the Environment

The OPEC-induced oil price rises of the 1970s brought home to the United States the need to be more self-sufficient in the production of energy. Even though there is now a worldwide glut in the production of oil, the desire is to become less dependent on foreign sources of energy. Energy independence — particularly with enormous coal reserves, a current surplus of oil, and the development of new sources of energy, for example, solar and wind[19] — appears to be possible, at least from a resource standpoint. However, to each approach to energy independence there is some opposition. For example, coal can be cheap to mine and consume when there is no concern for environmental standards but quite expensive to mine and consume when there are strict environmental standards. Environmentalists want coal mined and burned safely and cleanly without disturbing the typography at both ends.[20]

SUMMARY

Problems related to environmental pollution have attracted widespread attention only in recent years. This is not to say, however, that pollution is a relatively new phenomenon; on the contrary, pollution was a part of the American industrial and municipal scene during the last century. Recognition of this was expressed in the Refuse Act of 1899,

---

19. The Chernobyl disaster has probably, at least for the present, put an end to reliance on nuclear power as a source of energy.
20. Lester C. Thurow, *The Zero-Sum Society* (New York: Basic Books, 1980), p. 38.

which prohibited the discharge of waste into navigable waters. Nevertheless, most laws governing pollution are of recent vintage. The basic Water Pollution Control Act dates only from 1948, and the first Clean Air Act dates from 1956. The most important laws governing pollution were passed during the 1970s — the Clean Air Act of 1970 and the Water Pollution Control Act of 1972, both of which are amendments to the basic acts, and the Noise Control Act of 1972, which adds an entirely new dimension to the whole area of pollution control, with noise considered for the first time a major environmental pollutant. The Toxic Substances Control Act of 1976 regulates chemical substances, and the Hazardous and Solid Waste Amendments of 1984 protect ground water.

Pollution abatement entails both costs and benefits to society. There are three types of costs: opportunity, economic, and monetary. Monetary costs include the use of emission control devices. Air pollution expenditures account for almost half of total pollution abatement expenditures. The benefits that accrue to society from pollution abatement include improved health from the reduction of respiratory diseases. There are also economic and aesthetic benefits. Economic benefits include an improvement in agricultural production as soil acidity is reduced. Aesthetic benefits pertain to the senses. Air pollution creates offensive odors, and water pollution creates unsightly refuse on beach shores.

QUESTIONS FOR DISCUSSION

1. What are some of the causes of pollution?
2. Emission charges have an advantage over direct regulation of pollution in that there is less interference with the market mechanism. Discuss.
3. How is the term *opportunity cost* applied to the cost of cleaning up the environment?
4. What are some of the costs and benefits of cleaning up the environment?
5. Give an example of cost-benefit analysis as applied to cleaning up the environment.
6. What is the "bubble concept"?
7. Discuss how firms in a purely competitive market and in an oligopolistic market will react to environmental compliance costs.
8. Is there a conflict between the goal of economic growth and the goal of a clean environment?
9. What is the purpose of the Hazardous and Solid Waste Amendments of 1984?

10. In the final analysis, who ultimately pays most of the costs of cleaning up the environment?

RECOMMENDED READINGS

Bresnahan, Timothy, and Dennis A. Yao. "The Nonpecuniary Costs of Automobile Emission Standards." Technical Report 33, Stanford University, Center for Economic Policy Research, 1984.

Budlin, John, A. *The Economics of Environmental and National Resource Policy*, Boulder, Colo.: Westview Press, 1982.

Cooper, Charles. *Economic Evaluation and the Environment.* London, England: Hodder and Stoughton, 1982.

Council on Environmental Quality, *Fifteenth Annual Report.* Washington, D.C.: U.S. Government Printing Office, 1985.

Crandall, Robert W. *Controlling Industrial Pollution: The Economics and Politics of Clean Air.* Washington, D.C.: Brookings Institution, 1983.

Crandall, Robert W., Edward K. Gruenspecht, Theodore E. Keeler, and Lester B. Lave. *Regulating the Automobile*, Washington, D.C.: Brookings Institution, 1986.

Epstein, Samuel, Lester O. Brown, and Carl Pope. *Hazardous Waste in America.* San Francisco: Sierra Club Books, 1982.

Freeman, A Myrick. *Air and Water Pollution Control.* New York: John Wiley & Sons, 1982.

Ruff, Larry E. "Federal Environmental Regulation." In Leonard W. Weiss, and Michael W. Klass, eds. *Case Studies in Regulation.* Boston: Little, Brown, 1981.

White, Lawrence J. *The Regulation of Air Pollution Emissions from Automobiles.* Washington, D.C.: American Enterprise Institute, 1982.

PART V
DIRECT REGULATION OF BUSINESS

Part V discusses industries affected with the public interest, meaning simply they are too important to the public welfare to be allowed to function without regulation. Coupled with the public interest is a certain absence of competitive conditions in these industries, an example being the electric power industry, which provides a service necessary for society's well-being. Private property rules, which confer on individuals or groups the right and exclusive use and control of acquired economic goods, have been amended in the case of electric utilities and other industries affected with a public interest. These industries have become subject to regulation by regulatory commissions created at both the federal and state levels of government to set rates and prescribe services. These commissions also have judicial powers; that is, they are authorized to implement the law through judicial interpretation. Regulatory agencies, as agents of government, reflect group demands for positive action. Although they are not supposed to be arbiters like the courts, they can initiate policy in accordance with the law.

The regulation of business by such regulatory agencies as the Interstate Commerce Commission is economic rather than social and direct rather than indirect. However, there is a trend toward less direct government regulation of business. The Civil Aeronautics Board (CAB), which long regulated interstate air transportation, determining rates that could be charged and services that could be provided by carriers, is no longer in existence, and airline companies are now free to compete on the basis of price. Substantial price and service deregulation has also occurred in the natural gas, trucking, railroad, and banking industries to encourage more price and service competition. The move toward deregulation of industries previously regulated reflects a shift in attitudes toward the role of government, a belief that regulation has hampered productivity and job creation.

Chapter 14
The Regulated Industries

In an important minority of industries — transportation, communications, and electric and gas services — government intervenes actively and regulates business decisions more closely than in most private enterprises. These industries, classified under the general category of public utilities, provide all of us with services as essential to today's lifestyle as, perhaps, food or shelter. Yet, unlike the food or shelter industries, utilities are in a unique business category. From a legal standpoint, utilities are distinguished as a class of business affected with a deep public interest, which therefore makes them subject to regulation. What sets this segment of industry further apart is that in most areas it is considered desirable for a utility to operate as a controlled monopoly. As such, a utility is obligated to charge fair, nondiscriminatory rates and to render on demand satisfactory service to the public. The tradeoff is that a utility generally is free from direct competition and is permitted, though not assured of, a fair return on its investment.

The logic behind this kind of operating environment is reasonably straightforward. Utilities operate most efficiently as monopolies because they usually offer a single service or a quite limited number of services. A utility's operations are localized and limited by the necessary direct connection between the production plant and each piece of customer equipment. To a large degree, a utility plant can be used only for the service for which it is intended. There is concentration within a territory that permits the use of larger and more efficient equipment, hence a lower average expense per unit of output. Direct competition would be uneconomical because it would require duplicate investment and would clutter public property with distribution lines. This could lead to unnecessarily high rates or insufficient earnings, both unacceptable alternatives to the public and to the investor as well. There is some competition, but it is relatively diluted. Thus, a public utility operates under an exclusive franchise granted by a governmental unit.

CHARACTERISTICS OF A PUBLIC UTILITY

No set formula can be used to distinguish a public utility from other business enterprises, no definition that will include all the businesses that have been classed as public utilities and at the same time exclude those not generally considered as such. The most general definition of a public utility is that it is a business enterprise affected with a public interest although many companies affected with a public interest cannot be classified as public utilities. The oil companies are one example. The list of enterprises that have been declared to be public utilities or affected with a public interest is quite extensive. It includes gas companies, electric companies, telephone and telegraph companies, radio and television, railroads, water carriers, pipelines, air transportation companies, grain elevators, insurance companies, and stock yards. All these enterprises have been declared public utilities by a legislative body without subsequent contradiction by the courts.

The public utilities usually have certain economic and financial characteristics that separate them from other business enterprises. Generally, to be classified as a public utility, an enterprise must produce commodities or render services of general importance to the public. Furthermore, public utilities usually, but not always, have the important economic characteristics of being natural monopolies. Fire insurance companies have been held to be public utilities, but they are not monopolies. A natural monopoly is a legal monopoly established by the federal or a state government, usually because there can be increasing economies of scale over a wide range of output so that one firm can supply the market more efficiently than several, or because unrestricted competition among firms in the industry is deemed socially undesirable. Such public utilities as telephone companies, gas companies, electric companies, and waterworks are natural monopolies. Of course, it would be possible to duplicate these companies and have two or more of each occupying the same area and competing against each other, but this sort of duplication is not considered economical.

Economic Characteristics

Regulated industries such as public utilities have two economic characteristics. The first is that they generally are very capital intensive, since there is a very high ratio of fixed assets to total assets. A railroad has almost all of its assets concentrated in rolling stock, terminals, and warehouses; an electric company has almost all of its assets in power plants and transmission lines. These fixed assets lead to the second economic characteristic of regulated industries, namely, fixed costs that do not vary with output. Examples of these are rental payments, depreciation of plant and equipment, property taxes, wages and salaries of a skeleton staff that a firm would have to employ as long as it stayed in business — even if it produced nothing — and interest payments on debt. The last category is particularly important to a public utility, given the nature of its debt structure. Fixed costs are those costs that a firm would have to bear even if the plant were completely closed down for a time. A railroad, for example, has a tremendous investment in land, rolling stock, and repair shops. The expense of maintaining these properties continues regardless of the amount of traffic hauled by the railroad.

Because of certain technical factors, the expenses of many utility companies, particularly those in gas and electric power, decrease as the size of the plant increases. In most market areas the demand for electric power is insufficient to justify the construction of the optimum-sized production and distribution system. A firm considering building a new plant must decide on its size. A relatively small plant would have higher average costs than a larger plant would. For the firm, the average total costs usually drop over a certain range as the scale of operations is increased, then reach a minimum, and then increase when the scale of operations becomes too large. But since the total fixed cost remains the same regardless of output, the fixed costs are spread over more units of output, and consequently, each unit of output bears a smaller share of the fixed costs. Therefore, the average fixed cost curve is downward, sloping to the right throughout its entire length, and so firms with large fixed costs — railroads, for example, with their tremendous fixed costs for roadbeds and rolling stock — can substantially reduce their fixed costs per unit by producing larger outputs.

It is evident that firms operating very small plants are likely to be inefficient, that is, expensive to operate, in almost any line of production. The production unit is too small to take full advantage of the specialized labor and equipment. A good example of inefficient single-plant firms are small farms. They have proved to be inefficient in comparison with larger farms because they are not large enough to use mechanized equipment efficiently. It would hardly pay a wheat farmer with a ten-acre plot to purchase the combine that the farmer with a thousand-acre plot could use. But it also is true that firms operating very large plants are likely to be inefficient in almost any line of production. The production unit simply becomes too large for the job to be done properly. We can conclude, therefore, that the average total costs for the single-plant firm fall as the plant size is increased, reach a minimum, and then begin to increase as the plant grows larger. This is shown in Table 14–1.

Decreasing-cost industries are those for which the demand curve (represented by demand price) lies to the left of the point at which the average total costs are the lowest — that is, in the example, at an output of three thousand units. This means there is room for only one firm in this hypothetical industry. Under the existing conditions of demand, two or more firms would have such small outputs that their average total costs would be much higher than those of the single firm. Hence, they would probably be eliminated in a competitive struggle, until only one firm remained. If, on the other hand, the demand price were larger than the average total cost at three thousand units, there would be room in the industry for a number of competing firms to operate at their lowest average total cost output.

Diagram 14-1 illustrates the points made above. A company considering building a new plant must decide on its size. A relatively small plant, as for example a_1, would have higher average total costs than would a larger plant, a_2. The optimum-size plant would be a_5, which would produce an output of OL at an average cost per unit of OK. Past this point average total costs will increase. If the market is too small to justify a plant of this size, a smaller one should be constructed. If it is expected that fewer than OX units will be sold per period, plant a_1 is preferable to plant a_2. If the expected output is OM, that output can be produced by plant a_2 at a lower average cost than by a plant of any other size.

Let us assume the market is currently being served by a firm with a plant of the a_1 size. If demand is sufficient and a new company builds a plant of a_2 size, it will be able to undersell the first plant. This, of

Table 14-1 Cost and Price Figures of a Decreasing-Cost Firm (dollars)

Output (units)	Total Fixed Costs	Total Variable Costs	Total Cost	Average Total Cost	Marginal Cost	Demand Price
0	1,000					
100	1,000	400	1,400	14.00	4.00	9.00
200	1,000	750	1,750	8.75	3.50	8.00
300	1,000	1,050	2,050	6.83	3.00	7.00
400	1,000	1,300	2,300	5.60	2.50	6.00
500	1,000	1,500	2,500	5.00	2.00	5.00
1,000	1,000	2,400	3,400	3.40	1.80	3.00
2,000	1,000	4,000	5,000	2.50	1.60	2.00
3,000	1,000	6,000	7,000	2.33	2.00	1.00
4,000	1,000	9,000	10,000	2.50	3.00	.80
5,000	1,000	13,000	14,000	2.80	4.00	.60

$$\text{Average total cost} = \frac{\text{Total cost}}{\text{Output}} = \frac{\$1,400}{100} = \$14.00$$

$$\text{Marginal cost} = \frac{\text{Increase in total cost}}{\text{Increase in output}} = \frac{\$1,400 - \$1,000}{100} = \$4$$

Diagram 14-1 Natural Monopolies and Economies of Scale

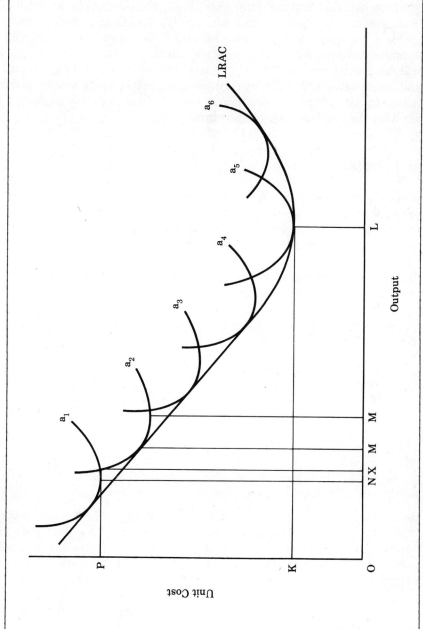

course, requires a lengthy period in which changes in plant capacities are possible. At any price below OP, the first plant will be selling below cost, whereas the larger plant will be able to sell at a price somewhat below OP and enjoy a considerable profit. If competition is allowed to operate without restriction in this situation, either the first company will be forced out of business or the two companies will get together and agree on a price that will bring monopoly profits to one or both firms. In neither case will the interest of consumers be protected by allowing the market forces to compete freely.

Public Utility Financing

Utility financing is unique in several respects. First, the amount of capital required is much greater than that in other industries and is several times the annual operating revenue. This requirement stems from the need for capital expenditures for various programs. For electric utilities, expenditures are needed to build and maintain generation and distribution facilities to meet projected demand, as well as pollution control equipment. The latter expense is of increasing importance, for public utilities are subject to regulation with respect to air and water quality and related environmental matters by various federal, state, and local authorities, which usually are authorized to require modifications of utility facilities and operations. Second, an unusually high percentage of utility capital is derived from the sale of bonds and preferred stock. The reasons for this reliance on long-term financing are

1. The relative stability of utility earnings, at least in the past, has made feasible the use of such sources without undue risk.
2. By using bonds and preferred stock whose interest and dividend rates are substantially less than the overall rate on investment, the return on the common stock of a public utility can be magnified to attract common stock capital.

Bonds normally account for about 50 percent of a public utility's capitalization. The most important type of bond is the first mortgage bond. Since the great bulk of a utility's assets are fixed, a mortgage permits the issuance of bonds against physical property. The first mortgage bond gives the owner, who is a creditor, the first lien against the property of the utility and, as such, can be sold to investors to yield a low rate of interest. But because of the uncertain market that has prevailed in the United States during this decade, interest rates on first mortgage bonds have increased precipitously. For example, a first mortgage bond that could have been sold to yield 3 percent on its par value twenty years ago now would have to yield 10 percent or more. This means that the ratio of interest charges to operating revenue and to earnings before interest charges has increased. Interest is a fixed charge that has to be paid out of operating revenue. High interest rates and other increased costs, among other things, have increased the need for rate increases, which in many instances have been subject to regulatory delays and consumer protests.

Preferred stock also is used commonly in public utility financing, particularly by electric and gas utilities. Since preferred stock usually carries no voting rights, the danger of management's losing control of either a public utility operating company or a holding company is reduced to a minimum. Furthermore, the safety of preferred stock, since it has preference over common stock in payment of dividends and prior claim on assets in the event of liquidation, makes it attractive to many investors. Public utility preferred stock is often cumulative; that is, if dividends on preferred stock have not been paid in one year because funds were not available, these back dividends must be paid up before any dividends can be declared on the common stock. But the dividends on preferred stock come out of the public utility's net earnings, which can be burdensome. As a general condition for the issuance of preferred stock, a public utility's net earnings for at least one year must be a minimum of one and one-half times the annual interest requirement on outstanding debt obligations plus annual dividend requirements on preferred stock.

PUBLIC UTILITY REGULATION

Public utility regulation, as we know it, is the consequence of many years of experimentation and change. As mentioned in Chapter 2, American public utilities first were regulated at the state level. In the 1870s, the agricultural states of the Middle West began to limit freight rates and curtail railroad rate discrimination in response to political pressures exercised by the Grange. The right of the states to regulate public utilities was made legitimate in 1877 when the United States Supreme Court, in the case of *Munn* v. *Illinois*, declared constitutional a law of the Illinois legislature that regulated the rates and practices of grain elevators. State public utility laws and advisory public utility commissions multiplied rapidly thereafter. But since most commerce was interstate, state legislation and regulation by themselves proved ineffective. So in 1887, the federal government created the Interstate Commerce Commission to prevent rate discrimination and various forms of monopoly agreements among railroads engaged in interstate commerce. Since that time regulation has continued to expand with the growth and technological advancements in the utility industry and the U.S. economy.

There are five types of regulation to which public utilities have become subject: regulation by the courts, regulation by state legislatures, regulation by local government units, regulation by state commissions, and regulation by federal commissions. Before the creation of regulatory commissions and in the absence of statutory or legislative control, certain industries were subject to a semblance of regulation by the courts. Under common law, they were required to give adequate service to all comers at reasonable rates and without discrimination. Individual grievances were handled by the courts. Then attempts were made to regulate public utilities directly through laws enacted by state legislatures. Rates and service conditions were fixed by law or by charter or franchise provisions. Legislatures, however, did not have the time or ability to handle the specialized problems constantly presented for attention. Furthermore, they were too close to the people and too mindful of political pressure from lobbies and the electorate to be able to maintain their objectivity. Today, only general legislation is enacted; administration is delegated to administrative commissions or to local governments as agents of the state. The latter may regulate their own local utilities within the powers granted to them by the state.

Of the several types of utility regulation, by far the most important is regulation by the state and federal commissions. In many cases, a public utility is subject to both state and federal regulations. For example, the Southwestern Public Service Company is a utility primarily engaged in the generation, transmission, distribution, and sale of electric energy.[1] More than 99 percent of its operating revenues was derived from these services during fiscal year 1986. The territory served by Southwestern, which covers approximately 45,000 square miles, includes the Texas Panhandle, extends north into the Oklahoma Panhandle and the southern half of Morton County, Kansas, and drops south into Texas over most of the South Plains region, as well as the Pecos Valley region in southeastern New Mexico and a portion of east central New Mexico. Its electric properties are an interconnected system, and approximately 80 percent of the company's operating revenues come from operations in Texas.

Southwestern is subject to the jurisdiction of the New Mexico Public Service Commission, the Corporation Commission of Oklahoma, and the Kansas Corporation Commission for its rates and service and the issuance of some of its securities; and the New Mexico Public Service Commission is empowered to certify the construction of its facilities. The Federal Power Commission governs some of Southwestern's activities, including its rates for reselling electricity, and the FCC's uniform system of accounts is the basis for Southwestern's books. In Texas, the Utility Commission, created by the Public Utility Regulatory Act of 1975, directs Southwestern's books and accounts and its rates and services. However, Southwestern's rates and services in the incorporated cities and towns in which it operates in Texas will continue to be

---

1. Southwestern Public Service, *Annual Report 1980.*

regulated by these municipalities unless a municipality elects to have the Utility Commission assume such jurisdiction. The Utility Act also establishes certain standards for the rates determined by the municipalities. Finally, the Securities and Exchange Commission governs the issuance of Southwestern's securities. The commission is authorized to require the filing of information concerning Southwestern's directors and officers, their remuneration, and the principal holders of Southwestern's securities.

Southwestern is subject to regulation of air and water quality and related environmental matters by various federal, state, and local authorities, which usually are empowered to require modifications of Southwestern's facilities and operations. The Texas Air Control Board and the New Mexico Environmental Improvement Board determine and enforce the permissible level of air contaminant emissions in their respective states. The Texas Water Quality Board and the New Mexico Water Quality Control Commission regulate water discharges and are required to set water quality standards and issue waste control orders covering water discharges that might affect the quality of their states' waters. Diversion of surface waters in Texas for cooling and other purposes is subject to the jurisdiction of the Texas Water Rights Commission, which is empowered to allocate such waters among users.

The Independent Regulatory Commissions

Congress has assigned much of the responsibility for implementing these laws to independent bodies known as regulatory agencies. With few exceptions, they are known as commissions. It is always somewhat difficult to define a regulatory agency because Congress has not distinguished the independent agencies from those in some executive departments. The regulation of stock exchanges, for example, has been delegated to an independent agency known as the Securities and Exchange Commission, whereas until recently the regulation of commodity exchanges had been under the jurisdiction of the executive branch of government. Similarly, the misrepresentation of articles, including drugs, is the concern of an independent agency, whereas the misleading labeling of food, drugs, and insecticides is the concern of an executive department.

In theory, these commissions were established by Congress to regulate and control the economy in accordance with Congress's will. The existence of such agencies is justified on the ground that the complexities of modern society demand regulation to avoid economic anarchy, monopoly, and irresponsibility. It has been argued, for example, that the advent of such phenomena as nuclear energy and jet aircraft calls for greater government surveillance in order to allocate these resources appropriately to meet the goals of modern society. From another perspective, the need for many regulatory agencies, such as the Interstate Commerce Commission, is often challenged on the grounds that such regulation hinders free enterprise and encourages waste. These agencies also are criticized because they are somewhat incompatible with the system of separation of powers. Their very existence represents a diffusion of executive power, which the constitution vests in the president. This separate existence, however, is justified because these bodies perform not only executive functions but also legislative and judicial ones.

The term *independent* suggests that the president has only limited control over these agencies and no direct responsibility for their decisions or actions. A few such agencies are in the executive department, but most are not. In nearly every independent agency, the governing body contains several persons and is headed by a chairperson. To encourage their independence from both the president and a single political party, Congress has decreed overlapping terms of office so that no one president can pack an agency with his or her followers. This attempt to keep the agencies above politics is further strengthened by congressional limitations on the number of commissioners who may be appointed from any one political party. In addition, the length of the terms tends to make even a president's own appointees somewhat independent, but despite this and their structural independence from the executive branch, the major regulatory agencies actually are open to a fair amount of executive influence. A member of the presidential staff may attempt directly to persuade a commissioner to adopt the president's position. Executive influence may also be asserted through the budgetary process. Agency requests for funds go through the Bureau of the Budget and are subject to executive surveillance.

The courts do not directly adjudicate the cases brought before the agencies. The cases decided by the agencies, however, may be appealed to the federal courts, giving the latter the power of judicial review of agency rulings. When an agency has acted in an adjudicative context, the courts can review its procedures to ensure that they are constitutionally valid, that the agency had proper jurisdiction, and that the statutory rules controlling the procedures have been observed. The courts may also review the agency's interpretation of the law, but they exercise substantial restraint in this area, and their powers are limited. Nevertheless, judicial review of agency actions is a valuable right for the business community to have. Review by the courts of agency decisions provides a safeguard against administrative excesses and the unfair or arbitrary action of overzealous officials. A court is most likely to set aside an agency ruling when an agency has erred in its interpretation of a statute, has acted outside the scope of its authority, or appears to have denied due process because of unfair agency procedures.

There are four federal commissions governing the interstate activities of the natural monopolies and the transportation industry: the Interstate Commerce Commission, Federal Energy Regulatory Commission, Federal Communications Commission, and Securities and Exchange Commission. Each regulates a specific industry — railroads, oil pipelines, television, and so forth. Their powers are broad, and they can make rules that have the force of law. For example, the Securities and Exchange Commission (SEC) has established many rules designed to protect buyers of securities. It regulates trading in securities on exchanges and in over-the-counter markets to eliminate abuses, and prosecutes companies and persons guilty of securities frauds, manipulations, and other violations. Table 14-2 presents an encapsulation of the characteristics of the SEC and other commissions that regulate utilities, transportation, and communication.

Table 14-2 Major Federal Regulatory Commissions

Agency	Date Established	Number of Members	Term (years)	Jurisdiction
Interstate Commerce Commission	1887	5	5	Railroads, motor carriers, shipping by coastal and inland waters, oil pipelines, express companies, freight forwarders
Federal Energy Regulatory Commission*	1920	5	5	Electric power, natural gas and natural gas pipelines, water power sources
Securities and Exchange Commission	1934	5	5	Securities and financial markets, electric and gas utility holding companies
Federal Communications Commission	1934	5	5	Radio, television, telephone, telegraph cables

*Formerly the Federal Power Commission

State Regulatory Commissions

Federal regulatory commissions are responsible for regulating public utilities and transportation in interstate commerce, and state commissions regulate intrastate activities. The individual state's authority to regulate is derived from the state's police power — the authority to legislate for the protection of the health, safety, morals, and general welfare of its citizens. The courts have given the states extremely wide latitude under these powers to regulate all kinds of business activities. In a 1934 case (*Nebbia* v. *New York*), the Supreme Court asserted that "a state is free to adopt whatever economic policy may reasonably be deemed to promote the public welfare and to enforce that policy by legislation adapted to its purpose."[2] Thus the right of federal and state governments to regulate economic activity — particularly to set prices or rates — is clearly established, although the Court recognizes that such regulation cannot violate individual rights safeguarded by the Constitution and that the activities of all regulatory bodies must be subject to judicial review. When the police power of the states conflicts with the power of the federal government, the states must yield.

State regulatory commissions were created to deal with special problems as they have arisen. For example, the development of state regulation of electricity offers interesting parallels to the history of railroad regulation. As such abuses increased, particularly in the form of high rates, consumer dissatisfaction laid the groundwork for regulation. As in the railroad industry, regulation came after the abuses had been disclosed and vested interests had become entrenched, and not as a means of guiding the growth of the industry. As with the railroads, regulation lagged behind the industry's developing geographic pattern. Statewide power was not invoked effectively until long after the industry had transcended state boundaries. Eventually, state commissions were created to regulate the electric utilities. As in the railroad industry also, regulation remained for a long time negative in character, concerned with discovering and penalizing abuses and checking excessive rates. Again, as with the railroads, regulation has become more positive, concerned with reshaping corporate structures, planning the development of new sources of supply, and controlling and directing marketing policies.

The constitution and laws of each state define more or less specifically the powers and duties of the utility commissions, and consequently, there is great variation in the utility laws of the states and the responsibilities of their commissions. In most states, the commissions have the power to regulate the rates charged by privately owned utilities, but the scope of jurisdiction is not the same for all states. In a

2. *Nebbia* v. *New York*, 291 U.S. 502 (1934).

few, the control is limited to fixing maximum rates only, leaving the companies free to set rates lower than the maximum fixed by the commission. In most states, the commissions can regulate the rates that the municipalities pay to privately owned utilities for street lighting, lighting of public buildings, and other public services. They also may regulate the rates that the federal government pays to a privately owned utility. The state commissions' authority to regulate contracts between municipal utilities and ultimate consumers is the same as that governing the private utilities in those states in which the commissions have jurisdiction over the municipal utilities. The power to regulate special contracts between utilities is granted under the commission's authority to regulate rates. Interconnection contracts must be approved by the commissions in many states, though in others such contracts do not require commission approval.

Members of state public utility commissions are either appointed by the governor with the approval of the legislature or elected by direct popular vote. There are defects in both approaches. Often appointments are based on factors irrelevant to the qualifications necessary to become a competent public service commissioner. Favoritism and politics are often involved in appointments. To some extent the state commissioners' overlapping terms prevent the appointment of purely political appointees beholden to special interests. Elected officials are presumed to be more responsive to the public will, although this is not necessarily the case. A commissioner who is a good campaigner may not possess the requisites necessary to understand the complex nature of the public utility commissions. In many states, salaries are inadequate to attract and hold the types of persons needed on the commissions. Because a state commissioner has complicated and technical duties, it requires three or four years for the typical appointee or elected official to acquire the experience and information necessary to handle properly the responsibilities of the office.

The main concerns of the state commissions are the intrastate electric, gas, telephone, water, and transit facilities. Their functions are similar to those of the federal regulatory commissions. State commissions act primarily as a legislative agency when they fix rates. When exercising judicial or quasi-judicial functions, commissions sit as a court to hear evidence on both sides of a complaint. They must judge the merits of the arguments presented by their own staffs, representatives of the public, and the utilities. In rate hearings, the commissioners find themselves in the conflicting position of being the legislative body whose duty it is to fix rates in the interests of consumers, while judging the adequacy of such rates to protect the rights of investors. Commissions also have administrative responsibilities, in that they must carry out the act of the state legislatures pertaining to regulation. A large part of the time of state commissions and their technical staffs is devoted to such duties.

RATE MAKING

The bread-and-butter responsibility of the federal and state regulatory commissions is rate making, establishing prices for the services provided by regulated firms. Public utilities usually are natural monopolies, and their business thus virtually excludes competition. The monopolistic power of a utility would enable it to overcharge unless curbed by public authority. Since it is the natural inclination of monopolies, if left unregulated, to enrich themselves at the expense of their customers, it is essential that the public be provided protection with respect to rates charged and services provided. One of the underlying principles to be kept in mind is that public utilities, since they are deeply affected with a public interest, are not considered legitimate instruments for reaping excessive profits; they should be limited to a fair and reasonable return to the operators and investors. But what a fair and reasonable return is, is debatable. From the consumer's standpoint, no rate is reasonable that yields more than a normal return to the utility or that assesses the costs inequitably among various classes of consumers.

Development of Rate Making

The first efforts to regulate public utility rates were made by the state legislatures. In the case of *Munn* v. *Illinois* (1877), the Supreme Court ruled that rate regulation was a legislative matter not reviewable by the courts.[3] But it became evident that the rapidity of economic change required constant, day-to-day regulation, and the legislatures were in session for only a few months of the year, many for only a few weeks. Jurisdiction over rate regulation therefore passed to the courts. In several railroad rate cases, the courts decided that the reasonableness of a rate was a matter for judicial investigation. The courts then redefined property as value rather than mere physical assets and extended the due process clause to protect this new concept of property. The courts forbade the confiscation of values and even went one step further: they asserted their right to determine value, not only as a matter of law, but also as a matter of precedent. But how was fair value to be ascertained?

Smyth *v.* Ames, *1898*

Along with *Munn* v. *Illinois*, *Smyth* v. *Ames* ranks as one of the two most important cases concerning public utility regulation.[4] In *Munn* v.

3. *Munn* v. *Illinois*, 94 U.S. 113 (1877).
4. *Smyth* v. *Ames*, 169 U.S. 466 (1898).

Illinois, the Supreme Court held that the legislative regulation of grain elevators and railroads did not violate the Fourteenth Amendment. In *Smyth* v. *Ames*, the Supreme Court declared that the rate — or price — charged for the product or service of a public utility ought to be calculated to yield "a fair return on the fair value" of the utility's holdings. In the dicta of *Smyth* v. *Ames*, the Court enumerated several factors to be considered in arriving at fair value: original cost of property, less depreciation; the amount spent on current improvements; the amount and market value of a utility's bonds and stocks; reproduction cost of new property, less depreciation; the probable earning capacity of the property under particular rates prescribed by statute; and the sum required to meet operating expenses. But the two most important criteria suggested in *Smyth* v. *Ames* for the determination of fair value were original cost of property, less depreciation, and reproduction cost new, less depreciation. Which should be used? If both are used, should one be favored over another? The Supreme Court did not answer these questions, nor did it define a fair return.

Original Cost Less Depreciation   The original cost method of property valuation can be used as a rate base. This method, which is also called the prudent historical cost method, is easy to determine and administer. The regulatory commission takes from the accounting records of a given utility the figures of the actual money outlay for the original plant and subsequent equipment. After the original cost has been ascertained, the accrued depreciation of the properties from all causes, both physical and functional, must be determined. This accrued depreciation must be deducted from the original cost to establish the net cost or investment devoted to the public service. From the physical point of view, the property wears out or otherwise deteriorates so that eventually it must be retired from service. This physical decline in service value can be determined by tests and measurements or can be estimated reasonably. When a proper charge has been made for depreciation using the straight-line method and included in the operating expenses, the full original investment is conserved.

Reproduction Cost Less Depreciation   The rate base also can be determined by the reproduction cost method: that is, a ten-year-old plant is given a value equal to the cost of replacing it at current prices less depreciation. The utilities generally have favored the reproduction cost method because of rising prices that have inflated the rate base, and the courts generally have favored it because to deny the public utilities the increase in property value owing to rising prices could be said to take property without due process of law. There are some problems with reproduction cost less depreciation. The hypothetical reproduction cost of a new plant that duplicates the old one is not valid even on a competitive basis, because a new plant, if actually built, would use more modern equipment, and the cost might be greater or less, but production would be more efficient. The use of the reproduction cost method when prices are falling would bankrupt many utilities. The service provided would be likely to deteriorate, and although the customers paid lower rates, they would receive less service. Finally, if the rate base determined by the reproduction cost method of valuation is revised by making changes in the price level, valuations become expensive, and the frequent changes in the rate base complicate the work of the regulatory commissions.

In *Smyth* v. *Ames*, as in subsequent decisions, the Supreme Court did not define a fair rate of return. Generally, the fairness of a rate of return on capital depends in large measure on the riskiness of the investment. The riskiness of investment in the public utility field, at least in the past, has been low — at least when the industry is a regulated public utility, because there is no close competition. Because of this, in the past a relatively low rate of return still would have made it possible for the utilities to attract capital as easily as more competitive fields where uncertainty is greater. But this has not been the case in recent years. Utility investors and officials are, of course, anxious to receive the highest possible rate of return on their investment. Administrative commissions and courts have no specific criteria to follow in determining a fair rate of return and most resort to largely arbitrary judgments that often are influenced by the amount of pressure brought to bear by special interest groups. The courts have asserted that no single rate is fair at all times and that regulation does not necessarily guarantee a fair rate of return to a utility. Thus it is still not very clear what a fair rate of return is.

Rates based on the fair return on fair value concept would be calculated by first determining the depreciated value of the physical property in accordance with the fair value rule. To this figure is applied a rate of return that would obtain a return to those who committed capital to the utility, whether bondholders or stockholders. Estimated operating expenses are added to the return, and the total is the amount that the rates should yield. Expressed as a formula,

$$R = E + (V - D)r$$

where

> R is the revenue to be obtained from the rates in question,
> E is the operating expense,
> V is the vaue of the physical property new,
> D is the depreciation to be deducted,
> r is the rate of return expressed as a percentage.

Hope Natural Gas, 1942

The Hope Natural Gas decision is important because in this case the Supreme Court departed from its past procedures in reviewing rates on the basis of a "fair return on the fair value" of property.[5] The Federal Power Commission ordered the Hope Natural Gas Company to reduce its wholesale rates by $3.6 million annually. The commission had valued the property of the company at $33 million after depreciation, on which it allowed a return of 6.5 percent. The company contended that it should be allowed a return of 8 percent on a reproduction cost rate base of $66 million. A lower court set aside the order of the Federal Power Commission because of its failure to give proper consideration to reproduction cost. The commission refused to include well drilling and other investment costs that totaled $17 million because these investments had been charged to operating expenses as they were made. The net operating income of the company from interstate rates was $5.8 million. Consequently, the reduction required was something over 62 percent.

In ruling against the company, the Supreme Court did not take a stand in favor of any rate base. Rather, it felt that if the end result was a rate that enabled the company to operate successfully, to attract capital, and to compensate its investors for risks assumed, the rate was sufficiently high. The effect of the Hope decision was to absolve the public utility commissions from having to set rates that provided a fair return on the present fair value of the utility property, as required by *Smyth* v. *Ames*. The Court upheld a valuation made substantially on the basis of original cost but stressed it was not endorsing or requiring any particular method. It stated: "It is the result reached not the method employed which is controlling...It is not theory but the impact of the rate order which counts."[6] This decision means the fairness of rates is to be judged primarily by their effects on the ability of a utility to furnish adequate service and provide needed capital. It also means the Court will not review a commission's rate orders or allow a utility to obtain a review except under extraordinary circumstances.

The Hope case means a "fair return on the fair value" of property will be used as a criterion for the reasonableness of rates, though the emphasis has shifted from the asset side of a utility's balance sheet to the liability side. Rate proceedings now tend to center more on the ability of rates to maintain the credit of the utility, to ensure fair treatment to its security holders, and to enable it to raise new capital. The rate of return ought to be sufficient to enable a utility to attract the financial capital needed for it to continue to operate. The return

5. *Federal Power Commission* v. *Hope Natural Gas Co.*, 320 U.S. 591 (1944).
6. Ibid.

should cover interest and preferred stock dividend requirements with enough to spare to yield an attractive but not unnecessarily large return on the common stock. This places a burden on the public utility commissions, for current interest rates must be computed and future ones estimated. Earnings-price and yield-price ratios for the stock of comparable utilities must be computed and compared. A comparability of earnings standard may also be used in rate making. This standard means the rate of return allowed a utility ought to be comparble to that prevailing in other industries with comparable risks.

Economic Principles of Rate Making

Monopoly is a market situation in which a single firm sells a product for which there are no close substitutes. There are no similar products whose price or sales will influence the monopolist's price or sales, and cross-elasticity of demand between the monopolist's product and other products will be either zero or small enough to be neglected by all firms in the economy. Indeed, the monopoly is the perfect industry from the producing point of view, and the market demand curve for the product is also the demand curve faced by the monopolist. Thus, the monopolist is able to exert some influence on price, output, and demand for the product. It is in a position to ascertain that point on the industry demand curve at which profits will be maximized. This has important implications for resource allocation because output restriction and higher prices are the end result. There is a possibility of long-run profits under monopoly because there is little or no entry into monopolized industries. When there are profits, consumers pay more for products than is necessary to hold the resources for making those products.

Diagram 14-2 represents the short-run marginal cost (MC) and the marginal revenue (MR) curves for a regulated monopoly. If the monopoly is allowed to operate under monopoly market conditions and attempts to maximize profits, it will produce OM units of output and sell them at a price of MP per unit. To maximize profits, the monopoly will produce at exactly the rate at which marginal cost and marginal revenue are equal. Up to this point, marginal revenue exceeds marginal cost, and it would continue to be profitable to produce any unit of output that adds more to revenue than it adds to cost, in other words, any unit for which marginal revenue exceeds marginal cost. Beyond this rate, marginal cost exceeds marginal revenue, and it would be pointless to produce additional units of output. At the output OM and the price MP, the monopoly is making a profit per unit of PS and a total profit of HPSR. From an economic and social point of view the result is undesirable, because consumers get less and pay more than would be the case under pure competition. This is so because the price under pure competition tends to equal the marginal cost of production, whereas the price under monopoly exceeds the marginal cost.

A fair rate of return, as allowed by a public utility commission, can be represented by the point OR, since this is the rate at which price equals average total cost (ATC), assuming that average total cost includes a normal or fair rate of return on capital investment. In economic theory, competitive long-run cost is defined to include the opportunity cost of all factors employed — what they could earn in their best alternative employment. In the case of capital supplied to a public utility, this means the rate of return should be comparable to that which could be earned in alternative investments. In Diagram 14-2, output under government regulation would be MN units greater than

Diagram 14–2 Monopoly Price, "Fair" Price, and Socially Optimum Price for a Public Utility

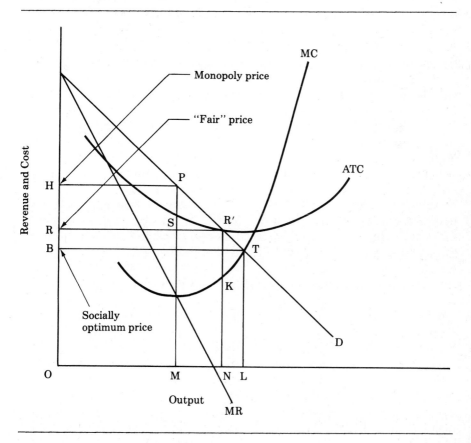

that which would exist in an unregulated monopoly situation, and the price would be lower by PS. Although the regulated price, NR', is equal to average total cost, it is greater than marginal cost. The price represents what can be called full cost or average cost pricing, the price at which the utility covers all its costs, both fixed and variable, and earns a normal profit.

The price OR is not the socially optimum price, however, for it is above marginal cost. Marginal cost at output ON is only NK. This indicates that output is still too low in terms of the ideal allocation of resources. This is true because marginal cost represents the amount of additional resources required to put an additional unit of service in the market; price represents the amount that consumers are willing to pay to secure the additional unit. As long as price is above marginal cost, more resources should be devoted to producing the service. The price OB illustrates marginal cost pricing, the price at which the utility's marginal cost equals its demand (D), or average revenue. Production is carried to the point at which marginal cost is equal to demand price and there are no customers to which the service is worth more than the additional cost of production. The marginal cost price is therefore the socially optimum price — the price that maximizes society's welfare — because at this price the value of the last unit to the marginal user is equivalent to the value of the resources used to produce that unit.

Under pure competition price equals marginal cost, and the optimum allocation of resources is achieved. But, under pure competition, price is also equal to average cost, and in the long run, firms neither make abnormal profits nor incur losses. Rate regulation for public utilities, therefore, poses a policy dilemma. If prices are set at average total cost levels (OR in the diagram), the output of the utility may be restricted below that which is most desirable socially for consumer sovereignty. But if the price is set at marginal cost levels, the utility company may be unable to cover average costs and therefore suffer losses, or it may make monopoly profits. In the diagram, marginal cost pricing would cause the utility company to incur losses, since the price falls below the average cost. If, however, the demand curve were to intersect the marginal cost curve somewhere to the right of the lowest point on the average cost curve, marginal cost pricing would enable the utility to secure an above-normal return.

In actual practice, utility commissions have tried to keep prices at average cost levels, though this can create a problem. Since a utility is legally entitled to a fair return, in other words, a normal profit above costs, there is little incentive for it to cut costs. If, by improving efficiency and curtailing all unnecessary expenses, the utility is able to reduce average costs, the old rates will then provide a surplus above costs, and the utility will enjoy monopoly profits. The utility will be making more than a fair return, and the logic of regulation would require that rates be lowered. But in fact, rates are not adjusted frequently; thus, an increase in efficiency may for a time increase the profits of the utility, and this may be sufficient to justify introducing a cost-reducing innovation. However, there are not the same incentives for cost cutting in a regulated monopoly that there are in a highly competitive industry, and sometimes the regulated industries are noticeably inefficient.

SUMMARY

Public utility enterprises are, to some degree, monopolies. For certain industries, operating as a monopoly rather than in open competition seems to be the most feasible way to produce and distribute a commodity or service. Economies of scale may make competition impractical and contrary to the efficient allocation of resources; hence the term *natural monopoly* is often applied to certain types of public utilities. It would be wasteful, particularly in regard to decreasing costs, for two or more firms to serve a given market when a single firm could provide the same service at a lower real cost. Competing electric power companies, for example, would result in unnecessary expense and duplication of services. It would also be wasteful to duplicate railway lines or even some air routes. What happens then is that a public utility usually operates under an exclusive franchise granted by a governmental unit. The utility thus becomes not only a natural monopoly but a legal monopoly as well; there can be no competition from another company for the life of the franchise.

Public utility enterprises are recognized by the courts as being affected with the public interest, as too important to be left exclusively to private enterprise to run as it sees fit. In return for the franchise privilege that allows a utility to provide a service to a particular area, the government establishes operating criteria that the utility must follow. It must render adequate service to all comers and charge reasonable rates. Regulatory agencies are given broad powers to establish prices charged and to control services provided. These agencies are usually referred to as independent regulatory commissions, and they exist at both the federal and state levels. They carry out legislative and judicial functions under a broad grant of power from Congress or from a state legislature. Public utility enterprises doing a purely intrastate business are subject to control by the public service or public utility commissions of the states in which they operate. If facilities are used for both intrastate and interstate business, the estimated property and expense devoted to each is calculated. Utility companies engaging in interstate commerce are subject to one of the several federal regulatory commissions or agencies.

Part of the regulation of public utilities is to establish a fair market price for the commodity or service being sold. This market price must allow for an equitable rate of return on the investment of the regulated firm. Since capital is the most important input to a utility, the issue of how to determine its fair value has been a significant one in regulatory proceedings. In the Hope Natural Gas case, the Supreme Court asserted that regulatory commissions are not bound to any special theory of valuation to determine the value of the utility's properties to be used to set rates. The original cost less depreciation method of property valuation is used by most commissions to establish the rate base. Once the base has been determined, a commission must decide what return to allow on it. Economic theory suggests that it should be a normal return, what the utility could earn on its capital in a competitive industry in long-run equilibrium.

QUESTIONS FOR DISCUSSION

1. What are some of the economic characteristics of public utilities?
2. Economies of scale accrue to firms operating under conditions of decreasing costs. Discuss.
3. Why are federal regulatory commissions called independent?
4. Discuss the functions of the four major federal regulatory commissions responsible for regulating natural monopolies and transportation.
5. Discuss the importance of the *Smyth* v. *Ames* case.
6. Which method of property valuation, original cost less depreciation or reproduction cost less depreciation, would a public utility prefer to use in a period of rising prices?
7. Distinguish between the concepts of monopoly price, fair price, and socially optimum price as applied to public utility rate making.
8. Distinguish between the concepts of average cost pricing and marginal cost pricing.

RECOMMENDED READINGS

Kahn, Alfred E. *The Economics of Regulation.* 2 vols. New York: John Wiley, 1970.

Lancaster, Angela. "Electric Utility Rate Making." Congressional Research Service, Library of Congress, March 26, 1976.

Phillips, Charles F., Jr. *The Economics of Regulation.* Homewood, Ill.: Richard D. Irwin, 1965.

Posner, Richard. "Theories of Economic Regulation." *Bell Journal of Economics,* 5 (Autumn 1974), pp. 335-357.

Samuels, Warren J. "Regulation and Valuation." *Public Utilities Fortnightly*, 96 (1973), pp. 35-48.

Stigler, George J. "The Theory of Economic Regulation." *Bell Journal of Economics*, 2 (Spring 1971), pp. 3-15.

U.S. Congress, House Committee on Interstate and Foreign Commerce, *A Short Primer on Rate Making and the Regulatory Process in the Electric Utility Industry: Report for the Energy and Power Subcommittee*, prepared by Douglas N. Jones, 94th Cong., 1st sess., March 18, 1976.

U.S. Congress, Senate Committee on the Judiciary. *Civil Aeronautics Board Practices and Principles: Report of the Subcommittee on Administrative Practices and Procedure*, 94th Cong., 1st sess., 1976.

Chapter 15
Deregulation and Competition

Competition is regarded as a principal desideratum of a market economy. It is thought to maximize productivity, encourage research and development, improve the position of the small businessperson, prevent excessive concentration of economic power, provide for attainment of consumer interests, and eliminate arbitrary barriers to market entry. There is also an interrelationship between competition in a free enterprise market economy and a democratic political structure, in that competition is supposed to prevent the growth of excessively powerful economic units, regardless of whether they are business or labor. This preventive aspect of competition will, it is believed, help maintain basic democratic institutions. In the *Wealth of Nations*, Adam Smith writes that self-interest works not only in the interest of the individual but also in the social interest, that is, it promotes the ends of society as well as those of the individual as long as there is competition in the economic system. When pure competition exists, no one person or firm can exercise economic control, for economic power comes from the ability to influence or control prices.

As we pointed out in the last chapter, competitive market structures sometimes can cause inefficient resource allocation and a socially undesirable market performance. This can happen when economies of scale are so extensive in relation to the size of the market that only one firm can operate efficiently within that market. It is not feasible to remedy this situation by means of structural modifications intended to create competitive conditions. Instead, direct regulation under the laws governing public utilities is used. Certain industries, including transportation, electricity, gas, telephone service, and the broadcast media, are exempted from the direct application of the antitrust laws on the theory that a regulatory agency protects the public interest and thus there is no rationale for what would be redundant intervention by antitrust enforcement agencies. But regulation differs greatly among the industries in which conditions of natural monopoly may exist, and public utility regulation often has been applied in cases in which a natural monopoly clearly does not exist.

CRITICISMS OF REGULATION

Criticisms of government regulation took a number of forms. Some critics felt the regulatory agencies acted more in the interest of the regulated firms than in the interest of the public. Regulatory agencies were blamed for "bending with the wind," changing policies and taking actions designed to curry favor whenever commissioners saw political tides going in a particular direction. Other critics thought there was too much regulation by the commissions. The results, they said, were that the individual, the economy, and in fact, society as a whole, were stifled. Often commissions, supposedly the experts, made decisions that hurt both regulated business and the consumer. For example, the Interstate Commerce Commission was accused of following policies detrimental to the interests of the railroad industry. Even though it was clear by the 1930s that the nineteenth-century concept of the railroads being responsible for offering complete service to every locality along every mile of track had become obsolete, the ICC refused to allow them to abandon unprofitable services.

There were other, more esoteric complaints about the regulatory agencies. In some agencies, the agency personnel not only made the rules and served as the judges but also decided to bring action. One highly esteemed American political tradition is the separation of legislative, judicial, and executive power; this tradition would seem to be violated when the decision to bring an action is not separated from its adjudication. In other agencies, the commissioners who made the ultimate decisions were removed from the actual fact-finding. Thus, they never really knew what was going on because they saw only a summary report when they made their decisions. They acted only on the basis of facts found by a trial or a hearings examiner of some kind, but they did not hear the actual testimony.[1]

Finally, critics have decried the effects of regulation on the efficiency of the market as a resource allocator. A price kept below the market price by regulation has the effect of creating a system of nonprice rationing in which excluded customers are forced to pay higher prices for substitutes. In some cases, price regulation leads to an excessively high level of some service characteristics because firms are prevented from competing on the basis of price. Because of price regulation by the Civil Aeronautics Board, for example, airlines competed primarily through frequency of flights, which led to low load factors and considerable excess capacity. Regulation of oil and natural

1. For a summary of the reasons for deregulation, see *The Economic Report of the President 1983* (Washington, D.C.: U.S. Government Printing Office, 1983), pp. 100–102.

gas prices has on occasion kept prices too low, causing shortages and inefficient choices among competing fuels.

DEREGULATION

A major deregulation effort was underway in the United States by the 1970s, which culminated in the passage of the Airline Deregulation Act of 1978, the Natural Gas Policy Act of the same year, and the Motor Carrier Act and the Staggers Railroad Act of 1980. These acts reflected a general distrust of big government, and regulatory agencies were part of the big government syndrome. With deregulation in such industries as air transportation and natural gas, firms have been able to set prices based on market demand but are constrained by competition. Further steps toward deregulation of industry occurred during the early 1980s, with the deregulation of the commercial banking industry. This deregulation has changed the nature of commercial banking and the competitive environment in which it operates.

Deregulation of Air Transportation

The main issue in the air transportation industry was whether competition or regulation would bring about more socially desirable results. When commercial aviation in the United States began, there were fears that ineffectively regulated competition would become cutthroat competition, to the detriment of both safety and the development of a commercial fleet that might serve as a national defense transport reserve. Originally, it was Congress's intent to place the airline industry under the jurisdiction of the Interstate Commerce Commission, but they then decided that the ICC was too close to the railroads and too judicial and regulatory in its approach to be able to provide the leadership necessary to promote a new means of transportation. In 1938, the Civil Aeronautics Act was passed, which created the Civil Aeronautics Board (CAB) and gave it regulatory authority over entry, routes, rates, airmail payments, and subsidies of common carriers. It was also empowered to grant or withhold the certificates of convenience or necessity needed for operating specific routes, as well as to approve mergers or pooling arrangements.

The CAB followed a general policy of fostering a mixture of competition and monopoly, mostly the latter. The competition was over service rather than price. As traffic grew on existing routes, the CAB approved applications from existing airlines to extend their routes and add new ones, thereby strengthening the weaker systems and permitting the duplication of service on major routes. The CAB was authorized to regulate domestic air fares and rates and to control entry into the air transportation industry. Its entry policy was restrictive with regard to the entrance of new airlines into the industry but permissive with respect to entry by existing carriers into specific markets. Thus the regulatory policies of the CAB were somewhat analogous to those that would be followed by a cartel — an agreement between legally independent enterprises that restrains competition. Except for self-imposed restraints on output, sales, or prices, the activities of the cartel members remain independent. Entry barriers are created and enforced by legal sanction, the market is divided formally among participants, and internal price competition is discouraged. As in an oligopoly, a cartel heeds other forms of competition. In the airline industry, this competition was primarily service — an excessive number of routes and product differentiation — elaborate cuisines, and attractive attendants.

The greatest criticism of the CAB's regulation of the air transportation industry was that it encouraged inefficient airline operation. In essence, the CAB established the fares that could be charged in various markets, and then the airlines tended to compete away the profits they could make through changes in scheduling. The absence of any real form of price competition, coupled with higher than competitive rates, works to the disadvantage of many consumers of air travel. Many passengers would prefer to be able to select airlines on the basis of price as well as type of service. Moreover, comparisons of CAB-regulated airlines with less-regulated intrastate airlines indicated that the latter were generally more efficient and could provide transportation over similar routes at a lower cost. A case in point was the Texas intrastate market, in which Southwest Airlines, a carrier licensed by the Texas Aeronautics Commission, directly competed with Braniff Airways, a CAB-regulated trunk carrier, and Texas International Airways, a CAB-regulated local service carrier. Despite having its service introduction postponed for nearly four years because of judicial challenges by Braniff and Texas International, Southwest Airlines was eventually allowed to serve the so-called golden triangle of Dallas, San Antonio, and Houston. It made a profit, charging fares that ran as much as 50 percent below comparable CAB fares.[2]

The Airline Deregulation Act of 1978

This desire to deregulate air transportation and return it to a competitive market resulted in the passage of the Airline Deregulation Act of 1978. One purpose of the act was to eliminate legal barriers to market entry, thus promoting competition. If profits are made in a competitive

---

2. Few frills were provided, and many flights were scheduled at off-hours.

market, new firms will be attracted into the industry. These new firms will endeavor to obtain a share of the profits by providing the same goods at lower prices, improved goods at the same price, or a combination of the two. Furthermore, should the industry have the productive characteristics that allow a purely competitive market structure to be approximated, the marginal cost of output will eventually equal the price of each good, thereby yielding economic efficiency in production and exchange. Consumers are better served, since they can get the same goods at a lower price, but a firm loses when new firms enter and reduce profits through competition. However, the surviving firms benefit in the long run by earning a market rate of return equal to that which they would get if they were producing their next highest valued alternative product.

The Airline Deregulation Act of 1978 had the following provisions:

1. The Civil Aeronautics Board was to be eliminated by 1985 (which it was), with economic regulation to be phased out by that time and other CAB functions were to be transferred to other agencies, such as the Federal Aviation Administration (FAA).

2. The act was designed to allow existing interstate carriers to enter new markets, and to make it easier for new firms to enter the air transportation industry.

3. The act allowed domestic airlines to cut or raise fares in single markets.[3] This freedom increased during a transition period, until, on January 1, 1983, all regulations on fares were eliminated.

Results of Air Transportation Deregulation

A Brookings Institution study indicates that, based on all efficiency grounds and most distributional grounds, airline deregulation has served the public interest much more effectively than regulation would have.[4] It found that deregulation air travelers have saved $6 billion annually as a result of lower fares and better service, and that airlines have improved their earnings by $2.5 billion. Because the industry is still tied to the capital structure created under government regulation, it has not fully adjusted to deregulation, so that benefits received by the public should be expected to increase in the future. Air carriers are now using more fuel-efficient, medium-size jets on their deregulated routes. These aircraft, with their more sophisticated electronics, are designed to

3. The act allowed domestic interstate airlines to cut fares in individual markets by as much as 50 percent in one year or to raise them by as much as 5 percent in fifty-eight days without CAB approval. This is now a thing of the past.
4. Steven Morrison and Clifford Winston, *The Economic Effects of Airline Deregulation* (Washington, D.C.: Brookings Institution, 1986.)

operate with two, rather than three pilots. This will lead to a reduction in industry costs, for labor will be used more efficiently.[5]

One common criticism of airline deregulation is that small cities served by airlines during regulation would be without air service. This has not necessarily proved so. Although there was a short-run loss of service resulting from deregulation as air carriers withdrew from cities they no longer had to serve, almost all small cities have picked up other carriers.[6] There has been a loss of air service to some small communities, and there has been some political fallout. However, deregulation may not be responsible. Rather, these losses may be explained by the increase in fuel prices and by cyclical macroeconomic conditions as better opportunities appeared elsewhere.[7]

One result of airline deregulation has been an increase in the number of mergers in the air transportation industry. In 1986, for example, Texas Air acquired Eastern Airlines, which could make it the largest U.S. domestic air carrier. United Airlines has acquired several Pacific routes from Pan American Airlines, and Trans World Airlines has acquired Ozark Airlines. Other industry consolidations include Southwest Airlines and Muse Air, Frontier Airlines, and People Express, and Piedmont Airlines and Empire Airlines. In 1983, the ten largest airlines in the United States had 99 percent of the domestic market as measured by revenue passenger miles.[8] Two of those airlines have been absorbed by other airlines. There is some concern that the airline industry of the 1980s may turn out to be like the railroad industry during the latter part of the last century. Faced with heavy fixed costs and recurring recessions, the railroad industry struggled for survival. There were many bankruptcies and last-ditch mergers. But this does not appear likely in the airline industry, and actual and potential competition appears sufficient to maintain benefits to consumers achieved by deregulation.

DEREGULATION OF NATURAL GAS

National gas is another example of special industry regulation in which competition and monopoly come into intricate interplay. To some

5. Ibid., p. 72.
6. Roanoke, Virginia, a city of one-hundred thousand, is a case in point. Before deregulation, it was served by Piedmont Airlines, the only airline certified to serve the city. There were a number of flights to and from Roanoke to such cities as Washington, most of which were half filled. After deregulation, Roanoke is now served by a subsidiary of Piedmont and by other carriers as well. There are fewer flights to Washington but more carriers from which to choose.
7. Morrison and Winston, p. 52.
8. "Summary of U.S. Major Carriers Domestic Traffic for 1983," *Aviation Daily*, March 2, 1984.

extent there is an interrelationship between the natural gas and the oil industries, in that some of the exploration for gas is conducted jointly with the search for crude oil, leading also to joint problems in defining and measuring the cost of exploration for gas. There are also common problems of production and distribution. The natural gas industry, however, differs from oil in that it resembles a public utility. Producers of natural gas search out and develop natural gas reserves and then contract with a pipeline company to deliver gas to them over some period. Generally, the pipeline companies purchase gas in the field, transport it to market and sell it, either to distribution companies for resale or directly to customers. Local distribution is a typical natural monopoly conducted under a public franchise, and facilities for gathering and transporting natural gas also tend to be monopolistic. At the same time, natural gas must compete with alternative energy sources, including oil. Thus, the mixture of competition and monopoly in the natural gas industry complicates the establishment of a sound public policy.

The natural gas industry is divided into three broad categories: the field market, the pipelines, and the distribution markets. The field market is the market for gas at the wellhead, and it centers on contracts under which petroleum companies set aside reserves of natural gas to channel into pipelines. The pipeline companies take the gas from the field to wholesale industrial users or retail distributing companies. Generally, the pipeline companies, which link the field and distribution markets, do not act as common carriers. Rather, the distribution companies are usually local public utilities that sell gas to residential, commercial, and industrial customers. Ultimately, more than 45 percent of natural gas production goes to commercial and residential consumers, and the rest is used as energy or process material in industry.

Natural gas was regulated first at the state and local levels of government. As the production and sale of gas was primarily intrastate, the problem of jurisdiction was not a barrier to state control. Markets were local, and gas had little or no commercial value. Eventually there were new industrial uses for natural gas, and through the construction of seamless pipes it became possible to transport gas over long distances. The demand for federal regulation of interstate movements of natural gas came initially from the states and cities, which found that their efforts to control rates were often thwarted by their lack of authority over companies transporting gas from other states or over the basic rates charged for such gas for local distribtuion. Only the federal government could reach into those interstate transactions, through which companies controlling a large proportion of the country's gas supply escaped regulation. In the absence of federal authority, no regulation was possible, and it was to fill this gap that the Natural Gas Act of 1938 was passed.

Rate Regulation at the Wellhead

Following the 1954 Supreme Court decision in *Phillips Petroleum Co.*
v. *Wisconsin*,[9] the wellhead prices of natural gas sold in interstate
commerce were regulated by the Federal Power Commission (FPC).
Since intrastate gas prices were not subject to regulation, a two-market
system resulted. In area rate proceedings, the FPC established a two-
tiered set of price ceilings — a higher price ceiling that applied to "new"
gas taken from gas wells, and a second, lower, ceiling that applied to
"old" gas from gas wells and all gas from oil wells. The rationale for
setting a lower price ceiling for old gas committed to the interstate
market was that it would transfer income from producers to consumers. In using this approach, the FPC assumed that the natural gas
found in conjunction with oil and old gas-well gas cost less to produce
than did new gas-well gas.

The main issue in the FPC regulation of natural gas was that rate
regulation had prevented prices from rising in response to a growing
demand for gas and thereby had prevented producers from responding
to this demand.[10] As a result, there was a shortage of natural gas.
Industrial use of natural gas was curtailed during periods of shortages,
and many potential users of gas, both at the industrial and residential
levels, were proscribed from using gas. The abnormally cold weather
of 1977 produced a severe interstate gas shortage. Many factories were
closed in major industrial states such as Ohio and Pennsylvania, with a
concomitant adverse effect on unemployment. The dependency of
American industry and American homes on natural gas was illustrated
graphically during the weather crisis. Transmission companies were
faced with insufficient pipeline capacity; they could not fit enough
gas into their systems to meet the burgeoning demand.

The Natural Gas Policy Act of 1978

The natural gas regulatory environment was changed substantially by
the Natural Gas Policy Act of 1978.[11] This act was intended to encour-

---

9. *Phillips Petroleum Co.* v. *Wisconsin*, 347 U.S. 622, 1954. In this case, the
   Supreme Court decided that the FPC was to have jurisdiction over the rates of
   all wholesale sales of natural gas in interstate commerce, whether or not by a
   pipeline company and whether occurring before, during, or after transmission
   by an interstate pipeline company.
10. Peter R. Merrill, *The Regulation and Deregulation of Natural Gas in the U.S.
    1938–1985* (Harvard University, Energy and Environmental Policy Center,
    John F. Kennedy School of Government, 1981).
11. Congress also passed the Powerplant and Industrial Fuel Use Act, which
    authorized nonprice rationing of gas to counter the problems inherent in
    continued price controls.

age production by deregulating the prices of newly discovered gas while restraining the growth of average gas prices through permanent controls on the price of older gas. It replaced the Federal Power Commission with the Federal Energy Regulatory Commission and extended price controls to gas sold in intrastate markets. It also provided for the phased deregulation of the wellhead price of most natural gas discovered after 1977, which was supposed to account for 40 to 60 percent of all gas by January 1985, whereas a smaller amount of natural gas was scheduled for deregulation in July 1987. Most gas to be deregulated in 1985 or 1987 was fixed until those dates at a price, in inflation-adjusted dollars, leading to the oil-equivalent adjusted price level existing in 1978. There were twenty regulated categories for natural gas pricing, which can be divided into four groups.

1. "New" (post-1977) gas, most of which received a 3 to 4 percent real price increase annually, until it reached the equivalent of fifteen dollars a barrel (in 1978 dollars) by 1985, when "new gas" was to be deregulated

2. "Old" (pre-1977) interstate gas, which remained price controlled at 1978 real prices until exhausted

3. "Old" (pre-1977) intrastate gas, some of which was deregulated in 1985 and the price-controlled remainder received a regulated price higher than that of old interstate gas

4. Certain high-cost gas was deregulated[12]

Evaluation of Natural Gas Deregulation

The phased deregulation of natural gas created many problems. Instead of producing the lowest cost natural gas supplies first and moving on to higher cost sources, producers were induced by the different price structures to produce high-cost gas first in many cases and generally to shift production efforts away from cost-minimizing alternatives. Another problem arose from the control of "new" prices. Since oil prices rose substantially after 1978, partial decontrol generated a continued increase in delivered price of natural gas as consumers bid up prices to levels equivalent with those of close substitutes such as oil. The field price of natural gas rose more than 40 percent in real terms from the passage of the National Gas Policy Act to the end of 1981.[13] The increases in the average price under the regime established by the act were larger than anticipated.

12. Wells deeper than fifteen thousand feet and unconventional gas other than tight sands gas.
13. Milton Russell, "Overview of Policy Issues: A Preliminary Assessment," in *The Deregulation of Natural Gas*, edited by Edward J. Mitchell (Washington, D.C.: American Enterprise Institute, 1983), p. 13.

Complexities and rigidities in the production and distribution of natural gas resulting from the act created problems from 1981 to 1983. Declining oil prices in 1981 meant that oil in some uses became less expensive than the gas available from many pipelines. Those energy users able to do so switched back to oil, lowering the demand for gas. Between 1981 and 1983, total natural gas sales declined by 14 percent. In a free market, this lower demand would have been translated into lower prices, but in fact, gas prices to pipelines continued to rise through 1983. Prices paid by residential consumers rose through 1984 and 1985. In January 1985, new gas prices were decontrolled as required by the Natural Gas Policy Act. Rather than rising as predicted, new gas prices actually declined.[14]

Massive changes in natural gas markets have occurred that have fundamentally changed the natural gas industry. One change was the end of cheap gas as was provided by regulation. At least in the early 1980s, there was excess demand for gas, and except for special circumstances, there was no trouble finding markets. A second change was field-price regulation itself and the economic and regulatory problems it carried with it. Regulation produced expectations about gas prices and availability of supply that affected the location of consuming industries, the criteria by which choices were made by consumers, growth strategies and financial structures of pipelines and distributors, terms of contract at every stage of the gas industry, and energy research and development programs. It affected the type of management style that prospered, the sorts of investors that were attracted, and state and local regulations that resulted.

DEREGULATION OF RAILROADS

No industry has had more impact on the economic and social development of the United States than the railroad industry. For many years, it was almost the sole source of transportation in the United States. It shortened the time of transportation between cities and stimulated the development of such industries as steel and meat packing. It opened up the development of the West and stimulated the expansion of agriculture. It remained the dominant form of transportation until well into this century, but fell on hard times, gaining the reputation of being one of the most inefficient and poorly run systems in the world. It is somewhat ironic that the British and German railway systems, both of which are state-owned and operated, have been more efficient than most of the privately owned railroads in the United States.

14. *Economic Report of the President 1986* (Washington, D.C.: U.S. Government Printing Office, 1986), pp. 170-171.

Regulation of railroads produced price structures largely unrelated to underlying cost and demand conditions. The United States changed dramatically after World War II.[15] Changing patterns of demand and supply called for adjusting railroad rates, but regulation found the task of efficiently controlling these rates to be impossible. The problem worsened in the 1970s when regulatory lag in adjusting rates during inflation resulted in rates moving up more slowly than the cost of doing business. Because of the varying degree of competition across the different commodities shipped and the changing demand and cost conditions for different types of traffic, adjusting all rates by the same percentage was inefficient. An end result of regulation was the bankruptcies of several railroads in the 1970s, including the Penn Central and the Rock Island.

The Staggers Railroad Act of 1980

Federal legislation enacted in 1976 gave the railroads increased rate flexibility.[16] The railroads were permitted to increase or decrease their rates by as much as 7 percent within a one-year period without seeking ICC authority. This initial dose of deregulation, however, proved inadequate, so the Staggers Railroad Act of 1980 brought additional changes to railroad regulation by giving the railroads increased pricing and operating flexibility. The act freed a major part of the rail rates from ICC regulations altogether and established a zone of flexibility within which railroads could raise, without ICC permission, the rates that remained regulated. Railroads were permitted to raise rates by 6 percent a year up to an 18 percent total by 1984 and 4 percent a year after that. If rates exceeded that range, the burden of proof was on the ICC to declare them excessive, unless a railroad achieved market dominance.

Results of Railroad Deregulation

There are some positive results to show for the short time since railroads have been deregulated.[17] Railroads have been able to increase profits, rates have declined moderately in real terms, and productivity has increased. Average real rates for all commodity groups as measured

---

15. The development of a national interstate highway system contributed to the decline of the railroads. Other forms of transportation also increased in importance.
16. The Railroad Revitalization and Reform Act of 1976.
17. *Economic Report of the President 1986*, pp. 163-165.

by the Bureau of Labor Statistics decreased by 1.6 percent between the third quarter of 1980 and the third quarter of 1985. Productivity as measured by ton-miles per employee hour was up by 44 percent in the first four years after the passage of the Staggers Act. Service quality has also improved as railroads have been able to invest in and upgrade track and equipment. Route-miles over which train speeds were reduced because of the poor quality of the roadbed went from thirty thousand miles in 1978 to twelve thousand miles in 1984.

There also have been some problems associated with railroad deregulation.[18] Electric utilities and coal companies have complained that railroads are able to exploit market power in shipping coal. One study estimated that 40 percent of coal shipments were captive to a single railroad, and another indicated that 13 percent were captive. However, coal rates as measured by the Bureau of Labor Statistics have declined by 0.7 percent in real terms since the passage of the Staggers Act. It is also necessary to point out that the ICC still has some regulatory controls over the railroads. If a shipper has no competitive shipping alternative, the ICC can review the reasonableness of the rail rate charged. The Staggers Act intended that there be limits on the ability of railroads to raise rates to captive shippers.

DEREGULATION OF TRUCKING

Trucks were first regulated by the states during the 1920s. Regulation was at first concerned with safety and the licensing of drivers, but then the rates and services of trucks and other common carriers were also regulated. However, the impossibility of regulating interstate motor carriers led to the passage of federal regulation. The Motor Carrier Act of 1935 included trucks and other forms of common carriers within the regulatory jurisdiction of the ICC. Common carriers operating in interstate commerce were required to obtain a certificate from the ICC that authorized them to serve particular routes. Rates, fares, charges, commodity classifications, and consolidations were subject to ICC control. Rates had to be published and were required to be reasonable and not discriminatory. The ICC was also charged with the enforcement of safety standards.

Disenchantment with regulation of the trucking industry developed for several reasons.[19] First, competition was limited within the industry because the ICC placed barriers to market entry on new carriers. It

---

18. Ibid., p. 164.
19. Martha Derthick and Paul J. Quirk, *The Politics of Deregulation* (Washington, D.C.: Brookings Institution, 1985), pp. 171-184.

often rejected applications by new carriers on the grounds that they would harm existing carriers. Regulation also benefited inefficient carriers while depriving efficient carriers of cost advantages, a result often tantamount to depriving them of all opportunities to compete for business. Like the air transportation industry, there was really no incentive for the trucking industry to be efficient, for competition was limited and excess costs could always be incorporated in rate increases. Trucks also compete against railraods, but both were regulated by the ICC. The main effect of this regulation was to reduce competition within the trucking industry and also to lessen and control its competitive impact on rival forms of transportation such as the railroads.

The Motor Carrier Act of 1980

The Motor Carrier Act of 1980, which was signed into law by President Carter, pared back forty-five years of extensive regulation of the trucking industry. It made it easier for new trucking companies to enter the business and for existing firms to expand their services. It also gave companies more freedom to raise or lower freight rates without government intervention. The act will also gradually limit the antitrust immunity that had enabled truckers to agree on the prices they will charge. In late 1980, the ICC adopted final rules relaxing much of the traditional trucking regulation; the new policies and procedures carry out directives in the act as interpreted by the ICC. One set of rules, which became effective in December 1980, eliminated the "gateway restrictions" that had required truckers to operate through certain cities, often prohibiting them from using the most direct routes. The rules also abolished the circuitous routing limitations often imposed in the past on one trucking company to protect the business of another. Now a trucking company may use any available routing to serve authorized points.

As there has not been complete deregulation of the railroad industry, nor has there been complete deregulation of the trucking industry. The process is gradual, with a goal of promoting competition while protecting users of the services against possible abuses and the pain of withdrawal from regulated rates. Published trucking rates are now subject to large and widely available discounts. About 90 percent of shipping rates are negotiated by individual shippers and carriers, with prices and services tailored to the needs of individual shippers. The ICC still exercises some control over the licensing of carriers and also can hear appeals from shipppers who feel they have been discriminated against.

Results of Trucking Deregulation

The results of trucking deregulation are similar to those for airline deregulation. The number of carriers has almost doubled since deregulation; as of 1984, more than two thousand had been granted general, nationwide authority.[20] As is also true of the air transportation industry, the new competition in trucking has had an impact on the wages of employees of carriers previously protected by regulation. Then, it was easy to give raises to workers without needing to be concerned about cost and efficiency, because labor costs could be automatically passed on to consumers in the form of rate increases. Today, nonunion firms and nonunion subsidiaries of established firms have proliferated in the transportation industry, exerting pressure on unionized firms, whose contracts have saddled them with high wages and restrictive work rules. Wage deferrals and freezes have occurred in both the airline and trucking industries. Many Teamsters locals have accepted wage cuts of 10 to 15 percent at small trucking companies.

Deregulation of the trucking industry has also not resulted in an increase in market dominance by a few large trucking firms, as some critics of deregulation had feared. The number of big carriers — those with operating revenues of more than $5 million a year — has remained stable under deregulation at around one thousand. Conversely, the number of intermediate carriers, with operating revenues between $1 million and $5 million a year, has shown a decline of almost 50 percent.[21] The smaller carriers have shown the greatest gain under deregulation. The number of these carriers has doubled, from roughly twelve thousand to twenty-four thousand. The growth in the number of small carriers can be attributed to ease of entry into the market, which was restricted under regulation, and to revenue they have been able to take away from the larger carriers. The trucking industry has also been made more efficient. Fewer trucks are empty on return trips, and rates are lower on average and are more nearly based on actual cost of service.

DEREGULATION OF TELECOMMUNICATIONS

The commercial history of telecommunications in the United States is synonymous with the development of the American Telephone and Telegraph Company (AT&T), which was created in 1900 and became dominant in its field by 1986. It achieved this dominance in several

20. "Industry Trends & Statistics," *Commercial Carrier Journal* (July 1984), p. 82.
21. Derthick and Quirk, pp. 4-5.

ways. The first was through control of patents. Licensing contracts with companies using Bell patents required them to turn over part of their stock to the Bell Company. Telephone apparatus was leased but not sold. Second, to control the manufacture and sale of telephone equipment, the Western Electric Company, a Bell subsidiary, refused to sell equipment to competing telephone companies. Third, the Bell Company eliminated competing companies through rate wars, refusals to connect with them or to sell them telephone equipment, attempts to block their franchises, and purchases of stock control.

The first attempt by government to regulate AT&T involved a threat to invoke the Sherman Antitrust Act. In 1913, AT&T agreed to get rid of Western Union and promised not to try to gain control of competing telephone companies. It also agreed to connect its toll-service system with independent companies. However, when the Willis-Graham Act of 1921 permitted the merger or consolidation of competing telephone companies, subject to state approval, AT&T was again acquiring competing companies. As a result, AT&T not only became the largest telephone company in the United States, it became the largest company in the world. By 1930, AT&T had 87 percent of the telephone facilities in the United States.[22]

Federal and State Regulation of the Telephone Industry

The states were the first to regulate the telephone industry. In most states, the established regulatory commissions were given the usual public utility control over intrastate telephone rates and services. This type of regulation was largely ineffective. For one thing, they were not equipped to deal with the complex problems of telephone regulation, and for another, they were not equipped to deal with AT&T, which had the financial resources to hire the best lawyers and public relations persons to circumvent regulation. The organizational structure of AT&T also made state regulation difficult because it presented jurisdictional obstacles, in particular the regulation of long-distance service. Then there were operating companies that served more than one state, which made state regulation even more difficult. So federal regulation of the telephone industry was inevitable.

General federal regulatory power over communications carriers was first vested in the Interstate Commerce Commission with the passage of the Mann-Elkins Act of 1910. However, at that time, most telephone service was intrastate and not subject to federal control. The ICC made little effort to regulate either telephone or telegraph rates and services;

22. Federal Communications Commission, *Investigation of the Telephone Industry of the United States*, H. Doc. 340. 76th Cong., 1st. sess., 1939, p. 14.

it was much more involved with the regulation of railroads. In 1934, the Federal Communications Commission (FCC) was created, to which was transferred all the duties, powers, and functions in communications formerly held by the ICC. The FCC was invested with jurisdiction over interstate telephone and telegraph rates and services. It, too, did not have the power to regulate all parts of the Bell System because some service was interstate and other service was intrastate. However, it and state commissions were able to exercise some control over the Bell System.

Deregulation of AT&T

Although the AT&T antitrust case was discussed in an earlier chapter, the deregulation aspects of the case need now to be discussed. The structure of AT&T was controversial not only because of its size, but also because it operated in both competitive and monopoly markets and owned most of the local telephone networks, which were needed by AT&T's competitors to provide their services. AT&T, it was felt, posed a threat to competition. To create an advantage for its own services, it could interfere with competitors' use of local networks by withholding technical information or providing inferior service. It was able to gain a competitive advantage over its rivals by cross-subsidizing its services. In a number of private antitrust suits, other companies had accused AT&T of using these and other anticompetitive tactics against them, and had won their cases in court.

Competition in the area of telecommunications had increased before the AT&T break-up in 1982. On terminal equipment, the FCC decided in 1977 to establish a program that would certify competitors' equipment for direct connection to the Bell network. Unrestricted competition in the long-distance markets was authorized through intervention by the courts. In a ruling that had enormous consquences for public policy and the development of the telecommunications industry, the Court of Appeals for the D.C. Circuit held that the FCC had erred in denying authorization to MCI to provide its "Execunet" service — a switched, or public, service intended for business firms.[23] The decision of the appeals court, which was upheld by the Supreme Court, left MCI and other competing carriers free to offer any kind of long-distance service they wished. Thus, the monopoly position of AT&T in terminal equipment and long-distance service was reduced.

In 1982, AT&T and the federal government jointly announced that they had reached an agreement in the antitrust case, and that, as a

---

23. *MCI Telecommunications Corporation* v. *Federal Communications Commission*, 580 F. 2d 590 (D.C. Cir., 1978).

part of it, the company would divest its twenty-two operating companies, representing about half of its total assets. This action severed the local operating monopolies from the competitive parts of AT&T's business operations. Competition, much of it deregulated, would extend throughout the industry and would be protected by structural reforms from unfair competition by AT&T. However, AT&T gained access to growing markets such as data processing; kept its research, development, and manufacturing subsidiaries; and to a considerable extent was deregulated itself. However, the settlement ended an era lasting almost a century in which a single firm was the dominant economic, social, and political force in the telecommunications industry.

DEREGULATION OF BANKING

The banking industry is another industry that has been deregulated. Commercial banks, the core of the U.S. banking system, are now free to compete directly with a variety of other financial and nonfinancial institutions. But it was not always this way, for in the 1930s, the collapse of the banking system and the Great Depression led to the passage of major banking and securities acts that set the basic structure of banking and financial regulation. In the financial crisis that occurred in the 1930s, depositors came to distrust banks; they withdrew funds and held them in the form of currency. Bank legislation passed during the 1930s was designed to protect depositors and to regulate what banks could do with their deposits. There were also regulations prohibiting the payment of interest on demand deposits and limiting the interest paid on time and savings deposits. The intent of interest rate ceilings was to restrain excessive price competition, which was thought to have contributed to the collapse of the banking system in the 1930s.

Reasons for the Deregulation of Banking

There were several reasons for the deregulation of commercial banking.[24] First, there were pressures exerted by consumer groups who argued that interest ceilings on time and savings accounts discriminated against small savers, including the elderly. They advocated the elimination of interest ceilings so that banks could pay market rates of interest. Technological change was a second reason for bank deregulation. With the developments that have occurred in electronic communication and

24. Kerry Cooper and Donald R. Fraser, *Banking Deregulation and the New Competition in Financial Services* (Cambridge, Mass.: Ballinger Publishing Company, 1984), pp. 17-20.

transportation, the geographic scope of the market for financial services broadened greatly, encompassing the entire United States. The ability of depository institutions, such as banks, to install the latest electronic equipment available to the financial services industry was limited by regulatory constraints. Third, banks as a group sought legislative changes that would allow them to compete with unregulated competitors. The money market funds, in particular, were able to offer higher rates of interest. Fourth, an economic and financial environment, characterized by volatile interest rates, contributed to deregulation in that more interest rate flexibility was needed by depository institutions.

Depository Institutions

Deregulation and Monetary Control Act of 1980 (DIDMCA)

The centerpiece of deregulation for deposit institutions is the DIDMCA. This legislation authorized NOW accounts nationwide, established uniform reserve requirements for all depository financial institutions, and empowered all depository institutions to pay interest on demand deposits. Title I of the act provided for the gradual elimination of the limitations on interest payable on accounts in depository institutions covered by the act. Interest rate regulations had been criticized as discriminatory against small savers. The phasing out of interest rate regulations was to occur over a six-year period.[25] The act also established the Depository Institutions Deregulation Committee (DIDC) to implement the phased deregulation of deposit rate ceilings. Title III of the act authorized all depository institutions to provide checking services. The act also contained other provisions, including the following:

1. It authorized Automatic Transfer Systems (ATSs) accounts, which provide for automatic funds transfer from interest-bearing to demand accounts, and negotiable order of withdrawal (NOW) accounts and share drafts for individual depository organizations.

2. It authorized savings and loan associations to expand greatly their consumer loan business, to issue credit cards, and to offer trust services.

3. It authorized mutual savings banks to make business loans and to accept demand deposits from business customers.

4. It eliminated the effects of state usury laws on certain types of loans, specifically agricultural, business, and mortgage loans.[26]

25. The time has now expired.
26. This provision was important because when the act was passed, the prime rate was 18 percent, which was above the usury rate that many states allowed.

The Garn-St. Germain Depository Institutions Act of 1982

The basic reason for the passage of the Garn-St. Germain Act was that managers of saving and loan associations and other thrifts feared their institutions would collapse because the high interest rates they had to pay to attract funds often exceeded the rates they earned on their portfolios. It was feared that should savings and loan associations fail in large numbers, it could result in a run on the commercial banking system, which might adversely affect the entire U.S. financial system. Congress was also concerned about the potential effects of a savings and loan industry collapse on the availability and cost of mortgage credit. There was also the realization that the deregulation of deposit rate ceilings and lending powers of savings and loan associations and other thrift organizations had not gone far enough. It was necessary to lift these ceilings to allow savings and loan associations to compete against money market funds.

The Garn-St. Germain Act has a number of important provisions. In Title I and Title II of the act, regulatory agencies were given power to deal with troubled banks and thrifts. The Federal Deposit Insurance Corporation (FDIC) or the Federal Savings and Loan Corporation (FSLIC) can make loans or purchase assets of any insured financial institution to prevent closing, or to restore normal operations. If an insured commercial savings bank closes and has assets of $500 million or more, the FDIC, as receiver, may sell the closed bank to an in-state insured depository institution owned by an out-of-state bank or bank holding company. By expanding the geographic and institutional barriers that constrained such mergers, this and other provisions of the act alleviated the problems faced by regulatory authorities in finding acquiring firms for failing financial institutions. The act also had other provisions, including the following:

1. It permitted Money Market Deposit Accounts with no interest ceiling for all depository institutions.

2. It permitted savings and loan associations to invest in consumer loans up to 30 percent of assets.

3. It authorized federally chartered savings and loan associations to offer demand deposits to persons or organizations with which they have a business association.

4. It permitted savings and loan associations to have much greater access to the commercial loans by allowing them to invest up to 55 percent of their assets in them.

Effects of Deregulation of Financial Institutions

Changes in banking laws, plus recent advances in communications and data processing technologies that have appeared to reduce the costs of managing multioffice banks, have led to a substantial increase in the level of interstate banking. Clearly, technological and economic forces, in conjunction with deregulatory actions and a new pattern of competition, have resulted in nothing less than a revolution in the market for financial services. The banking sector of the American economy has been supplanted by a financial services industry of which depository institutions, such as commercial banks and savings and loan associations, are only a segment. The regulatory framework for commercial banks and thrift institutions was narrowed considerably by the landmark legislation of DIDMCA and the Garn-St. Germain Act. State banking laws have also been passed that have affected deregulation of banking. It is necessary to review the changes that have occurred in the operation of financial institutions.[27]

Interstate Banking

In 1970, changes in the Bank Holding Company Act permitted most banking-related services to be offered interstate, except for deposit taking. The 1970 changes also narrowed the definition of "bank" to include only institutions that both accepted deposits and made commercial loans. As a result, bank holding companies and others were able to establish interstate networks of consumer finance companies, mortgage companies, and the like that escaped regulation by either not accepting deposits or not making commercial loans. The Garn-St. Germain Act empowered bank regulatory agencies to permit the acquisition of failing institutions across state lines. States then passed laws to facilitate interstate banking. In 1983, South Dakota passed a law that allows out-of-state bank holding companies to own state chartered banks, which can own insurance companies. Massachusetts passed an interstate banking law that allows local banks to expand into other New England states on a reciprocal basis.

Supply of Financial Services

Developments in the electronic computer industry have served to reduce greatly the costs of transmitting, storing, and processing information. Computer advances have made electronic banking feasible. This incorporates automated clearinghouses, automated teller machines, and point-of-service terminals into an electronic funds transfer system (EFTS), which is now spreading rapidly. The development of EFTS involves the substitution of capital for labor and, to a considerable extent, the substitution of fixed costs for variable costs. The equipment

27. Ibid., pp. 195–202.

needed to operate an EFTS efficiently involves a substantial monetary outlay. It is apparent that the expense of EFTS and other technological advances requires economies of scale. Larger financial institutions have an advantage in being able to muster the capital resources necessary to meet the equipment requirements mandated by the new technology.

Deregulation and the Supply of Financial Services

Before deregulation, several constraints were placed on banks, one of which was a restriction on the price of deposits. A result of deregulation has been the virtual elimination of pricing restrictions on entry and expansion into financial markets as well as on the scope and nature of financial activities. Before deregulation, there were restrictions on geographic expansion, but this, too, has been eased. Constraints on entry and geographic expansion had acted to limit competition among depository institutions. This restriction on expansion tended to create local markets for financial services, with limited competition among the suppliers of such services. It encouraged vertical integrated operations in which banks both produced and distributed financial services.[28] Relaxation of geographic restraints, in conjunction with deregulation of activity restraints, should make feasible new strategies for depository institutions in the provision of financial services.

Deregulation and Nonbank Competition

There has been an expansion into the financial services industry by nonbank institutions. This competition has occurred in both the credit and deposit markets. In the credit market, competition is particularly intense for consumer loans.[29] For example, the single largest consumer lender in the United States is General Motors. Sears is also a large consumer lender, as is Ford. Nonbank lenders also provide business loans. Competition from nonbank organizations is also intense for commercial mortgage loans. Nonbanks also compete for sources of funds. Money market funds have offered the widest substitute for deposits. Deregulation of financial institutions reflected the growth in competition from nonbank firms and will enable banks to compete against them in interest rates for loanable funds and also in a wider number of services.

---

28. Dwight B. Crane, Ralph C. Kimball, and William T. Gregor, *The Effects of Banking Deregulation*, Association of Reserve City Bankers, (July 1983), pp. 1-12.

29. Federal Reserve Bank of Atlanta, "Signals from the Future: The Emerging Financial Services Industry," *Economic Review* (September 1983), pp. 20-32.

Bank Mergers

The deregulation of depository institutions has led to an increase in bank mergers. This can be attributed in part to the competition of other forms of financial services and in part to the cost of new technology. Mergers facilitate economies of scale and an increase in the average size of many depository institutions. That there will be a decline in the number of commercial banks in the United States, particularly those not affiliated with a chain, appears likely. Some experts on banking predict the banking and financial services industry will evolve into a three-tiered structure.[30] The first tier will consist of a few national financial institutions offering a wide range of financial services. This would include both large commercial banks and nonbank organizations such as American Express. The second tier would consist of low-cost producers of financial services. Many would be new entrants into the industry using the latest technology. The last tier would be those firms that specialize in particular segments of the financial market.

SUMMARY

The deregulation of certain industries traditionally subject to regulation began during the latter part of the 1970s and accelerated during the early 1980s. Criticism of regulation aided the passage of the Airline Deregulation Act of 1978, the National Gas Policy Act of the same year, and the Motor Carrier Act and the Staggers Railroad Act of 1980. Many persons had been discontented with the subordination of competition by the regulatory process, and others felt there were better substitutes for existing regulation. In the airline industry, events in Texas and elsewhere suggested that competition both in terms of price and entry would work to the ultimate benefit of consumers. There was also criticism of the anticompetitiveness of the railroad and trucking industries, and Congress committed itself to competitive principles by deregulating them.

Depository financial institutions — commercial banks, savings and loan associations, mutual savings banks, and credit unions — have also been affected by deregulation. Two major laws were passed — The Depository Institutions Deregulation and Monetary Control Act of 1980 and the Garn-St. Germain Depository Institutions Act of 1982. These acts not only eliminated many regulatory constraints on the management of depository institutions but also allowed nonbank depository institutions to alter the nature of deposit and lending

30. Ibid., pp. 215-216.

services offered to their customers. Deregulation has changed the nature of the whole financial services industry. Financial deregulation has affected the price and availability of financial services to the benefit of most consumers. A greater number of firms providing a given financial service has produced more competition. The elimination of ceilings on interest rates permits consumers to receive market rates of interest on their deposits. Similarly, greater competition in the credit market has produced a greater amount of credit at a lower cost.

QUESTIONS FOR DISCUSSION

1. What are some of the principal criticisms of deregulated markets?
2. Discuss some of the reasons for the deregulation of the airline industry.
3. From your own point of view, has the deregulation of the airline industry been a success?
4. What are some of the criticisms of airline deregulation?
5. What was the purpose of deregulating natural gas?
6. What are some of the problems that have occurred in natural gas deregulation?
7. Why would some groups oppose the deregulation of natural gas?
8. Discuss some of the reasons for the deregulation of the railroad and trucking industries.
9. What are some of the advantages and disadvantages of railroad and trucking deregulation?
10. Discuss the reasons for the deregulation of the telecommunications industry using AT&T as an example.
11. Discuss the reasons for the deregulation of depository institutions such as commercial banks.
12 Discuss the Depository Institutions Deregulation and Monetary Control Act of 1980.
13. Discuss the Garn-St. Germain Depository Institutions Act of 1982.
14 What are some of the results of financial deregulation?

RECOMMENDED READINGS

Cooper, Kerry, and Donald R. Fraser. *Banking Deregulation and the New Competition in Financial Services.* Cambridge, Mass.: Ballinger Publishing Company, 1984.

Derthick, Martha, and Paul J. Quirk. *The Politics of Deregulation.* Washington, D.C.: Brookings Institution, 1985.

Economic Report of the President 1986: Washington, D.C.: U.S. Government Printing Office, 1986, pp. 159-187.

Federal Reserve Bank of Atlanta. "Signals from the Future: The Emerging Financial Services Industry." *Economic Review* (September, 1983), 20-32.

Friedlander, Ann F., and Richard H. Spady. *Freight Transportation Regulation: Equity, Efficiency, and Competition.* Cambridge, Mass.: MIT Press, 1981.

Koran, Donald William. "The Welfare Effects of Airline Fare Deregulation in the United States." *Journal of Transport Economics and Policy*, 17 (May 1983), 177-189.

Mitchell, Edward J., ed. *The Deregulation of Natural Gas.* Washington, D.C.: American Enterprise Institute, 1983.

Morrison, Steven, and Clifford Winston. *The Economic Effects of Airline Deregulation.* Washington, D.C.: Brookings Institution, 1986.

Roussakis, Emmanuel N. *Commercial Banking in an Era of Deregulagion.* New York: Praeger Publishers, 1984.

PART VI
GOVERNMENT AS A PROMOTER
OF BUSINESS

The federal government runs a number of programs that offer financial assistance to private enterprise. Some of these programs are of a permanent nature, whereas others are of limited duration and are intended to help a firm or industry through a temporary crisis. The permanent programs give assistance to agriculture, housing, transportation, small business, and banks, among others. Many federal programs are an important source of credit for certain sectors of the economy. For example, the housing industry relies on the various federal mortgage credit programs and the Federal Home Loan Board for a good portion of its funds, particularly when money is tight. Agriculture receives credit assistance from the Farmers Home Administration and government sponsored credit corporations such as the Federal Land Banks and Federal Intermediate Credit Banks. Exporters also can obtain financial assistance from the Export-Import Bank. Many of these programs were created during the 1930s to help various sectors of the economy through the Depression. Instead of being abolished after this economic crisis, they have continued to operate and have become an important part of the nation's credit structure. The temporary programs, though, have not become an institutionalized source of funds and, with the ending of a particular financial crisis, have lapsed.

Taxation is another area in which government affects business. It can be used as a stimulus or a deterrent to methods of doing business or to the kind of business being done. A tax can be used as a subsidy or a negative tax to encourage a specific course of action. The agricultural price-support program is a large-scale example of this. Other examples are subsidies to airlines and to the merchant marine. Then there are tariffs that protect domestic industries from foreign competition, though this goes against the grain of competition. The consumer pays higher prices for protected goods, and efficiency may suffer because the producer is spared the necessity of striving to reduce his or her costs. There is much public support for protection, however, because many persons regard themselves as having primarily a producer's rather than a consumer's interest. They are, therefore, more concerned about the possibility of losing profits or becoming unemployed because of foreign competition than they are about being able to buy the imported commodity at a lower price.

Tax incentives are used to stimulate many activities. At the federal level, tax credits and accelerated depreciation are used to encourage business investment. Depletion allowances are used to encourage oil and mining companies to explore for new sources of energy. The foreign tax credit is said to be an incentive for U.S. firms to invest abroad. At the state and local level, there are also a variety of tax incentives, the most common being an exemption from the property tax as an inducement to encourage the location of industry. In fact, states use this device to compete against one another in attracting industry. The examption of interest on state and local bonds for federal income tax purposes also has been used to stimulate industrial development, with states or localities using the proceeds from tax-exempt bonds to build a plant to be leased to industry. Both the federal and state governments grant special tax concessions to firms that comply with environmental protection laws by acquiring pollution control equipment. Some states permit the deduction of pollution control costs as a credit against state income taxes.

Chapters 16 and 17 examine several areas of government support of business. In Chapter 16, various forms of federal credit programs will be discussed. These programs are an important, but neglected, area of government and business relations and are influential in allocating capital in domestic credit markets. The federal government is the largest financial intermediary in the United States. At the end of 1985, it held $257 billion in its direct loan portfolio, and it had guaranteed another $410 billion in loans. Government-sponsored enterprises lent another $370 billion. Thus, directly or indirectly, the federal government is responsible for one seventh of the total debt of the United States. Another area in which government has an impact on business is through taxes, which have an effect on the decision-making process. Finally, there is government support of business in the area of foreign trade. Business is protected against foreign competition by the use of such devices as tariffs and import quotas.

Chapter 16
Government Loan and Tax Policies

The public, if it thinks about government and business relations at all, conceives of the government as the tax collector, trust buster, consumer advocate, and protector of the environment, all of which place business on the receiving end of a number of requirements that generally do not have pleasant connotations. There is, however, another area in which government influences business, and this is in the area of direct and indirect financial aid. This aid dates back to the time of Alexander Hamilton, who identified the prosperity of the nation with the prosperity of the business class. It was government's duty to dispense privileges to business; the resulting economic benefits would percolate throughout the whole economy. Hamilton wished to establish a strong central government that would dedicate its energies to promoting business enterprise. To do this, he set up a program that was enacted, in the main, during President George Washington's first term in office. This program provided for the assumption of federal and state debts by the federal government, the creation of a national bank that would make loans to business, and the passage of a protective tariff that would shield business from foreign competition.

Government aid to business came in a number of forms in the nineteenth century. The tariff was one that proved highly effective in stimulating the development of business because it essentially guaranteed a domestic market free from foreign competition. Tariffs are, in effect, taxes that raise consumer prices. The subsidy was another form of direct government aid to business, particularly in the field of transportation. In 1845, Congress authorized subsidies for ships carrying mail, with preference given to steamships, which could be converted into warships. Various other forms of subsidies have been used for ocean transportation, right up to the present. Grants also were used as an aid to business, particularly to the railroads. Between 1862 and 1866, Congress gave more than 100 million acres of public lands to the railroads. This was the period of the Pacific railway charters, when the rush to span the continent was in full swing. Loans to business were a fourth source of government aid and were first used to encourage the construction of inland waterways, a branch of commerce in which private enterprise depended completely on government support.

In addition to these forms of government aid, a number of federal agencies have been created to assist business. Almost all this assistance is provided by the Department of Commerce, which was established in 1903 and has become a general service agency for American business. Its subordinate units include the Bureau of the Census, the Office of Business Economics, the Patent and Trademark Office, and the Bureau of Foreign Commerce. A second agency is the Small Business Administration, which makes loans to small business firms and offers various consulting services. In foreign trade, the Export-Import Bank has been an important source of credit since its creation in 1934. Its functions have been expanded to include the financing of general foreign trade to exporters and their foreign customers when private funds are not available on reasonable terms. Other agencies, such as the Federal National Mortgage Association and the Public Housing Administration, offer credit, which directly or indirectly, aids business. The overwhelming majority of the guaranteed and insured loans of these two agencies benefit the housing sector. Other federal agencies also offer services to business.

We shall explore in detail some of the more important areas of government assistance to business. One area is credit, which can be divided into two categories — direct federal loan programs and loan insurance. Of course, the credit extended in the federal credit programs goes into several economic activities. Business is the direct beneficiary of a few of these loans, though the sheer volume of federal loans has an impact on business through the loans' effect on the total volume of spending in the economy and on the interest rate. A second area is subsidies, which also are of two types — direct subsidies to business that come out of the federal budget and subsidies that do not involve direct payments. Many credit programs offer loans or insurance at rates below those that would be charged by a private firm for comparable services and at rates below those at which the government itself borrows money. If a business firm can borrow from a federal agency at 6 percent interest, but the Treasury is paying 8 percent on the money it borrows, this, in effect, is a subsidy. This is not necessarily bad, for the end result of the subsidy may be the promotion of some socially useful activity.

FEDERAL LOAN PROGRAMS

Federal loan programs exist to erase imperfections from the direct market, to provide subsidies for socially desirable activities, and to stimulate the economy when there are idle resources. Imperfections in the credit market occur because borrowers differ in size, geographic location, and types of activity. Federal loans are designed to fill certain gaps in the private lending market. In addition, many economic transactions benefit not only the principal participants in the transaction but other members of society as well. Home ownership, which increases social stability, and education, which increases productivity and economic growth, are two examples of activities with external benefits. When there is a difference between the total costs and benefits and the private costs and benefits, federal loan programs can supply credit for socially desirable purposes at less than the market interest rates. This has a subsidy effect, in that subsidies reduce the private cost of a particular transaction. By setting the subsidy at an appropriate level, the government can induce the level of activity that would prevail if social benefits were taken into consideration by the market process.

Direct Loans

Direct federal loans have several characteristics. First, they are designed to promote socially useful activities rather than to remove imperfections in the credit market. Second, they contain a subsidy element. For example, loan programs of the Rural Electrification Administration and loans for the construction of higher-education facilities and college housing offer borrowers subsidies at around 50 percent of the total value of the loan. Third, direct loans are financed directly out of the federal budget. Through the tax-transfer mechanism of the federal budget, the government can influence the amount — and presumably the allocation — of credit extended in the private market. Fourth, foreign loans are by far the largest single component of direct loans, accounting for more than 40 percent of the total loans outstanding in 1985. In quantity, the most important types of outstanding foreign loans are development loans and loans of the Export-Import Bank. Both types create a foreign demand for the products of American business. An example of a foreign loan that benefits business is the military sales credit extended to countries to assist them in purchasing military equipment from the United States, which benefits firms making aircraft, tanks, and so forth.

Table 16-1 presents the amount of new direct federal loans made by major government agencies in 1985. Excluded from the table are the loans of the federally sponsored agencies that are also not included in the federal budget. Government-sponsored agencies were originally financed by subscriptions of government capital, but this capital now has been retired and the agencies are entirely privately owned. Direct loans financed out of the federal budget include business loans made by the Small Business Administration, loans made by the Economic Development Administration of the Department of Commerce, and loans made for ship construction by the Maritime Administration. In addition, the Export-Import Bank, a federally owned enterprise, lends directly to exporters and importers and insures and guarantees loans extended by private lenders.

Economic Impact of Direct Loans

Since direct loans are included in the federal budget, we shall examine their possible economic impact. The method of financing used in the budget is important. If there is a deficit in the budget, the whole process, including the loans, can have an income-generating effect, particularly if new money is created to finance the deficit. This would affect both consumption and investment. The impact on consumption may be divided into income and wealth effects. The income effect comes about because the government spends and consumers receive income. The wealth effect comes about because savings accumulate as income increases. Assuming that income and consumption continue to expand for a long enough period, consumption increases also will produce increases in investment. And because the deficit was created by means of new money, interest rates will remain low, which also should encourage an increase in investment spending unless, of course, the investment schedule is interest inelastic.

Table 16-1 New Direct Loans by Federal Agency, 1985
(millions of dollars)

Agency	Amount
Funds appropriated by the president	6,339
Agriculture	21,256
Commerce	106
Defense	1,533
Education	1,315
Housing and Urban Development	15,072
Transportation	443
Other agencies	
Small Business Administration	1,017
Export-Import Bank	660
Other	5,113
Total new direct loans	52,847

Source: Executive Office of the President, Office of Manpower and Budget, *Budget of the U.S. Government, Fiscal Year 1987* (Washington, D.C.: U.S. Government Printing Office, 1986), p. 6D–192.

There would be a similar effect if the federal government borrowed directly from the Federal Reserve or from the excess reserves of the commercial banks to finance the deficit. In all three cases, the money supply is increased, the income and wealth effects operate on both consumption and investment, and there should be little or no pressure exerted on interest rates. Thus, federal lending conceivably could have a double-barreled effect with respect to stimulating gross national product. The deficit incurred in the budget, financed by any of the three methods referred to above, would provide one stimulus to the economy, and the loans supported by the budget from deficit financing would provide the other stimulus.

On the other hand, increases in taxes to finance budgetary outlays, including loan programs, would reduce directly disposable income and the level of consumer spending. The effect of loans could be counter-balanced by the effect of decreased spending. Federal borrowing through the sale of bonds to the nonbank public also could reduce the expansionary effect of federal loans if interest rates were raised and cash balances reduced, both of which tend to discourage private spending. Then, of course, loans could also generate a reverse flow of income to the government. It is possible for the expansionary effect of loan disbursements to be equaled by the contractionary effects of loan repayment. This would require comparison of the reduction in spending associated with a decrease in disposable income resulting from loan repayments, with the increase in spending associated with an increase in disposable income resulting from loan disbursements. But in some cases, the reduction in spending associated with loan repayments may be nil. For example, a loan is used to finance the construction of a building. In later years, during the life of the loan, the building yields a return sufficient for the borrower to repay the loan. Society thus has an asset it otherwise would not have had, but the loan repayments, being in a sense self-financed, do not have any contractionary influence on the gross national product.

We also should consider the case of the borrower who, in the absence of the federal loan, presumably would have been able and willing to obtain funds from private lenders. But we can assume that the borrower would not borrow as much from the private lender, since the interest rates on federal loans are typically lower than those on private loans. In this case, it would no longer be possible to equate the effects of the loan with the entire amount of the increase in gross national product that may be attributable to the loan. To determine the net increase in gross national product that may be attributable to the federal loan, one first would have to subtract the increase that would have occurred if a private loan had been made instead of the government loan. And second, one would have to add the effect of the increased funds available to private lenders.

One issue in the federal credit programs is the existence of subsidies. Many of these credit programs offer loans or insurance at rates below those that would be charged by a private firm for such services and at rates below those that the government itself would have to pay to borrow money. The subsidy can be defined as the difference between the amount the borrower has to pay for a government loan and the price he or she would have to pay for a similar loan from a competitive private lender. In essence, the subsidy circumvents the forces of the free market. In the market for loanable funds, the interest rate is supposedly determined by the interaction of the supply of funds with the demand for the funds. An equilibrium point is reached when supply and demand are in balance at a given rate of interest. In a competitive market economy, borrowers are free to obtain loans at the going interest rate If this market rate is 6 percent and the government charges 2 percent to a specific set of borrowers, there is a subsidy that, in the final analysis, is paid by the taxpayers. The effectiveness of the market as an allocator of loanable funds is circumvented.

The Small Business Administration and the Export-Import Bank are examples of agencies that make direct loans to business. In 1985, the total loans of the Small Business Administration (SBA) amounted to more than $1 billion, and the loans of the Export-Import Bank (Eximbank) amounted to $660 million.[1] Both agencies were created to achieve specific economic objectives, the SBA to offer loans and assistance to small business firms and the Eximbank to stimulate business involvement in foreign trade.

The Small Business Administration — SBA

The principal governmental agency concerned with the problems of small business is the Small Business Administration (SBA). The SBA was created by the Small Business Act of 1953, which had as its objective the assistance of small business firms to ensure fair competition. The common problem of small business firms is securing capital, and so the act authorized the SBA to provide two types of financial assistance to small firms — loans for plant construction and the acquisition of land, equipment, and materials, and disaster loans to business concerns that suffer financial loss from floods, hurricanes, drought, or other natural catastrophes. In addition, the SBA was responsible for helping small business firms secure a larger share of government contracts for materials, construction, and research and development. The

1. Executive Office of the President, Office of Manpower and Budget, *Budget of the U.S. Government, Fiscal Year 1987* (Washington, D.C.: U.S. Government Printing Office, 1986), p. 6D-192.

SBA was also supposed to provide counseling for small firms. In applying for a loan, a small business concern must submit credit data, and in evaluating these data, SBA officials often are able to advise on alternative ways of solving a problem.

In 1958, the Small Business Investment Act was passed by Congress to help small businesses secure additional equity capital and long-term loan capital. This law, which is administered by the SBA, provides equity capital and long-term capital through privately owned and operated small business investment companies and state and local development corporations. Small business investment companies operate by supplying equity capital in exchange for convertible debentures under conditions approved by the SBA. These securities give the investment company the privilege of converting such debentures into the small business firm's common stock. The investment company also may make long-term loans to small business concerns for up to twenty years, with provision for an additional ten years for repayment. State and local development corporations have been formed to assist the development of small business, and loans made to them by the SBA are used to make loans to small business firms. In its community development work, the SBA works closely with the Department of Commerce's Economic Development Administration to establish, expand, and assist in financing local industries in areas designated for redevelopment.

The Export-Import Bank — Eximbank

The Export-Import Bank (Eximbank) is a wholly federally owned enterprise, and its mission is to promote U.S. exports. It does this by making direct loans to exporters and importers and by insuring and guaranteeing loans made by private lenders. It is authorized to have outstanding at any one time dollar loans, guarantees, and insurance in an aggregate amount of not in excess of $40 billion. Since it concentrates on areas where private financing is not available and on meeting foreign competition, its programs are generally intended to supplement private credit financing. To match the special terms that foreign governments provide to subsidize their exporters, terms and credits on the use of its funds are more favorable than those available in the private sector. Eximbank receives its financial support from the federal budget, with authorizations in the 1987 budget set at $949 million.

Direct loans extended by Eximbank are dollar credits made to borrowers outside the United States for the purchase of U.S. goods and services. Disbursements under the loan agreements are made in the United States to the suppliers of the goods and services, and the loans plus interest must be repaid in dollars by the borrowers. The purposes for which the loans can be used are:[2]

1. To supplement private sources of financing when the private financial source is unwilling or unable to assume the policital and commercial risks under current conditions

2. To extend credit on terms longer than those private lenders can provide

3. To enable U.S. suppliers to provide terms on major projects that are competitive with those offered by government-sponsored export financing institutions in other exporting countries

In addition, Eximbank has financial guarantee programs under which it can guarantee, backed by the full faith and credit of the United States, the repayment of credits extended by private lenders to foreign purchasers of U.S. goods and services. In this respect, the bank's role is comparable to that of the many foreign institutions that provide guarantees and insurance to aid their countries' exporters and safeguard them from undue risk from overseas sales. Under the financial guarantee loan authority, the Eximbank will unconditionally guarantee repayment by a borrower of up to 100 percent of the outstanding principal due on such loans, plus interest equal to the U.S. Treasury rate for similar maturities, plus 1 percent per annum, on the outstanding balances of any loan made by an American financial institution to a buyer in another country for the purchase of U.S. goods and services.

Insured Loans

From the standpoint of the amount of money involved, insured loans are by far the most important segment of federal government credit. In 1985, for example, insured loans by the federal government amounted to $410 billion, compared with $257 billion for direct federal loans.[3] The government may either insure or guarantee loans made by private lenders. The best-known example of the former is Federal Housing Administration mortgage insurance, in particular, the Veterans Administration's mortgage guarantee program. The major difference between loan insurance and loan guarantees is that a fee generally is charged for insurance.

Loan insurance is of particular importance in the housing market. In fact, when FHA mortgage insurance was introduced, it led to a revolu-

---

2. Export-Import Bank, *Description of Eximbank Export Financing Programs and Services*, 1983, pp. 5–8.
3. *Economic Report of the President 1986* (Washington, D.C.: U.S. Government Printing Office, 1986), p. 192.

tion in home mortgages and home ownership. Before its introduction, home mortgages for the average family were difficult to obtain. The typical home mortgage was a medium-term loan — on the average of three to five years — and covered only a relatively small portion of the price of the house. In addition, these mortgages were typically non-amortizable; that is, the monthly mortgage payments covered only interest on the loan, and these payments did not reduce the principal of the loan. The FHA insurance permitted private lenders to extend mortgages with much higher loan-to-value ratios than before, without incurring any more risk than they assumed by making uninsured mortgage loans of considerably less value. The higher loan-to-value ratio associated with the FHA mortgages implied that a correspondingly lower down payment would be required to take possession of a house, and the mortgages thus undoubtedly stimulated the demand for, and the construction of, private housing.

Federal loan insurance is subject to fiscal offsets, just as direct federal loans are. For those types of insurance that carry a premium and are just self-supporting, the premium itself is not an offset. Funds collected as premiums are used to cover administrative costs and to settle claims. The settlement of claims does not offset the income and loan-generating effects of loan insurance; it redirects these effects. Premiums are collected from one group of lenders and distributed to another group of lenders. It is in the case of loan guarantees, in which no premiums are charged and losses are financed out of general revenues, and in the case of loan insurance programs that do not break even, that the possibility of fiscal offsets arises. The analysis of offsets to insured loans is identical with that made for direct loans.

Table 16-2 on the following page presents new loan guarantees by federal agencies for 1985. Almost all the loan guarantees were made by two agencies — the Department of Housing and Urban Development (HUD) and the Veterans Administration. The Small Business Administration and the Export-Import Bank are also in the business of making loan guarantees.

The Credit Budget

The purpose of the federal credit budget, which was introduced in 1980, is to measure and control the volume of new loans and loan guarantees extended to borrowers. It is a supplement to the regular, or unified, budget for two reasons. First, the regular budget does not include loan guarantees because they are contingent liabilities that do not result in a monetary outlay by the federal government, except in the case of default. Then it is the responsibility of the federal government as the loan guarantor to make restitution to the bank or agency that made the loan. Second, neither loan guarantees nor direct loans can be fully controlled by the appropriations of the budget authorities.

Aid to Business — The Chrysler Bailout

A classic example of the use of government loan guarantees to help business was the Chrysler bailout of 1979.[4] Back-to-back financial losses in 1978 and 1979 brought an appeal to the federal government for financial assistance. Chrysler and its supporters had several arguments. First, its problems were in large part due to government regulation. It argued that it cost it twice as much to comply with pollution control requirements than it did General Motors. Second, a Chrysler failure would have caused numerous dislocations in the U.S. economy. Thousands of jobs would have been lost, and both federal and state tax revenues would have declined. Third, rigorous competition, and the corresponding benefits of lower prices, product innovation, and the efficiency that came with it, required three, no fewer, large U.S. auto-

Table 16-2 New Loan Guarantees by Federal Agency, 1985 (millions of dollars)

Agency	Amount
Agriculture	3,910
Education	8,888
Housing and Urban Development	47,441
Veterans Administration	12,140
Other agencies	
Small Business Administration	2,810
Export-Import Bank	7,849
Federal Savings and Loan Insurance Corporation	900
Other	773
Total new loan guarantees	84,771

Source: Executive Office of the President, Office of Manpower and Budget, *Budget of the U.S. Government, Fiscal Year 1987* (Washington, D.C.: U.S. Government Printing Office, 1986), p. 6.

4. The following sources provide the background for the bailout: U.S. Congress, House Committee on Banking, Finance and Urban Affairs, *The Chrysler Corporation Financial Situation: Hearings on the Chrysler Corporation Loan Guarantee Act*, 96th Cong., 1st sess., 1979, pts. 1, 2; U.S. Congress, Senate Committee on Banking, Housing and Urban Affairs, *Chrysler Corporation Loan Guarantee Act of 1979*, 96th Cong., 1st sess., 1979, pts. 1, 2.

makers.[5] With only two auto companies left, the U.S. auto industry would have become more concentrated.

Opponents of the Chrysler bailout also had their arguments. First, Chrysler was not well managed. It had made a series of mistakes over time that were responsible for its losses. A major problem was poor timing of product introduction. In the 1970s, Chrysler's market position suffered from three ill-timed new model introductions. It restyled its 1971 intermediate models when demand was swinging back toward full-sized models. It introduced new full-sized models when demand shifted to small cars following the Arab oil embargo and subsequent oil crisis. Later in the decade, Chrysler stuck with its large cars when smaller Japanese cars were becoming popular. Second, there was the free market argument. Senator William Proxmire of Wisconsin best summed up the rationale for opposing aid to Chrysler when he said that a free market economy meant the freedom to fail as well as to profit.

Aided by lobbyists and public relations experts that most firms could not afford, Chrysler was able to obtain a $4 billion package consisting of $1.25 billion in loan guarantees and $2.75 billion in outside financing.[6] The latter was obtained from a variety of sources, including the UAW pension fund and the Canadian government. Wage concessions were also made by the UAW, but in return, Douglas Fraser, the president of the UAW, was made a member of Chrysler's board of directors. Chrysler lost close to $2 billion in 1980, again achieving the distinction of being the biggest money loser for the year and setting an all-time record in the process. However, Chrysler began to turn the corner in 1981, and made record profits in 1984 and 1985. The loans were repaid ahead of time. However, whether the Chrysler turnaround was due to the charismatic personality of its president, Lee Iacocca, or to the imposition of import quotas on Japanese automobiles is debatable. Restricting the flow of Japanese automobiles into the United States certaintly gave the U.S. automakers a larger share of the market and enabled them to raise their prices.[7]

5. This was not a particularly good argument. The U.S. automobile industry was an oligopoly that had been dominated by General Motors, Ford, and Chrysler for fifty years. These firms were not exactly noted for their competition, nor were they noted for quality of product innovation.
6. Large firms can afford to hire lobbyists. The importance of lobbying is discussed in Harrison W. Fox and Martin C. Schnitzer, *Doing Business in Washington* (New York: Free Press, 1981).
7. The impact of import quotas on Japanese cars on American consumers will be discussed in Chapter 17.

Government-Sponsored Financial Institutions

A third way in which the federal government allocates credit, although indirectly, is through privately owned government sponsored financial enterprises. These enterprises have been created by the government to perform specialized credit functions. Three of them, the Federal National Mortgage Association (Fannie Mae), the Federal Home Loan Mortgage Bank (Freddie Mac), and the Federal Home Loan Banks, serve the housing financial market. The Farm Credit System finances agriculture, and the Student Loan Market Association (Sallie Mae), makes a secondary market in federally guaranteed student loans. Each issues securities and uses the proceeds to finance its lending activities, and their earnings are exempt from state and local income taxes. They have greatly increased their activities in the domestic credit market in the past few years. In 1980, lending by government sponsored enterprises amounted to $153.4 million; by 1985, it has increased to $370.0 billion.[8] These enterprises have an effect on the national economy and also on business in several ways.

   1. Government-sponsored loan enterprises can borrow at interest rates significantly lower than even the best-rated private borrowers. Thus, they can make loans at interest rates below prevailing market rates. This provides a subsidy to borrowers.
   2. The loans have some impact on business. More than half of their total amount has gone to support housing construction, which benefits a variety of industries.
   3. By creating a national market for mortgages, Fannie Mae and Freddie Mac have provided a method for diversifying away much of the geographically specific risk in mortgage lending, thereby lowering the cost of return required by the lender.

Other Forms of Financial Assistance

Government aid to business extends far beyond credit assistance. There are also direct cash benefits that the federal government pays to a particular firm or industry to accomplish a particular objective. For example, the government pays the sugar beet and sugar cane growers a subsidy to produce sugar even though sugar could be purchased far more cheaply from foreign countries. Cash payments are also used to help support the privately owned U.S. merchant marine. For financial and security reasons, the federal government has determined that it is necessary to have a domestic merchant marine capable of carrying a

8. *Budget of the U.S. Government, Fiscal Year 1987*, p. 6c-9.

part of the U.S. oceangoing trade. Nearly every aspect of the merchant marine industry is affected by a public measure, such as paying of seaman's wages, instruction costs, and moth balling, intended to promote the U.S. fleet. Without subsidies, there would probably be no U.S. fleet and no U.S. shipbuilding industry; with the subsidies, the cost of U.S. ships is more than double the price of those built in foreign shipyards.[9]

Government research and development expenditures also have an impact on business. There are expenditures on basic research in science and engineering. Then there is space research, which will amount to $7.0 billion in 1987,[10] in space science and the application of space technology. There are also weapons research and development expenditures, a part of national defense, which will amount to an estimated $9.3 billion in 1987.[11] Government procurement expenditures were $96 billion in 1985 and go for a wide variety of expenditures, including the purchases of planes, aircraft carriers, tanks and other military hardware, all of which is produced by private industry. Funding for the construction of highways, set at $7.8 billion for 1987, benefits private construction firms. Government expenditures on airports and airways benefit business firms, as do expenditures on aeronautic research and technology.

TAXATION AND THE CONTROL OF BUSINESS

Taxation is often used as an instrument of regulation to supplement the state's police power. Every tax necessarily exerts some kind of effect on the ability or willingness of an individual or a business firm to undertake an economic act. If an individual or firm pays the tax, there is less purchasing power to use for other things. If the tax is avoided by a decision not to perform a taxable action, the tax has conditioned the action of the individual or firm. Usually a tax is used to combine revenue and regulation. In some cases, however, the revenue and regulatory aspects of a tax can conflict. An example of this would be a moderate tax on the undistributed profits of corporations. The effect of such a tax might be to increase dividends, but not to eliminate undistributed profits altogether. Therefore, some revenue would be collected, but at the same time, revenues would be sacrificed if the firms responded to the tax by declaring dividends.

The tax instrument is used extensively to control business and commerce. Taxes are imposed to affect the form of business enterprise,

---

9. Operating subsidies for the U.S. maritime industry amounted to $338 million in 1985.
10. *Budget of the U.S. Government, Fiscal Year 1987*, pp. 3-6.
11. Ibid., p. 5-13.

as well as the methods of doing business and the kind of business done. For example, in an attempt to protect the dairy industry, discriminatory taxes have been levied on oleomargarine, and to protect the independent grocer, special taxes have been imposed on chain stores. Moreover, a tax can often become a subsidy when the explicit intention is to encourage a specific course of action. One example of this is a tax reduction for a particular type of business firm. An exemption of a few thousand dollars of corporate income from the corporate income tax may be granted in an effort to encourage the growth of small business firms. Firms engaged in favored forms of output may be allowed to reduce their income tax liability for a few years by taking accelerated depreciation of plant and equipment for tax purposes. Oil and mineral producers are permitted deductions, called depletion allowances, from taxable profits, presumably to encourage the opening up of new sources. Firms having good employment records also are granted lower payroll tax rates under state unemployment insurance systems.

Taxes can be used to effect new methods of achieving worthy social ends. In the environmental area, for example, tax incentives could be used to replace many of the present direct controls. Sumptuary excise taxation — to which consumers have grown accustomed for tobacco products and alcoholic beverages — could be used to alter basic production and consumption patterns. The desired results would no longer be accomplished by fiat, but by making the higher-pollutant product or service more expensive than the low-pollutant product or service. The guiding principle would be that people and institutions pollute because it is easier, cheaper, or more profitable to do so, and not because they enjoy messing up the environment. Instead of a corps of inspectors or regulators, it would then be possible to use the price system to make pollution harder to accomplish, more expensive, and less profitable. The growing scarcity of energy sources provides another opportunity for choosing between greater government control of industry and the use of markets to achieve the same results. This could be achieved by imposing heavier taxes on the use of energy and thereby reducing the demand for it.

Federal Income Taxation

Although all levels of government — federal, state, and local — use various forms of direct and indirect business taxes, the federal government has the most effect on business. One tax used by the government is the corporate income tax. For the fiscal year 1987, corporate income taxes are estimated to amount to $75 billion, or about 9 percent of the total federal budget income from all sources.[12] However, for business,

12. Ibid., p. 1-1.

it is not the corporate income tax as a revenue source for the federal government that is important, but the structure of the tax — exclusions, exemptions, deductions, credits, preferential rates, and deferrals. This is true because there is a major link between the corporate income tax and the investment of business firms. Investment is one of the key components of national income and is a fundamental determinant of economic growth in that it defines the potential for production in any economy.

Probably the most important influence the federal goverment has on private investment expenditures is that effected through taxes and tax laws. The marginal efficiency, or rate of return, of capital is concerned with the profitability that additional amounts of capital will bring to the business enterprise, and so the businessperson or entrepreneur will be acutely aware of the influence of anything as direct as taxation on the expected rate of return of capital assets. Investment expenditures depend on the expected rate of return over cost, and thus presumably taxes, because they lower the expected returns, will lower investment expenditures. Taxes, to put it another way, can impinge on incentives, and therefore tend to affect the decision to invest. With respect to incentives, tax considerations may determine how a thing is to be done rather than whether it is to be done.

Tax Incentives and Investment

Tax incentives are given to business to encourage specific economic or social objectives, for example, to encourage oil exploration and production and to hire and train minorities. Liberal depreciation policies are one example of a tax incentive that can have a direct impact on private capital investment. Without a tax on business income, the rate at which a firm chooses to charge off the depreciation of its capital goods is purely a matter of statistical information; the enterprise generally tries to obtain as realistic a picture of costs and current net income as possible. On the other hand, when business income is taxed, there are certain advantages for the firm to depreciate its capital goods over a shorter time than it would normally. The rate at which depreciation can be charged in computing business income is regulated by the tax statutes. Liberal or accelerated depreciation policies can affect investment demand in the sense that they can reduce the impact of taxation on investment.

Another type of tax incentive that can influence investment is the investment credit, a credit against the income tax liability of a person or corporation that is allowed by the government for amounts invested in particular assets that meet specific requirements. It can be thought of as a negative tax in that it provides, through the reduction of income taxes, a direct increase in after-tax profits to a business firm investing in new plants and equipment that fall within the law's guideline. It ordinarily comes about, as the one now in use in the United States did, through the desire of a government to stimulate economic growth. The investment credit, along with accelerated depreciation, can be used as an instrument of countercyclical fiscal policy.

In considering the economic effects of tax policies on investment, it is crucial to distinguish between measures that apply only to new investment, such as accelerated depreciation and the investment tax credit, and measures that reduce the tax burden on all kinds of income, such as a reduction in the rates of the personal and corporate income taxes. Measures that apply only to new investment affect only marginal decisions to invest; no tax benefit is conferred on the owners of existing capital. Therefore, at least in the short run, more investment is stimulated per dollar of immediate revenue loss when tax benefits apply only to investments in new capital than if the benefits were conferred on all capital.

The Reagan Administration and Tax Incentives for Business

In July 1981, Congress passed massive tax cuts for both individuals and business. The rationale of the tax cuts was to generate a wave of saving and investment that would carry the country to economic prosperity. Specifically, business was to benefit by more liberal tax incentives, which were supposed to help redress the nation's lagging rate of corporate investment. The Economic Recovery Tax Act permitted business firms to depreciate most purchases of equipment according to an accelerated five-year schedule. It preserved the investment tax credit on equipment. Some changes were made in 1982 in both accelerated depreciation and the investment credit. For example, in 1985, a regular investment credit against the federal corporate income tax was allowed for 10 percent of investment in new capital, which was limited to $25,000 plus 85 percent of the tax in excess of $25,000. Accelerated depreciation for most tangible property is for five years and is recovered at the rate of 15 percent the first year, 22 percent the second year, and 21 percent in each of the remaining three years.[13]

Tax incentives are also used to stimulate exports. The income a firm gets from exporting is taxed by the federal government in the year it is earned. There are ways the tax can be reduced. Until 1984, exporters were allowed to form a Domestic International Sales Corporation (DISC), which allowed them to defer or postpone federal income taxes

13. Price Waterhouse, *Corporate Income Taxes: A Worldwide Summary*, 1985, p. 377.

on one-half of export profits. This deferred income was not taxed until it was distributed to DISC shareholders. Deferred earnings retained by the DISC could be reinvested in its export business, or used to extend export financing to its foreign customers. The Foreign Sales Corporation Act of 1984 allows for the creation of Foreign Sales Corporations, which are to replace the DISCs and will receive greater tax benefits. The main benefit is a tax exemption on income earned from foreign trade. The maximum tax exemption on income from foreign trade is 1.27 percent of gross receipts, or 16 percent of combined taxable income.

Benefits and Costs of Tax Incentives to Business

All too often the cost of government action is ignored, and attention is focused on the action's benefit. Tax benefits to oil companies are supposed to encourage oil exploration, which more likely than not, does not turn out to be profitable, but there is also a cost to the U.S. Treasury in revenues lost. These lost revenues have to be made up from other tax sources, usually the general body of taxpayers. The benefits gained by society from, for instance, the provision of more energy, can more than offset the loss of tax revenue to the Treasury and the cost of the subsidy to the taxpayer, but then again, they may not. Any subsidy, regardless of the type, has an income redistribution effect, and tax breaks for business serve to redistribute income to business. For example, investment incentives while raising the rate of return on new investments may actually penalize holders of old investments. This is not necessarily bad because there are times when it is in the national interest to stimulate the rate of capital formation. In recent years, the rate of capital formation in the United States has lagged relative to world competitors, who also offer tax incentives to their business firms.

Nevertheless, a number of tax breaks have enabled corporations to reduce payment of their tax to the point where corporate income taxes have become increasingly less important as a source of federal tax income. In 1970, the corporate income tax accounted for 20 percent of federal tax income; by 1985, the amount was around 10 percent.[14] Moreover, some corporations have ended up paying little or no income taxes, whereas others have paid at the regular 46 percent rate. A total of 128 large U.S. corporations paid no federal income taxes for at least one of the years between 1981 and 1983.[15] Almost all tax breaks have favored basic manufacturing and real estate firms, which have used

14. *Economic Report of the President 1986* (Washington, D.C.: U.S. Government Printing Office, 1986), p. 246.
15. *The Washington Post*, Sunday, June 29, 1986, p. 12.

them to reduce their taxes to as little as zero, whereas service industries and high-tech firms have reaped little advantage. These firms pay up to the maximum corporate income tax rate of 46 percent on their income, which has the effect of distorting resource allocation.

Tax Reform

Tax reform has become one of the major issues of 1986. Both the Senate and the House of Representatives have introduced legislation that would revise the tax system.[16] Both personal and corporate income tax rates will be changed. The Senate would replace the fifteen tax rates on individual income with two rates — 15 percent on taxable income up to $29,300 and 27 percent on taxable income more than that amount.[17] The House would replace the fifteen rates with four rates — 15 percent on taxable income up to $22,500, 25 percent on income up to $43,000, 35 percent up to $100,000, and 38 percent on income more than that amount. The corporate income tax under the Senate proposal would be reduced to 33 percent from the existing rate of 46 percent; the House proposal would reduce the rate to 36 percent. Taxes on small business firms would also be reduced to a lower rate under both proposals.

A number of proposed changes in the tax laws could have a direct impact on business. One change is the elimination of special depletion allowances for the oil and natural gas industries. Proponents of depletion allowances argue that they are necessary to encourage drilling for oil, but the benefit from exploration has to be measured against the loss of revenue to the Treasury from the tax break. On capital gains, the Senate would repeal the 60 percent exclusion from taxable income of gains from investments held more than six months and tax all gains as ordinary income. The House would keep the exclusion but at a lower rate. Write-offs for depreciation, particularly on real estate investment is also subject to change.

SUMMARY

The federal government has become the nation's largest banker. Through a myriad of agencies, it raises funds or directs their flow to provide credit on terms it specifies to borrowers it selects. Federal credit pro-

---

16. The final version of the tax bill should be reached by the end of 1986, or probably earlier. The rate changes should be similar to those that have been proposed.
17. The taxable income is for those who file jointly.

grams have two primary effects on credit markets. First, they provide subsidies transferring income to government-favored borrowers from the rest of the public. These subsidies may create distortions in the economy by reallocating resources from higher to lower valued uses. Second, these credit programs can disperse lending risk nationally. This can provide a more broadly based loan portfolio that diversifies away a portion of lending risk, and the remaining nondiversifiable lending risk can be more easily borne if widely dispersed rather than concentrated in one region or one institution.

Taxes also have an impact on business. The most important business tax is the corporate income tax, which is considered a cost of production, and in part, is passed off to consumers in the form of higher prices. However, its importance as a revenue source to the federal government has declined. Tax incentives to accomplish certain economic and social objectives have narrowed the base of the tax. Business firms have been given more liberalized depreciation schedules and other incentives designed to stimulate saving and investment. But there are gains and losses that have to be considered in calculating the effectiveness of these incentives. If plant modernization and productivity are stimulated by the tax incentives, there is a gain to the economy. But counterbalanced against this gain is a loss of revenue to the U.S. Treasury, which then has to find alternative sources of revenue. Major tax reform has been initiated in both the Senate and the House of Representatives, and a change in the rate of the corporate tax and the elimination of some of its loopholes can be anticipated.

QUESTIONS FOR DISCUSSION

1. Federal loans to business often contain a subsidy element. Discuss.
2. Distinguish between the objectives of direct loans and those of insured loans.
3. What types of risks are covered by federal loan insurance?
4. From the standpoint of a free enterprise market economy, the Chrysler loan was indefensible. Do you agree?
5. Under what circumstances would it be in the public interest to avoid a potential bankruptcy on the scale of Chrysler?
6. Have the interests of the general public been served as a result of the Chrysler bailout?
7. What is the purpose of government-sponsored financial institutions such as the Federal National Mortgage Association?
8. There are costs as well as benefits when government offers tax breaks to business. Discuss.
9. The Reagan administration has emphasized tax incentives to stimulate business investment. Give examples.

10. Tax breaks for business serve no useful purpose and should be eliminated. Do you agree?

RECOMMENDED READINGS

Aaron, Henry, and Michael J. Boskin. *The Economics of Taxation.* Washington, D.C.: Brookings Institution, 1980.

Bosworth, Barry P., Andrew S. Carron, and Elisabeth B. Phyne. *The Economics of Federal Credit Programs.* Washington, D.C.: Brookings Institution, 1986.

Economic Report of the President 1986. Washington, D.C.: U.S. Government Printing Office, 1986, chapter 6.

Fox, Harrison W., and Martin C. Schnitzer. *Doing Business in Washington.* New York: Free Press, 1981.

Galper, Harvey, and Joseph J. Cordes. *Tax Shelters: Analysis and Policy.* Washington, D.C.: Brookings Institution, 1986.

Meising, Paul. "The Chrysler Corporation Loan Guarantee Act of 1979." Cleveland, Ohio: Case Research Association, 1981.

Ornstein, Norman J., and Shirley Elder. *Interest Groups, Lobbying and Policy Making.* Washington, D.C.: Congressional Quarterly Service, 1978.

U.S. Executive Office of the President, Office of Manpower and Budget. *Budget of The U.S. Government, Fiscal Year 1987.* Washington, D.C.: U.S. Government Printing Office, 1986.

Chapter 17
International Trade Policies

The reasons for the importance of international trade between nations have been recognized by economists since the time of Adam Smith. He attacked the mercantilist view that only exporting countries gained from trade. More recently, political scientists and international affairs specialists have come to recognize the political and strategic importance of foreign trade to a country's national security. Exports of goods and services that are highly valued by consumers around the world and that can be produced by one country more efficiently than it can produce other goods raise a nation's productivity and create employment. Imports of goods from other countries increase the choices of consumers and add to a nation's standard of living. Exports and imports are linked together in that each contributes to economic growth and rising living standards throughout the world.

For thirty years following the end of World War II, most of the world existed under a Pax Americana. Like the Roman Empire of old, American economic and political dominance extended over a wide area. But times have changed, worldwide competition has been growing more severe, and the relative competitive strength of the United States has declined. The rest of the industrial world has either caught up or is in the process of catching up with the United States. U.S. business firms no longer have a monopoly on business conducted in the world or even in the United States. German steel, Japanese cars, and Chinese textile products compete with American industry in its own home territory. Furthermore, foreign competition in the U.S. domestic market has expanded rapidly during recent years, particularly in certain product areas. An example is the automobile market, where Japanese imports now account for more than one-fifth of automobile sales.

One of the major political issues that has developed in the United States is a demand for protection measures against the import of certain foreign products. Segments of the American economy have taken a beating from foreign competition. Factories ranging from textile plants in North Carolina to machine-tool plants in Ohio have shut down. In many cases, older installations have been replaced by hundreds of smaller, more competitive plants, but many industrial towns are dying, and the number of blue-collar jobs has dramatically declined. The villain is foreign competition, and restrictive trade measures, aimed at sheltering a wide variety of American industries from foreign competition, have been introduced in Congress. Some argue that deindustrialization of key American industries such as steel will occur unless they are protected, and that protectionism is necessary to rebuild the competitiveness of U.S. manufacturing. However, it also can be argued that deindustrialization is not occurring, that there is, instead, a shift from large and heavily unionized companies to smaller, more productive enterprises in which labor plays a less important role.

THE RATIONALE FOR INTERNATIONAL TRADE

If there were no restrictions on the free movement of productive factors from one region to another or from one nation to another, the total world production of goods and services would be maximized when the marginal products of similar units of each production factor were equal in all uses and all places. Resources are attracted to those areas in which they are the most productive, and the total output of goods and services is maximized when similar units of resources produce marginal products of equal value in all regions. From this it is easy to see that if the whole world were one economic unit and the maximization of world production were accepted as the appropriate policy goal, the same principles would apply. This suggests that from the consumers' standpoint, free international trade is beneficial, contributing to higher living standards. The interest of the consumers and the general welfare would be identical if there were free mobility of resources from one area to another.

Of course, in the real world, productive resources do not readily move across international boundaries in response to economic concerns; rather, the impetus for trade across national boundaries is increased. This is because differences in the efficiency and proportion of labor and capital make it profitable for nations and regions to specialize in the production of those goods and services for which the resource situation is the most advantageous. A major benefit of trade between nations is that it allows them to capitalize on any advantage they may have in cost of production. This advantage may be absolute or comparative, and each plays a significant role in foreign trade theory.

Absolute Advantage

The law of absolute advantage states that there is a basis for trade when one nation can produce a good or service more cheaply than another nation can. The latter should buy from the former. To put it simply, if the Japanese can produce automobiles more cheaply and of better quality than the United States, we should buy their automobiles; conversely, if the United States can produce farm products more cheaply and of better quality than the Japanese, they should buy our farm products. Consumers in both countries stand to benefit from the specialization of trade, though the American auto producers and the Japanese farmers do not. By concentrating on that one thing it does best, each country gains. Resources are allocated to those areas in which they can be used most efficiently and away from those areas in which they are used inefficiently.

Comparative Advantage

The law of absolute advantage ought not to be confused with the law of comparative advantage. The latter holds that if one country enjoys an advantage over another country in the production of several goods, it should produce the good in which it has the greatest advantage and buy the good in which it has the least advantage from the other country.[1] For example, assume Brazil has an advantage over the United States in the production of both coffee and sugar. Brazil can produce five units of coffee for every unit of coffee produced by the United States, and Brazil can produce two units of sugar for every unit produced by the United States. Brazil has a greater advantage over the United States when it comes to producing coffee, and the United States has less of a disadvantage when it comes to producing sugar. Therefore, Brazil should produce coffee, and the United States should produce sugar. The exchange between the two countries should be coffee for sugar.

The principle here is that a country should not produce all the goods it can make cheaper but only those it can make cheapest. Even if a country is inefficient, it should not cease all production simply because labor and other costs are more expensive. It should drop only those lines in which its performance is most expensive. In the example, Brazil has a five-to-one advantage over the United States when it comes to producing coffee and only a two-to-one advantage when it comes to producing sugar. Brazil would specialize in the commodity it could make with the greatest relative efficiency, and the United States would concentrate on the commodity it could produce with the least relative inefficiency.

1. David Ricardo, an important classical economist of the last century, is associated with the concept of comparative advantage.

Restraints on Trade

In the real world, the aforementioned American auto companies and Japanese farmers are not going to stand by idly while the other side wins. Each will ask its government for assistance, and that is precisely what has happened. The U.S. auto industry has lobbied extensively for protection against Japanese auto imports, and Japanese farmers have demanded and received government protection from U.S. farm imports. American business firms may praise the virtue of free competition in their annual reports to their stockholders and in their pronouncements to the general public, but all too often they lobby in Washington for protection against foreign competition. Competition thus has a double standard: it is fine if we win but wrong if foreigners win. Trade restrictions are by no means limited to the United States; other countries also use them.

Forces and events have created a world much different from the one that existed thirty years ago. Before discussing U.S. foreign trade policies, it is necessary to examine the changes that have taken place in the world and how they have affected the American economy. As other economic processes have emerged, it has become progressively more difficult for the United States to continue to ignore economic practices that have taken their toll on the economy. But U.S. government policies to protect American industries further undermine the whole process of trade.

THE UNITED STATES AND THE NEW ECONOMIC ORDER

Since its inception, the United States has generally followed a policy of trade protection designed to protect domestic producers from foreign competition. In this respect, it is no different from other countries. Trade protection reached its peak during the Depression of the 1930s when all the major industrial countries used tariffs and other restrictive devices to restrict imports. This was self-defeating, for as soon as one country placed restrictions on the imports of another country, the other country would retaliate. The rationale of protection was to protect home industries and workers from the impact of the worldwide Depression, but the benefits of trade protection on unemployment were short-lived because of the retaliatory protection measures that offset any short-term gain. The Depression also brought about the use of many different kinds of trade restrictions, including exchange controls and import quotas.

The General Agreement on Tariffs and Trade (GATT) was signed in 1947 by twenty-three countries, including the United States. Its purpose was to reduce the trade barriers between countries by reciprocal trade agreements and to ensure that all nations would be treated the same. The objectives of unrestricted and nondiscriminatory trade were intended to increase economic efficiency. Since production costs and production structures in the various advanced countries were thought to converge, it was believed that expanded trade would result in greater specialization. Consequently, trade between nations could grow without the pains of economic dislocation. The implication was that countries should produce what they could make most efficiently and trade for the rest. Product specialization and higher incomes for all trading nations would result from expanded exchange.

The world monetary system was also reordered after the end of World War II. The gold standard was replaced by a mixed standard under the Bretton Woods Agreement of 1945. Countries that signed the agreement agreed to maintain stable exchange rates, to abstain from exchange controls, and to avoid competitive currency devaluation. All member currencies were freely convertible against the dollar, which was the only currency backed by gold. The exchange rates of other currencies were linked to the dollar. Each nation established a par value for its currency, with the price of gold the yardstick by which par value was measured. In this way, exchange rates could fluctuate only within limits.[2] However, the mixed standard was eventually abandoned in favor of floating exchange rates where supply and demand forces determine the value of a country's currency.

The Changing World Economy

The liberal economic order in which trade between countries could move freely and exchange rates would remain stable has been affected by a number of changes that have occurred in the world. The task of promoting free trade between countries has become more difficult because of state-centered practices that have developed in response to changes in production and in the international division of labor, as well as to the economic problems of the 1970s and 1980s. State strategies to shape world markets have become more prevalent, more powerful, and more central to the future shape of the world economic order. It is desirable to look at some of the changes that have occurred and how they have had an impact on the U.S. economy.

---

2. Under the gold standard, the exchange rate for the currency of a country was fixed in terms of gold into which the currency could be converted. Gold inflows and outflows were the correction mechanism that held fluctuations in exchange rates to a minimum.

The Oil Crisis of 1973

The oil crisis of 1973 caused the greatest transfer of wealth in the history of humankind; the surpluses of the oil exporting countries were channeled into those importing countries with the greatest need. Meanwhile, those countries that imported oil soon developed large trade deficits, which set off a round of double-digit inflation. The high rate of inflation made floating exchange rates inevitable. Under floating exchange rates, a decrease in the price of a nation's currency relative to other currencies would encourage that country's exports and discourage its imports; an increase in the price of its currency relative to other currencies would have the opposite effect. Since the market determines the value of currencies, some are overvalued and some undervalued. In countries whose currencies become undervalued, import prices rise and export prices fall; in countries whose currencies become overvalued, import prices fall and export prices rise. A good example of the latter has been the strength of the U.S. dollar relative to other currencies. Imports have increased, and exports have declined.

Government Economic Development Strategies

A second factor that has undermined the objective of the free trade order of the GATT system was the development of government strategies to shape markets. Japan is a case in point. Since the end of World War II, it has pursued policies that have moved the economy from the production of labor intensive goods such as textiles, to capital intensive goods such as steel, through consumer durables such as television sets and automobiles, to the advanced technology sectors of computers. Japanese economic development can be catalogued in periods.[3] During the 1950s, emphasis was placed on the development of the ship building industry. The central purpose was to facilitate the external development of Japan through exports. In the 1960s, priority was given to the development of a modern world-class steel industry, which was to provide the industrial base required for the expansion of the entire economy. The development strategy of the 1970s involved the expansion of the Japanese automobile industry; by the end of the decade, Japan was the world's largest producer of automobiles. The strategy for the 1980s is the development of the high technology industries.

It is one thing to have a development strategy and quite another to implement it. But the Japanese have succeeded in their strategy and in the process have increased the animosity of their trading partners, who

3. Ezra Vogel, *Comeback* (Cambridge: Harvard University Press, 1985), chapter 2.

accuse them of unfair trading practices and blocking all competing foreign products from entering the domestic market. There is an enormous imbalance in trade with the United States. In 1985 alone, Japanese exports to the United States exceeded imports from the United States by close to $60 billion. Japan has also become the world's major creditor nation and by degrees is becoming the nexus of the world banking system. It has achieved this success in a relatively short time and is serving as a model for other East Asian countries such as South Korea, Singapore, and Taiwan.

Japan is an example of state-directed capitalism. There is no question that the government has played an important role in the development of the economy but not the paramount role, as many Americans think. One thing that has contributed to the success of Japan is savings — government, corporate, and personal. The savings rate of the Japanese is the highest of all major industrial countries (the United States is the lowest). In part, this can be attributed to government tax policies designed to encourage savings, which are funneled through government-owned investment banks to industry.[4] There has also been a close working relationship between business and government that dates back to the first century.[5] This has resulted in working to achieve common ends. Japanese exports are encouraged through the use of tax breaks.[6] At the same time, domestic industries are protected by an elaborate system of tariffs and quotas.[7]

The Developing Industrial Countries

A number of countries are in the process of achieving industrial development. South Korea is one example, and Brazil is another. These and other developing countries have attempted to achieve a state-directed comparative advantage in the production of such goods as steel and automobiles.[8] The capacity of governments to act as players in the market in pursuit of development goals rests on the provision of specific financial and administrative arrangements. Traditional trade theory, which is based on the assumption of pure competition, does not

---

4. Peter F. Drucker, "Behind Japan's Success," *Harvard Business Review*, January-February, 1981, p. 83-90.
5. There are far more businessmen in politics in Japan than there are in the United States.
6. The United States, Canada, and the Western European countries also do this.
7. The Japanese domestic economy is highly competitive, with an element of social Darwinism involved. It is sort of a training ground for international competition. But few outsiders are allowed to compete.
8. The South Koreans are now able to undercut the Japanese in terms of price, and their quality is equally good.

take into consideration the role that a government can play in creating comparative advantage. It can define and pursue detailed industrial goals, setting not only general objectives but also specific ones involving the organization of particular sectors. A government dominated financial system also allows state intrusion into the marketplace, as does the government budget.

The developing industrial countries have affected the advanced industrial countries such as the United States in several ways. First, they have cut into the exports of those countries. Brazil and South Korea have made a conscious effort to develop a steel industry. Given an advantage of low-cost labor, exports of steel from these countries have cut into the shares of the world steel market held by such producers as Japan and West Germany. Second, they have substituted domestic production for imports from the advanced industrial countries. Mexico, for example, has pursued a policy of import substitution, which means restrict imports to encourage the development of domestic manufacturing. This obviously reduces the market available to the advanced industrial countries. Third, these and other development stragegies have enabled the developing countries to concentrate on developing low-cost producer and consumer goods, which they are able to sell to less-developed countries.

Excess Capacity

The entry of producers from the developing industrial countries increases the world output of many manufactured goods. The end result is excess capacity for industries in both the developed and developing industrial countries. When there is a drop in world demand for a product such as steel, producers have to battle over a diminishing market. Each country, developed and developing, is going to take some sort of action to preserve jobs and protect its industries. Subsidies, import protection, and currency devaluation are devices that can be used to preserve jobs and company earnings, while exporting the problem elsewhere. But these actions violate the principles of free trade in that each country raises its trade barriers to protect its own industries.

The developing countries have a production cost advantage over the developed countries because their labor costs are lower. This is particularly true in the production of such products as shoes and textiles. This advantage enables them to increase their exports to the markets of the developed countries, which has critical implications for profitability of home industries and for employment for each country. Each country may react in a different way. Western European countries protect their industries through the use of subsidies or through market sharing arrangements. American policy response is usually through some form of external protection such as a tariff or import quota. Internal readjustment usually occurs as a result of shifts in resources from one sector to another, forced by the need for firms to depart from industries affected by excess capacity or shifts in competitive advantage. Given the changing world economy, export and import policies have become an important component of government economic policy.

POLICIES TO PROMOTE EXPORTS

Several types of government policies are used to promote exports. Of these, tax policies are probably the most important. A government can manipulate taxes to grant exemptions and special rates to certain types of activities, corporations, or persons. Favorable tax treatment of certain types of income can influence shifts in economic behavior.[9] Governments also sponsor exports through loans financed out of budget revenues or by commercial banks. Subsidies may also be used to aid export industries. Export cartels, international associations of firms in the same industry, are often used to set prices in foreign markets and to restrict output.

Subsidies

Most governments, including the United States, subsidize some exports. Export bounties have been paid by some European governments on one product or another since the seventeenth century. Some countries subsidize the output of farm products. Europe, a major importer of sugar on the world market since 1975, has turned into one of the largest subsidizers in the world, second only to Cuba. Farmers in the European Community countries received a subsidy in 1985 of eighteen cents a pound for their sugar, which was sold in the world market for five cents a pound.[10] Sugar production in the United States is also subsidized. The United States sells beef to Brazil at thirty cents a pound. The economic effect of these and other subsidies is that a country's resources are allocated less efficiently than would be the case if competition and the free flow of resources were permitted between countries. According to World Bank estimates, subsidies of farm products for export cost taxpayers in the United States, Western Europe, and Japan $104.1 billion in 1985 — almost twice the $55.6 billion the farmers of these countries gained from farm exports.[11]

9. Tax incentives were discussed in Chapter 16.
10. The World Bank, *World Development Report 1986*, p. 8.
11. Ibid., p. 24.

Cartels

A cartel is an agreement, formal or informal, entered into by firms situated in different countries or in one country and doing business across international boundaries when the purpose of the agreement is to increase profits by reducing or eliminating competition. Firms may enter into an agreement to control prices. They may also allocate markets among their members, or they may assign sales to an international trade association. They may exchange patents and secret processes. They may also control the use of trademarks, with each cartel member granted the right to use a trademark in its territory. The European countries and Japan tend to manage excess capacity at home through cartels or cartellike arrangements, which have government support. These cartels operate in international markets. Such arrangements are legally more difficult in most cases in the United States.[12]

IMPORT POLICIES

International trade is a two-way street. Countries export goods and services to other countries and import goods and services from them. Consumers gain because there are a wider variety of goods and services from which to choose. Although consumers gain from imports, domestic producers can lose from increased competition because they will sell less, and they may have to sell at a lower price. Competition is a hard taskmaster, for there are losers as well as winners. Over time, individuals and groups have altered the rules of the competitive marketplace when they didn't like the results. Chrysler is one example of a company that sought government help, but it is hardly the only one. Because foreign competition causes some domestic firms, their employees, and their suppliers to lose, they have an incentive to seek government protection from imports, and this is where the whole concept of free trade breaks down. Governments have to respond to the demands of their various constituencies.

Since the end of World War II, the United States has led the world toward a more open and free world trading system. But times have changed, and protectionist sentiment is stronger in the United States than at any time since the Depression. It is necessary to discuss in some

12. The Export Trading Company Act of 1982 permits a form of cartel called the export trading company. The law, which is designed primarily to benefit small and medium-sized companies, grants antitrust immunity to a trading company as long as the foreign operations do not inhibit U.S. competition or undercut domestic prices.

detail the causes of this sentiment, the use of various import restriction devices such as tariffs and import quotas, and the effect of these restrictions on the welfare of consumers, for consumers will carry the results of restrictions, whereas domestic producers may gain, at least in the short run.

Arguments for Protectionism

Despite the benefits that can accrue from an open trading system between countries, sentiment for protection against foreign competition has grown strong in the Untied States. Major legislation has been introduced in Congress aimed at imposing general and specific country barriers on imports. Those who argue for protection advance four reasons for its use. First, it should be used to reduce the deficit in the U.S. merchandise trade account, which amounted to $148.5 billion in 1985.[13] Second, protectionism is necessary to preserve U.S. jobs that are being lost to foreign competition. Third, it is needed to prevent the deindustrialization of important segments of American industry, notably the steel industry. Fourth, it is needed because other countries don't play fairly in that they subsidize exports and restrict imports.

Protectionism and the U.S. Trade Deficit

Trade between countries can be measured by the exports and imports of goods and services. These are a country's current account, which is a part of its balance of payments.[14] Exports and imports of goods are listed in the merchandise trade account, and services and the payments for them are listed in the service account. When merchandise exports and imports are compared, the United States had an unfavorable balance of trade of $-148.5 billion in 1985, and for 1986, it could be as large or larger. This negative balance was offset somewhat by a positive balance in the service account, which reduced the deficit to $-74.4 billion in 1985.[15] U.S. service exports of 1985 amounted to $157.3 billion. Services such as data processing, computer programming, scientific research, and engineering and consulting have become an important and rapidly growing element in U.S. foreign trade.

13. U.S. Department of Commerce, International Trade Administration, *Business America*, March 1985, p. 3.
14. Balance of payments is an account measuring all inflows and outflows of a country.
15. *Economic Report of the President 1986* (Washington, D.C.: U.S. Government Printing Office, 1984), p. 253.

In 1985, U.S. merchandise exports amounted to $213.1 billion, and merchandise imports amounted to $361.6 billion. Table 17-1 presents the ten leading country markets for U.S. exports and the ten leading U.S. suppliers of imports for 1985. From the table, it can be seen that the United States has a deficit in its merchandise trade accounts with all ten countries. However, the major part of the total deficit is concentrated in two trading areas — the East Asian countries and Canada. In fact, half of the merchandise trade deficit for 1985 was with four East Asian markets — Japan, Taiwan, Hong Kong, and South Korea. Demand for protection has been directed against imports from these countries and from Canada.

A primary contributing factor to the trade deficit has been the strength of the U.S. dollar relative to other currencies. This has had an effect on both exports and imports. As far as exports are concerned, price competitiveness has been reduced because foreign countries have had to exchange more of their currencies to obtain U.S. dollars to pay for American products. U.S. exports become more expensive and decline; conversely, U.S. imports have increased because the U.S. dollar can acquire more foreign currency. Foreign products become cheaper for Americans. Imports have increased relative to exports, and the trade deficit has widened to a record $150 billion for 1985. Even though the dollar has depreciated in value relative to the Japanese yen, the Korean won, and other world currencies has not eased the deficit in the first half of 1986.

Table 17-1 Major U.S. Export Markets and Import Suppliers for 1985 (billions of dollars)

Export Markets	Amount	Import Suppliers	Amount
Canada	$ 47.3	Japan	$ 72.4
Japan	22.6	Canada	69.9
Mexico	13.6	West Germany	21.2
United Kingdom	11.3	Mexico	19.4
West Germany	9.0	Taiwan	17.8
Netherlands	7.3	United Kingdom	15.6
France	6.1	South Korea	10.7
South Korea	6.0	Italy	10.4
Austria	5.4	France	10.0
Belgium	4.9	Hong Kong	9.0
World Total	$213.1	World Total	$361.6

Source: U.S. Department of Commerce, International Trade Administration, *Business America*, March 17, 1986, p. 5.

Protectionism and Jobs

One of the strongest arguments advanced for protectionism is that it preserves American jobs being lost to foreign competition. Some supporters of protection claim that each additional billion dollars of imports costs the United States 25,000 to 30,000 jobs.[16] Many textile mills in North Carolina and other southern states have closed down because they cannot compete with low-cost foreign labor. Steel mills and other heavy manufacturing firms in the so-called rust-belt of America also are being put out of business by foreign imports for the same reason. Providing protection for American textile and steel mills will lead to greater domestic spending for their products and preserve jobs for American workers. However, this argument ignores what will happen on the other end. Foreign imports create jobs for Americans, and U.S. exports to foreign countries also create jobs for Americans. U.S. restraints on foreign imports invite retaliation against our exports.

It also can be argued that the U.S. economy has done better than the economies of other industrial countries when it comes to job creation. During the period 1980–1985, in the United States, around eight million jobs were created, more than the combined total for Western Europe and Japan.[17] However, most of those created jobs are in the service industries, and many of them pay less than the blue-collar jobs that have been lost when steel mills close down. Much of this change is inevitable as the United States has matured into a service-oriented economy. The U.S. unemployment rate for 1985 was 7.2, a rate lower than its major competitors, with the exception of Japan. But Japan has a static labor market and does not have to worry about creating jobs for new entrants into the labor force.[18]

Protectionism and Deindustrialization

Sociologist Daniel Bell wrote a book called *The Coming of Post-Industrial Society*, which is a society based on two dimensions — the centrality of theoretical knowledge and the expansion of the service sector as against a manufacturing economy.[19] An industrial society is organized around the axis of production and machinery. There are several characteristics of a post-industrial society, one of which is the gathering of information and another is the creation of new intellectual

16. Ibid., p. 107.
17. Ibid., p. 290.
18. In fact, in Japan there is a shortage of labor as the population is aging.
19. Daniel Bell, *The Coming of Post-Industrial Society* (New York: Basic Books, 1976).

technology, which has created a knowledge class. The fastest growing group in society is the technical and professional class, which according to Bell, will be the largest single group in the U.S. economy by the end of this century. The mode of production shifts from the use of energy and machine technology for the manufacture of goods to the use of telecommunications and computers for the exchange of information and knowledge. Bell contends that the United States has already reached the postindustrial stage of development.

Nevertheless, some groups are concerned that the United States is losing its industrial base to other countries. They argue that protectionism is necessary to preserve the basic manufacturing industries such as steel, without which the American economy risks losing its position as the world's industrial leader. There is also concern that without protection, U.S. workers will lose their manufacturing skills as products are made abroad. In some major export- and import-competing industries, output has declined or has expanded less rapidly than in the rest of the economy. Total employment in manufacturing has not regained the level reached in 1979. These circumstances are also viewed as proof of the deindustrialization of America. The answer, in the minds of critics, is the establishment of a national industrial policy in which the government aids key industries in the same way it helped Chrysler.[20]

Table17-2 presents the performance of the manufacturing sector of the U.S. economy for the period 1973–1984. As the table indicates, employment in manufacturing has declined, but this cannot be interpreted as proof that U.S. producers are losing out to foreign competition. Instead, it can be part of the process where U.S. producers become more efficient and competitive in the world economy. Furthermore, in a competitive market, productivity will continue to grow as firms introduce new technologies when they become economically profitable. Manufacturing employment will continue to decline as productivity grows. In this respect, there is a similarity to agriculture in that agriculture in the United States is far more productive today than it was forty years ago although there are far fewer farmers.

Other Countries Play by Different Rules

It is argued that other countries provide a wide variety of assistance to their export industries while erecting trade barriers against imports. These practices are somewhat similar to the mercantilist policies pursued by Western European countries for around three hundred years. A characteristic of mercantilism was a policy of encouraging exports and discouraging imports, for it was believed a country's wealth

20. Industrial policy will be discussed more in detail in Chapter 19.

Table 17-2 Manufacturing Sector Indicators, 1973–1984

Year	Import Penetration (percent)	Industrial Production (1977 = 100 percent)	Employment (thousands)	Productivity (1977 = 100 percent)	Average Hourly Earnings (dollars)	Real Net Capital Stock (billions of 1982 dollars)
1973	6.2	94.0	20,154	93.4	4.09	554.2
1974	7.2	92.6	20,077	90.6	4.42	581.1
1975	6.5	83.4	18,323	92.9	4.83	597.2
1976	6.7	91.9	18,997	97.1	5.22	612.5
1977	6.9	100.0	19,682	100.0	5.68	630.5
1978	7.8	107.1	20,505	101.5	6.17	655.1
1979	7.9	111.5	21,040	101.4	6.70	681.4
1980	8.2	108.2	20,285	101.4	7.27	707.2
1981	8.5	110.5	20,170	103.6	7.99	729.7
1982	8.9	102.2	18,781	105.9	8.49	741.3
1983	9.3	110.2	18,434	112.9	8.83	741.1
1984	10.9	123.9	19,412	118.5	9.18	752.9

Source: *Economic Report of the President 1986* (Washington, D.C.: U.S. Government Printing Office, 1986), p. 111.

and self-sufficiency depended on exports exceeding imports. Aid was given to local producers by taxing imports and paying subsidies on exports. As was pointed out earlier, the developed and developing industrial countries of today support their export industries in a variety of ways — subsidies, cartels, tax breaks, and so forth.

However, the assumption is that the United States is free from sin in that it plays by the rules of free trade, whereas other countries do not. This is only partially true, for the United States also aids its export industries while protecting domestic industries from foreign imports. It is also assumed that U.S. exports have suffered because other countries have erected trade barriers to keep out our products. But there are also other reasons the United States exports less than it imports. A strong U.S. dollar is one reason, but another reason is the attitude of American management, which has been accused of being out of touch with the world outside the United States and indifferent to export opportunities.[21] Despite the merchandise trade deficit, American labor costs in manufacturing are still the highest in the industrial world.[22]

It is also argued that the Foreign Corrupt Practices Act has an adverse impact on U.S. foreign trade.[23] The act makes various forms of payments illegal even if they break no law where paid. No other country has such a law. As was pointed out in Chapter 9, U.S. antitrust laws also may have an inhibiting effect on U.S. exports. The United States has also failed to stimulate service exports, an area in which it has a comparative advantage over the rest of the world.[24] For example, manufacturers receive investment tax credits and accelerated depreciation, but no such tax favors assist the service industries. As a rule, the service industries pay higher taxes than the manufacturing industries.[25] Research and development tax breaks are given to manufacturing industries but not to the service industries.

Protective Tariffs

The tariff is probably the most common device used by the United States and other countries to restrict foreign trade. It is simply a tax

21. U.S. Joint Economic Committee. Subcommittee on Trade, Productivity, and Economic Growth. *American Exports; Why Have They Lagged?* 99th Cong., 1st sess., 1985, p. 16.
22. Ibid., p. 17.
23. U.S. General Accounting Office, Comptroller General, *Impact of Foreign Corrupt Practices Act on U.S. Business* (Washington, D.C.: U.S. Government Printing Office, 1981), pp. 12–17.
24. *American Exports: Why Have They Lagged?* p. 16.
25. In 1986, it was announced that a number of large U.S. manufacturing firms have paid no income taxes over several years. Many service firms paid the full tax rate.

levied on foreign goods coming into the country. The result is to make imported goods more expensive than comparable domestic goods, which, of course, are not subject to the tax. If the tariff is sufficiently high, American consumers will find imported goods too expensive to buy; if they buy at all, they will probably buy the domestic goods. The main effect of a tariff is that it raises the prices of the commodities protected by it; if it did not raise prices, it would afford no protection. The increase in prices represents a gain to domestic producers, at least in the short run, and a loss to consumers. The higher price for the product is likely to mean a greater income for producers and a reduction in living standards for consumers, for consumers are denied the opportunity of buying foreign goods, which could come into this country at a lower cost and with greater quality than comparable American goods.

Import Quotas

Compared with tariffs, which have been used by countries since the days of mercantilism, import quotas are relatively new. Introduced in France in the 1930s as an antidepression measure, the import quota has become a significant part of most countries' international commercial policy. As the name implies, a quota places limits, numerical or other, on the amount of a product that can be imported. For example, one country decides to restrict its auto imports from another country to two million cars a year. An import quota is generally considered more restrictive than a tariff. With a tariff, there is still the option of buying the foreign product, albeit at a higher price, but the import quota limits even this option. Prices cannot be forced by a tariff to rise by more than the amount of the tariff, but there is no upper limit to the price increase that can result from a quota. The prices to consumers are raised, and the restrictions placed on imports take away the incentive of domestic producers to innovate and promote efficiency.

U.S. Protection of the Automobile Industry

The U.S. automobile is a classic example of an oligopoly. Since Chrysler was created in 1925, the domestic automobile industry has been dominated by three firms — General Motors, Ford, and Chrylser. Their total share of the market ranged from 75 percent to 90 percent for fifty years. But during the 1970s, the once irrevocable oligopoly showed signs of cracking. In 1980, two of the three companies, Chrysler and Ford, lost more than $3 billion between them. Chrysler was close to financial collapse, and only Ford's foreign allies kept it from collapse as well. Japan's penetration of the U.S. auto market was a prime contributor to the U.S. auto industry's problems. In 1970, Japanese imports represented less than 8 percent of the total U.S. purchases of all cars, but by 1980, one out of every four cars purchased by American consumers was Japanese. Foreign imports accounted for 30 percent of all cars sold in the United States.

Several factors contributed to the problems of the U.S. automobile industry during the 1970s.[26] One was regulation. Safety regulation began in the late 1960s, and emission control standards were mandated by the Clean Air Act. The costs of safety and emission control regulations were substantial, adding about $2,000 more to the price of a new car during the period 1966–1981. A second factor was that the automobile industry had problems in adopting the technologies of emissions control. For several years, they used relatively inefficient devices to control emissions. Poor performance, severely depressed fuel economy, and widespread consumer dissatisfaction were the results. A third factor was the two oil shocks of the 1970s, which changed consumer buying attitudes in favor of the smaller fuel economy cars. The fourth factor was the arrival of the Japanese cars. The Japanese were able to adjust more readily to U.S. regulatory requirements because they didn't have to downsize their product lines. The quality of Japanese cars was superior to American cars, and the gap had widened by the end of the decade.[27]

One factor that gave the Japanese auto firms a production advantage over their American competitors was lower labor costs. Table 17-3 compares labor costs in the U.S. and Japanese automobile industries for the period 1975–1983. Comparisons are also made of wages in the U.S. and Japanese automobile industries to the wages in all U.S. and Japanese manufacturing industries. It can be seen that there is a far greater gap between autoworkers wages and all manufacturing wages in the United States than there is in Japan. Moreover, the gap widened in the United States particularly for the period 1979–1983. Wage differentials gave the Japanese a competitive cost advantage of from $1,300 to $2,500 per car. This cost advantage did not reflect the quality advantage that Japanese cars had over American cars. Japanese quality control standards were superior to those of the American car companies.

26. Robert W. Crandall, "Import Quotas and the Automobile Industry: The Costs of Protection," *The Brookings Review*, Vol. 2, No. 4 (Summer 1984), pp. 8–10.
27. Ibid., p. 11.

The Automobile Industry and Import Quotas

In 1981, the U.S. auto companies asked Congress and the Reagan administration for quotas against the Japanese automobile industry. At stake, the U.S. auto industry claimed, was the survival of the industry and the necessity to preserve jobs. Import quotas would provide a time-out or respite, so to speak, while the auto industry could recuperate, retool, and come out with new cars that could compete successfully against Japanese cars. Precedents for import quotas had already been established. Beef quotas have assisted cattle raisers, sugar quotas have kept high-cost domestic sugar cane and sugar beet growers in business, and quotas and other forms of support have been used to protect domestic steel producers from further losses to Asian and European steel producers. The Reagan administration made a compromise in that it reached an agreement with Japan whereby Japanese auto companies would voluntarily limit their exports to the United States.

These quotas, set at 1,680,000 cars a year over a three-year period, ended in March 1984. A new quota, which raised the number of cars the Japanese could ship to the United States to 1,850,000 cars, was applied from April 1, 1984 to March 31, 1985. The allocation of import shares among Japanese automobile manufacturers was determined by the Japanese government on the basis of each company's

Table 17-3 Total Hourly Compensation in the Motor Vehicle Industry and All Manufacturing, United States and Japan (dollars per hour)

	United States		Japan	
Year	Motor Vehicles	All Manufacturing	Motor Vehicles	All Manufacturing
1975	9.44	6.35	3.56	3.05
1976	10.27	6.93	4.02	3.30
1977	11.45	7.59	4.82	4.03
1978	12.67	8.30	6.85	5.54
1979	13.68	9.07	6.90	5.49
1980	16.29	9.89	6.89	5.61
1981	17.28	10.95	7.65	6.18
1982	18.66	11.68	7.18	5.70
1983	19.02	12.31	7.91	6.24

Source: Robert W. Crandall, "Import Quotas and the Automobile Industry: The Costs of Protection," *The Brookings Review*, Vol. 2, No. 4 (Summer 1984), p. 10.

share of the U.S. market before the quota was imposed. The breakdown of the market was as follows:[28]

Toyota	31 percent
Nissan	27 percent
Honda	21 percent
Mazda	9 percent
Mitsubishi	7 percent
Subaru	4 percent
Isuzu	1 percent

Results of the Import Quota on Japanese Cars

The import quota had a number of results, few of which were of benefit to American consumers. As the market allocation indicates, the quota benefited those Japanese auto firms that had already established a market for their cars in the United States. Toyota was assured of a market share of around one-third of the quota. Conversely, Japanese car companies that had not established a market share before the quota were virtually shut out of the U.S. car market. U.S. consumer choice was limited to a choice of the cars produced by Toyota, Nissan, or Honda, or the U.S. cars, or the cars of countries to which the import quota did not apply. However, the import quota on Japanese cars also had other effects on American consumers:[29]

1. It raised the prices of both American and Japanese cars to U.S. consumers. One estimate was that the price of Japanese imports increased an average of $920 to $960 per car in the 1981–1982 period. Since restrictions were placed on Japanese cars, the companies shipped their top-of-the-line models. It was estimated that Japanese producers and their dealers benefited by as much as $2 billion a year during the quota.

2. The prices of U.S. automobiles also increased by an estimated $1,300 for each new U.S. car sold during the period 1981–1983. The estimated additional costs to consumers for new American and Japanese cars was $4.3 billion in 1983.

3. One intent of the import quota was to protect American jobs. An estimated 20,000 to 25,000 jobs were saved in the automobile industry at a cost to consumers of $160,000 a year per job.

4. Another purpose of the import quota was to enable the U.S. car companies to improve the quality of their cars. There is little evidence that this has happened.

---

28. Information provided by the Office of the U.S. Special Trade Representative.
29. Crandall, pp. 11-16.

5. The U.S. automobile companies increased their market shares and made record profits. In 1984, Chrysler's profits were the highest in its history. Automobile profits were $6.3 billion for 1983 and close to $10 billion in 1984.

6. With such profits, the automobile companies paid their executives and some employees substantial bonuses. Chairman Philip Caldwell of Ford Motor Company received a 1983 salary and bonus of $1.4 million plus $5.9 million in long-term compensation. Chrysler Chairman Lee A. Iacocca received stock options valued at $17 million.

Protectionism and the U.S. Steel Industry

The U.S. steel industry has fallen on hard times. Its plants are old, its profits low, its prospects uncertain. In July 1986, LTV filed for bankruptcy, and other producers are under pressure to lower costs or face bankruptcy.[30] Bethlehem Steel, one of the largest steel companies in the United States, has lost $2 billion since 1981. In 1985, it lost $196 million on total sales of $5.1 billion. LTV lost $724 million on total sales of $8.2 billion.[31] Inland Steel had a loss of $178 million on total sales of $3.2 billion. Wheeling-Pittsburgh Steel lost $303 million on total sales of $681 million. U.S. Steel earned a profit of $409 million on total sales of $18.4 billion.[32] However, the profit reflected a credit of 10 percent of its net income. The growth rate of U.S. Steel was a negative 9.4 percent annually for the period 1975–1985.

The industry has taken a beating in world competition from the Germans and Japanese, and lately from the steel industries of the developing industrial countries such as South Korea and Brazil. The U.S. share of world production slipped from 26 percent in 1960 to 14 percent in 1980; conversely, Japan's share of world steel production increased from 6 percent to 16 percent over the same period. During that period, the Japanese steel industry became the world's largest and most sophisticated. The Japanese steel industry has possessed two characteristics that have been absent in the U.S. steel industry — a devotion to quality and a willingness to invest a large amount of money in projects that might not show profits for years.[33] The most modern Japanese steel mills are models of efficiency. High-pressure gases leaving the blast furnaces turn electrical generators. A computer may regulate

30. *U.S. News & World Report*, July 28, 1986, p. 31.
31. *Fortune*, April 28, 1986. The data were taken from *The Fortune 500*, pp. 182–201.
32. U.S. Steel is now USX.
33. U.S. Congress, Office of Technology Assessment, *U.S. Industrial Competitiveness: A Comparison of Steel, Electronics, and Automobiles* (Washington, D.C.: U.S. Government Printing Office, 1981).

the flow of energy to every part of the plant. Computer-controlled cranes automatically lift and store bars and sheets of steel. And even the steel itself meets the highest standards of purity and the tightest specification.

Reasons for Decline

Several factors are responsible for the decline of the U.S. steel industry.[34] First, government regulations, such as those pertaining to environmental protection, required significant capital expenditures by the industry. At the same time, the government has not attempted to offset such expenditures so that the industry could update its plants and equipment. This is one reason why most of the productivity growth in the American steel industry has come piecemeal through improvements to existing facilities. A second reason for the decline of the U.S. steel industry is an increase in wages exceeding its productivity. Furthermore, the industry's plants and equipment have not been modernized rapidly enough to give efficiency improvements that would keep up with rising wages. A third reason is the feeling that the managers of the U.S. steel industry are just not as good as the managers of the foreign competitors. Fourth, demand for steel has fallen as more products are designed to use less steel.

Import Restraints

Several forms of import restraints have been used to reduce the flow of foreign steel into the United States. Voluntary import quotas have been used against both the European and Japanese steel industries. A set of reference, or trigger, prices were also used. They were based on the cost of production for the world's most efficient steel industry, the Japanese steel industry. The Japanese cost of production was calculated at a five-year average rate of capacity utilization, which was 85 percent.[35] Prices could be set at or above this reference price, based on the Japanese unit cost of production plus freight from Japan. Any steel shipped to the United States below this reference price was monitored to determine if there was prima-facie evidence of dumping. The reference price established a price below which steel imports were restricted into the United States.

34. Robert W. Crandall, *The U.S. Steel Industry in Recurrent Crisis* (Washington, D.C.: Brookings Institution, 1981).
35. Ibid., p. 43.

Several bilateral export restraint agreements were negotiated with foreign steel producing countries in 1985. An earlier agreement with the European Community (EC) was renegotiated, but the United States unilaterally imposed import quotas on semifinished steel from the EC. A countervailing duty case was brought against several European steel producers that were either state-owned or heavily subsidized. A limitation placed on market shares from these countries was intended to reduce the ability of subsidized imported steel to drive down prices in the U.S. market. It might be added that there has been a complete restructuring of the steel industry in Europe, which has found it difficult to compete against imports from Japan and South Korea.

The Performance of the U.S. Steel Industry

Table 17-4 presents the performance of the U.S. steel industry for the period 1975-1984. As the table indicates, employment in the steel industry has declined by more than 200,000 workers since 1975. Wages have doubled, and the ratio of steel workers' wages to wages of all manufacturing workers has increased. The rate of import penetration by foreign steel products has shown an increase but cannot be considered the prime cause of unemployment. There has been some decline in steel output and a gain in productivity.

In the United States, two steel industries have developed. There is the older steel industry — characterized by old plants, high labor and other costs, and a declining demand — which is losing out to the more efficient steelmaking companies in Japan, South Korea, and Brazil. But then there is a new type of steel producer in the United States that is competitive.[36] These are the "minimills," which are small-scale plants producing steel from scrap instead of iron ore. They have reduced costs by operating more efficiently and by expanding their array of products. They do not require trade protection to survive and, in fact, are highly competitive with foreign steel producers. They have been as important as foreign competition in contributing to the decline of the large-scale integrated producers of steel. By 1990, they are expected to account for 40 percent of the steel produced in the United States.

In addition to the minimills, there are also the reconstituted mills of steel companies that have gone through bankruptcy or its threat — such as Wheeling-Pittsburgh, Weirton, McLough, and now LTV. These companies also provide competition for the large integrated companies, such as USX, Bethlehem, and Armco. Reconstituted steel mills now

---

36. Donald F. Barnett and Robert W. Crandall, *Up from the Ashes: The Rise of the Steel Minimill in the United States* (Washington, D.C.: Brookings Institution, 1986).

Table 17-4 Indicators of Performance in the U.S. Steel Industry, 1975–1984

Year	Import Penetration (percent)	Output (millions of tons)	Employment (thousands)	Productivity (1977 = 100 percent)	Weekly Wages (dollars)	Ratio to Manufacturing
1975	10.6	80.0	548	93.3	$274.13	168
1976	9.0	89.4	549	99.0	305.88	174
1977	10.8	91.1	554	100.0	338.58	179
1978	11.4	97.9	561	108.3	389.69	191
1979	10.4	100.3	571	106.9	428.89	195
1980	10.9	83.9	512	102.9	448.77	191
1981	13.8	88.5	506	112.0	509.04	199
1982	16.8	61.6	396	90.9	505.97	189
1983	12.3	67.6	341	116.8	509.16	181
1984	16.7	73.7	334	132.0	527.39	179

Source: *Economic Report of the President 1986* (Washington, D.C.: U.S. Government Printing Office, 1986), p. 115.

make half as much steel as traditional integrated mills but can produce steel for a much lower price. Since steel tends to be priced at the level of the lowest cost producer, the possibility for increased insolvency of other firms in the steel industry remains distinct, with or without trade protection.[37]

SUMMARY

Everyone is in favor of trade between countries as long as the results are of equal benefit to all concerned. However, this is not usually the case. Although to consumers, trade between countries is clearly beneficial because it contributes to higher living standards, some producer groups may be adversely affected. Import of textiles and the decline of the U.S. textile industry is an example. Those whose sales are reduced by foreign competition and those whose incomes are reduced if foreign goods are made available to domestic consumers will want protection against foreign imports. It is imporant to keep in mind that any change generates a conflict among economic groups in any country. Policy-makers in the field of international trade have to determine what groups are to be helped at the expense of other groups.

For centuries, governments have been involved in actively promoting foreign trade. Exports have been stimulated through a variety of devices ranging from military conquests to cartels. Home industries have been protected by means of tariffs and, more recently, import quotas. The United States traditionally followed a high-tariff policy designed to help certain domestic producers. After World War II, however, tariff rates were significantly lowered and, other forms of trade restrictions were relaxed. American trade policies were far more liberal than those of other industrial countries. However, the decline of the U.S. automobile and steel industries during the 1970s and early 1980s promoted a demand by U.S. producers for protection against foreign competition. The government responded by imposing voluntary import quotas on Japanese cars and by creating a wide variety of policies intended to insulate U.S. steel firms from foreign competition. The demand for protection has spread over into other U.S. industries, including textiles and shoes. At best, these policies have had or will have limited success, with U.S. consumers paying higher prices for the protected products.

37. Alan Wm. Wolff, "International Competitiveness of American Industry: The Role of U.S. Trade Policy," in *U.S. Competitiveness in the World Economy*, Bruce R. Scott and George C. Lodge, eds. (Boston: Harvard Business School Press, 1986), pp. 310-314.

QUESTIONS FOR DISCUSSION

1. What are some of the reasons that world trade has turned away from the principles of free trade as promoted by GATT?
2. What is the principle of absolute advantage? How would it apply to the American and Japanese auto industries?
3. What is comparative advantage? Can a country create comparative advantage?
4. What is a tariff? What effect does it have on consumers?
5. What is an import quota? What effect does it have on consumers?
6. What are some of the reasons for the demand in the United States for protection against foreign competition?
7. What impact did the import quota on Japanese cars have on the U.S. automobile industry? What impact did it have on car buyers?
8. What are some of the reasons for the decline in the international competitive position of the U.S. steel industry?

RECOMMENDED READINGS

Arndt, Sven, Richard J. Sweeney, and Thomas D. Willett, eds. *Exchange Rates, Trade, and the U.S. Economy.* Washington, D.C.: The American Enterprise Institute, 1985.

Barnett, Donald F., and Robert W. Crandall. *Up from the Ashes: The Rise of the Steel Minimill in the United States.* Washington, D.C.: Brookings Institution, 1986.

Crandall, Robert W. "Import Quotas and the Automobile Industry: The Costs of Protection." *The Brookings Review*, Vol. 2, No. 4 (Summer 1984), pp. 8-16.

Economic Report of the President 1986. Washington, D.C.: U.S. Government Printing Office, 1986, chapter 4.

Lawrence, Robert L. *Can America Compete?* Washington, D.C.: Brookings Institution, 1984.

U.S. Congress, Office of Technology Assessment. *U.S. International Competitiveness: A Comparison of Steel, Electronics, and Automobiles.* Washington, D.C.: U.S. Government Printing Office, 1981.

U.S. Joint Economic Committee. *The Foreign Trade Dilemma: Fact and Fiction.* 98th Congress, 2d Session, 1984.

U.S. Joint Economic Committee. Subcommittee on Trade, Productivity, and Economic Growth. *American Exports: Why Have They Lagged?* 99th Congress, 1st Session, 1985.

PART VII
GOVERNMENT AND BUSINESS: OTHER ISSUES

Much has happened to the United States during the twentieth century: involvement in two global wars, the Great Depression of the 1930s, and an inflation that was the most virulent in the nation's history. As the United States entered the 1980s, it had reached a crossroad in its development as the world's leading economic power, for there had been an erosion of U.S. industrial strength in the world, particularly during the 1970s. In this decade, the United States lost 23 percent of its share of the world market, compared to a 16 percent decline during the 1960s. The losses in the 1970s were particularly telling because they came in the wake of a 40 percent decline in the value of the dollar, which made U.S. exports cheaper and foreign imports more expensive. There is also evidence that the ability of U.S. industry to innovate — to convert ideas into commercial products and processes — is slipping. Declining investment has helped to reduce U.S. productivity; this has become serious in the industrial sector where the United States once reigned supreme. The rest of the industrial world, especially Germany and Japan, is rapidly closing the gap.

The election results of 1980 and 1984 may prove to have far-reaching consequences as far as economic policy is concerned. The Reagan administration, armed with a mandate to reduce the role of the federal government in the economy, has made an attempt to make a lasting imprint by reducing its functions. The implementation of supply-side economics in the early 1980s favored measures designed to increase the total output of goods and services. Taxes were lowered to stimulate savings and the rate of capital formation, and various tax incentives to stimulate business were introduced into the tax system. The administration has attempted to make the states assume responsibility for various programs by reducing expenditures on entitlements. Meanwhile, the deficit in the federal budget has more than doubled, with neither the administration nor Congress willing to assume any responsibility for its reduction. Reagan economic policies have had some favorable results, particularly in reducing the rate of inflation.

Chapter 18
Government Stabilization Policies

Probably the most important development in the role of the federal government, at least in the last thirty years, has been its explicit assumption of responsibility for the nation's general economic health. A high level of employment, price stability, and an adequate rate of economic growth are accepted as goals that the government must attempt to fulfill. To these goals, a fourth, a more equitable distribution of income, may be added. Each goal in itself has proved somewhat difficult to attain. Moreover, the attainment of one may not necessarily assist in the achievement of the others. For example, efforts to achieve full employment and price stability often are at cross-purposes with each other: achieving one goal usually has meant sacrificing the other.

Government responsibility for economic stability is a relatively recent phenomenon, dating from the end of World War II when the Employment Act of 1946 was passed. The Depression of the 1930s was the catalyst for the government to change from being passive to being active in using economic policy measures to achieve prosperity. Before and even during the Depression, the government was expected to maintain a neutral or laissez-faire attitude toward the general working of the American economy. The Depression, however, was unprecedented in both size and duration. Almost one-fourth of the labor force was unemployed in 1932, and throughout the decade unemployment remained higher than ever before in this century. The feeeling grew that something was inherently amiss in the market system and that the country might be facing permanent economic stagnation. It was thus only a short step to formally accepting the government's responsibility for overall economic growth and stability, a step symbolized by the Employment Act of 1946.

Taxes and transfer payments and in some cases government purchases of goods and services serve as incentives or disincentives to the private sector of the economy. Changes in existing rules and norms for taxation and transfer payments may thus have, in a broad sense, incentive, or substitution, effects. An increase in the progression of the personal income tax may, for instance, lead to the substitution of leisure for work. An increase in the rate of payroll taxes may lead to the substitution of resources in production, and a change in depreciation allowances may affect the expected rate of return on investment. Moreover, any payment between the federal budget and the private sector will correspondingly change the wealth and liquidity position of the private sector's assets and may thus affect private spending with regard to liquidity or assets, either directly or via the reactions of the credit market.

As mentioned earlier, monetary and fiscal policies are the instruments for controlling or influencing economic activity. The most pervasive instruments are a part of monetary policy. Changes in the legal reserve requirements of member banks in the Federal Reserve System can be made by its board of governors to influence the supply and cost of loanable funds. Almost all the contraction or expansion in the nation's supply of money occurs as a result of changes in the volume of bank credit. Commercial banks expand the money supply by making loans and creating new deposits, though legal reserves must be held against deposits. When reserve requirements are raised, there is a contraction in the amount of funds that banks can make available for loans; the reverse holds true for a lowering of legal reserve requirements. The Federal Reserve Banks' open-market operations also expand or contract the money supply. When a Federal Reserve Bank buys government securities from a commercial bank, the payment increases the latter's deposits and enhances its lending capabilities. And when a Federal Reserve Bank sells government securities to a commercial bank, it has the reverse effect. Changes in the rediscount rate by the board of governors influence the level of interest rates. Since the interest rate is the price paid for borrowed capital, its level in turn affects the volume of business investment.

Fiscal policy measures — changes in government expenditures and taxes — directly change aggregate demand by altering income and expenditures flows, whereas monetary policy measures indirectly change aggregate demand by altering prices and the absolute and relative supplies of different kinds of financial assets. Fiscal policy makes deliberate changes in government expenditures and taxes as a means of controlling economic activity. The budget of the federal government is the key instrument through which fiscal policy is effected, and it can be used as a flywheel to change the level of economic activity. Taxes are a withdrawal of income from the income stream, and government expenditures are an injection of income into it. When a government's income, as represented by taxes and other revenues, exceeds it expenditures, the net effect is to damp down the level of economic activity. But when government expenditures exceed revenues, the net effect is economic stimulation. Budgetary surpluses or deficits, then, can be used to effect changes in the level of economic activity. Fiscal policy controls the provision of public goods and services through expenditures, and income redistribution through taxes and transfer payments.

Government stabilization policies have an important impact on the operations of business firms. Monetary policy influences the rate of interest and the supply of loanable funds. When interest rates are high and loanable funds scarce, business firms will be forced to postpone certain types of investments that would have been profitable during a period of lower interest rates and easy credit. Fiscal policy relies on changes in taxation and expenditures to effect changes in the level of economic activity. Changes in taxation will touch any business firm; for example, a reduction in the rate of the corporate income tax would give business firms more funds to invest or pay out to stockholders.

THE IMPACT OF THE DEPRESSION ON ECONOMIC POLICY

The Depression did more to reshape the American economy than any other event has since the nation was created. As mentioned in Chapter 3, there was massive government intervention in a number of areas affecting business. Banks were made subject to closer regulation and supervision. The program of government support for prices of agricultural products was greatly enlarged to prevent losses and bankruptcy for farmers already hurt by market forces in the form of falling prices. Labor unions were encouraged by new legislation so that workers would no longer have to bargain individually in the market for labor. For a time, through the National Industrial Recovery Act, business firms were encouraged to join together to plan how to avoid subjecting their products to the vagaries of supply and demand. Legislation was passed requiring compulsory contributions to retirement funds through a government-operated social security system, which had the effect of partly replacing people's voluntary savings, in response to market forces such as the level of interest rates. Legislation also was passed imposing compulsory costs on business to finance automatic payments to unemployed workers.

Perhaps most important, however, the Depression persuaded the United States and nearly all other Western democratic governments to commit themselves to the goal of full employment. This was in response to the Depression's most unforgetable feature, mass unemployment, both at home and abroad. In 1933, for example, 24.9 percent of the American civilian labor force was unemployed; one out of every four workers was out of work. Even as late as 1939, ten years after the onset of the Depression, unemployment was still at the high figure of 17.2 percent of the labor force. To many, it appeared that the capitalistic system was in a state of collapse and that the Marxist predictions of capitalism's demise were about to come true.[1] Unemployment had also contributed to social upheaval in other countries. In Germany, the main reason for the rise of Adolph Hitler was social discontent caused by an unemployment rate of more than one-fourth of the labor force. The choice for many Germans was Hitler's National Socialism or communism. The result was that fascism replaced parliamentary democracy in Germany.[2]

Classical Economic Theory and Unemployment

Until the 1930s, the American economy had never experienced a deep and prolonged depression. Everything about the past supported the view of classical economic theory that full employment of labor and other resources could be accepted as the norm.[3] There could be lapses from full employment, but self-correcting market forces would pull the economy back to the normal state. Classical economic theory was based on many assumptions. First, there was a competitive market system, in which resources were mobile. There were many buyers and sellers in both the product and resource markets, and prices were free to move either upward or downward. Second, income was spent automatically at a rate always consistent with full employment. There could not be too much saving, for saving was channeled into investment through the mechanism of the interest rate. If there was excessive saving, the interest rate would fall and investment would increase. Conversely, if there was too little saving, the interest rate would rise and investment would decrease. An equilibrium point would always be reached at full employment. Both saving and investment seemed in fact to be functions of the interest rate. Since saving was just another form of spending, according to classical theory, all income was spent on either consumption or investment.[4]

1. Karl Marx, *Das Kapital* (New York: Modern Libary, 1949), pt. VII, pp. 671-688.
2. William L. Shirer, *The Rose and Fall of the Third Reich* (Greenwich, Conn.: Fawcett Publishers, 1973), p. 215.
3. The term *classical economics* was invented by Karl Marx to refer to the writings of David Ricardo and his predecessors, including Adam Smith. Later the term was applied to the writings of John Stuart Mill, Alfred Marshall, and A. C. Pigou.
4. For a good description of classical economics, see Dudley Dillard, *The Economics of John Maynard Keynes* (Englewood Cliffs, N.J.: Prentice-Hall, 1960), chap. 2.

Say's Law of Markets

The catalyst, so to speak, in classical economic theory was Say's Law of Markets.[5] Say's Law states, in effect, that supply creates its own demand. Whatever is produced represents the demand for another product. Additional supply creates additional demand; hence, any increase in production is an increase in demand, and any general over-production is impossible. This assertion is supported by the argument that goods really exchange for goods, money being merely a medium of exchange. Say reasoned that whenever workers and other resources are hired to create goods and services, a demand equal in value to the incomes paid to the factors of production is created automatically. Since the purpose of earning income is to spend it on output, income will automatically equal that output. In an exchange economy, Say's Law means there will always be a rate of spending sufficient to maintain full employment.

The crucial assumption underlying Say's Law is that free competition and flexible prices, wages, and interest rates are part of the economic system. For example, all income received by labor may not necessarily be spent on consumption. Overproduction is possible, with the result that incomes decline and unemployment occurs. But the nonexpenditure, or saving, of income creates no problem, for all saving is transformed into investment spending through the mechanism of the interest rate. The increased saving will cause interest rates to decline, which will encourage business firms to invest. This in turn will cause the demand for goods and services to grow, which will counterbalance the decline in demand caused by consumer saving. Thus, the act of saving cannot lead to a deficiency of total demand or an interruption in the flow of income and expenditure.

The classical assumption of full employment was made easier to accept by making the concept consistent with voluntary unemployment. In classical economic theory, involuntary unemployment did not exist. Voluntary unemployment existed when workers were unwilling to accept the going wage. If there was competition and the market system was allowed to function, supply and demand would eventually drive wages down to a point at which unemployed workers could find employment. If they did not accept the wage, they were unemployed by choice and were not to be counted in the unemployment statistics. But this was obviously inconsistent with the facts. In 1932, there were fifteen million unemployed workers; most were hardly unemployed as a

5. Jean Baptiste Say was a French economist who lived during the time of Adam Smith. His major work, entitled *Treatise on Political Economy*, was the first popular book on economics published on the European continent.

matter of choice. The classical rationale for this situation was that labor markets had been made imperfect by union and government intervention in supply and demand. Wage rates were therefore not free to fall to a competitive level, at which point all who were willing to work could find employment.

Policy Implications for Government

The classical theory of employment has a predilection for laissez faire, the policy that minimizes the extent of government intervention in the economy's operation. The reason is readily apparent. Classical economic theory asserted that the normal market situation is one of full employment of all resources. If there was a departure from full employment, self-adjusting market forces would move the economy to the full employment level. Given the classical assumption of a competitive market economy, with a flexible system of prices and free mobility of resources, no depression could be prolonged. Interest rates would decline to a point at which business firms would be encouraged to borrow and spend on capital goods to expand productive capacity. Savers, in response to declining interest rates, would save less and spend more. With these market adjustments freely functioning, mass unemployment could not be sustained. Through price flexibility and the free play of market forces, there eventually would be an automatic adjustment to a level of full employment.

Keynesian Economic Theory

An economic theory is valid until events prove otherwise, and the facts of economic life simply did not correspond to the way the economy was supposed to act in the classical system. The automatic adjustment toward a level of full employment did not occur; on the contrary, as the Depression of the 1930s continued, serious and prolonged unemployment became the normal condition of the economy. Under these conditions, not even the staunchest defenders of classical theory could maintain seriously that there existed within the economy forces that automatically would generate continuous full employment. The classical theory offered little help to policymakers responsible for devising measures to combat unemployment, and it was no consolation to those unemployed to be told that unemployment was temporary and that eventually market forces would effect the conditions necessary for full employment. What was needed was a new theory that would explain the causes of unemployment and offer solutions for the policymakers to follow.

In 1936, the British economist John Maynard Keynes published the *General Theory of Employment, Interest, and Money.*[6] Only Adam Smith's *Wealth of Nations* and Karl Marx's *Das Kapital* have had as much impact on economic and political thinking as the *General Theory* did, but it was some years before its analysis was accepted by economists and its prescriptions for unemployment accepted by policymakers both in the United States and in other countries. The purpose of the *General Theory* was twofold. First, Keynes explained why classical economic theory was wrong to assume there would be full employment of labor and capital. Second, and much more important for government policy purposes, Keynes constructed an alternative theory of how employment is determined in a complex industrial society. Keynes took the position that there was nothing inherent in the market system that would assure an equilibrium of resources at a level of full employment. In fact, an equilibrium position could be attained at a high level of unemployment. Moreover, as the Depression demonstrated, this position could remain relatively unchanged for a long time.

In classical economic theory, the flexibility of wages and the rate of interest could be counted on to keep an economy in balance at a high level of employment. The classical economists reasoned that unemployment would eventually disappear because the workers' competition for jobs would drive wages down to the point at which it would be profitable for employers to hire them. But Keynes contended that the volume of employment depended on aggregate demand, not flexible wages. Obviously, a drop in wages meant a drop in aggregate demand. In classical rubric, the flexibility of interest prevented a glut of savings. An oversupply of savings could reduce consumption and the level of demand, but the increase in saving would lower the interest rate and thus stimulate investment. The increase in investment would counterbalance the decrease in consumption. But Keynes claimed that the rate of saving bore little relation to the interest rate.

In Keynesian economic theory, the level of employment is linked to the business firms' volume of output of goods and services. The volume of output, in turn, depends on the level of income and aggregate demand. The catalyst in the Keynesian analytical framework is aggregate demand, for it determines, at least in the short run, the extent to which an economy's productive capacity will be used. It is at one and the same time the source of total income and the basis on which the level of employment is determined. If demand is not sufficient to employ all available resources, income will be lower than it need be. As demand falls, so will income, and as income falls, so will output and

6. John Maynard Keynes, *The General Theory of Employment, Interest, and Money* (New York: Harcourt, Brace & Co., Inc., 1936).

employment. The key to economic stability is to maintain income at a level consistent with high employment of labor and other resources.

Since income is derived from demand, we shall consider the components of aggregate demand. The two main components of Keynesian analysis are the consumers' demand for goods and services and the private business firms' investment demand for capital goods. To these parts, a third component, the government's demand for goods and services, may be added. Both the consumer and investment demands are based on certain determinants. Income is the prime determinant of consumption expenditures. Income, for practical purposes, is disposable income, or income after taxes. As disposable income increases, so will consumption, but not at the same rate. This functional relationship between income and consumption has been formalized in the concept of the consumption function, or the propensity to consume, which has become one of the key analytical tools of modern income and employment theory. A high propensity to consume is favorable to employment.

Investment expenditures have complex determinants. Investment is the application of productive resources to the manufacture of capital goods. Capital goods are valuable because of the services they are expected to yield in the future. The efficiency of a capital good, or the rate of return over cost, is the capital good's rate of yield. This rate of yield is called the marginal efficiency of capital, a term denoting the discount necessary to equate the expected future earnings derived from the most profitable capital asset that can be added to an existing stock of capital goods with the cost of reproducing that added capital asset. The marginal efficiency of capital in conjunction with the interest rate determines the level of investment. The interest rate is the cost of borrowing money. There is a relationship between the marginal efficiency of capital and the interest rate — one is the rate of return on a capital asset, and the other is the cost of borrowing to acquire the asset. A functional relationship can be expressed as follows: Investment, $I = f(n, i)$, where n = marginal efficiency of capital, and i = rate of interest.

Consider, for example, a simple situation in which a business firm is considering an investment that has an initial cost of $1,000 and an estimated length of life of only one year. Assume that the proceeds expected from the investment are $1,200 and the rate of interest is 5 percent. The business firm compares the expected rate of return, or the marginal efficiency of capital, with the cost of borrowing to acquire the asset or, if it chooses to use its own money, the interest it could receive. The marginal efficiency of capital is 20 percent, which is much greater than the rate of interest. As long as the marginal efficiency of capital is greater than the rate of interest, or $n > i$, the investment project is worthwhile to the business firm, for it will yield a rate of return greater than the cost of borrowing $1,000 to acquire the asset, or the interest forgone if it uses its own money. On the other hand, if the marginal efficiency of capital is less than the rate of interest, or $n < i$, the project will be rejected.

Keynes's Basic Thesis

The basic thesis of Keynes's *General Theory*, then, is that in the short run, both the level of income and employment are determined by aggregate demand, which in turn, depends on the propensity to consume and the amount of investment. This relationship can be expressed by the equation $Y = C + I$, where Y = total output, C = consumption expenditures, and I = investment expenditures. Y is referred to as the aggregate supply determined by the income that business firms receive from consumption and investment expenditures. In the short run, such fundamental conditions of supply as capital accumulation and population growth remain stable enough to permit the assumption that aggregate supply is determined mainly by aggregate demand. Aggregate supply and aggregate demand interact with each other to determine an equilibrium level of income and employment. They are made equal when expenditure or demand equals income or supply.

This most basic Keynesian macroeconomic model is illustrated in Diagram 18-1. The vertical axis measures aggregate demand, such as consumption and investment expenditures, and the horizontal axis measures output, real gross national product. The 45° line is the aggregate supply schedule, which shows, in effect, that the total cost of national output must be matched by an equivalent amount of sale proceeds if producers as a whole are to justify total output. The line implies there always must be an equal vertical amount of expenditure for each horizontal cost of national output. The aggregate demand line is a schedule associating spending decisions with different levels of real income. It shows, in other words, the amounts that will be spent for output at each and every possible level of income. Given the aggregate supply and aggregate demand schedules for the economy, the equilibrium level of income and employment will be detemined by the intersection of the two schedules. This equilbrium is represented by the fundamental identity equation, $Y = C + I$. At any point below the equilibrium point, aggregate demand exceeds aggregate supply, and so business firms in total would be induced to increase the level of output. At any point above the equilibrium point, aggregate supply exceeds aggregate demand, and the revenue that business firms receive does not cover the cost of total output.

Implications for Government Policy

Keynesian economic theory repudiates laissez faire and accepts government intervention as the prime requisite for economic stability. The policy implications are clear: there has to be more government participation in economic life. This participation, however, does not have to be a total reconstruction of society along socialist lines. On the contrary, Keynesian economics tries to create a better economic and social milieu in which industrial capitalism can survive. The first desideratum of such a better environment is the abolition of unemployment,

Diagram 18-1 Aggregate Demand and Aggregate Supply

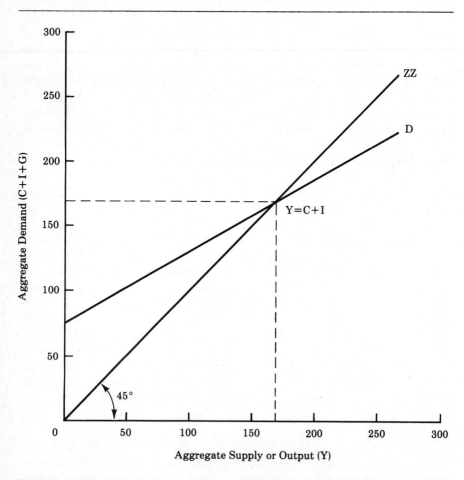

through government fiscal and monetary policies that stimulate consumption and investment expenditures. The second desideratum of a better system is a more equitable and less arbitrary distribution of income, through progressive income taxation and various social welfare measures designed to increase consumption. Prosperity can be achieved more easily by stimulating the consumers' purchasing power. The Keynesian view that inequality of income is a barrier to the creation of new wealth reversed the traditional notion that the accumulation of wealth depends on the savings of the rich. In fact, Keynes advocated what he called the euthanasia of the rentier class.[7]

WORLD WAR II AND ITS AFTERMATH

World War II had a rather salubrious effect on the American economy. For one thing, it cured unemployment. Despite the efforts of President Franklin D. Roosevelt's New Deal, unemployment continued at a high level, although well below the peak unemployment rate of 24.9 percent in 1933. By 1937, the unemployment rate had declined to 14.3 percent; however, in 1938, the rate increased to 19.0 percent, and in 1939 the year Hitler marched into Poland, the rate was 17.2 percent.[8] In 1940, even with Lend-Lease and the eventual realization that in one way or another, the United States would be drawn into the war, the unemployment rate was 14.0 percent. In 1941, the year of Pearl Harbor, the rate was 9.9 percent, but in 1942, the rate declined to 4.7 percent and in 1943, to 1.9 percent. The war also cured unemployment in Great Britain and Germany.

After the war was over, the governments in this and other countries were less than sanguine about the future, as they realized that the problems created by the Depression, particularly unemployment, had not been solved. In the United States, there was no reason to doubt that the unemployment ratio of the 1930s would return. Demobilization itself would create an enormous readjustment. How would the vast majority of the veterans be assimilated into the labor market? History offered horrible examples. In the United States in the immediate post-World War I period, there was a recession and a high rate of unemployment. In the United Kingdom between 1919 and 1939, the average annual rate of unemployment was more than 10 percent. Germany after World War I was in a state of chaos, as unemployed war veterans

7. Keynes, *The General Theory of Employment, Interest, and Money*, p. 376.
8. *Economic Report of the President, 1975* (Washington, D.C.: U.S. Government Printing Office, February 1975), p. 276.

joined various private armies to fight anyone.[9] The authority of the state was subverted, and eventually mass unemployment led to the rise of Hitler.

The Employment Act of 1946

The Employment Act of 1946 is a landmark act in that it gave legislative sanction to the view that the federal government has a direct responsibility for the level of employment and income prevailing in the economy. This marked a complete departure from the government's laissez-faire idea that broad segments of American society had supported as late as 1929. Before the onset of the Depression, the major explicit goal of American public economic policy was to maintain price stability. Little intervention by the federal government was needed to achieve this goal. If this goal was achieved, it was credited to the natural forces operating in the economy that would assure expanding employment and economic growth. But the Depression was a trauma without a parallel in U.S. history, and the old order broke down. The act reflected the hope, derived from the war experience, that the proper use of fiscal and monetary policies could help stabilize the economy at a level above that of the Depression years.

The significance of the act is in the general direction it gives to economic policy and the machinery it established to enable both the executive and legislative branches of the federal government to assume responsibility for the overall functioning of the American economy. The act makes maximum employment only one of three public policy objectives.[10] The other two are maximum production and purchasing power, which are to be advanced conjointly with maximum employment.[11] To facilitate the pursuit of these objectives, the act created a Council of Economic Advisers to the president, consisting of three members charged with the responsibility of gathering and analyzing information on current and prospective economic trends and of formulating and recommending national economic policy. The president, with the assistance of the Council of Economic Advisers, is required to transmit annually an economic report, which analyzes current economic conditions and presents a program for carrying out the public policy objectives expressed in the act. On the legislative side, the act

---

9. John Maynard Keynes, *The Economic Consequences of the Peace* (New York: Harcourt, Brace & Co., Inc., 1920). This book lists the mistakes the Allies made in the Treaty of Versailles, which led to disruption and eventually chaos in the German economy.
10. Section 2 of Public Law 304, 79th Cong., 1st sess.
11. Section 2 of Public Law 304, p. 1.

created the Joint Economic Committee, composed of eight members of the Senate and eight members of the House of Representatives. Its task is to advise Congress on the president's recommendations.

The effectiveness of the Employment Act of 1946 was never tested. Contrary to expectations, the economy did not revert back to Depression conditions. First, the period between 1942 and 1945 had been one of austerity for American consumers. Although money was fairly abundant, consumer goods were either rationed or not produced at all. There were also forced savings, which took the form of compulsory war bond purchases. After the war was over, there was a massive accumulation of savings and a pent-up demand for consumer goods, which were in short supply. Many veterans were absorbed into the defense industries, which were reconverted into capital and consumer goods industries to satisfy the demand for goods and services. Other veterans enrolled in schools under the G.I. Bill and did not become a part of the labor force. The Marshall Plan stimulated exports to Europe. The period of détente with the Soviet Union came to an abrupt end with the Berlin Blockade, and the renewed fear of war stimulated defense spending. The federal government's expenditures on goods and services had declined from a 1944 high of $165.4 billion to $19.1 billion in 1947 but by 1952 these expenditures had increased to $63.8 billion.[12]

Acceptance of Keynesian Economics in the United States

It is commonly believed that Keynesian economics, or the new economics, as it came to be called by many, was introduced into the United States during the Kennedy administration. There was an intellectual revolution in policymaking at that time, based on the belief that a steadily growing, fully employed economy was both desirable and attainable; that fiscal and monetary policies could contribute greatly to full employment and economic growth; and that these policies should be dedicated to economic objectives rather than to other ends.[13] Fiscal policy measures, as practiced by the Kennedy and Johnson administrations, were directed largely toward influencing the level of aggregate demand so as to bring it into line with the economy's changing productive capacity. One requirement of this approach was a massive reduction in both personal and corporate income taxes. It was expected

12. *Economic Report of the President, 1976*, p. 245.
13. James Tobin, "The Intellectual Revolution in U.S. Economic Policy-Making," Noel Buxton Lecture at the University of Essex, England, January 18, 1966, published in *Public Finance and Public Policy Issues*, ed. Martin Schnitzer and Yung-Ping Chen (Scranton, Pa.: International Textbook Company, 1972), pp. 72-91.

that these tax cuts would stimulate both consumption and investment spending, thus increasing output and the level of employment.

Reasons for the Acceptance of the New Economics

Two economic factors contributed to the election of John F. Kennedy as president. One was the United States' low rate of economic growth in comparison with that of the Soviet Union, Japan, and most of the Western European countries. It was little consolation that only the United Kingdom, among the major industrial countries, had a lower rate of economic growth. Much more serious was that the growth rate of the United States was lower than that of the Soviet Union. In 1958, the Soviet Union sent Sputnik into orbit, to the horrified disbelief of the United States. The lower growth rate seemed to confirm Nikita Khrushchev's statement that the Soviet Union would bury the United States: he must have been referring to economic competition. The growth rate was an issue in the 1960 campaign, and the Democratic Party's national platform promised to raise it to 5 percent a year.

The second factor was unemployment. Although the rate of unemployment during the post-World War II period had never reached the unemployment rates of the 1930s, there had been several business recessions. The peak unemployment rate in the 1949 recession was 8.1 percent, but it was of short duration and recovery was rapid. During the 1953-1954 recession, the peak was not as high but was of longer duration. Further, the level of unemployment during the following recovery period was substantially higher than during the previous recovery period. The unemployment rate during the 1957-1958 recession was significantly higher than during the previous recession. In addition, the rate during and after recovery was again much higher than during the same period following the 1953-1954 recession. The rates during 1959 and 1960 averaged 5.5 and 5.6 percent, respectively. The average rate of unemployment was higher after each of the postwar recessions, and thus, the unemployment situation became progressively worse after each recession. Moreover, a balance of payments problem constituted an important new policy constraint not noticeably present in the earlier postwar recessions.

There was a fourth recession in the 1960-1961 period, which overlapped the Eisenhower and Kennedy administrations. The average unemployment of 5.6 percent in 1960 increased to an average rate of 6.8 percent in 1961. Kennedy took office confronted by a stagnant economy and a rising rate of unemployment. Further, there were policy constraints imposed by more than a century of tradition. One constraint was the strong instinctive American opposition to government spending, especially deficit spending. It was an article of faith, a matter of fiscal rectitude, among most Republicans and some Democrats that the federal budget should be balanced. A second constraint was the general disagreement over the causes of unemployment. Some people felt unemployment could be attributed to structural changes in the economy. Automation was alleged to be rapidly eliminating old jobs while creating new ones for which neither the displaced workers nor the new entrants to the labor markets were qualified by skill, experience, or location. But other people believed unemployment was due to a lack of aggregate demand. Moreover, the national unemployment rate was not widely regarded as a politically urgent problem.

During the Kennedy administration, the traditional concepts of public finance underwent a major change: government fiscal policies came to be viewed as instruments for influencing the magnitude and direction of income flows throughout the economy. The impact of these policies on business was considerable. The acceleration of the economy's rate of growth was a prominent national objective, and the key to stimulating economic growth was to increase investment, both public and private. But to increase private investment during a period of unemployment and underutilization of productive capacity required an increase in profits and an upward revision of business expectations. Policy measures were needed to stimulate investment, and some, in fact, were adopted: a tax credit for investment and a liberalization of depreciation rules.[14]

The Revenue Act of 1964

The Revenue Act of 1964 is a classic example of the application of Keynesian economic policy. The purpose of the act was to provide a stimulus to the American economy through the use of tax cuts. Income tax rates were reduced for all individual and corporate taxpayers. Personal income taxes were cut by more than 20 percent and corporate income taxes by about 8 percent. Before the cut, the marginal personal tax rates ranged from 20 to 91 percent; afterwards, the range was 14 to 70 percent. For most corporations, the rates fell from 52 to 48 percent. For calendar-year liabilities, tax rates were cut in two stages, with part of the cut postponed until 1965. Personal withholding rates were reduced by the full amount by as early as March 1964. The Revenue Act was aimed at the demand side rather than the supply side of the nation's economy, and its main objective and achievement were to put productive capacity to work by raising the level of private aggregate demand. Effects on the productive capability of the country were largely incidental, but nonetheless important.

14. These measures had the effect of stimulating business investment and increasing the rate of economic growth.

The tax cuts proved successful in terms of their impact on the economy.[15] They created business incentives for growth-oriented activities, which were apparent in the subsequent investment boom, with its widening and updating of capital equipment, particularly in such areas as transportation, and in heavy industry, such as steel. The tax cuts also enabled the fuller employment of labor, which can be attributed to increases in both consumption and investment expenditures. It is estimated that personal income taxes were cut by $10 billion and corporate income taxes by $3 billion.[16] The overall gain in gross national product as a result of the cuts was $36.2 billion — $28.4 billion in consumption and $7.8 billion in business fixed investments. Of this $36.2 billion gain in gross national product, $25.9 billion came from the personal income tax reduction and $10.3 billion from the corporate tax cut. The estimated multiplier for the personal tax cut was 2.59, and the estimated multiplier for the corporate tax cut was 3.4.[17] The stimulus of the cut lasted through 1964 and 1965 and into 1966. Of course, the overall stimulus to economic expansion in this period was not limited to the cut in income taxes; it also included the delayed effects of the investment credit and liberalized depreciation allowances.

THE 1970s — A DECADE OF TURBULENCE

The Golden Age of the Consumer Ends

The 1970s will not be remembered as one of the better decades of this century, particularly in comparison with the three preceding ones. The golden age of ever-increasing living standards came to an end, with rising prices offsetting increases in income. Between 1967 and 1973, real disposable income per person increased by 17.5 percent, but over the next six years, the gain fell to 5.5 percent.[18] In 1979, median family income rose by 11.6 percent over 1978, but the rate of inflation increased by 11.3 percent.[19] The purchasing power of the median family rose at an average annual rate of 3.3 percent in the 1950s, by 3 percent in the 1960s, and by only 0.7 percent in the 1970s.[20] What

15. Arthur M. Okun, "Measuring the Impact of the 1967 Tax Reduction," in *Perspectives on Economic Growth*, ed. Walter Heller (New York: Random House, 1966), pp. 27–49.
16. Ibid., p. 34.
17. Ibid., p. 45.
18. *Economic Report of the President, 1981*, p. 198.
19. Ibid., p. 202.
20. The Bureau of the Census reported that although money median income doubled during the 1970s, there was no gain in real income. "ABC Nightly News Report," April 19, 1982.

all this means is that the standard of living began to shrink in the 1970s after more than a quarter century of unprecedented economic growth. This goes against the American grain of always "more." The political slogan "a chicken in every pot, a car in every garage," which was fine for 1928, would be ineffective in more recent years as rising living standards demanded Cornish hens in every pot, two cars in every garage, and two houses. But the golden age of the consumer may be gone forever.

The 1970s also witnessed the worst combination of unemployment and inflation in modern U.S. experience. The average rate of unemployment ranged from a high of 8.5 percent in 1975 to a low of 5.3 percent in 1973.[21] The unemployment rate for the decade, however, was over 6 percent — the highest rate for any decade since the 1930s. During the same decade, the inflation rate was the worst for any decade in this century. In fact, the rate of inflation was 12 percent in 1974, the highest peacetime rate since the Civil War. The rate of inflation decreased to less than 6 percent by 1976, but was back to double-digit levels by 1978. By 1980, the misery index, a term coined by former President Carter during the 1976 presidential campaign, was more than 20 percent — an unemployment rate of 7.8 percent plus an inflation rate of 12.4 percent. Both unemployment and inflation have deleterious effects on the American economy — unemployment because of the loss of income that can never be regained, and inflation because of the impact it has on both consumer purchasing power and business investment.

Government Economic Policy: Supply-Side Economics

Supply-side economics has received considerable attention in the early 1980s. The term *supply-side economics* represents a reaction against the demand-side economics of John Maynard Keynes, which has guided government stabilization policies in most countries since the end of World War II. The Keynesian prescriptions — tax tinkering and government spending to stimulate aggregate demand — became an article of faith in the Western world. Everything worked fine when demand was slack and unemployment was on the increase. But times have changed, and inflation, not unemployment, has become the bête noire of Western society. The economic pendulum has swung from underutilization of capacity to an overstraining of resources, and policies designed to stimulate demand simply fire up inflation. Economies have

21. U.S. Congress, House Committee on the Budget, *Economic Policies: The Historical Record, 1962-76* (Washington, D.C.: U.S. Government Printing Office, 1978) p. 15.

become more complex, and techniques have to be adapted to provide solutions to "stagflation" — low growth and high inflation. One thing that is necessary is an increase in investment in the United States. Investment spending that results in expansion of capital and in increases in productivity will result in increases in the nation's productive capacity.

There is nothing new about supply-side economics. Supply was an important component of nineteenth-century classical economics with an emphasis on increasing total output by concentrating on the quantity and quality of such productive elements as labor, natural resources, physical plant and equipment, and financial capital. This emphasis has been updated, and today supply-side economics is proposed as a solution to the problem of stagflation. Attention is placed on the supply side of the economy, where certain impediments to economic growth have developed. Foremost among them is a low rate of saving and investment, which has retarded capital formation and reduced the growth rate of productivity. The solution, according to the supply-side economists, is to reduce taxes, particularly those that impinge on saving and investment. Incentive and response logic is at work: cut taxes, and saving and investment will increase. Given the right incentives, the free market is better equipped than the government to bring about lower prices and more supplies of what people want and need. Output and productivity will go up, and inflation will go down.

REAGANOMICS

Reaganomics, the term used to describe the economic policies instituted since the election of Ronald Reagan, has had five components — a large across-the-board tax cut, a cut in social welfare spending, an increase in defense spending, less government regulation, and restricted growth in the money supply. The tax cut reflected a belief in the efficacy of supply-side economics. The cuts were designed to favor those persons who made fifty thousand dollars or more, for they provide the bulk of savings in the United States. Savings were supposed to increase and to be channeled into investment. This created a tax cut flow from savings to investment to increased productivity. Cuts in social welfare expenditures were designed to limit increases in entitlement programs. Increases in defense spending were not designed for economic reasons but had the effect of increasing the deficit in the federal budget because they were larger than cuts in civilian spending. Antitrust and other forms of government regulation were relaxed because they discouraged investment and were too costly to business. The slow rate of growth in the money supply was designed to reduce inflation.

The Economic Recovery Tax Act of 1981

The cornerstone of Reagan's tax policy was the Economic Recovery Tax Act, ERTA, which was signed into law in August 1981. The act legislated sweeping changes in both the individual and corporate income taxes. It provided for an across-the-board reduction in individual income tax rates amounting to 23 percent over three years, and an immediate cut in the top bracket from 70 to 50 percent. These reduced marginal rates were designed to increase the incentive to invest. There was a shift in emphasis away from using the tax system to redistribute income and toward the creation of national income through economic growth. The corporate income tax was also reduced from 48 to 46 percent, and ERTA allowed accelerated depreciation of new capital assets and a system of tax credits for investment. Both of these provisions decreased the effective tax burden on new investment.

Changes in Federal Expenditures

The composition of federal expenditures by the Reagan administration reflected its objectives. As a share of GNP, defense expenditures grew from 4.9 percent in 1980 to 6.3 percent in 1985, as total federal expenditures increased from 21.6 percent of GNP in 1980 to 23.7 percent in 1985. The federal deficit rose from 2.7 percent of GNP in 1980 to 5.3 percent in 1985. Changes in tax laws reduced receipts as a share of GNP to the range that had existed during most of the 1970s — from 21.1 percent in 1981 to an estimated 19.1 percent in 1985.[22] Given the increase in expenditures and the decrease in tax revenues, it is obvious why the federal budget deficit increased. However, without tax law changes, GNP growth during the 1983–1985 recovery would probably have been lower.

Monetary Policy

There were four changes in monetary policy in the period from 1981 to 1985. The first change, which extended to mid-1982, saw the Federal Reserve pursue a restrictive monetary policy designed to reduce inflation. The second change began in the late summer of 1982. Prompted by accumulating evidence that the recession would be deeper and longer than had been expected, the Federal Reserve began to ease credit and the money supply. Interest rates fell sharply as the growth in the

22. Office of Management and Budget, *Budget of the United States Government, Fiscal Year 1986* (Washington, D.C.: USGPO, 1985), pp. 48–57.

money supply accelerated in 1982 and early 1983. The third change began in the spring of 1983 and ran to the latter part of 1984. The concern was that too rapid a recovery of the economy would lead to inflation. Interest rates were permitted to rise and money supply growth was substantially reduced. The fourth change began in late 1984 and has continued through mid-1986. Fear that the economic recovery was running out of steam led the Federal Reserve to increase the money supply, and interest rates fell to one of their lowest points in the decade.

Regulatory Policies

A number of federal regulatory agencies were created during the 1970s, and regulation increased in such areas as consumer protection and the environment. But by the end of the decade, the feeling was there was too much regulation of the U.S. economy. During the election campaign of 1980, Reagan promised to get the government off the people's backs. Regulatory approaches to environmental and health and safety problems raised production costs and created considerable uncertainty because rules and regulations continually changed. It was also felt that antitrust regulation was out of step with the times and that concentration of output in the hands of a few large firms in a given industry could not automatically be considered bad. The Reagan administration did not eliminate any of the major regulatory agencies, but it did attempt to cut back on the extent of their enforcement. In the area of antitrust policy, a number of major mergers were permitted, including mergers involving Standard Oil of California, Gulf, Texaco, and Getty, four of the largest oil companies in the United States.

The Laffer Curve

The centerpiece of supply-side economics is the Laffer curve and its concept of incentive effects. Diagram 18-2 illustrates the Laffer curve. Its shape, which is backward bending, is based on the concept that if government levies no taxes, it collects no revenues. If it levies 100 percent taxes, it collects no revenues — because no one would work. Tax rates are plotted on the vertical axis, and tax revenues on the horizontal axis. As tax rates first rise, so do government revenues. However, the curve eventually bends backward as increased taxes cause a decline in work and investment large enough to reduce tax revenues. The assumption was made that the U.S. economy was at an upper point on the curve. The increase in income that a tax cut was supposed to generate would raise government tax revenues so much that the loss of revenue from the tax cut would be more than offset. However, this plan did not work; instead, the budget deficit increased.

Table 18-1 shows the deficit in the federal budget for the period from 1970 to 1985. The budget was not balanced for any of these years; in fact, it has been balanced only four times in the last fifty years. In President Carter's last year in office, the deficit was $73.8 billion. There was little change during President Reagan's first year in office, and then there were sharp jumps in 1982 and 1983, in part because of an increase in government defense expenditures. Despite the tax cuts, there was not the increase in government receipts necessary to cover the increase in government expenditure. The economy was also in sharp recession, which militated against any increase in tax revenues.

Diagram 18-2 Laffer Curve

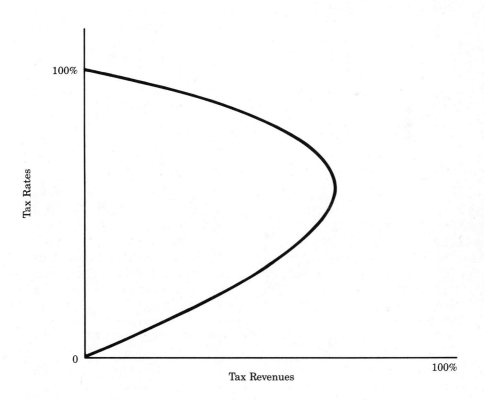

The Results of Reaganomics

When Ronald Reagan was elected president in 1980, the most important problem confronting the U.S. economy was inflation. The consumer price index increased at a rate of 13.3 percent in 1979 and 12.4 percent in 1980. However, by 1982, the consumer price index had decreased to 3.9 percent, and for any year since has not been in excess of 4.0 percent.[23] The real rate of economic growth ranged from a high of 6.5 percent in 1984, which was one of the better performances for any one year since World War II, to a low of -2.5 percent in 1982. On a comparative growth rate basis, the U.S. economy has performed better than the economies of the major free market countries with the exception of Japan.[24] Productivity, as measured by output per hour of all persons, showed some gain. Using a 1977 index of 100, the 1980 index was 99.2. By 1985, the index had increased to 105.0.[25] The

Table 18-1 Federal Governmental Total Receipts and Expenditures, 1970-1985 (billions of dollars)

	Receipts	Outlays	Deficits
1970	$192.8	$195.6	$- 2.8
1971	187.1	210.2	- 23.0
1972	207.3	230.7	- 23.4
1973	230.8	245.7	- 14.9
1974	263.2	269.4	- 6.1
1975	279.1	332.3	- 53.2
1976	298.1	371.8	- 73.7
1977	355.6	409.2	- 53.6
1978	399.7	458.7	- 59.0
1979	463.3	503.5	- 40.2
1980	517.1	590.9	- 73.8
1981	599.3	678.2	- 78.9
1982	617.8	745.7	- 127.9
1983	600.6	808.3	- 207.8
1984	666.5	851.8	- 185.3
1985	734.1	946.3	- 212.3

Source: Office of Management and Budget, *Budget of the United States Government, Fiscal Year 1986* (Washington, D.C.: USGPO, 1985), p. 60; and *Economic Report of the President, 1986* (Washington, D.C.: USGPO, 1986), p. 241.

23. *Economic Report of the President, 1986*, p. 319.
24. *Economic Report of the President, 1986*, p. 378.
25. Ibid., p. 302.

unemployment rate, which was 7.0 percent in 1980, increased to 8.5 percent for 1982 and 1983 but declined to 7.1 percent for 1985 and is projected to be around the same for 1986.[26]

Nevertheless, the federal deficit is a problem that confronts the U.S. economy, and the trade deficit is also a problem. By the end of 1985, the United States became a debtor nation for the first time. Within the framework of international competition, the United States is in the process of losing its competitive edge over other countries. The debtor status of developing countries such as Mexico and Brazil is cause for concern; indeed, many forces at work in the world have had and will continue to have an impact on the U.S. economy and on U.S. business firms.

SUMMARY

Momentous turning points in economic and social history can occur with amazing speed. The last great upheaval in peacetime Western society occupied a single decade, the thirties, and it put its lasting imprint on the political, economic, and social trends of the succeeding decades. Whatever might be said about the continuity of historical forces, the Depression caused a radical change in a number of areas of Western society. Bad times spread throughout the world, and societies most akin to our own were coping poorly. The strain proved too strong in Germany, and democracy was replaced by a totalitarian state. Unemployment was proving to be an intractable problem in the United States and elsewhere. Existing policies appeared incapable of lifting the Western economies out of the unemployment rut, for classical economic theory and nineteenth-century laissez-faire ideology allowed government only a limited role in shaping economic policy. Classical theory maintained that full employment was normal; lapses were due to wage rates that were too high, to monopoly, or to similar causes. Laissez-faire ideology taught that the least government is the best government; the government's budget always should be balanced; the lowest levels of taxes and expenditures are the best level; and the self-regulating free market is the best guide to the efficient allocation of a country's resources.

A new theory on which a set of economic policies could be based was needed. This theory was presented by John Maynard Keynes in 1936, when his book, *The General Theory of Employment, Interest, and Money*, was published. Before his theory could be digested adequately and new economic policy measures tried, World War II intervened. However, after the war, the theory was generally accepted

26. Ibid., p. 293.

as the framework for economic policy in the major Western industrial countries. The central objective of this policy was the maintenance of a high level of employment. The basic premise of Keynes was that unemployment is caused by an insufficiency of aggregate demand. Therefore, to increase the level of demand consistent with the level of full employment, it was necessary to increase the role of the public sector. Both fiscal and monetary policy measures could be used to stimulate demand. But Keynesian economics, by premise, required increased intervention by the state into economic affairs, which meant laissez-faire ideology was obsolete.

In the U.S. economy, Keynesian economics was accepted as a foundation of economic policy during the Kennedy administration. Kennedy surrounded himself with economists who favored an active, expansionary fiscal policy to stimulate the rate of economic growth and to reduce the level of unemployment. Fiscal policy measures were used to increase the level of spending. In 1961, there was an increase in the volume of government spending. In 1962, the investment tax credit was instituted to stimulate investment and thus promote a more rapid rate of economic growth. In 1964, personal and corporate income tax rates were reduced for the purpose of stimulating aggregate demand. The Kennedy period produced a greater than ever consensus that a steadily growing, fully employed economy is both desirable and attainable; that the government's fiscal and monetary policies can contribute greatly to achieving full employment, steady growth, and price stability; and that these policies should be dedicated to economic objectives. The shibboleth that the federal budget was like a household budget that must be balanced year in and year out was discarded. Budget deficits to stimulate the economy were accepted as a matter of course.

The decade of the 1970s witnessed the contradiction of a low growth rate accompanied by inflation, a condition called stagflation by economists. Keynesian economic prescriptions, which had worked when demand was slack, did not seem to work anymore. A new group of economists provided new prescriptions on how to fix the economy. Their approach came to be known as supply-side economics because they believed increasing supply was the only solution for stagflation. When Ronald Reagan was elected president, he made a number of important economic policy decisions that incorporated elements of supply-side economics. The Economic Recovery Tax Act included tax cuts for individuals and corporations. Government expenditures on various entitlement programs were reduced, whereas government expenditures on national defense were increased.

QUESTIONS FOR DISCUSSION

1. What is meant by the term *classical economics*, and why was the full employment of resources automatically assumed?
2. Distinguish between monetary and fiscal policy.
3. Present a good case againt Keynesian economic policy.
4. What is supply-side economics?
5. Why is the Employment Act of 1946 considered an important act?
6. What is the purpose of the Economic Recovery Act of 1981?
7. What is the causal relationship between the Depression of the 1930s and the kind of economic system the American nation found itself with several decades later?
8. Why is Keynesian economics called demand-side economics?

RECOMMENDED READINGS

Chase Manhattan Bank. "Getting Serious About Supply." *Business in Brief*, 150 (March–April 1980).

Economic Report of the President, 1986. Washington, D.C.: U.S. Government Printing Office, 1986.

Feldstein, Martin S., ed., *The American Economy in Transition.* Chicago: University of Chicago Press, 1980.

Keynes, John M. *The General Theory of Employment, Interest, and Money.* New York: Harcourt, Brace, 1936.

Lodge, George C. *The American Disease.* New York: Alfred E. Knopf, 1984.

Rohatyn, Felix G. *The Twentieth Century.* New York: Random House, 1983.

Thurow, Lester C. *Dangerous Currents.* New York: Random House, 1983.

Vogel, Ezra. *Comeback.* New York: Simon & Schuster, 1985.

Chapter 19
Business and Government in a Global Environment

German philosopher Oswald Spengler wrote a book called *Decline of the West*, in which he forecasted the decline of Western civilization.[1] Spengler claimed to be able to discern the outline of a life cycle through which, he believed, all civilizations must pass. Western civilization was compared with Greco-Roman civilization in terms of form, duration, and meaning. According to Spengler, whose view of Western civilization was a gloomy one, the West had already passed through the creative stage of culture into a period of material comfort. The end of a creative impulse begins the process of decline. Of reversing the decline, there is no prospect, for civilizations blossom and decay like natural organisms, and true rejuvenation is impossible. Spengler used a biological metaphor to describe the fateful trajectory of a civilization: "For everything organic the notions of birth, youth, age, lifetime, and death are fundamental."

It may be that the United States has reached a watershed in its history. Spenglerian prophesies of gloom and doom have become commonplace. Articles in the major newspapers have cited the declining status of the American middle class, stating that the current generation of income earners will witness a lower standard of living than their parents.[2] The Joint Economic Committee of Congress has stated that the United States has gone from a nation where virtually all families could expect increased purchasing power to one in which few can maintain purchasing power even with increased participation in the work force. Another article has stated that America's financial bubble is likely to burst, and that there is a parallel between today's stock market and the stock market of 1929.[3] The world economy is in precarious shape. Because the world's financial network is so intertwined and

1. Oswald Spengler, *Decline of the West* (New York: Knopf, 1939).
2. For example, see the following articles: John Hess, "Our Horn of Plenty Is Running Out," *The Washington Post*, Sunday, July 6, 1986, p. D1; also Steven Greenhouse, "The Average Guy Takes It on the Chin," *The New York Times*, Sunday, July 13, 1986, section 3, p. 1.
3. Jim Rogers, "We've Had Our Boom; Does a Bust Come Next?" *The Washington Post*, Sunday, July 13, 1986, p. B1.

fragile, a small, unconnected disruption could cause a collapse of the world banking system.

Assuming that all the dire portents and prophesies have some validity, decisions have to be reached about what should be done. One popular approach is to blame somebody else for your problems. Here, the Japanese and, more recently, the South Koreans and other Asians have come in handy. That we are having our problems in the world economy is the fault of Japan because they don't play fairly and we do. A second approach is more realistic. Shakespeare once wrote: "The fault, dear Brutus, is not in our stars, but in ourselves, that we are underlings."[4] There is more than a germ of truth to that quote as far as the United States is concerned. But then who do we blame? Usually the other person or the political party that happens to be in power.

A number of problems have an impact on the world economy. One is the competitive position of the United States in the world economy. Many feel the U.S. position has slipped compared to other economies, particularly Japan. Then there is the Third World debt problem and its implications for the U.S. economy. And the balance of trade deficit with Japan, Canada, and other countries shows no sign of going away. The trade deficit is linked to the deficit in the federal budget, estimated to be in excess of $200 billion for the fiscal year 1986-1987. For the first time since 1914, the United States has become a debtor nation — owing $107 billion more than it is owed to foreign creditors.

INDUSTRIAL COMPETITIVENESS

In 1985, the Harvard Business School published a compendium of research papers that described and evaluated America's changing position in the world economy. The following conclusions were arrived at:[5]

1. For the last fifteen years, the United States has been losing its capacity to compete in the world economy. This loss is felt most acutely in the manufacturing sector and is serious because there is an increasing dependence on international trade.

2. The decline in U.S. competitiveness has been reflected in a shift from a trade surplus to a trade deficit, eroding world market shares and declining profits.

3. The principal competition to the United States comes from five East Asian countries — Japan, South Korea, Taiwan, Singapore, and Hong Kong. These countries provide a challenge because they have

4. *Julius Caesar*, 1.2. 133-134.
5. Bruce R. Scott and George C. Lodge, eds., *U.S. Competitiveness in the World Economy* (Boston: Harvard Business School Press, 1985), pp. 1-2.

adopted national strategies through which each mobilizes its resources to achieve economic growth and global competitiveness.

4. The United States and Western Europe do not have similar development strategies. Instead, they place emphasis on economic security and income redistribution at the expense of market rigidities, and current consumption at the expense of investment for long-term benefits.

5. The United States has to reexamine its current economic policies, for if it does not, it cannot sustain the performance necessary to finance its world commitments, increase domestic living standards, and improve income distribution.

A somewhat similar conclusion concerning the competitive position of the U.S. economy in the world was reached by the President's Commission on Global Competitiveness. Warning that the United States is losing its ability to compete in world markets, it cited several problems, not the least of which is declining productivity.[6] Since 1960, Japanese productivity growth increased at a rate five times that of the United States. The East Asian countries have focused attention on developing manufacturing expertise, and their products are often more attractive, in both price and quality, than those made in the United States. They represent a challenge in the global environment in which U.S. firms operate. Japan's productivity now exceeds that of the United States in automobiles; steel; transportation equipment; and electrical, general, and precision machinery.

U.S. Competitiveness

For more than twenty years, almost all major U.S. competitors have been gaining on the United States in terms of real living standards. To some extent, this was inevitable, for the United States was the only major industrial country not damaged or destroyed by World War II. It had an enormous start over the rest of the world after the war ended. However, since 1960, there has been a slippage of the performance of the U.S. economy in comparison to its major competitors. For example, between 1950 and 1980, America's share of world GNP declined from 40 percent to 21.5 percent, its portion of world trade declined from 20 percent to 11 percent, and its holdings of gold and gold reserves fell from 32 percent to 6 percent, even though its share of world population declined only from 6 percent to 5 percent.[7] The American share

---

6. The Report of the President's Commission on Industrial Competitiveness, *Global Competition: The New Reality*, Vol. 1, pp. 11-15.
7. Bruce R. Scott, "U.S. Competitiveness: Concepts, Performance, and Implications," in *U.S. Competitiveness in the World Economy*, pp. 18-19.

of world merchandising exports declined from 16.5 percent in 1955 to 11.1 percent in 1984.[8]

International Comparisons of Growth and Productivity

Economic growth refers to increases through time in either real per capita GNP or real total GNP. Among the chief immediate causes of economic growth are enlargement of the stock of real capital through the process of saving and investment, improvement in the quality of the people as workers and entrepreneurs through education and training, and advances in technology. Table 19-1 presents a comparison of real per capita growth rates for the major industrial countries and the developing East Asian countries. As the table indicates, the perform- ance of the U.S. economy was poor.

A related problem, declining productivity, has lessened the ability of the United States to compete in global markets. Manufacturing pro- ductivity growth in the United States has lagged behind its major competitors. America's industrial base has been unable to produce the kinds of financial returns that attract productive investment. Over the past twenty years, real rates of return on manufacturing assets have declined. Pretax returns on manufacturing assets are well below alter- native financial investments and make many investors question the

Table 19-1 Average Annual Growth Rates for Selected Countries, 1965–1983

Country	Percent Real Growth Rate
Japan	4.7
France	3.0
West Germany	2.7
United States	1.7
United Kingdom	1.6
Taiwan	6.8
Singapore	7.8
South Korea	6.6
Hong Kong	6.2

Source: The World Bank, *World Development Report 1986*, table 1, p. 181.

8. Robert E. Lipsey, *Recent Trends in U.S. Trade and Investment* Report No. 565 (Cambridge, Mass: National Bureau of Economic Research, 1984), p. 70.

wisdom of putting funds into manufacturing. For example, during most of the 1960s, the pretax rate of return on manufacturing assets averaged around 10 percent which was well above the bond and prime rates.[9] During the 1970s, the pretax rate of return on manufcturing assets declined while the bond and prime rates increased. The growth rate of net fixed investment per workers and per hour of time worked also showed a marked decrease over the same period.

Table 19-2 presents one measure of productivity, real gross domestic product per employed workers for selected countries for the period 1960-1983. As the table indicates, the average annual productivity gains for Japan and South Korea were four to five times greater than for the United States. Superior productivity has long been a comparative advantage that the United States has enjoyed over other countries. It has also been one of the prime causes for the high standard of living that Americans have so long enjoyed. Despite some improvement in the 1980s, the living standard of the average American worker has continued to deteriorate.

Reasons for the Decline in U.S. Competitiveness

A number of reasons have been suggested to explain the declining performance of American industry both at home and abroad.[10] Many believe the strong dollar has been the main cause of the declining U.S.

Table 19-2 Real Gross Domestic Product Per Employed Person, 1960-1983

Country	Average Annual Percent Change
South Korea	5.3
France	3.7
West Germany	3.4
Japan	5.9
United Kingdom	2.3
United States	1.2

Source: The Report of the President's Commission on Industrial Competitiveness, *Global Competition: The New Reality*, 1985 Vol. 1, p. 11.

9. Scott, p. 36.
10. Raymond Vernon, "Can U.S. Manufacturing Come Back?" *Harvard Business Review*, 64 (July-August, 1986), pp. 98-101.

position in world trade. A second reason is that the United States has become a service economy, so it is natural that manufacturing is in the process of decline. A third reason places the blame on American managerial practices, which are considered inferior to those of the Japanese. Included is the contention that American managers have lost both the desire and the ability to produce competitive products.[11] A fourth reason cites the unwillingness or inability of the U.S. government to target and support favored industries, although this is done in Japan and other countries. Many argue that the United States needs a coherent industrial policy to compete with the successful industrial policies of other countries.

The Strong U.S. Dollar

Compared to other world currencies the U.S. dollar has been strong. A combination of interrelated factors were responsible for its strength. One has been the high real rate of interest in the United States relative to real interest rates elsewhere. A high real rate of interest increases the demand for U.S. assets. To buy U.S. assets, foreigners must first buy U.S. dollars. The increased demand for dollars drives up the value of U.S. dollars relative to other currencies. Second, a potpourri of economic, social, and political factors contributed to the strength of the U.S. dollar. In particular, the unsettled state of the world economy — especially in Europe and Latin America — created a desire on the part of investors for a safe haven for their funds. Third, financial officers of multinational corporations look for those areas with the highest real rates of interest to deposit money. The United States has had a higher real rate of interest than other areas, so corporate holders of liquid assets moved into dollar securities.

The strength of the U.S. dollar had a concomitant effect on both exports and imports. As far as exports were concerned, price competitiveness was reduced because foreign countries had to exchange more of their currencies to obtain U.S. dollars to pay for American products.[12] U.S. exports became more expensive and declined. Expecting the dollar to remain overvalued, U.S. manufacturing companies shifted production abroad and outsourced or purchased components and finished products from foreign suppliers. Conversely, U.S. imports increased because the U.S. dollar acquired more foreign currency.

11. Robert H. Hayes and William J. Abernathy, "Managing Our Way to Economic Decline," *Harvard Business Review*, 58 (July-August, 1980) pp. 67-73.
12. U.S. Joint Economic Committee, Subcommittee on Economic Goals and Intergovernment Policy, *Impact of the Dollar on U.S. Competitiveness*, 99th Cong., 2d sess., 1985.

Foreign products became cheaper for American consumers, and foreign companies built distributive networks here to increase their export volume. The strong U.S. dollar coupled with high real interest rates also caused an inflow of foreign money into the United States to finance the federal deficit.

In September 1985, a meeting was held in New York by financial representatives of each of the five major industrial countries — France, Japan, the United Kingdom, the United States, and West Germany — in which steps were to be taken to devalue the dollar relative to the values of the other major currencies. In negotiations with the Japanese, the Bank of Japan, which is the central bank, agreed to sell dollars in the world market. Since the Bank of Japan held 50 percent of the dollars in the world market, the effect of selling them was to drive down their price and drive up the price of the yen. The central banks of the other countries, particularly the Deutsche Bundesbank, did the same thing. By appreciating the values of the other currencies relative to the dollar, the intended effect was to increase U.S. exports while decreasing U.S. imports. But things have not turned out that way, and the U.S. merchandise trade deficit is expected to be higher in 1986 that it was for 1985.[13] It appears that the recent period of an over-valued dollar seems simply to have aggravated a tendency that had deeper causes and antecedents dating back for more than twenty years.[14]

The Development of a Service Economy

A second factor cited for the decline of U.S. world competitiveness is that the United States is in the process of becoming a service economy. The concept of a service economy has a pejorative connotation in the minds of many persons, for they visualize an economy where everyone works at hamburger stands and pizza parlors for scant wages. This is far from reality, for a service economy encompasses a wide variety of activities, ranging from medicine to banking. Many service jobs require a high degree of education and skill, and wages are far from being low. Moreover, it is in the service industries that the United States enjoys a comparative advantage over other countries. Were it not

13. Complicating the problem are such countries as South Korea, Singapore, and Taiwan whose currencies, which did not appreciate in value, are pegged to the dollar. They have gained over Japan in the falling dollar because their exports have been unaffected. Goods from these countries are also priced low in comparison to Japan. Japanese companies have also shaved profit margins to hold on to their U.S. customers and have not raised their prices to reflect the rise in the price of the yen.
14. Vernon, p. 99. The dollar was overvalued only from 1982 to 1985.

that the United States exports more services than it imports, there would be a greater deficit in its current account and balance of payments. Some services, such as research in biotechnology, are building blocks for future economic growth.

It is also necessary to distinguish between manufacturing in general and in specific areas. It is true that there is a decline in output and employment in a number of manufacturing industries. For example, both output and employment have declined in the steel industry over the last twenty years. In the shoe manufacturing industry, there has been even more of a decline in output and employment. In 1973, the U.S. shoe industry produced 490 million pairs of shoes; in 1984, it produced 298 million pairs.[15] Overall manufacturing, however, has not shown a decline. The index of industrial production, which was 100 percent in 1977, was 123.9 percent in 1984, and the number of workers employed in manufacturing amounted to 19.7 million in 1977 and 19.4 million in 1984.[16] As was pointed out in Chapter 17, the steel industry has become more efficient because steel producers are specializing in the production of high quality steel products.

Business Management Practices

A third reason for low productivity and the declining competitiveness of the U.S. economy is said to be the practices of U.S. business managers. Other countries, particularly the Japanese, have more flexible management techniques. Of U.S. management practices, there are several criticisms. The first is that American managers have placed too much emphasis on the attainment of short-term objectives instead of planning over a long term. They are judged on the basis of achieving and maintaining profits. A second criticism of American managers is that the marketing orientation of U.S. companies encourages a reduced emphasis on technological competition.[17] A third criticism is that the background of American managers, their modes of training and orientation, and the increasing diversification of large U.S. companies tend to encourage detached, analytical, and often superficial understanding of the businesses they manage. Finally, American managers are accused of knowing little about the global economy in which they have to compete.

15. *Economic Report of the President 1986* (Washington, D.C.: U.S. Government Printing Office, 1986), p. 113.
16. Ibid., p. 111.
17. U.S. Joint Economic Committee, *Business Management Practices and the Productivity of the American Economy*, 97th Cong., 1st sess., 1981, pp. 9-13.

The criticism of American managers extends into the area of labor-management relations. It is argued that managerial practices, such as the assembly line, have become obsolete, and that the more flexible management techniques, such as quality circles, used by Japan and other countries are superior.[18] Japanese managers allow more participation in the decision-making process by workers. This participation makes the workers feel as though they are a part of a team. However, it is difficult to attribute the high productivity of Japanese industry to that one factor alone. High productivity in Japanese industries is due to a number of explanations, including the high literacy of Japanese workers and cultural factors. Moreover, it is difficult to prove that American managers are a major cause of the decline in U.S. world competitiveness.

Unwillingness of the U.S. Government to Target Favored Industries

The final reason advanced for the decline of U.S. competitiveness is that Japan has an industrial policy in which they target key industries for development, whereas the United States does not. Again, Japan is used as a frame of reference, for it does have an industrial policy based on the goals of the economy.[19] For example, in 1980, the Japanese Ministry of International Trade and Industry (MITI) published a document that set Japanese priorities for the 1980s.[20] It recognized that the Japanese economy was being adversely affected by forces over which it had little control. High energy costs had affected industries that depended on the import of oil and coal. Japanese success in exporting automobiles to the United States and Europe had increased the resentment of U.S. and European automakers and their unions. Thus, the Japanese planned to base their economic future on high-technology industries, which require far less energy, with the main thrust in semiconductors, communication, and information processing.

In Chapter 17, we mentioned that a number of countries have succeeded in creating comparative advantage through either import substitution or other government policies. Traditional trade theory assumed that comparative advantage rested largely on resources that were on hand rather than created. That has proved not so, for one thing that has happened is that Japan and other East Asian countries have

18. William Ouchi, *Theory Z* (Reading, Mass.: Addison-Wesley, 1981).
19. U.S. Joint Economic Committee, Subcommittee on Economic Goals and Intergovernmental Policy, *Policies for Industrial Growth in a Competitive World*, 98th Cong., 2d sess., 1984, pp. 7-11.
20. Ministry of International Trade and Industry, *Visions of Industry in the Eighties* (Tokyo, March 1980).

been able to mobilize their limited resources to create a dynamic theory of comparative advantage. These countries use national development strategies that incorporate the mobilization of technology, capital, and skilled labor as a way of nurturing the whole industrial sector toward areas of growth and opportunity in the world market. Furthermore, they can create policies and institutions that can accelerate the development of new sectors and the abandonment of old sectors.

Much has been made of the development of Japan into a world economic power, but the so-called Four Tigers — South Korea, Taiwan, Singapore, and Hong Kong — are also becoming formidable competitors in world markets. One-half of the U.S. merchandise deficit is with Japan and these countries. South Korea is in about the same position today that Japan was twenty years ago. It began its initial economic development by emphasizing import substitution, which provided an initial impulse for economic growth. Then South Korea changed its policy toward export promotion. Government policy included a uniform exchange rate, unrestricted access to intermediate and capital goods, tax exemptions for exporters, reduced prices on inputs, and access to credit for investment. Subsidies through credit to selected industries were used to encourage capital formation.[21]

Industrial Policy

Some people advocate an industrial policy to restore the competitive position of the United States in the world economy.[22] Claiming that the reason the United States is lagging behind Japan, West Germany, and other industrial countries is that it has no coherent strategy for economic development, they call on the U.S. government to take on a new role as the promoter of industrial adjustment using the vehicle of an industrial policy. These analysts argue that since companies and industries have failed to adjust to international competition, the government has to step in to reduce the frequency and cause of market failure and take a more constructive role in solving industrial problems. Instead of dealing with its problems, the United States has responded with a mixture of ad hoc policies and a lack of an explicit strategy to promote competitiveness.

Industrial policy can be defined as a form of strategic planning. It outlines the basic strategy a nation intends to follow in maximizing economic growth and meeting foreign competition. It analyzes how changes in technology and human needs are going to alter the industrial

21. *Policies for Industrial Growth in a Competitive World*, pp. 11-12.
22. Ira Magaziner and Robert Reich. *Minding America's Business* (New York: Harcourt Brace Jovanovich, 1982).

structure. Industrial policy would involve an increase in the role of government in three ways:

1. A government agency is created to partially finance private industrial research on new products or new production processes. In Japan, it is the Agency of Industrial Science and Technology.[23] It consults with Japanese industry to encourage the use of new technologies that will further the national interest, and it sponsors research that will make the needed technology available.

2. The government systematically seeks to reduce the costs and increase the availability of capital to industrial firms. Included are tax incentives and measures to increase the rate of saving. The net result in countries that use an industrial policy is a real cost of capital much lower than that found in the United States. To stimulate savings in Japan, interest income from savings deposits up to $13,700 is tax exempt. These savings are funnelled into various government financial institutions, such as the Japan Development Bank, which lends to industry.[24]

3. A government has a systematic procedure for dealing with declining or financially troubled industries. If an industry comes to the government asking for financial aid or protection against foreign competition, it must come up with a development plan to make itself more competitive. Then the government examines the plan to see if it is feasible. In some cases, the government may not provide financial assistance, requiring instead that the industry work out its problems itself. Some countries may allow the creation of a recessionary cartel.

It should be emphasized that industrial policy is not a form of central economic planning. Instead, it is more of a cooperative arrangement between business, government, and labor to achieve certain industrial goals. In Japan, considered a model for industrial policy, the most important and powerful government agency is the Ministry of International Trade and Industry (MITI). Its mandate is to determine a basic course of action to improve Japan's comparative advantage and to mobilize each sector to make a contribution to the whole. It offers guidance to Japanese industry in terms of providing an industrial strategy consistent with Japan's national interest, but it does not have the power to coerce industry into following this strategy.[25] It does have the power to make recommendations to Japanese lending institu-

---

23. Ezra Vogel, *Comeback* (New York: Simon and Schuster, 1985), p. 65.
24. U.S. Congress, Joint Economic Committee, *Japanese Taxation Policy*, 98th Cong., 2d sess., September 1984, p. 21.
25. Chalmers Johnson, *MITI and the Japanese Miracle* (Stanford, Calif.: Stanford University Press, 1982).

tions with respect to giving credit priorities to industries that are a part of its development strategy.

Criticism of Industrial Policy

There are a number of problems with industrial policy. For one thing, it is assumed that what works well for Japan will also work for the United States. Imitation is said to be the sincerest form of flattery, and the Japanese have copied and improved on many American technological developments such as quality control. Ipso facto, it follows that we can copy from the Japanese. Industrial policy has worked in Japan in part because there has been a cooperative arrangement between business and government dating back for more than one hundred years. Conversely, the relationship between business and government in the United States has been adversarial for most of this century, and there is no reason to assume that this will quickly change. Moreover, the political, economic, and social structure of Japan is not at all similar to that of the United States. Japan is a homogeneous society, but the United States is not. The political system of Japan is centralized, and the United States is a federal republic. The business-banking structure in Japan is interlocked, whereas in the U.S. it is not.

Another problem is identifying industries that are going to be successful in the future. The selection of firms and industries that would be entitled to special government financial support would be determined by a special government agency for industrial competitiveness and a government-created lending institution.[26] However, Charles L. Schultze, who was a chairman of the Council of Economic Advisers during the Carter administration, contends that there does not exist a set of economic criteria that determine what gives different countries preeminence in particular lines of economic activity.[27] Nor is it clear what the substantive criteria would be for deciding which older industries to protect or restructure. A serious problem of industrial policy is that it could end up being nothing more than a systematic protector of inefficiency. It would encourage politicians, unions, declining industries, states, and localities to apply for favorable treatment at the expense of those not so treated. It would become another entitlement program managed by the same special interest groups.

26. The Industrial Competitiveness Act (H.R. 4360), which was introduced in the House Committee on Banking, Finance, and Urban Affairs, would create a Council on Industrial Competitiveness and a Bank for Industrial Competitiveness.
27. Charles L. Schultze, "Industrial Policy: A Dissent," *The Brookings Review*, 1 (Fall 1983), pp. 3-12.

Other Approaches to Industrial Competitiveness

The subject of U.S. industrial competitiveness is too important and complex to be left to simplistic free market or government solutions. It should be pointed out that the U.S. competitive position has not declined vis-à-vis the Western European countries; to the contrary, most of them have more economic problems than we have. Their inflation and unemployment rates are higher, and their rate of economic growth, at least in this decade, has not been as good as ours. Instead, comparisons have to be made to Japan and the other East Asian countries. The theory of comparative advantage assumes diminishing marginal returns and a law of increasing costs, as well as full employment, costless factor mobility, and universal access to production technologies. But the theory, which was formulated almost two hundred years ago, has to be adjusted to conform to the realities of today's world. Being endowed with a natural resource does not translate into comparative advantage, unemployment is high in many industrial countries, and labor and other factors are not mobile.[28]

As already mentioned, Japan and other countries have pursued a dynamic policy of creating comparative advantage. Had Japan used the resource in which it had the greatest comparative advantage after the end of World War II, namely labor, it would have specialized in labor-intensive industries and would have been unable to break away from the Asian pattern of stagnation and poverty.[29] Instead, the Japanese government rejected static comparative advantage theory in favor of creating comparative advantage by mobilizing technology, capital, and skilled labor to develop opportunities in selected sectors. But Japan is a development state where the government has given high priority to promoting economic development, that is, baking the pie before dividing it.[30] The United States is a regulatory state that emphasizes the rules and procedures of competition, not substantive outcomes. Nevertheless, the regulatory state can play a constructive role in promoting industrial competitiveness.

Education

The U.S. educational system has been subjected to much recent criticism, and there have been a number of proposals for reform. Education practices at both the primary and secondary school levels

28. Bruce R. Scott, "National Strategy for Stronger U.S. Competitiveness," *Harvard Business Review*, 62 (March–April 1984), pp. 77–91.
29. Ibid., p. 86.
30. Johnson, p. 18.

have failed to produce the skills needed for a modern industrial society despite federal funding. It can be said that America produces too many lawyers and not enough engineers to the detriment of national productivity.[31] It has been said that the United States is a nation at risk in that its ability to maintain a higher living standard will depend on the development of a literate labor force.[32] One reason that Japan has performed so well in the world economy is that it has a literate and skilled labor force capable of performing complex, demanding tasks.

A key issue today is how to improve the U.S. educational system to where large segments of the population are brought up to the level of literacy that is consistent with the maintenance of economic competitiveness and high living standards. There are problems though. Federal funding of education has not been any panacea, and reliance on state and local governments means that variation in the quality of education can be expected to grow. Then there are questions about how to address the problem of education. Is simply paying higher salaries to teachers the answer? A wide variety of solutions have been proposed such as creating a national teacher certification board, strengthening teacher preparation, and restructuring the profession to give a few highly experienced and highly paid teachers the opportunity to lead the instruction of their schools.

Modification of Antitrust Laws

Antitrust laws were passed in the United States to prevent monopolistic abuses, to promote competition, and to promote consumer welfare. The two major laws, the Sherman Act and the Clayton Act were passed in 1890 and 1914, when the United States and the world were decidedly different from how they are today. It is felt that antitrust laws today have an adverse effect on the ability of the United States to compete in the world market.[33] In the new world economy, U.S. firms are going to face strong foreign competition with active govern-

---

31. In 1986, the United States had close to one million lawyers, and Japan had around twenty thousand. On the other hand, Japan had twice as many engineers as the United States.
32. National Commission on Excellence in Education, *A Nation At Risk* (Washington, D.C., April 1983).
33. Lester C. Thurow, *The Zero-Sum Solution* (New York: Simon and Schuster, 1985), pp. 182; also Bruce R. Scott, "National Strategy for Stronger U.S. Competitiveness," pp. 82-84; Raymond Vernon, "Can U.S. Manufacturing Come Back?" pp. 82-84; and The Report of the President's Commission on Industrial Competitiveness, *Global Competition: The New Reality*, pp. 197-205.

ment backing even if they are large and dominant compared to other U.S. firms. No longer is it simply IBM versus smaller American computer firms; it is Japanese competitors that are reducing IBM's competitive position in the world. That U.S. antitrust laws are anachronistic and discourage managerial initiative is argued by some.[34]

Increase Incentives for Research and Development

A third recommendation to increase the industrial competitiveness of U.S. firms is that more incentives should be provided to encourage research and development. Government policies can stimulate research and development. The U.S. aircraft industry has depended on the military budget for most of its research and development. It has been suggested that the United States create a cabinet-level Department of Science and Technology to promote policies for research and development. By making clear the national importance of science and technology in meeting long-term national goals it would increase the effectiveness of research and development. It is also suggested that research and development should be encouraged through enhanced tax incentives by making permanent a research and development tax credit in the tax laws and broadening the definition of research and development that qualifies for the credit.

However, the problem in stimulating research and development is that technology crosses national boundaries; therefore, technology resulting from research and development expenditures at home not only helps the productivity of the United States but also of other countries. Foreign firms able to imitate this technology are often able to capture market shares from those countries that developed the technology. The advantage of imitator firms is enhanced if they are in countries where they have access to cheaper capital for production or for market probing and expansion. Japan is an excellent case in point. An imitative strategy can also enable countries such as Japan and South Korea to enter the market at a later stage in the product life cycle, when simplification and standardization are possible and competitive prices and production costs become a more important factor in market penetration.[35]

34. Vernon, p. 101.
35. Harvey Brooks, "Technology as a Factor in U.S. Competitiveness," in *U.S. Competitiveness in the World Economy*, pp. 335-342.

The Need for More Saving

For decades, America has been consuming, rather than saving, and since 1976, the process has accelerated dramatically. Consumer debt, business debt, and government debt have increased as the United States has engaged in an orgy of consumption and instant gratification. This consumption has led to a balance of payment deficit. For the first time since 1914, the United States has become a debtor nation. In and of itself, a balance of payments deficit would not be disastrous if there is something to show for it in terms of investment that increases productive capacity. A railroad or a steel mill does that, but national defense and entitlement expenditures do not. The current deficit in the federal budget comprises expenditues for entitlement programs such as Medicare and military spending, both of which are unproductive consumption.

Table 19–3 presents data for net saving and net investment. Both have been affected by the deficit in the federal budget. As the deficit has increased, it has had an adverse effect on capital formation because it absorbs a large part of private saving. Net foreign investment has changed from positive to negative, which reduces net investment. If the federal budget and the nation's balance of payments accounts were balanced, the share of the economy's output available for capital formation would simply be the share set aside as net private savings. If the deficit in the federal budget continues in the range of 4 to 6 percent of GNP, as now seems likely, it will absorb more than half of the private sector's rate of net saving. In the absence of an increase in government saving at the state and local level, the federal deficit will depress capital formation.

Several studies have indicated that the cost of capital in the United States is much higher than it is in such countries as West Germany and Japan.[36] These studies indicate that the cost difference is at least as great as the wage differences relative to those competitors and that this difference — if allowed to continue — threatens the capacity of U.S. firms to maintain the necessary investment to compete in the world. The high cost of this capital can be attributable in part to U.S. tax policies, which have had the effect of stimulating consumption at the expense of investment. Consumer credit is subsidized by the tax deduction of interest on mortgages and other kinds of debt. Among industrial countries, the United States has taken a firm hold on last place in terms of the rate of personal saving. In Japan it is a matter of national strategy to specifically target incentive to save.

36. George N. Hatsopoulus, *High Cost of Capital: Handicap of American Business*, study sponsored by the American Business Conference, April 1983.

Table 19-3 U.S. Net Saving and Net Investment as a Percent of GNP for Selected Periods

	1971–1975	1975–1980	1981	1982	1983	1984	1985
Total net saving	6.4	5.7	5.1	1.9	1.9	4.3	3.0
Net private saving	7.6	6.5	6.1	5.3	5.8	7.3	6.4
Personal saving	5.6	4.2	4.6	4.1	3.5	4.6	3.2
Corporate saving	2.0	2.3	1.5	1.2	2.4	2.7	3.2
State and local government surplus	0.6	1.2	1.2	1.0	1.5	1.6	1.5
Federal government surplus	-1.8	-2.0	-2.2	-4.8	-5.5	-4.6	-4.9
Total net investment	6.7	5.8	5.0	1.5	1.8	4.3	3.0
Net foreign investment	0.3	-0.2	0.1	-0.3	-1.0	-2.4	-2.8
Private domestic investment	6.4	6.0	4.9	1.8	2.8	6.7	5.8

Source: *Economic Report of the President 1986* (Washington, D.C.: U.S. Government Printing Office, 1986), table B-12, p. 266; table B-15, p. 270; and table B-27, p. 284.

Labor-Management Relations

The potential for polarization between labor and management has increased. The U.S. automobile industry is a case in point. At a time when wage concessions and other givebacks were imposed on the autoworkers to save the auto industry from Japanese competition, U.S. auto executives were rewarding themselves handsomely. To justify such compensation as the impersonal outcome of the play of market forces is hard; indeed, that market forces had anything to do with these rewards is highly doubtful. This and other situations promise to exacerbate divisions between labor and management. Average hourly earnings adjusted for inflation boomed during the 1950s and 1960s, but they fell during the 1970s and have had no real growth in the 1980s.[37] Average weekly wages, held down slightly by a shorter work week, have declined by 14.3 percent since 1973, after allowing for inflation. Much of the problem is that workers can increase their real earnings in the future only through steady and strong productivity growth.

So, in terms of labor-management relations, several things have to be done. Mechanisms should be built for achieving consensus between labor and management, which given the history of adversarial relations between labor and management, will be difficult. American management can make use of a broad array of incentive mechanisms, including compensation plans, to reward the efforts of individual employees and to strengthen the linkage between pay and performance.[38] Management can invest in employee training. Regaining competitiveness means retaining production in the United States through a high productivity solution based on new technology and worker commitment. The challenge of American business and labor is clearly defined. They need to improve productivity and quality so that a higher degree of competitiveness can be achieved. Whether or not they have the commitment remains to be seen.

THE CHANGED WORLD ECONOMY

Peter Drucker argues that the world economy has changed irrevocably in three fundamental ways.[39] These changes have rendered international and macroeconomic theories obsolete in that the United States is tied into the global economy, and almost all macroeconomic theories are based on domestic manipulation of fiscal and monetary policies.

37. Greenhouse, section 3, p. 1.
38. *Global Competition: The New Reality*, pp. 53–56.
39. Peter Drucker, "The Changed World Economy," *Foreign Affairs*, April 1986, pp. 37–52.

1. The primary products economy has come "uncoupled" from the industrial economy. In contrast to predictions by the Carter administration's Global 2000 report and the Club of Rome, there are not the shortages in food supplies and raw materials that were predicted by the 1980s. With regard to primary products, the ratio between prices of raw materials and manufactured goods has increased, resulting in a fundamental change in the relationship between these goods. Previously, a prolonged drop in the price of primary products would precipitate a depression in the industrial economy. Today, world demand for primary products has decreased because less is needed per unit of industrial production than before. Industrial production has moved toward more sophisticated high-technology industries. In sum, as a result of a shift to knowledge-based industries, there is a global oversupply of food and raw materials. This has resulted in problems for developing countries, which depend on world prices for their primary products to meet their loan obligations.[40]

2. In the industrial economy, manufacturing production has come "uncoupled" from manufacturing employment. There has been a constant decline in the number of blue collar workers per unit of production as industry becomes more capital intensive. The increasing reliance on automation and data processing has resulted in a decreased importance of labor as a comparative cost in production. Hence, Drucker argues that it is the American labor force and not the American economy that is becoming deindustrialized. This is a trend that cannot be reversed.

3. The third major change in the global economy is the emergence of the "symbol" economy — defined as the flywheel of transnational money flows and their uncoupling from the real economy of goods and services. Capital movements that are unconnected to and largely independent of trade greatly exceed trade finance. Major causal factors are a shift from a fixed to a floating exchange rate, the surge of funds to petroleum producers after the two oil shocks of the 1970s, and the U.S. federal government deficit. Capital flows do not fit the traditional international trade theory or Keynesian theory in which the symbol economy determines the real economy. Therefore, exchange rates must be treated as a comparative advantage factor.

Trends in the Global Economy

The Japanese are formidable competitors, and they are now being joined by other East Asian countries. It is common knowledge that the

---

40. Mexico is an example. The fall in the world price of oil has reduced revenue from oil exports, which means it has less money with which to pay its foreign debts.

Japanese have superseded the United States as the world leader in a number of manufacturing industries. Less well known, however, is that the Japanese have now replaced the United States as the world's largest bankers.[41] In less than a century, dominance of international banking has passed from the British to the Americans to the Japanese. The largest bank in the world is now Japanese, and Japanese banks are now financing the U.S. federal deficit. The Japanese banks are so formidable because they belong to industrial groups made up of dozens of interconnected companies. They own stock in these companies and extend them as much credit as they need. So when foreign auto firms take on Toyota, they are also competing against a Japanese bank.

We can safely predict that, by the end of this century, the U.S. share of world GNP and world markets will decline, and the world shares of Japan and the other East Asian countries will increase. What the contribution of China will be in the future is difficult to predict. It is conceivable that China could become an industrial giant in the next century. Some projections of the future are presented in Table 19–4. As the table indicates, Japan's share of world GNP will increase, and the U.S. share will decline. The share of world GNP for Japan and the

Table 19–4 World GNP Shares of Selected Countries and Regions (percent)

	Share of World GNP			Real Growth Rate Per Annum	
	1960	1980	2000	1970–1979	1980–2000
Japan	3	10	12	5.2	4.0
United States	33	22	20	3.1	2.5
Industrial countries	62	63	58	3.3	2.8
LDCs*	11	11	13	5.7	4.0
Developing countries	14	15	20	6.3	4.6
Union of Soviet Socialist Republics	15	13	12	5.1	3.0
Eastern Europe	4	5	5	5.9	3.0
China	5	4	5	5.8	4.0
Communist bloc	24	22	22	5.4	3.2

*Less-developed countries

Source: *Japan 1984: An International Comparison* (Tokyo: Mitsubishi Research Institute, 1984), p. 16.

41. *Time*, August 11, 1986, p. 43.

developing East Asian countries will be larger than that for Western Europe. The highest real growth rates for the period 1980–2000 are projected for Japan and other East Asian countries, including China, which is in the process of initiating a series of major economic reforms.

SUMMARY

There are several issues that involve business and government relations as of mid-1986. One is the deficit in the federal budget, projected to be $230.2 billion for 1986. The one ray of hope in reducing this deficit is tax and spending reform. The Gramm-Rudman-Hollings Act gave the illusion that spending was to be reduced, but the Supreme Court has thrown out the operative part of the act. A positive step that would have had an impact on business and the deficit was reforming the tax system to encourage more saving and investment. But this is unlikely to happen; to the contrary, corporate income taxes will be raised, and personal income taxes will be lowered. Protectionist sentiment has increased and Congress, as usual, overreacts by introducing protectionist legislation. If enacted, two things will happen. Other countries will retaliate, which will be disastrous in itself. Even more disastrous, production costs in the United States will increase, U.S. consumers will pay more, and we will price ourselves out of world markets.

Of equal importance is the position of the United States in global economy. The United States is now much more interdependent with other economies, and its competitive position as the world leader has decreased. Competitiveness in the world has become more and more a matter of national strategies where comparative advantage is created by government policies. National competitiveness depends increasingly on technology, capital skills, and labor skills, all of which can be shaped and mobilized if not created. In addition, these resources, unlike natural resources, move across national boundaries. It is said that the United States is at a competitive disadvantage in comparison to other countries because it has no coherent industrial policy. Advocates of industrial policy, which involves the promotion of growth industries through the use of various forms of government assistance, claim that it is the necessary cure for U.S. competitiveness. However, the problem of U.S. competitiveness appears to be the emphasis on promoting growth through government spending and personal consumption, which has had an adverse impact on saving and capital formation.

QUESTIONS FOR DISCUSSION

1. Give several reasons for the decline of the competitive position of the United States in the world economy.

2. What is an industrial policy?
3. Comparative advantage no longer needs to be based on natural endowments but can be created. Discuss.
4. How has Japan created comparative advantage?
5. Discuss the relationship between education and productivity.
6. It has been said that American managerial practices have contributed to the decline in U.S. industrial competitiveness. Discuss.
7. What are some of the policy recommendations to improve U.S. industrial productivity?
8. According to Peter Drucker, what are the three ways in which the world economy has changed?

RECOMMENDED READINGS

Drucker, Peter. "The Changed World Economy." *Foreign Affairs*, April 1986.

Economic Report of the President 1986. Washington, D.C.: U.S. Government Printing Office, 1986.

Lawrence, Robert Z. *Can America Compete?* Washington, D.C.: Brookings Institution, 1984.

Magaziner, Ira, and Robert Reich. *Minding America's Business*. New York: Harcourt Brace Jovanovich, 1982.

Reich, Robert. "Why the U.S. Needs an Industrial Policy." *Harvard Business Review*, 60 (February–March 1982), pp. 74–81.

Schultze, Charles L. "Industrial Policy: A Dissent." *The Brookings Review*, 1 (Fall 1983), pp. 3–12.

Scott, Bruce R., and George C. Lodge, eds. *U.S. Competitiveness in the World Economy*. Boston: Harvard Business School Press, 1985.

Scott, Bruce R. "National Strategy for Stronger U.S. Competitiveness." *Harvard Business Review*, 62 (March–April 1984), pp. 77–91.

The Report of the President's Commission on Industrial Competitiveness. *Global Competition: The New Reality*, Vols. 1 and 2, 1985.

The World Bank. *World Development Report 1986*.

U.S. Joint Economic Committee. *Impact of the Dollar on U.S. Competitiveness*. 99th Cong., 1st sess., 1985.

Vernon, Raymond. "Can U.S. Manufacturing Come Back?" *Harvard Business Review*, 64 (July–August 1986), pp. 98–106.

Appendix A
Federal Regulatory Commissions

Table A-1 Regulation of Banking and Finance

Organization	Year Established	Primary Regulatory Functions
Office of the Comptroller of the Currency	1863	Licenses and regulates national banks
Board of Governors of the Federal Reserve System	1913	Determines monetary and credit policy for the system and regulates member commercial banks
Federal Home Loan Bank Board	1932	Provides credit reserves for and regulates federally chartered savings and home-financing institutions
Federal Deposit Insurance Corporation	1933	Insures deposits of eligible banks and supervises certain insured banks
Federal Savings and Loan Insurance Corporation	1934	Insures savings in thrift and home-financing institutions
Securities and Exchange Commission	1934	Requires financial disclosure by publicly held companies; regulates practices of stock exchanges, brokers, and dealers; regulates certain practices of mutual funds, investment advisers, and public utility holding companies
National Credit Union Administration	1970	Charters, supervises, and examines all federal credit unions
Farm Credit Administration	1971	Supervises and regulates all activities of credit disbursed through the Farm Credit System

Table A-1 (continued)

Organization	Year Established	Primary Regulatory Functions
Commodity Futures Trading Commission	1975	Licenses all futures contracts and the brokers, dealers, and exchanges trading them
International Trade Commission (formerly U.S. Tariff Commission, established in 1916)	1975	Investigates and rules on tariff and certain other foreign trade regulations

Table A-2 Regulation of Energy and Environmental Matters

Organization	Year Established	Primary Regulatory Functions
Army Corps of Engineers	1824	Issues permits for all construction in navigable waterways; constructs and maintains rivers and harbor improvements
Mississippi River Commission	1879	Approves plans for and constructs flood control projects in lower Mississippi River Basin
Bureau of Reclamation	1902	Establishes criteria for use, development, and pricing of resources obtained from reclamation projects
Forest Service	1905	Manages U.S. forest preserves by determining amounts of land eligible for harvest, conditions of cutting, need for reforestation, etc.
National Forest Reservation Commission	1911	Rules on requests from Secretary of Agriculture for authority to acquire or exchange national forests
Federal Power Commission	1930	Regulates wholesale rates and practices in interstate transmission of electric energy and regulates transportation and sale of natural gas

Table A–2 (continued)

Organization	Year Established	Primary Regulatory Functions
Tennessee Valley Authority	1933	Operates river control systems and sets rates for power generated from TVA hydroelectric projects
Bonneville, Alaska, Southeastern, and Southwestern	1937 (abolished 1967)	Sets prices and markets federally generated hydroelectric power
Bureau of Land Management	1946	Classifies, manages use of, and disposes of all federal lands
Delaware River Basin Commission	1961	Develops and/or approves all plans for control and utilization of water resources in Delaware River Basin
Environmental Protection Agency	1970	Develops environmental quality standards, approves state abatement plans, and rules on acceptability of environmental impact statements
Susquehanna River Basin Commission	1970	Develops and/or approves all plans for utilization and control of watershed resources in Susquehanna River Basin
Federal Energy Administration	1973	Regulates price and allocation of certain petroleum products under emergency energy legislation
Mining Enforcement and Safety Administration	1973	Sets and enforces mine safety standards
Nuclear Regulatory Commission (formerly Atomic Energy Commission, established in 1946)	1975	Promotes and regulates civilian use of atomic energy
Ocean Mining Administration	1975	Supervises leasing of ocean resources and regulates ocean mining

Table A–3 Regulation of Commerce, Transportation, and Communications

Organization	Year Established	Primary Regulatory Functions
Patent and Trademark Office	1836	Administers patent and trademark laws
Interstate Commerce Commission	1887	Regulates rates, routes, and practices of railroads, trucks, bus lines, oil pipelines, domestic water carriers, and freight forwarders
National Bureau of Standards	1901	Establishes standards of measurement in trade, public safety, technical, and scientific performance
Coast Guard	1915	Sets and enforces safety standards for merchant vessels and navigable waterways
Federal Communications Commission	1934	Licenses civilian radio and television communication, and licenses and sets rates for interstate and international communication by wire, cable, and radio
Foreign Trade Zones Board	1934	Grants authority to public or private corporations to establish and/or utilize foreign trade zones within United States
Federal Maritime Commission	1936	Regulates fares, rates, and practices of steamship companies engaged in U.S. foreign commerce
Maritime Administration	1936	Determines eligibility for merchant marine subsidies, and regulates construction and operation of certain merchant ships
Civil Aeronautics Board	1938	Promotes and subsidizes air transportation, and regulates airline routes, passenger fares, and freight rates

Table A-3 (continued)

Organization	Year Established	Primary Regulatory Functions
Appalachian Regional Commission	1965	Approves state plans for projects in Appalachian area before requests for funds can be considered by federal departments
Federal Highway Administration	1966	Determines highway safety standards and administers federally funded highway construction programs
Federal Railroad Administration	1966	Administers high-speed railroad development program and the railroad and oil pipeline safety programs formerly administered by the ICC
Office of Telecommunications Policy	1970	Sets standards for broadcast technology and performance and assigns federal telecommunication frequencies

Table A-4 Regulation of Food, Health, and Safety, and Unfair or Deceptive Trade Practices

Organization	Year Established	Primary Regulatory Functions
Federal Trade Commission	1914	Administers some antitrust statutes, and laws concerning advertising misrepresentation, flammable fabrics, packaging, and labeling of certain products
Packers and Stockyards Administration	1916	Regulates fair business practices in livestock and processed meat marketing
Food and Drug Administration	1931	Administers laws concerning purity, safety, and labeling accuracy of certain foods and drugs

Table A-4 (continued)

Organization	Year Established	Primary Regulatory Functions
Commodity Credit Corporation	1933	Finances and determines farm price supports and administers production stabilization programs
Social Security Administration	1933	Determines eligible medical expenses under Medicare/Medicaid
Agriculture Marketing Service	1937	Sets grades and standards for most farm commodities, inspects egg production, administers product and process safety acts, licenses and bonds warehouses
Agricultural Stabilization and Conservation Service	1953	Administers commodity stabilization programs, and rules on eligibility of participants
Animal and Plant Health Inspection Service	1953	Sets standards, inspects and enforces laws relating to meat, poultry, and plant safety
Federal Aviation Administration	1958	Certifies airworthiness of aircraft, licenses pilots, and operates air traffic control system
Federal Insurance Administration	1968	Sets standards for all insurance programs related to natural disasters and similar occurrences
Office of Interstate Land Sales Registration	1968	Requires disclosure and regulation for interstate sales of land in quantities of over fifty lots
Interim Compliance Panel	1969	Grants permits for noncompliance with health standards in underground coal mines
National Highway Traffic Safety Administration	1970	Establishes safety standards for trucks and automobiles and certifies compliance with emission standards for pollution control

Table A–4 (continued)

Organization	Year Established	Primary Regulatory Functions
Occupational Safety and Health Review Commission	1970	Adjudicates all enforcement actions when OSHA rulings are contested
Consumer Product Safety Commission	1972	Establishes mandatory product safety standards and bans sale of products that do not comply
Occupational Safety and Health Administration	1973	Develops and enforces worker safety and health regulations
Professional Standards Review Organization	1973	Reviews and sets private medical practice and health care standards
Foreign Agricultural Service (absorbed Export Marketing Service, established in 1969)	1974	Determines eligibility price and terms of payment for commodities allocated to export market
National Transportation Safety Board	1974	Investigates transportation accidents, and rules on needed improvements in airline, rail, and highway safety

Table A–5 Regulation of Labor, Housing, and Small Business

Organization	Year Established	Primary Regulatory Functions
Civil Service Commission	1833	Sets job standards and classifications for most federal employees and enforces Equal Employment Opportunity Act within federal government
National Mediation Board	1926	Conducts union representation elections and mediates labor-management disputes in the railroad and airline industries

Table A–5 (continued)

Organization	Year Established	Primary Regulatory Functions
Employment Standards Administration	1933	Sets and administers standards under laws relating to minimum wages, overtime, nondiscrimination, etc.
Unemployment Insurance Service	1933	Reviews state unemployment insurance laws to ensure compliance with federal standards
Federal Housing Authority	1934	Sets and enforces standards for federally insured residential and commercial properties
National Labor Relations Board	1935	Conducts union representation elections and regulates labor practices of employers and unions
Railroad Retirement Board	1935	Administers retirement and insurance acts for railroads, and rules on eligibility of retiring or disabled workers
General Services Administration	1949	Establishes critical needs for national stockpile and regulates purchase/sale of required/surplus materials
Renegotiation Board	1951	Sets standards for private contracts with federal government and rules on contractors' liabilities
Small Business Administration	1953	Makes loans and gives advice to small businesses
Labor-Management Services Administration	1963	Determines (with Treasury) eligibility of employee welfare and pension plans and sets standards for financial disclosure
Equal Employment Opportunity Commission	1964	Investigates and rules on charges of racial and other discrimination by employers and labor unions

Table A–5 (continued)

Organization	Year Established	Primary Regulatory Functions
Federal Labor Relations Council	1969	Oversees and prescribes regulations pertaining to labor-management relations programs in federal government
Cost Accounting Standards Board	1970	Promulgates rules and regulations for implementation of cost accounting standards to be included in federal defense contracts and subcontracts

Appendix B
Deregulation and
the Airline Industry

The interstate air transportation industry was deregulated in 1978, with the intent of promoting competition between air carriers. Prior to deregulation, the major interstate airlines had been protected from competition by the Civil Aeronautics Board. Since its creation in 1938, the CAB had 79 applications from companies that wanted to become long-distance interstate airlines; not one was approved. During the time they were protected from competition, the regulated airlines had become high-cost unionized operations. There was no incentive to become cost efficient, for increased costs could be readily absorbed by rate increases granted by the CAB. The Airline Deregulation Act of 1978 had as its intention the elimination of legal barriers to market entry, thus promoting competition from new entrants into the air transportation industry.

However, things have not worked out as well as the deregulators had hoped. Right after the deregulation, the major airlines were at a serious cost disadvantage. New entrants into the industry were able to employ cheaper nonunion labor and use smaller crews on their aircraft than the major airlines did. Price competition occurred, which put the major carriers at a disadvantage. There were a number of new entrants into the airline industry; most went broke. Some 150 airlines went bankrupt during the period 1978–1985, and there were years when the industry lost money. In 1985 air carriers had an average profit margin of 2 percent, and in the first half of 1986 the industry lost $765 million; airlines went bankrupt, and in order for others to survive, a spate of mergers occurred. The following table presents mergers that have been consummated or are pending as of September 1986.

There are those persons who see a parallel between the airline industry of the 1980s and the railroad industry during the latter part of the last century. Faced with heavy fixed costs and recurring recessions, the railroad industry struggled for survival. Price wars were frequent and there were many bankruptcies or last-ditch mergers. By the end of the last century, six major railroad companies controlled most of the railroads in the United States. Similarly, airlines have gone bankrupt and an increase in the number of mergers has occurred. The airline industry is well on its way to becoming an oligopoly. It is predicted by some

Buyer	Target	Value of Merger (millions)
Northwest	Republic	$884
Delta	Western	860
Texas Air	Eastern	607
TWA	Ozark	250
Texas Air	Frontier	197
Texas Air	People	125

Source: USA Today, September 12, 1986, p. 1. Used by permission.

experts that the airline industry will have no more than six carriers by the end of this decade some with twenty-four feeder carriers. The table below presents the share of the market held by the major airlines, assuming that some of the pending mergers, such as Texas Air and People Express are approved.

Major airline groups and their share of the market*
(if mergers are approved)

Texas Air	20.1%
Eastern	9.6%
Continental	5.4%
People Express	3.3%
Frontier	1.2%
New York Air	0.6%
United	15.7%
American	13.5%
Delta	11.9%
Delta	8.8%
Western	3.1%
Northwest	9.4%
Northwest	6.6%
Republic	2.8%
TWA	8.1%
TWA	7.2%
Ozark	0.9%
Pan American	5.7%
USAir	3.0%

*Measured in revenue passenger miles, through July.
Source: Shearson Lehman Bros. TIME chart by Renee Klein. Reprinted from *Time*, September 29, 1986, p. 57. Copyright 1986 Time Inc. All rights reserved. Reprinted by permission from TIME.

It remains to be seen whether or not this trend toward concentration will result in higher fares to air travelers. In a pure oligopoly there would be little or no price competition. However, it may be that price competition will continue to exist. One reason is the airline industry's overcapacity, especially during off-peak travel seasons, like the fall. Overcapacity means continued fare wars. Moreover, if any air carrier raised prices too high, it would be easy for a competitor to enter that market with lower fares. There are also some aggressive smaller companies that will challenge the major carriers. Piedmont Airlines, which bought the New York-based Empire Airlines, is an example. There are also small carriers that are entering the market. McClain Airlines plans to offer jet service between Chicago and Los Angeles, catering to business travelers with premium services at coach-class prices.

Index

DATE DUE

JUL 1 ~~1988~~			
GAYLORD			PRINTED IN U.S.A